Palgrave Studies in Sustainable Business
In Association with Future Earth

Series Editors
Paul Shrivastava
Pennsylvania State University
University Park, PA, USA

László Zsolnai
Corvinus University Budapest
Budapest, Hungary

Sustainability in Business is increasingly becoming the forefront issue for researchers, practitioners and companies the world over. Engaging with this immense challenge, Future Earth is a major international research platform from a range of disciplines, with a common goal to support and achieve global sustainability. This series will define a clear space for the work of Future Earth Finance and Economics Knowledge-Action Network. Publishing key research with a holistic and trans-disciplinary approach, it intends to help reinvent business and economic models for the Anthropocene, geared towards engendering sustainability and creating ecologically conscious organizations.

More information about this series at
http://www.palgrave.com/gp/series/15667

Annabeth Aagaard
Editor

Sustainable Business Models

Innovation, Implementation and Success

Editor
Annabeth Aagaard
Aarhus University
Herning, Denmark

Palgrave Studies in Sustainable Business In Association with Future Earth
ISBN 978-3-319-93274-3   ISBN 978-3-319-93275-0 (eBook)
https://doi.org/10.1007/978-3-319-93275-0

Library of Congress Control Number: 2018952451

© The Editor(s) (if applicable) and The Author(s), under exclusive license to Springer Nature Switzerland AG 2019
This work is subject to copyright. All rights are solely and exclusively licensed by the Publisher, whether the whole or part of the material is concerned, specifically the rights of translation, reprinting, reuse of illustrations, recitation, broadcasting, reproduction on microfilms or in any other physical way, and transmission or information storage and retrieval, electronic adaptation, computer software, or by similar or dissimilar methodology now known or hereafter developed.
The use of general descriptive names, registered names, trademarks, service marks, etc. in this publication does not imply, even in the absence of a specific statement, that such names are exempt from the relevant protective laws and regulations and therefore free for general use.
The publisher, the authors, and the editors are safe to assume that the advice and information in this book are believed to be true and accurate at the date of publication. Neither the publisher nor the authors or the editors give a warranty, express or implied, with respect to the material contained herein or for any errors or omissions that may have been made. The publisher remains neutral with regard to jurisdictional claims in published maps and institutional affiliations.

Cover illustration: Peter Pöhlein / EyeEm / Getty

This Palgrave Macmillan imprint is published by the registered company Springer Nature Switzerland AG
The registered company address is: Gewerbestrasse 11, 6330 Cham, Switzerland

About the Book

Global sustainability issues and requirements present unique, new business opportunities, but at the same time also challenge the existing structures of companies and the way value is created and measured in businesses today. These changes influence and force organizations to change their ways of organizing, managing, collaborating, and engaging with new and different types of stakeholders and ecosystems. This presents a need for new theoretical models and empirical understandings of business modeling in today's interconnected society across institutional boundaries and international borders.

The current rates of change are intensifying and involve a growing number of codependent dynamic variables (Inyang et al. 2011; Aagaard 2016). Greater global interconnectedness, technologically enabled transparency, customer transience, and cultural diversity have all converged (Rosethorn 2009; Garavan and McGuire 2010; He 2012), generating market pressures companies can no longer ignore. With new demands and the quest for competitive advantage still a dominant driver (He 2012), organizations are being forced to find new ways to achieve success. In order to stay competitive, organizations are under pressure to respond to social changes (Wang et al. 2011) and sustainable business model innovation is suggested as a new and different perspective on creating and ensuring the sustainability and longevity of business models and business success in the short and long run.

The research gaps surrounding the identification, application, and implementation of this new concept of sustainable business models stress the necessity for the development of existing and new theories, models, and theoretical and practical frameworks in understanding and using the concept in theory and practice, in academia and industry. Thus, a key contribution and aim of *Sustainable Business Models: Innovation, Implementation and Success* is to contribute to the knowledge of the concept, design, implementation, management, and evaluation of the different aspects of sustainable business models, as this is stressed as an insufficiently researched area by a number of researchers (e.g., Tukker and Tischner 2006; Wells 2008; Schaltegger et al. 2012; Boons and Lüdeke-Freund 2013).

Another contribution of this book is to bridge between the theoretical frameworks of sustainable business models to empirical findings and cases of how this concept is applied and integrated in practice. While this book focuses on the potential of sustainable business models in research, the question is also highly relevant for practitioners, as the business model perspective reveals a number of components that need to be actively managed to "create customer and social value by integrating social, environmental, and business activities" (Schaltegger et al. 2012, p. 112). Therefore, the book incorporates a number of cases and case examples to explain and illustrate how sustainable business models are developed, integrated, and actively managed in creating sustainable value (Bocken et al. 2014; Aagaard and Ritzén 2018).

Sustainable Business Models: Innovation, Implementation and Success is one of the first international and comprehensive contributions to the field of sustainable business models, which explores the identification development and application of sustainable business models from a theoretical and empirical angle to benefit academia and students as well as industry and organizations. We hope this book will help elevate and further develop the discussion, research streams, and practices in sustainable business models and wish you, the reader, happy reading!

Aarhus University, Denmark   Annabeth Aagaard

References

Aagaard, A. 2016. *Sustainable Business: Integrating CSR in Business and Functions*. River Publishers.
Aagaard, A., and S. Ritzén. 2018. Creating and Capturing Sustainable Value through Sustainable Business Models and Service Innovation. In *25th IPDMC: Innovation & Product Development Management Conference*, Porto, Portugal, June 10–13, 2018.
Bocken, N.M.P., S.W.A. Short, P. Rana, and S. Evans. 2014. A Literature and Practice Review to Develop Sustainable Business Model Archetypes. *Journal of Cleaner Production* 65 (2014): 42–56.
Boons, F., and F. Lüdeke-Freund. 2013. Business Models for Sustainable Innovation: State-of-the-art and Steps Towards a Research Agenda. *Journal of Cleaner Production* 45: 9–19.
Garavan, T., and D. McGuire. 2010. Human Resources Development and Society: Human Resource Development's Role in Embedding Corporate Social Responsibility, Sustainability and Ethics in Organisations. *Advances in Developing Human Resources* 12: 487–507.
He, N. 2012. How to Maintain Sustainable Competitive Advantages: Case Study on the Evolution of Organizational Strategic Management. *International Journal of Business Administration* 3 (5): 45–51.
Inyang, B., H. Awa, and R. Enuoh. 2011. CSR-HRM Nexus: Defining the Role Engagement of the Human Resources Professionals. *International Journal of Business and Social Science* 2 (5): 118–126.
Rosethorn, H. 2009. *The Employer Brand: Keeping Faith with the Deal*. Surrey, UK: Gower Publishing.
Schaltegger, S., F. Lüdeke-Freund, and E.G. Hansen. 2012. Business Cases for Sustainability—The Role of Business Model Innovation for Corporate Sustainability. *International Journal of Innovation and Sustainable Development* 6 (2): 95–119.

Tukker, A., and U. Tischner, eds. 2006. *New Business for Old Europe. Product-Service Development, Competitiveness and Sustainability*. Sheffield: Greenleaf.

Wang, W., C. Lin, and Y. Chu. 2011. Types of Competitive Advantage and Analysis. *International Journal of Business and Management* 6 (5): 100–104.

Wells, P. 2008. Alternative Business Models for a Sustainable Automotive Industry. In *Perspectives on Radical Changes to Sustainable Consumption and Production 1. System Innovation for Sustainability*, ed. A. Tukker, M. Charter, C. Vezzoli, E. Stø, and M.M. Andersen, 80–98. Sheffield: Greenleaf.

Contents

1 **Identifying Sustainable Business Models Through Sustainable Value Creation** 1
  Annabeth Aagaard

2 **Research on Sustainable Business Model Patterns: Status quo, Methodological Issues, and a Research Agenda** 25
  Florian Lüdeke-Freund, René Bohnsack, Henning Breuer, and Lorenzo Massa

3 **Designing Sustainable Business Models: Exploring IoT-Enabled Strategies to Drive Sustainable Consumption** 61
  Nancy Bocken, Emilia Ingemarsdotter, and Diana Gonzalez

4 **Sustainability Goal Setting with a Value-Focused Thinking Approach** 89
  Kaisa Manninen and Janne Huiskonen

Contents

5 **Sustainable Business Model Ideation and Development of Early Ideas for Sustainable Business Models: Analyzing a New Tool Facilitating the Ideation Process**   119
Ulla A. Saari, Leena Aarikka-Stenroos, Leena Köppä, Jörg Langwaldt, Stina Boedeker, and Saku J. Mäkinen

6 **Business Models for Multiple Value Creation: Exploring Strategic Changes in Organisations Enabling to Address Societal Challenges**   151
Jan Jonker and Niels Faber

7 **Managing Innovation for Circular Industrial Systems**   181
Sofia Ritzén

8 **Leveraging Sustainable Business Model Innovation Through Business-NGO Collaboration**   211
Annabeth Aagaard and Lise Lodsgård

9 **Sustainable Business Models in an Entrepreneurial Environment**   239
Raz Godelnik and Jen van der Meer

10 **Organizational Identity and Value Triangle: Management of Jungian Paradoxes to Enable Sustainable Business Model Innovation**   277
Roberto Biloslavo, David Edgar, and Carlo Bagnoli

11 **Performance Management and Enterprise Excellence Through Sustainable Business Models**   317
Rick Edgeman

12 **Summary and Concluding Remarks: The Next Step for Sustainable Business Models**   361
Annabeth Aagaard

Index   371

Notes on Contributors

Annabeth Aagaard, PhD, MSc, is an Associate professor at Aarhus University in Denmark. She conducts international research and teaches Executive, Master and Bachelor courses in digital and sustainable business models, innovation management, strategic management and open innovation. She is the Centre Director of Centre for Business Development at Aarhus University, which bridges research and projects combining digital technologies and business development in a sustainable way. Furthermore, she is the CEO and owner of a consultancy company, KnowledgeHouse, which has designed and implemented strategies, business development and innovation projects among top 100 companies in Scandinavia. She has 20 years of experience working in these academic fields drawing on her experiences in the academic, public, and private sectors, where she was formerly a manager and management specialist. She has published nine textbooks and management handbooks and over 200 scientific papers, conference papers, and public articles on management, business models, innovation, and sustainability, and has published her scientific work in acclaimed, peer-reviewed journal articles including the *Journal of Product Innovation Management*, *Creativity & Innovation Management*, and the *Scandinavian Journal of Management*.

Leena Aarikka-Stenroos, PhD (Econ. and Business Administration), is an associate professor at the Laboratory of Industrial and Information Management, CITER (Center for Innovation and Technology Research), at Tampere University of Technology (TUT), Finland. Her research focuses on the commercialization of innovations, innovation networks and ecosystems, innovation process, business-to-business marketing, technology start-ups, and business approach to circular economy. Her articles have been published in various journals, for example, *Industrial Marketing Management, Journal of Business Research, Journal of Cleaner Production, Journal of Service Management, International Journal of Technology Marketing, Journal of Business and Industrial Marketing*, and international books.

Carlo Bagnoli, PhD, is Professor of Strategy Innovation at the Department of Management Ca' Foscari University of Venice. He is the proponent and scientific coordinator of "Technology & Design Strategy Innovation Master" and of "Strategy Innovation Hub": an innovation center located within the Economic Campus of Ca' Foscari University. He is also the founder and scientific director of Strategy Innovation Srl: a Ca' Foscari University spin-off focused on action research. Among his institutional assignments, he is the Rector delegate for strategy innovation. His areas of interests are strategy innovation, business strategy, knowledge management, and social and entrepreneurial innovation. He participated and coordinated several national and European research projects.

He presented several papers at international top conferences and won the Kizok best paper award on SME at 3rd EIASM Workshop on Intangibles and IC—Ferrara, 2007 and the 3rd Best Paper Award at the SMS (Strategic Management Society) conference, Glasgow, 2013. He is distinguished International Business Scholar, at Angelo State University College of Business and Norris Family Endowment for International Business, October 2013. He won several University of Venice—Faculty of Economics best teacher awards (2006–2007, 2007–2008, 2008–2009) and the University of Venice best teacher awards for innovative teaching (2012–2013). He is a member of the editorial board of different international journals. He was also a member of the scientific committee of several national and international conferences.

Roberto Biloslavo is Professor of Management at the Faculty of Management, the University of Primorska. His research work is focused on strategic management, sustainable development, and wisdom. He is a former Vice-Rector for Academic Affairs and Vice-Dean for Research. Beside teaching and researching, he consults to different domestic and international companies about strategic planning, sustainable business models, CSR, knowledge management, and leadership development.

He has a wide range of academic experience from program development at all levels to international collaboration and academic management and leadership. He is on the editorial board of a range of journals and regularly reviews for journals and conferences. In addition, he is involved in different international research projects and acts as an external advisor for Slovene Qualification Framework and Slovene Network for Corporate Responsibility. For one year, he was involved as an external academic expert in Marie Curie Project on business model development for electric mobility.

Nancy Bocken is Professor in Sustainable Business Management and Practice at The International Institute for Industrial Environmental Economics, Lund University, Sweden. She is also an associate professor at Delft University of Technology (Netherlands) and fellow at the Cambridge Institute for Sustainability Leadership, U). Her main areas of interests around sustainability are business models, business experimentation, innovation for sustainability, scaling up sustainable businesses, circular economy, and closing the "idea-action" gap in sustainability.

Stina Boedeker, M.Soc.Sc., BBA, is a research funding specialist at the University of Tampere. She has a background in world-leading international business. In academia, her passion is Human-Computer Interaction (HCI), where she has proved her ability to receive EU Framework Programme funding. For ten years, she has coordinated European and global project funding initiatives. Her present commitment is to share her expertise in strategic proposal preparations, where research from any field of science can make a difference.

René Bohnsack is Assistant Professor of Strategy and Innovation at Católica-Lisbon, Portugal, and international faculty fellow at MIT Sloan School of Management. He studies the diffusion of technologies as well as how business models can accelerate this process. Bohnsack has published his research in various international innovation and management journals such as *Research Policy*, *Journal of Business Venturing*, *Journal of Product Innovation Management*, *California Management Review*, or *Technovation*. Furthermore, he is founder and director of the Smart City Innovation Lab (SCIL), a multi-disciplinary research team working on cutting-edge knowledge related to improving well-being in urban areas via sustainable technologies and digital transformation. Under his guidance, six researchers work for two major European energy research projects in which SCIL is the lead partner. SCIL is also developing the platform www.smartbusinessmodeler.com on which firms can create disruptive business models. Next to the academic accomplishments, he co-founded several start-ups.

Henning Breuer is the founder of UXBerlin—Innovation Consulting and Professor for Business and Media Psychology at the University of Applied Sciences for Media, Communication and Management in Berlin, Germany. His academic research and consulting work for corporate clients from automotive, internet, and telecommunication focuses on innovation management, business anthropology, futures research, and customer research. Together with Florian Lüdeke-Freund, he published a textbook on values-based innovation management. As a visiting professor and an adjunct researcher, he worked at the Waseda University, Tokyo, the University of Chile, Santiago, and the University of Applied Sciences in Potsdam on interaction design and learner-centered environments. He studied psychology, philosophy, and law at the universities of Magdeburg, Berlin, and Tübingen.

David Edgar is Professor of Strategy and Business Transformation and member of the Department of Business Management at Glasgow School for Business and Society. His main areas of research and teaching are in the field of strategic management, specifically dynamic capabilities, responsible management, business uncertainty and complexity, and innovation. He has worked with a range of organizations on business transformation projects in particular relating to e-Business strategies, innovation, ethical sustainability and knowledge or talent management. His interest in innovation relates to innovation as an element of dynamic capabilities and the design of business models.

He has a wide range of academic experience from program development at all levels, to international collaboration and academic management and leadership. Edgar has successfully supervised 26 PhD students and has 5 more nearing completion. He is on the editorial board of a range of journals and regularly reviews for journals and conferences. In addition, he regularly contributes to international conference organizing committees, has a number of large research projects, and acts as a specialist advisor for a range of organizations and grant awarding bodies.

Rick Edgeman is Professor and Chair of the Management Department in the Robbins College of Business and Entrepreneurship at Fort Hays State University (Kansas). He is concurrently Professor of Sustainability and Enterprise Performance in the Department of Business Development and Technology (BTECH) at Aarhus University (Denmark), and Honorary Professor of Engineering Operations Management in the Department of Technology & Innovation—Faculty of Engineering at Southern Denmark University.

Edgeman's inter-, multi-, and transdisciplinary orientation contributed to prior posts spanning schools of business, engineering, and science. Among those were Shingo Institute Research Director and Professor of Management in the Jon M. Huntsman School of Business at Utah State University—Home of the Shingo Prize for Operational Excellence; QUEST Professor and QUEST

Honors Fellows Program Executive Director in the Robert H. Smith School of Business and A. James Clark School of Engineering at the University of Maryland; Professor of Computer Information Systems and Center for Quality and Productivity Improvement Director at Colorado State University; Statistical Science Department Professor and Chair at the University of Idaho; and Professor of Quality Sciences in the Industrial Engineering and Management Department—Uppsala Engineering School at Uppsala University (Sweden).

Sustainable enterprise excellence, six sigma innovation and design, quality management, and social-ecological innovation define his research domains. He has authored 125 plus journal articles and book chapters and another 125 plus published book reviews and conference articles.

Globally, Edgeman is one of only six academics selected for inclusion in 21 Voices of Quality for the 21st Century (American Society for Quality: 2000).

Niels Faber is a researcher at Radboud University Nijmegen and a lecturer at Hanze University of Applied Sciences in Groningen. His research focuses on the organizational aspects of sustainability. This translates into three related themes: the transition toward a sustainable society and toward a circular economy in particular, new forms of organization for sustainability, and measuring sustainability. He has produced more than 50 publications, including books, book chapters, and articles and conference contributions.

Faber and Jan Jonker have been working on various research projects regarding business modeling, the circular economy, and blockchain. In recent years, they also have cop-edited a series of academic columns on the circular economy. With Florian Lüdeke Freund (and others), they form the organizing committee of the annual international conference on new business models. Two of these conferences have taken place in Toulouse (2016) and Graz (2017), respectively. The forthcoming conferences will take place in Sofia (2018), Berlin (2019), and Nijmegen (2020).

Raz Godelnik is Assistant Professor of Strategic Design and Management and the Co-Director of the MS in Strategic Design & Management Program at Parsons School of Design—The New School in New York. He teaches undergraduate and graduate courses in innovation, leadership, the sharing economy, sustainability, and strategic design. His research explores connections between innovation, sustainability, business, and design strategies. He is involved in projects focusing on developing resilient business models, the sharing economy and sustainable lifestyles, and the impact of organizational culture on business strategy. He is also leading a collaboration between Parsons students and refugees in

Berlin working together on entrepreneurial initiatives to address refugee needs in cities and refugee camps. He is the co-founder of two green start-ups—Hemper Jeans and Eco-Libris, and a regular contributor to Triple Pundit, writing about issues related to sustainable business, the sharing economy, and design. He holds an MBA from Tel Aviv University and a BA in Communication and Economics from the Hebrew University.

Diana Gonzalez is a user experience and interaction designer residing in Austin, Texas. She graduated from Delft University of Technology (The Netherlands) in 2017 with a MSc in Design for Interaction. She previously received a Bachelor's degree in Industrial Design and worked as a researcher and ship designer for four years in Colombia. She is passionate about sustainability, Internet of Things, and behavior change and is working as a consultant for start-ups in the Silicon Hills high-tech hub. See: https://dianagonzalez.myportfolio.com/

Janne Huiskonen is Professor of Supply Chain Management in Lappeenranta University of Technology (LUT). His research focuses on sustainable business models and operations management in supply chains, networks, and service systems. He has published over 60 articles in scientific conferences and journals.

Emilia Ingemarsdotter is a PhD researcher at Delft University of Technology in the field of Design for Circular Economy, as part of the Marie Curie Innovative Training Network Circuit. Her research explores how emerging digital technologies, in particular Internet of Things (IoT), can act as enablers for the development and implementation of circular products and services. She holds a MEng in Engineering Physics, and a MSc in Industrial Ecology, both from Chalmers University of Technology, Sweden.

Jan Jonker is Professor of Sustainable Enterprise at Radboud University (Nijmegen School of Management). His work focuses on the development of three closely related themes: the emergence of the WEconomy, the development of business models focused on the community and the circular economy, and the exploration and development of value transaction systems with more than money alone. Along with over 40 people, he wrote the bestseller "Nieuwe Business Modellen; Samen Werken aan Waardecreatie" (2014), the English translation of which was published as an e-book [New Business Models; Working Together on Value Creation].

Leena Köppä is a Coach for Entrepreneurship and Impact at the Innovation Services/Y-kampus, Tampere University of Technology. She is an experienced coach with a demonstrated history of working in the university, business, and municipality environment in close connection with entrepreneurial-minded people and entrepreneurs. Skilled in innovation management, coaching, and new business development, her passion is to coach and support lean experiments and meetings with different talents and experts. Her mission is to coach researchers to see the impact of their research on society and to make them aware of the possibility of commercialization of their research results.

Jörg Langwaldt, Dr.Tech., is a research liaison officer at the Research Services, the Tampere University of Technology. He has more than 20 years' experience in acquisition of external funding and writing of research proposals. His focus on provided services to researchers lies on strengthening communication of the foreseen impact of research and innovations actions. He has an interest in the benchmarking of pre-award support services at universities and research organizations.

Lise Lodsgård is a PhD student at Department of Business Development and Technology, Aarhus University. Her PhD dissertation investigates the area of strategic value creation through business-NGO partnerships, including empirical studies of key drivers and challenges across different types of partnerships and how they are managed, organized, and measured optimally. She has been a lecturer within CSR, scientific methods, entrepreneurship, and project management for several years. Formerly she was a manager within municipals and public organizations, including development and implementation of public-NGO partnerships within the social area, from which she also draws her experience.

Florian Lüdeke-Freund is a lecturer at ESCP Europe Business School, Berlin, Germany, where he also holds the Chair for Corporate Sustainability, and he is a research fellow at the Centre for Sustainability Management (CSM), Leuphana University, Lüneburg, Germany. His research deals with corporate sustainability, sustainable entrepreneurship, business models, and values-based innovation. Besides publishing on these topics, he is a guest editor of journal special issues with *Organization & Environment, Business & Society*, and the *Journal of Business Models*. He is serving on different advisory boards, including the *Journal of Business Models* and the annual International Conference on New Business Models. In 2013, Florian founded the research hub www.SustainableBusinessModel.org.

Saku J. Mäkinen, Dr.Tech, is Vice Dean of Research and Professor of Industrial Management at the Tampere University of Technology (TUT), Finland, and Research Director at University of Helsinki/CERN, Switzerland. Previously Mäkinen has also been with the Columbia University at the City of New York, USA, the University of New South Wales, Australia, and the National University of Singapore. His research has appeared in leading journals, including *Technological Forecasting and Social Change, Journal of Product Innovation Management,* and *Technovation.* He works in the intersection of technology and innovation management, and strategic management.

Kaisa Manninen, MSc, Tech., is a junior researcher and a PhD student at the Lappeenranta University of Technology (LUT). Her research topic is related to sustainable business models and she is interested in integration of sustainability in business strategy. She has several years' research experience from the field of environmental sustainability and life cycle assessment. She has published eight scientific international peer-reviewed articles.

Lorenzo Massa Is a scientist at the Collège du Management at École Polytechnique FÉdÉrale de Lausanne (EPFL), Lausanne, Switzerland, and adjunct faculty at the Department of Management, University of Bologna, and at the Bologna Business School (BBS). His research lies at the intersection between strategy, innovation, and sustainability.

He has published research on business models in prestigious outlets, including *Journal of Management, Oxford Handbooks,* and *Academy of Management Annals.* He completed his Master's degree and PhD in Management at IESE Business School. During his PhD, he has been a research fellow at the Rocky Mountain Institute, Boulder, Colorado, United States, working on business model design for the diffusion of renewable energies. He holds graduate degrees, both with distinction, in Mechanical Engineering from the Dublin Institute of Technology (B.Eng.) and the University of Genoa (M.Sc. Eng.).

Jen van der Meer is Assistant Professor of Strategic Design and Management at Parsons School of Design—The New School in New York. A former Wall Street analyst and economist, She is an entrepreneur who cultivates leadership potential in students, start-up founders, and corporate innovation clients. She is in equal parts data-driven and creative in her approach to understand and apply the opportunities for technology and design to transform the economy, society, and culture. She is founder of Reason Street, a consultancy that designs innovation systems for Fortune Global 500 companies, helping board and C-suite executives evaluate and manage their full portfolio of growth opportunities. The consultancy also advises start-ups seeking transformational growth in health, social justice, and environmental impact. In 2008, she joined, as a partner, Drillteam, a consumer advocacy consultancy where she created a digital platform for managing large-scale design research projects, and grew the organization, resulting in subsequent acquisitions by venture-backed Powered, Inc. and by Dachis Group. She has previously taught at NYU's Interactive Telecommunications Program (ITP) and the School of Visual Arts. She has an MBA from HEC Paris and a BA from Trinity College.

Sofia Ritzén is Professor in Integrated Product Development at the Royal Institute of Technology (KTH) in Stockholm, Sweden. Her research focuses on strategic business issues in industry and the need to deliver radical innovations, both for reaching a sustainable development and to be a competitive actor in an innovation system. The research is made in collaboration with industry or public organizations and research impact is an important characteristic in Ritzén's research. Ritzén is also teaching in Integrated Product Development and Head of Department of Machine Design at KTH.

Ulla A. Saari is a postdoctoral researcher at the Center for Innovation and Technology Research (CITER), the Laboratory of Industrial and Information Management at the Tampere University of Technology (TUT), Finland. She holds a DTech degree in Industrial Engineering and Management from TUT and a MA degree in Languages and Social Sciences from the University of Helsinki. Her research topics include sustainability, eco-friendliness, stakeholder management, entrepreneurship, and business ecosystems. She has 20 years' experience in the high-tech industry in various senior manager level roles in international organizations.

List of Figures

Fig. 1.1	Business models' value creation framework. Source: Bocken et al. (2015, p. 71)	9
Fig. 1.2	The SBM pyramid framework for evaluating sustainability of BMs. Source: Aagaard (2017)	12
Fig. 1.3	Assessing the sustainability of the 11 dimensions of business models. Source: Aagaard (2017)	12
Fig. 1.4	Evaluating the sustainability level of Grundfos Lifelink's value proposition. Source: Aagaard (2017)	14
Fig. 1.5	Evaluating the sustainability level of Grundfos Lifelink's value creation. Source: Aagaard (2017)	15
Fig. 1.6	Evaluating the sustainability level of Grundfos Lifelink's value capture. Source: Aagaard (2017)	16
Fig. 2.1	Illustration of connections between business model patterns (Source: own illustration; "Business Model Canvas" based on Osterwalder and Pigneur 2009)	40
Fig. 2.2	The BIK "playground" and facilitation cards	49
Fig. 2.3	Possible pattern combinations of revenue methods and pricing schemes	51
Fig. 2.4	Value proposition of the Smart Business Modeler	53
Fig. 2.5	IA-enabled business modelling with the Smart Business Modeler	55
Fig. 4.1	The relationship types of profit and sustainability (reproduced from Lankoski and Smith 2017) combined with the	

	"Financial Logic", "Integrated Logic" (Gao and Bansal 2013), "Environmental Dominant Logic" (Montabon et al. 2016), and "Sustainability Logic" (e.g., Gao and Bansal 2013; Greenwood et al. 2015)	93
Fig. 4.2	Corporate responsibility and sustainability science perspectives to support sustainability management at the organizational level	96
Fig. 4.3	Sustainability management levels (based on Baumgartner (2014) supported by sustainability science-based principles)	101
Fig. 4.4	Possible value profiles of a company (based on the range of alternative objective functions by Lankoski and Smith (2017))	102
Fig. 4.5	Framework for effective Values-Driven Sustainability Management	103
Fig. 4.6	Connection of the Value-Focused Thinking (VFT) approach (Keeney 1992, 1996) and the Values-Driven Sustainability Management Framework. The values of decision makers are identified and structured based on the techniques of the VFT. The phases of the VFT presented with dotted lines are excluded	106
Fig. 4.7	The connection of Future-Fit Business Benchmark (adapted from Future-Fit Foundation 2017) and the Values-Driven Sustainability Management Framework. The System Conditions and 23 Break-Even Goals are used as a basis to correlate sustainability objectives with science-based sustainability principles. The phases of the FFBB with dotted lines are excluded from the study	112
Fig. 5.1	Impact Canvas tool and a built-in iteration with Status—Target—Test and Do for each section of the canvas	126
Fig. 5.2	The development timeline and iteration cycles of the Impact Canvas tool	135
Fig. 7.1	The critical resource efficiency parameters in relation to the life cycle perspective of a physical product	190
Fig. 7.2	Logical chain of actions, necessary steps for closing material loops while finding new business models	192
Fig. 7.3	Value creation, delivery, and capture will be different with different orientations in developing product service systems (after Tukker 2004)	193

Fig. 7.4	A number of resource efficiency parameters should inspire each element in a business model, and specifically the value proposition and the revenue model must be carefully considered to secure a business aligned to closing material loops	195
Fig. 7.5	Different driving forces push for different innovation	197
Fig. 8.1	The collaborative continuum of business-NGO collaborations. Source: Austin and Seitanidi (2012, p. 736)	218
Fig. 9.1	SBM in startups at the intersection of SBM and SE	242
Fig. 9.2	The lean SBM framework	257
Fig. 10.1	The value tetrahedron	279
Fig. 10.2	Value triangle business model canvas	287
Fig. 10.3	Impact of strategic meanings on the building blocks of Muji's VT BM canvas	308
Fig. 11.1	The house of sustainability	337
Fig. 11.2	A generic sustainable enterprise excellence model	339
Fig. 11.3	Sustainable enterprise excellence, resilience and robustness model	346
Fig. 11.4	SEER2 strategy assessment dial	352
Fig. 11.5	SEER2 deployment assessment dial	353
Fig. 11.6	SEER2 results assessment dial	353
Fig. 11.7	Generic SWOT Plot narrative	354
Fig. 11.8	SEER2 NEWS Report Assessment Dashboard	354

List of Tables

Table 2.1	Business model pattern definitions	34
Table 2.2	Pattern example "House Cluster"	36
Table 2.3	SBM pattern example "Product-Oriented Service"	37
Table 3.1	Different PSS and potential impacts	66
Table 3.2	Design interventions and strategies for sustainable behavior	70
Table 3.3	Overview of IoT capabilities suitable for sustainable PSS	74
Table 3.4	Framework to support PSS design to encourage sustainable behavior using IoT strategies	75
Table 3.5	Cases reviewed for study	76
Table 3.6	Washing machines snapshot case summary	79
Table 3.7	Car-sharing snapshot case summary	82
Table 4.1	Relationships between the variables of profit and social welfare	92
Table 4.2	Future-Fit Break-Even Goals (Future-Fit Business Benchmark 2017)	110
Table 5.1	Results from the first version of the feedback survey focusing on testing the user-friendliness and usefulness of the tool in multidisciplinary teams	141
Table 5.2	Results from the second version of the feedback survey focusing on the content elements	142
Table 9.1	Comparing the lean startup "shop" vs. the sustainable business model "shop"	255

Table 10.1	Definitions of SBM	286
Table 10.2	Paradoxes and sustainability	294
Table 11.1	The United Nations Global Compact 10 principles	340
Table 11.2	United Nations Sustainable Development Goals for agenda 2030	342
Table 11.3	Business sector alignment with United Nations Sustainable Development Goals	344
Table 11.4	Three most important business sectors relative to each United Nations Sustainable Development Goal	345
Table 11.5	Representative SBM and SEER2 strategic emphases	347
Table 11.6	Selected means by which strategy may be deployed, usually in combination	348
Table 11.7	Representative results targeted by SBM and SEER2 models	349
Table 11.8	Example maturing scale for the systems, processes, and tools deployment means	351

1

Identifying Sustainable Business Models Through Sustainable Value Creation

Annabeth Aagaard

1   Introduction

Over the last decade, research on sustainable businesses (SBs) and sustainable innovations has increased rapidly, as sustainability has become a new premise for doing business (Dryzek 2005; Birkin et al. 2009a, b). However, applying business model innovation (BMI) as a way to create sustainable value requires several alterations of our ways of understanding and evaluating businesses and their business models (BMs). Yet, in exploring the theoretical concepts of sustainable business models (SBMs), the starting point would have to be the original definitions of BMs.

BMs and BMI have been the focus of substantial attention from both academics and practitioners (e.g., Amit and Zott 2001; Chesbrough and Rosenbloom 2002; Christensen and Raynor 2003; Govindarajan and Trimble 2005; Markides 2008; Teece 2010; Ritter and Andersen 2014;

A. Aagaard (✉)
Aarhus University,
Herning, Denmark
e-mail: aaa@btech.au.dk

Foss and Saebi 2017) and have been the subject of a still growing number of academic and practitioner-oriented studies. The extensive stream of work on BMI has generated many important insights. However, our understanding of BMs remains fragmented, as stressed by Zott et al. (2011). One thing the authors in this field seem to agree on is that a BM is a model of the way in which a business does business (Taran 2011). However, while there is consensus on the meaning of "doing business," namely creating and delivering value so as to generate value and achieve a SB position, there is less agreement on the "model" part (Taran et al. 2013). Another key challenge of performing studies in BM and BMI relates to the issue addressed by David J. Teece, who states that "the concept of a business model lacks theoretical grounding in economics or in business studies" (Teece 2010, p. 174).

BMs appear in many different forms. They can be applied as a core unit of analysis extending beyond the business boundaries (e.g., Zott and Amit 2007). In addition, BMs may be viewed as a construct between strategy and implementation (Baden-Fuller and Morgan 2010). BMs can also be a means for commercializing new technologies (Chesbrough and Rosenbloom 2002; Chesbrough 2007, 2010) and as an intermediary between different innovation actors such as businesses, financiers, and research institutions, that is, actors who shape innovation networks (Doganova and Eyquem-Renault 2009). BMs can therefore be subject to innovation themselves or be a template for implementing managerial initiatives (Zott and Amit 2010). Furthermore, they can be used to depict current realities ("as is") or used for simulations to decide on a preferred future ("to be") (Osterwalder 2004; Chatterjee 2013), that is, as role exemplars (Baden-Fuller and Morgan 2010). Existing BMs can then be seen as a representation of strategic decisions, which have been implemented through tactical choices (Casadesus-Masanell and Ricart 2010), which may create self-enforcing "virtuous circles" in processes and resources, as stressed by Casadesus-Masanell and Ricart (2011).

BMs can also have a narrative role (Magretta 2002), serving as boundary objects (Doganova and Eyquem-Renault 2009) and as conventions (Verstraete and Jouison-Lafitte 2011) or theories of performative actions (Perkmann and Spicer 2010) in which stakeholders become motivated to participate in the joint realization of a venture. As such, the core idea of the

BM concept addresses many classic questions of strategic nature, such as market relevance (value proposition), what customers to serve and how to serve them, how to make a profit, and what technology to use (Magretta 2002; Sandberg 2002; Morris et al. 2005; Verstraete and Jouison-Lafitte 2011). Thus, in defining BMI we apply the following definition by Casadesus-Masanell and Zhu (2013, p. 464): "The search for new business logics of the firm and new ways to create and capture value for its stakeholders."

2 From Traditional to Sustainable Business Models

Baden-Fuller and Morgan (2010) underline that from a holistic and systemic concept, a BM perspective may be expected to contribute to a sustainable business model innovation (SBMI) agenda by opening up new approaches to overcoming internal and external barriers. Although there is a growing body of literature analyzing and discussing sustainability and sustainable development on the political and society levels (Dryzek 2005), the operationalization of the concept in relation to business and on the corporate level is still rather weak (Bansal 2005; Stubbs and Cocklin 2008; Zink et al. 2008; Carroll and Shabana 2010).

Furthermore, studying the concept of sustainability is challenged by the fact that it is a fragmented concept, and some researchers even question whether sustainability is a concept or a political discourse (Dryzek 2005) or an artifact (Faber et al. 2005). In the so-called Brundtland report, "Our Common Future" by World Commission on Environment and Development, sustainable development is defined as follows: "Sustainable development is the kind of development that meets the needs of the present without compromising the ability of future generations to meet their own needs." One attempt of how to transfer the general and rather vague Brundtland definition of sustainability into corporate level is presented by Dyllick and Hockerts (2002, p. 131), who define sustainable development as "meeting the needs of a firm's direct and indirect stakeholders without compromising its ability to meet the needs of future stakeholders as well." This explicit focus on stakeholder needs emphasizes the importance of businesses responding to their ecosystem and the primary stakeholders such as shareholders, employees, and customers, but also secondary stakeholders such as non-governmental organizations (NGOs) in order to gain and maintain legitimacy and license to operate with regard to various sustainable issues (Zink et al. 2008; Lodsgård and Aagaard 2016).

The application of a long-term perspective to the needs of future stakeholders underlines the complexity of long-term management practices and SBMs combined with short-term requests from shareholders for increased profits, which is a key challenge that needs to be addressed at the corporate level (Poncelet 2001). The most common translation of sustainability into business on corporate level is the triple bottom line, which consists of three sustainable dimensions: people, planet, and profit (Elkington 1997) and is described as three equally important managerial principles of SBMs (Hansen et al. 2009; Bradbury-Huang 2010; Schaltegger and Wagner 2011). As this approach is both well established and applied in the Corporate Social Responsibility (CSR)-reporting of many international companies reporting to global reporting initiative (GRI), the same methodology will be applied in the frame designed to evaluate the level of sustainability of BMs and their value creation. The three evaluation criteria or dimensions are also referred to as people, planet, and profit and are explained as follows:

- *People*—the social dimension refers to equity for all human beings and their opportunities in gaining access to resources with regard to basic needs such as water, food, and development through improved living conditions such as health care and education (Bansal 2005).
- *Planet*—the environmental dimension refers to the ecosystem of the Earth and to reductions of human-created footprints and ecological imbalances in terms of pollution, the ozone layer, greenhouse gases, non-biodegradable waste, deforestation, overfishing, and so on.
- *Profit*—the profit dimension emphasizes that production of goods and services is a prerequisite to improve the living conditions globally (Bansal 2005).

With a focus on integrating sustainability into business systems, Charter and Clark (2007, p. 9) offer a definition of sustainable innovation embracing all of these three elements: "Sustainable innovation is a process where sustainability considerations (environmental, social and financial) are integrated into company systems—business systems—from idea generation and development (R&D) and commercialization. This applies to products, services and technologies, as well as to new business and organizational models."

This definition is closely aligned with business strategies, where social and environmental issues are seen as commercially profitable options and as sources to increase future competitiveness. Nevertheless, as Charter and Clark's (2007) definition builds on Elkington's (1997) triple bottom line and the Brundtland (1987) definition, which are anchored in sustainable development, it is necessary to elaborate further on the differences and similarities between the concept of sustainable development and that of sustainable innovation. In the perspective of sustainable development, BMI is merged into sustainability and seen as means in pursuing sustainable objectives (Ferauge2013). The main question here is, therefore, "what can innovation do for sustainability?" In this context it is no longer enough for an innovation to be novel and original in its technical features—it has to be novel and original in terms of environmental or social sustainability as well (Phills et al. 2008). In the other perspective, sustainability is merged into innovation, where sustainable problems are seen as sources of inspiration for businesses in generating new innovations and business opportunities (Ferauge2013; Lodsgård and Aagaard 2017). This is summed up by Bocken et al. (2014, p. 44) in their definition of BMIs for sustainability: "Innovations that create significant positive and/or significantly reduced negative impacts for the environment and/or society, through changes in the way the organisation and its value-network create, deliver value and capture value (i.e., create economic value) or change their value propositions."

A number of researchers stress that disruptive circumstances through external stakeholder pressures often lead to the creation of radical sustainable innovations, while sustaining circumstances where, for example, customers are willing to accept minor product adjustment typically lead to incremental sustainable innovations (Christensen 1997; Steketee 2010). Research indicates that businesses recently have moved beyond eco-efficiency compliances and extended the focus to the adaption of disruptive innovative processes where businesses respond with new game-changing

BMs (Schaltegger and Wagner 2008; Loorbach et al. 2009; Boons et al. 2013). This evidence emphasizes the potentials for businesses in pursuing both incremental innovations though the perspective of eco-efficiency in products and processes and in pursuing more radical innovations though SBMIs.

3   Understanding the Concept of Sustainable Business Models

The definitions of SBMs and SBMI originate from different scientific areas. Looking into the literature on sustainable entrepreneurship and corporate sustainability management, the concept of SBMs is still used in a fuzzy way (Stubbs and Cocklin 2008; Lüdeke-Freund 2009; Schaltegger et al. 2012; Aagaard 2016, 2017). In addition, BM research often neglects to take a dynamic perspective to understand how firms' BMs evolve over time (Pereira Da Costa and Levie 2014). Thus, "the relationship between business model and time is little discussed… it is a snapshot and description at a specific moment in time" (Osterwalder et al. 2005, p. 15). This is a challenge when studying SBMs, as what is considered sustainable changes over time. Baden-Fuller and Morgan (2010) stress that from a holistic and systemic concept a BM perspective may be expected to contribute to a SBMI agenda by opening up new approaches to overcoming internal and external barriers.

Chou et al. (2015, p. 50) argue that sustainability is considered to be an integrated part of company value propositions and state that "Company policies and brand image are driven by value propositions. The company mission reflects the core business value and competitive strategy, and the sustainability vision implies the direction of social responsibility the company intends to pursue. These two factors should be linked in order to produce clear, sustainability-led value propositions." Birkin et al. (2009a, b) identified in their study on North European and Chinese businesses that societal and cultural demands of sustainable development evolve outside the economic sphere as drivers for BM change in businesses. Their findings reveal that as social and natural needs become institutionalized as concrete societal and cultural demands, BMs will change radically, as businesses are expected to ensure adaptations in order to secure legitimacy, legality, and business success.

Earlier work reveals the first developments in mapping the concept of and movements toward SBMI. Lovins et al. (1999), for example, propose a four-step agenda to align business practice with environmental needs, which they labeled "Natural Capitalism." The four steps constitute increase of natural resources' productivity, imitation of biological production models, change of BMs, and reinvestment in natural capital. Important for our review and mapping of the concept is the fact that Lovins and colleagues see a fundamental change toward SBMs as crucial to realizing Natural Capitalism and business potentials in the future. Another interesting early contribution that emphasizes the same understanding of SBMI is Hart and Milstein's (1999) paper, which views sustainable development as a force of industrial renewal and progress. They conclude that "simply transplanting business models" (p. 29) from one economy to another will run counter to sustainable development. Common for these two classic articles is how they see changing BMs as a way to reduce negative social and ecological impacts as well as a way to achieve sustainable development.

More recent scientific contributions mapping the SBMI concept reveal a more elaborate understanding of the components involved. For example, Yunus et al. (2010) reason that for social businesses to evolve, a specific BM framework is needed that integrates a social profit equation. They present a number of key components, which go into explaining and developing a social BM (p. 319):

1. Social profit equation (social profit and environmental profit),
2. Value constellation (internal value chain and external value chain),
3. Value propositions (stakeholders and product/services), and
4. Economic profit equation (sales revenues, cost structure, and capital employed).

According to their concept, social businesses apply BMs that above all recover their full costs and pass profits on to customers, who benefit from low prices, adequate services, and better access to maximize the social profit equation. Yunus et al. (2010) refer to this as: "a no-loss, no-dividend, self-sustaining business that offers goods or services and repays investments to its owners, but whose primary purpose is to serve society and improve the lot of the poor" (p. 311). Another interesting contribution in mapping SBMI addresses different typologies of SBMIs and comes from Boons and Lüdeke-Freund (2013). They define three different types of SBMs that create social value and maximize social profit while focusing on three different areas (pp. 14–15):

- *Technological innovation*: creating a fit between technology characteristics and (new) commercialization approaches that both can succeed on given and new markets
- *Organizational innovation*: implementing alternative paradigms that shape the culture, structure, and routines of organizations and thus change the way of doing business toward sustainable development
- *Social innovation*: helping to create and further develop markets for innovations with a social purpose

Other streams of literature emphasize that the SBMI typology changes depending on the kind of partnerships (e.g., public-private and business/NGO collaboration) that are required to create social value and maximize social profit (Kanter 1999; Chesbrough et al. 2006; Dahan et al. 2010; Lodsgård and Aagaard 2016). The ultimate holistic approach toward the sustainable business case is to combine economic-oriented value propositions with environmental- and social-oriented value propositions (Emerson 2003; Bocken et al. 2015). In understanding SBMs as a way to build linkages between actors that are necessary to successfully market a sustainable product or service (Boons and Mendoza 2010), various elements being open to multiple interpretations may be considered strengths rather than weaknesses. In other words, the so-called "fuzziness" of the concept of sustainability may actually be a useful quality in developing sustainable innovations (e.g., Tukker and Tischner 2006; Hansen et al. 2009; Boons et al. 2013), as what is considered sustainable will change over time.

In conceptualizing SBMs and SBMI, the acclaimed frameworks of Osterwalder et al. (2005) and Richardson (2008) as portrayed in Bocken et al. (2014, 2015) are applied. In the further interpretation by Bocken

Identifying Sustainable Business Models Through Sustainable...

Fig. 1.1 Business models' value creation framework. Source: Bocken et al. (2015, p. 71)

et al. (2014, 2015), BMs are explored through the sustainable value they generate and consist of three core elements: the value proposition, value creation and delivery, and value capture as illustrated in Fig. 1.1.

- Value proposition is concerned with the product and service offerings in generating economic return. In a sustainable business, the value proposition provides measurable ecological or social value together with economic value (Boons and Lüdeke-Freund 2013).
- Value creation emphasizes how businesses capture value by seizing new business opportunities, new markets, and new revenue streams (Teece 2010; Beltramello et al. 2013).
- Value capture relates to how a business earns its revenues from the provision of goods, services, or data/information to customers and users (Teece 2010).

4 Sustainable Value Creation in Sustainable Business Models

The concepts of value and value creation have been discussed extensively in literature on strategic management, organizational and partnership theory, and more recently in the discussion of how to realize financial goals in combination with social performances through sustainability and BMs. Contributions in the value field count Bowman and Ambrosini

(2000), Makadok (2001), and Makadok and Coff (2002), who discuss value creation as value capture derived from value in use and value in exchange from a classic economic perspective on an organizational level. Lepak et al. (2007) extend the concept beyond the classical economic perspective, applying the individual and society level as sources and targets of value creation and value capture in a more holistic perspective, which supports the idea of (sustainable/holistic) value creation through SBMs.

This implies that the concept of value in use is extended from customer perceptions as target users into a broader context where target users and subjective assessments are found among several stakeholders on all levels—individual, organizational, and society. Stakeholders and entities on all levels may benefit from the transformation of value in use into value in exchange, which means value beyond pure economic gains may be captured on more levels as well (Lepak et al. 2007) and value is defined as shared value on more levels (Porter and Kramer 2011). Thus, the value construct is reframed from the one-dimensional shareholder logic of profit maximization toward more stakeholders and levels of attention (Pedersen et al. 2016; Schaltegger et al. 2016; Upward and Jones 2016).

The concept of value is closely related to valuable resources, which are necessary for companies to develop, access, and bring into play in order to create value though exploitation of opportunities, and elimination of threats and to stay at the competitive forefront (Bowman and Ambrosini 2000). As such, Barney (1991) explains that resources are considered valuable if they are rare, imperfectly imitable, and imperfectly substitutable. In a classic economic perspective, resources are only considered valuable if they are exploited into products and services that are perceived as valuable by customers/end users. Thus, the value proposition of a company reveals the value to be created and the stakeholders it is created for (Upward and Jones 2016). In sustainable business thinking, value propositions go beyond these conventional product, service, and process considerations and are referred to as the triple bottom line logic (Bocken et al. 2015; Pedersen et al. 2016).

Consequently, the optimal approach toward SBM is to combine economic-oriented value propositions with environmental- and social-oriented value propositions (Emerson 2003; Bocken et al. 2015). This is further underlined by Chou et al. (2015), who emphasize that sustainability is to be considered as an integrated part of a company's value propositions: "Company policies and brand image are driven by value propositions. The company mission reflects the core business value and competitive strategy, and the sustainability vision implies the direction of social responsibility the company intends to pursue. These two factors should be linked in order to produce clear, sustainability-led value propositions" (p. 50). For companies to define or redefine their value propositions in the context of environmental and social issues may provide them with new business opportunities and reduction of negative impacts on, for example, stakeholders with no voice of their own, such as the environment and marginalized groups and individuals (Bocken et al. 2014; Upward and Jones 2016). However, a business may also overlook value that is captured by unintended stakeholders and miss out on future value opportunities in its value propositions.

As discussed above, several authors have attempted to define the characteristics of sustainable value creation and the SBM concept. It appears from the literature review that the majority of the contributions in this scientific field take on a more macro, technological, or environmental approach toward the SBM and relate it to the advantages of the business, the customers, the society, or the world. For the conceptual BM framework (as presented in Fig. 1.1) to be applied in evaluating sustainability of BMs, we need to combine it with a set of evaluation criteria of sustainability. In the framework, the acclaimed, empirically applied (e.g. in CSR reporting), and previously mentioned criteria of Elkington (1997)—people/social, planet/environmental, and profit—are applied and the following conceptual evaluation framework is derived (Fig. 1.2).

In the SBM pyramid framework, sustainable value creation is defined as the resources, activities, and partnerships that companies apply and implement in order to realize their sustainable value propositions. Consequently, sustainable value capture is explained as a company's economic and non-economic value gains tightly linked to its sustainable value propositions. It is important in studying a company's sustainable value propositions and sustainable value creation to step inside the company's inner logics to explore which targets and levels of attention SBM

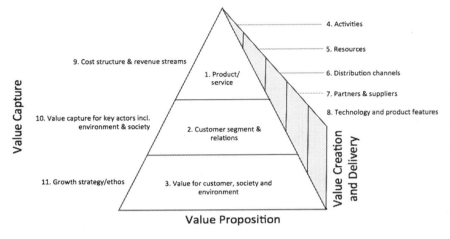

Fig. 1.2 The SBM pyramid framework for evaluating sustainability of BMs. Source: Aagaard (2017)

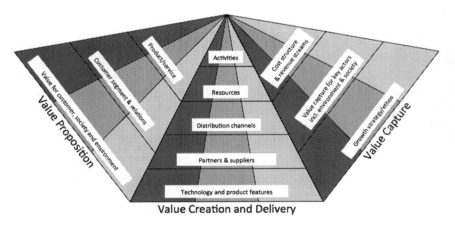

Fig. 1.3 Assessing the sustainability of the 11 dimensions of business models. Source: Aagaard (2017)

are aimed at and which specific activities are carried out in order to realize the company's SBM (Lodsgård and Aagaard 2017).

The SBM pyramid framework is depicted folded as well as unfolded to show all the 11 dimensions included in sustainable value propositions, sustainable value creation, and sustainable value capture in SBMs (Fig. 1.3).

In the case example below, the framework for evaluating sustainability in BMs is applied in identifying and evaluating the actual level of sustainability of BMs across four case studies in different industrial contexts.

5 Case Example Using the SBM Pyramid Framework

In exploration of the framework, an empirical case of a company's BM is applied. The selected case is Grundfos Lifelink. The company Grundfos was founded in 1945 and is a traditional pump manufacturing company that employs around 18,500 people and has departments in 56 countries. Over the year, the company has tried to develop new BMs based on their core pump technology and competences, while including sustainability in the value propositions, value creation, and value capture of the product and service offerings related to the BM. The specific BM of Grundfos explored in this case example is Lifelink, which is widely known as a SBM and therefore selected as a case example. As a business Grundfos Lifelink produces water solutions that combine technology with professional service networks to support operations on the ground. Through partnerships across sectors Grundfos Lifelink develops, sells, and offers services for automatic water systems, primarily aimed at rural areas in developing countries.

5.1 Grundfos Lifelink Value Proposition

Grundfos Lifelink's value proposition consists of manufacturing and offering water solutions for developing countries and communities generally characterized by poor access to clean water and through collaborations with NGOs such as the Red Cross. The Lifelink products include AQtap (an intelligent water dispenser that is operated by smartcard), AQpure (an ultrafiltration-based water treatment system optimized for producing drinking water), and SQflex (an submersible solar energy–based pumping system). The value proposition of these water systems is clearly stated by the manager informant #1 *"Our main mission and business is to provide reliable access to clean water in the developing world."* The value proposition

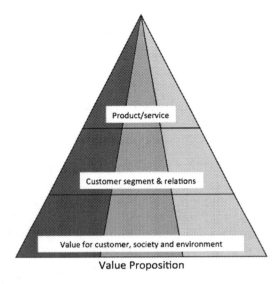

Fig. 1.4 Evaluating the sustainability level of Grundfos Lifelink's value proposition. Source: Aagaard (2017)

of Grundfos Lifelink addresses the *social dimension* (e.g., providing clean water to people in developing countries, who seldom have easy access), the *environmental dimension* (e.g., ensuring water quality by cleaning it through unique water cleaning techniques), and *the profit dimension* (emphasizes that the business aim of Lifelink is to generate a business (profits), while providing sustainable water solutions to people in need of clean water) (Fig. 1.4).

5.2 Grundfos Lifelink's Value Creation

Grundfos Lifelink products and services are primarily sold through development organizations that make water projects or to water supply companies working in Kenya or Africa. It creates value through a sustainable value chain approach, where NGOs play a central part. This is emphasized by manager informant #1 in the following statement: "*NGOs have a role as a customer in reality. In an expanded customer relationships, where you can also go in and implement projects together, as we did with the Red Cross for example.*" The specific challenges of combining NGOs and social and profit dimensions in the value creations are stressed by manager informant #2: "*We had the problem that when the projects involved the Red Cross, all the people expected that it was free... We are therefore about to establish a separate unit that we call 'trade-water,' which is actually a non-profit water company, but instead of donating hardware for free to the village, our new partnership with NGO, Water Missions International, ensures that we maintain ownership of the hardware, but establish the organization in charge of the daily operation of the project and ensures that they sell water credits for the project, etc.*" Developing Grundfos Lifelink has required new technologies, new partners, and new ways of making profits to ensure that the social, environmental, and profit dimensions were present at all five dimensions of value creation at Grundfos Lifelink (Fig. 1.5).

5.3 Value Capture of Grundfos Lifelink

Grundfos Lifelink is a new business for Grundfos and has in many ways altered the way Grundfos captures value, as revenue streams have not been the major focus, as stressed by manager informant #1: "*As a businessman I should probably have closed the project down a long time ago, but*

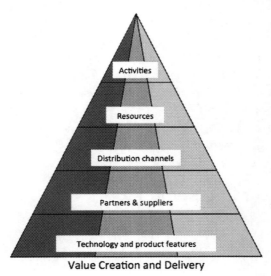

Fig. 1.5 Evaluating the sustainability level of Grundfos Lifelink's value creation. Source: Aagaard (2017)

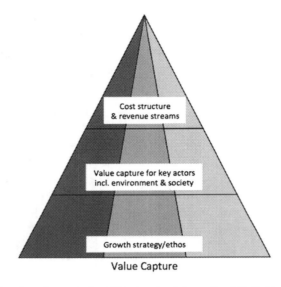

Fig. 1.6 Evaluating the sustainability level of Grundfos Lifelink's value capture. Source: Aagaard (2017)

the vision behind is simply too big to do so." Sustainability is part of Grundfos growth strategy and part of the value captured by the key actors, as emphasized in this quote by manager informant#2: *"Sustainability is a central part of our innovation internally, which was defined in 2011, when we made three guiding stars: 'Put stability first,' 'try new technologies,' and 'be there for/take care of a better world.' Grundfos has usually focused more on climate- or energy-based sustainable innovations and less on the social side. But with Grundfos LIFELINK we go more into the social sphere."* Thus, value capture at Grundfos Lifelink incorporates the environmental, social, and profit dimensions (Fig. 1.6).

6 Concluding Remarks

Having a conceptual framework for SBMs is one thing; evaluating how sustainable the BMs actually are is quite another issue. In creating a SBM or in transforming an existing and non-sustainable business into a sustainable business, the SBM framework provides an overview of which dimensions of the BM are sustainable and on which of the three P-dimensions (people, planet, profit). Illustrating the entire BM and evaluating all 11 dimensions on the three sustainability parameters also provide inspiration as to where a company's BM(s) may potentially develop and innovate to provide new and sustainable business opportunities through, for example, new customer segments, new resources, new partners and suppliers, or new technologies. The framework also makes it possible to compare BMs and their sustainability across industrial context and company sizes.

Furthermore, the framework can also determine the level of sustainability of any BM or BMI over time, as the people, planet, and profit evaluation criteria follow the level of corporate sustainability as expected by society at any given time. This is also visible in CSR reporting, which applies the same three sustainability criteria, as what is considered a "good" CSR report, and performance of companies today will change for tomorrow, as societal expectations rise to the level of the best performers, which stakeholders then compare to other companies' sustainability efforts. One further development of the SBM pyramid in assessment of the level of sustainability of BMs would be to include metrics, for example, 1–5 or low, medium and high levels of sustainability of each BM dimension. However, this is a challenging task as what is considered sustainable in one industry may be considered mainstream in another. And in a global context, what may be considered sustainable in one country for example, the developing countries, may not be considered sustainable in developed, western countries or vice versa. Thus, one should explore/apply the frameworks within the given (industrial and/or geographical) context and assess sustainability in the norm of the specific context. This could for example, include the best practices/high performers of the industry as representatives of the "high" levels of sustainability in the BM dimensions.

The chapter presents a three-dimensional SBM framework that can assist researchers and practitioners in understanding and mapping SBM/SBMI and evaluating the level of sustainability of all businesses and BMs across industrial contexts and dimensions and over time. SB and SBM practices can lead to a renewed vision of the function of a BM. The proposed framework provides users with the tools to describe, categorize, and compare their SB, SBM, and SBMI on a valid foundation.

This chapter has attempted to close the research gap of mapping and understanding SBs and SBMs as addressed earlier by Kanter (1999), Eppinger (2011), and Venn and Berg (2013). Another theoretical contribution of the chapter is the operationalization of the concept in relation to business and on a corporate level, as research in this area is still rather weak, as stressed by Bansal (2005), Stubbs and Cocklin (2008), Zink et al. (2008), and Carroll and Shabana (2010). With the presented literature overview, the evaluation parameters, and the presented SBM framework, a new theoretical tool is provided to improve our understanding and the theoretical and empirical discussion and evaluation of SBs and SBMs.

This model is designed in such a way that it can be applied across companies and organizations of different sizes and industrial backgrounds to identify and illustrate the sustainability of a specific BM or BMI and its 11 different BM dimensions. The empirical contribution is therefore captured in the applicability of the framework across contexts as well as over time, while making sustainability in BMs much more tangible and detectable. The managerial implications of the chapter (1) provide managers with an overview to better understand and evaluate their BMs in relation to sustainability, (2) illustrate where existing and new BMs can be developed and innovated through the identified "unsustainable" dimensions of existing BMs or BM systems and ecosystems to gain potential competitive advantages through sustainability, and (3) enable managers to compare the level of sustainability of their BMs to competing BMs.

The research field of SBM and SBMI is still at a very early stage, which does present a limitation and challenge in the design of a framework for understanding and evaluating the level of sustainability of a BM or BMI. This is also why the framework is designed on the basis of one of the most empirically applied BM frameworks, the BM canvas. One could easily challenge whether the same dimensions are of equal interest in an SBM compared to a traditional and potentially unsustainable BM. However, in this study it is assumed that the same dimensions are of relevance in describing a (sustainable) BM. Another limitation of the present study relates to the fact that the presented framework has only been explored through one case company in this chapter and where the selected BM is sustainable.

However, the model has been explored across other case companies (Aagaard 2017) and showed that it is applicable across different industries, company sizes and levels of sustainability in the companies BMs. The present case example was applied to illustrate how sustainability of BM dimensions is exemplified and illustrated through actual sustainable activities. Thus, venues for further research lie in testing the framework through an elaborate and longitudinal case study to explore SBMI and the SBM framework across non-sustainable and sustainable businesses, over time, and across different national, organizational, and industrial contexts.

References

Aagaard, A. 2016. *Sustainable Business: Integrating CSR in Business and Functions*. River Publishers.

———. 2017. Understanding and Evaluating Sustainable Business Models: A Cross-Industry Case Study. In *The 24th Innovation and Product Development Management Conference (IPDMC)*, Reykjavik University, Reykjavik, Iceland, June 11–13.

Amit, R., and G. Zott. 2001. Value Creation in e-Business. *Strategic Management Journal* 22 (6–7): 493–520.

Baden-Fuller, C., and M.S. Morgan. 2010. Business Models as Models. *Long Range Planning* 43: 156–171.

Bansal, P. 2005. Evolving Sustainability: A Longitudinal Study of Corporate Sustainable Development. *Strategic Management Journal* 26: 197–218.

Barney, J. 1991. Firm Resources and Sustained Competitive Advantage. *Journal of Management* 17 (1): 99–120.

Beltramello, A., L. Haie-Fayle, and D. Pilat. 2013. *Why New Business Models Matter for Green Growth*. Paris: OECD Publishing.

Birkin, F., A. Cashman, S.C.L. Koh, and Z. Liu. 2009a. New Sustainable Business Models in China. *Business Strategy and the Environment* 18: 64–77.

Birkin, F., T. Polesie, and L. Lewis. 2009b. A New Business Model for Sustainable Development: An Exploratory Study Using the Theory of Constraints in Nordic Organizations. *Business Strategy and the Environment* 18: 277–290.

Bocken, N.M.P., P. Rana, and S.W. Short. 2015. Value Mapping for Sustainable Business Thinking. *Journal of Industrial Production Engineering* 32 (1): 67–81.

Bocken, N.M.P., S.W.A. Short, P. Rana, and S. Evans. 2014. A Literature and Practice Review to Develop Sustainable Business Model Archetypes. *Journal of Cleaner Production* 65: 42–56.

Boons, F., and F. Lüdeke-Freund. 2013. Business Models for Sustainable Innovation: State-of-the-Art and Steps Towards a Research Agenda. *Journal of Cleaner Production* 45: 9–19.

Boons, F., and A. Mendoza. 2010. Constructing Sustainable Palm Oil: How Actors Define Sustainability. *Journal of Cleaner Production* 18: 1686–1695.

Boons, F., C. Montalvo, J. Quist, and M. Wagner. 2013. Sustainable Innovation, Business Models and Economic Performance: An Overview. *Journal of Cleaner Production* 45: 1–8.

Bowman, C., and V. Ambrosini. 2000. Value Creation Versus Value Capture: Towards a Coherent Definition of Value in Strategy. *British Journal of Management* 11: 1–15.

Bradbury-Huang, H. 2010. Sustainability by Collaboration: The Seer Case. *Organizational Dynamics* 39: 335–344.

Carroll, A.B., and K.M. Shabana. 2010. The Business Case for Corporate Social Responsibility: A Review of Concepts, Research and Practice. *International Journal of Management Reviews* 12 (1): 85–105.

Casadesus-Masanell, R., and J.E. Ricart. 2010. From Strategy to Business Models and onto Tactics. *Long Range Planning* 43: 195–215.

———. 2011. How to Design a Winning Business Model. *Harvard Business Review* 89: 100–107.

Casadesus-Masanell, R., and F. Zhu. 2013. Business Model Innovation and Competitive Imitation: The Case of Sponsor-Based Business Models. *Strategic Management Journal* 34: 464–482.

Charter, M., and T. Clark. 2007. *Sustainable Innovation: Key Conclusions from Sustainable Innovation Conferences 2003–2006*. The Centre for Sustainable Design, University College for the Creative Arts, May. www.cfsd.org.uk.

Chatterjee, S. 2013. Simple Rules for Designing Business Models. *California Management Review* 55: 97–124.

Chesbrough, H. 2007. Business Model Innovation: It is Not Just About Technology Anymore. *Strategy and Leadership* 35 (6): 12–17.

———. 2010. Business Model Innovation: Opportunities and Barriers. *Long Range Planning* 43: 354–363.

Chesbrough, H., S. Ahern, M. Finn, and S. Guerraz. 2006. Business Models for Technology in the Developing World: The Role of Non-governmental Organizations. *California Management Review* 48: 48–61.

Chesbrough, H., and R. Rosenbloom. 2002. The Role of the Business Model in Capturing Value from Innovation. *Industrial and Corporate Change* 11 (3): 529–556.

Chou, C., C. Chen, and C. Conley. 2015. Creating Value Through Service Offerings: Creating Sustainably-Led Service Offerings Requires Integrating Customer Context with Sustainably Values. *Research-Technology Management* 58 (2): 48–55.

Christensen, C.M. 1997. *The Innovator's Dilemma: When New Technologies Cause Great Firms to Fail*. Boston, MA: Harvard Business School Press.

Christensen, G.M., and M. Raynor. 2003. *The Innovator's Solution*. Boston, MA: Harvard Business School Press.

Dahan, N.M., J.P. Doh, J. Oetzel, and M. Yaziji. 2010. Corporate-NGO Collaboration: Co-creating New Business Models for Developing Markets. *Long Range Planning* 43: 326–342.

Doganova, L., and M. Eyquem-Renault. 2009. What Do Business Models Do? Innovation Devices in Technology Entrepreneurship. *Research Policy* 38: 1559–1570.

Dryzek, J.S. 2005. *The Politics of the Earth: Environmental Discourses*. Oxford: Oxford University Press.

Dyllick, T., and K. Hockerts. 2002. Beyond the Business Case for Corporate Sustainability. *Business Strategy and the Environment* 11: 130–141.

Elkington, J. 1997. *Cannibals with Forks: Triple Bottom Line of 21st Century Business*. Oxford: Capstone Publisher Limited.

Emerson, J. 2003. The Blanded Value Proposition: Integrating Social and Financial Returns. *California Management Review* 45 (4): 35–51.

Eppinger, S. 2011. The Fundamental Challenge of Product Design. *Journal of Product Innovation Management* 28 (3): 399–400.

Faber, N., R. Jorna, and J. Van Engelen. 2005. The Sustainability of 'Sustainability'—A Study into the Conceptual Foundations of the Notion of 'Sustainability'. *Journal of Environmental Assessment Policy and Management* 7 (1): 1–33.

Ferauge, P. 2013. The Complementarity of Corporate Social Responsibility and Innovation: Evidence from Belgian Firms. *Global Journal of Business Research* 5 (5): 99–113.

Foss, N.J., and T. Saebi. 2017. Fifteen Years of Research on Business Model Innovation: How Far Have We Come, and Where Should We Go? *Journal of Management* 43: 200–227.

Govindarajan, V., and G. Trimble. 2005. *Ten Rules for Strategic Innovators: From Idea to Execution*. Boston, MA: Harvard Business School Press.

Hansen, E.G., F. Große-Dunker, and R. Reichwald. 2009. Sustainability Innovation Cube: A Framework to Evaluate Sustainability-Oriented Innovations. *International Journal of Innovation Management* 13: 683–713.

Hart, S.L., and M.B. Milstein. 1999. Global Sustainability and the Creative Destruction of Industries. *Sloan Management Review* 41: 23–33.

Kanter, R.M. 1999. From Spare Change to Real Change: The Social Sector as a Beta Site for Business Innovation. *Harvard Business Review* 77: 123–132.

Lepak, D.P., K.G. Smith, and M.S. Taylor. 2007. Value Creation and Value Capture: A Multilevel Perspective. *Academy of Management Review* 32 (1): 180–194.

Lodsgård, L., and A.Aagaard.2016. The Four Archetypes of Business-NGO Collaborations in Creating Sustainable Innovation. Paper presented at the *23rd IPDMC Innovation & Product Development Management Conference*, Glasgow, UK.

Lodsgård, L., and A. Aagaard. 2017. Creating Value Through CSR Across Company Functions and NGO Collaborations: A Scandinavian Cross-Industry Study. *Scandinavian Journal of Management* 33 (3): 162–174.

Loorbach, D., J.C. van Bakel, G. Whiteman, and J. Rotmans. 2009. Business Strategies for Transitions Towards Sustainable Systems. *BusinessStrategy and the Environment* 19 (2): 133–146.

Lovins, A.B., L.H.Lovins, and P.Hawken.1999. A Road Map for Natural Capitalism. *Harvard Business Review*, 1–14 (HBR paperback reprint 2000).

Lüdeke-Freund, F. 2009. *Business Model Concepts in Corporate Sustainability Contexts. From Rhetoric to a Generic Template for 'Business Models for Sustainability'*. Lüneburg: Centre for Sustainability Management.

Magretta, J. 2002. Why Business Models Matter. *Harvard Business Review* 80: 86–92.

Makadok, R. 2001. Appointed Commentary on Priem and Butler. *Academy of Management Review* 26: 498–499.

Makadok, R., and R. Coff. 2002. The Theory of Value and the Value of Theory: Breaking New Ground Versus Reinventing the Wheel. *Academy of Management Review* 27 (1): 10–13.

Markides, C. 2008. *Game-Changing Strategies: How to Create New Market Space in Established Industries by Breaking the Rules*. San Francisco, CA: Jossey-Bass.

Morris, M., M. Schindehutte, and J. Allen. 2005. The Entrepreneur's Business Model: Toward a Unified Perspective. *Journal of Business Research* 58: 726–735.

Osterwalder, A. 2004. *The Business Model Ontology: A Proposition in a Design Science Approach*. PhD thesis, Université de Lausanne, Lausanne.

Osterwalder, A., Y. Pigneur, and C.L. Tucci. 2005. Clarifying Business Models: Origins, Present, and Future of the Concept. *Communications of the Association for Information Systems* 16 (1): 1–25.

Pedersen, E.R.G., W. Gwozdz, and K.H. Hvass. 2016. Exploring the Relationship Between Business Model Innovation, Corporate Sustainability, and Organizational Values Within the Fashion Industry. *Journal of Business Ethics*. https://doi.org/10.1007/s10551-016-3044-7.

Pereira Da Costa, A.S., and J. Levie. 2014. Effectual and Causal Behaviors, Business Model Change, and Performance of Early-Stage Firms. *Academy of Management Annual Meeting Proceedings* 2014 (1): 14305–14305.

Perkmann, M., and A. Spicer. 2010. What are Business Models: Towards a Theory of Performative Representations. *Research in the Sociology of Organization* 29: 265–275.

Phills, J.A., K. Deiglmeier, and D.T. Miller. 2008. Rediscovering Social Innovation. *Stanford Social Innovation Review* 6 (Fall): 34–44.

Poncelet, E.C. 2001. A Kiss Here and a Kiss There: Conflict and Collaboration in Environmental Partnerships. *Environmental Management* 27 (1): 13–25.

Porter, M.E., and M.R. Kramer. 2011. Creating Shared Value. *Harvard Business Review* 89 (1–2): 62–77.

Richardson, J. 2008. The Business Model: An Integrative Framework for Strategy Execution. *Strategic Change* 17 (5–6): 133–144.

Ritter, T., and H. Andersen. 2014. A Relationship Strategy Perspective on Relationship Portfolios: Linking Customer Profitability, Commitment, and Growth Potential to Relationship Strategy. *Industrial Marketing Management* 43 (6): 1005–1011.

Sandberg, K.D. 2002. Is It Time to Trade in Your Business Model? *Harvard Management Update* 7: 3.

Schaltegger, S., E.G. Hansen, and F. Lüdeke-Freund. 2016. Business Models for Sustainability: Origins, Present Research, and Future Avenues. *Organization & Environment* 29 (1): 3–10.

Schaltegger, S., F. Lüdeke-Freund, and E.G. Hansen. 2012. Business Cases for Sustainability: The Role of Business Model Innovation for Corporate Sustainability. *International Journal of Innovation and Sustainable Development* 6 (2): 95–119.

Schaltegger, S., and M. Wagner. 2011. Sustainable Entrepreneurship and Sustainability Innovation: Categories and Interactions. *Business Strategy and the Environment* 20 (4): 222–237.

Steketee, D.M. 2010. Disruption or Sustenance? An Institutional Analysis of Sustainable Business Network in West Michigan. In *Facilitating Sustainable Innovation Through Collaboration: A Multi-stakeholder Perspective*, ed. J. Sarkis, D.V. Brust, and J.J. Cordeiro. Springer.

Stubbs, W., and C. Cocklin. 2008. Conceptualizing a Sustainability Business Model. *Organization & Environment* 21 (2): 103–127.

Taran, Y. 2011. *Re-thinking It All: Overcoming Obstacles to Business Model Innovation*. PhD thesis, Center for Industrial Production, Aalborg University.

Taran, Y., H. Boer, and P. Lindgren. 2013. A Business Model Innovation Typology. *Journal of Decision Science* 46 (2): 301–331.

Teece, D.J. 2010. Business Models, Business Strategy and Innovation. *Long Range Planning* 45 (2–3): 172–194.

Tukker, A., and U. Tischner, eds. 2006. *New Business for Old Europe: Product-Service Development, Competitiveness and Sustainability*. Sheffield: Greenleaf.

Upward, A., and P. Jones. 2016. An Ontology for Strongly Sustainable Business Models: Defining an Enterprise Framework Compatible with Natural and Social Science. *Organization and Environment* 29 (1): 97–123.

Venn, R., and N. Berg. 2013. Building Competitive Advantage Through Social Entrepreneurship. *South Asian Journal of Business Research* 2 (1): 104–127.

Verstraete, T., and E. Jouison-Lafitte. 2011. A Conventionalist Theory of the Business Model in the Context of Business Creation for Understanding Organizational Impetus. *Management International/International Management/Gestión International* 15: 109–124.

World Commission on Environment and Development (WCED). (1987). *Our Common Future* (Brundtland Report). Oxford University Press.

Yunus, M., B. Moingeon, and L. Lehmann-Ortega. 2010. Building Social Business Models: Lessons from the Grameen Experience. *Long Range Planning* 43: 308–325.

Zink, K.J., U. Steimle, and K. Fisher. 2008. Human Factors, Business Excellence and Corporate Sustainability: Differing Perspectives, Joint Objectives. In *Corporate Sustainability as a Challenge for Comprehensive Management*, ed. K.J. Zink. Physica-Verlag.

Zott, C., and R. Amit. 2007. Business Model Design and the Performance of Entrepreneurial Firms. *Organization Science* 18: 181–199.

———. 2010. Business Model Design: An Activity System Perspective. *Long Range Planning* 43: 216–226.

Zott, C., R. Amit, and L. Massa. 2011. The Business Model: Recent Developments and Future Research. *Journal of Management* 37 (4): 1019–1042.

2

Research on Sustainable Business Model Patterns: Status quo, Methodological Issues, and a Research Agenda

Florian Lüdeke-Freund, René Bohnsack,
Henning Breuer, and Lorenzo Massa

> *"The people can shape buildings for themselves, and have done it for centuries by using languages which I call pattern languages. A pattern language gives each person who uses it, the power to create an infinite variety of new and unique buildings, just as his ordinary language gives him the power to create an infinite variety of sentences."*
> (Alexander 1979, p. 167)

F. Lüdeke-Freund (✉)
ESCP Europe Business School, Berlin, Germany
e-mail: fluedeke-freund@escpeurope.eu

R. Bohnsack
Católica Lisbon School of Business & Economics, Lisbon, Portugal
e-mail: r.bohnsack@ucp.pt

H. Breuer
HMKW Berlin & UX Berlin Innovation Consulting, Berlin, Germany
e-mail: henning.breuer@uxberlin.com

L. Massa
Ecole Polytechnique Fédérale de Lausanne, Lausanne, Switzerland
e-mail: lorenzo.massa@epfl.ch

© The Author(s) 2019
A. Aagaard (ed.), *Sustainable Business Models*, Palgrave Studies in Sustainable Business
In Association with Future Earth, https://doi.org/10.1007/978-3-319-93275-0_2

1 Introduction and Motivation

Ever since the Internet boom of the mid-1990s, firms have been experimenting with new ways of creating, delivering, and capturing value, which has led to a branching of the scholarly literature on business models and business model innovation (Massa et al. 2017; Wirtz et al. 2016; Zott et al. 2011). At a general level, a business model is "a description of an organization and how that organization functions in achieving its goals (e.g., profitability, growth, social impact, …)" (Massa et al. 2017, p. 73). Often, these goals are associated with value creation, so that business models mostly represent "the rationale of how an organization creates, delivers and captures value" (Osterwalder and Pigneur 2009, p. 14). Substantial research in the area of business models has focused on identifying and describing different types of business models (e.g., e-commerce) and recurrent business model patterns (e.g., freemium) that support this value creation function (Amshoff et al. 2015; Gassmann et al. 2014; Remane et al. 2017). This search for recurrent patterns is not limited to "conventional" business models. Similar approaches are currently emerging in the field of sustainable business model (SBM) research and practice.[1]

An increasing number of scholars and practitioners go beyond value creation in economic or financial terms and explore the potential of business models to help solve ecological and social problems, and in particular the challenge to move towards corporate sustainability (Bocken et al. 2014; Lüdeke-Freund and Dembek 2017; Schaltegger et al. 2016). Several authors describe iconic cases of companies that aim at reducing the pressure on ecological and social systems through their business models (e.g., Bohnsack et al. 2014; Boons and Lüdeke-Freund 2013; Rauter et al. 2017; Stubbs and Cocklin 2008), while others propose archetypal business models for sustainability (Bocken et al. 2014; Clinton and Whisnant 2014). All these cases and business model types bear the potential to provide inspiration or even useful solutions for established companies and start-ups facing similar challenges. They also bear the potential to allow for comparative evaluations of different models to assess their business success and sustainability potential. Identifying and systematically describing and generalising the characteristics of SBMs can thus support both creative and analytical purposes.

In a similar vein, Girotra and Netessine (2013, p. 538) argue that business models often share similarities that are independent of industries, which allows for knowledge transfer and learning from best practices: "These similarities highlight that, to create new business models that promote sustainability, we can often repurpose innovations from other industries. What is often missing is a unifying approach that allows one to see this commonality and enable this translation process." Several questions result from their observation: What types of SBMs can be identified? Which reusable solutions to ecological, social, or economic challenges do these types propose? How to develop an overview of these types? And how to provide a common "language" to describe, compare, and evaluate these types? Identifying and describing the assumed similarities of SBMs, as proposed by Girotra and Netessine (2013), leads to different questions related to the *selection* and *classification* of SBMs and an appropriate *notation system*.

To answer these questions we propose a pattern-theoretical approach to identify, classify, and document business models that provide potentially reusable solutions to ecological, social, and economic problems. The pattern-theoretical approach follows the seminal works on a pattern "language" for the design of towns, houses, and construction by Alexander et al. (1977). Their work, which mainly deals with the design of the environments in which people live, offers a rich theoretical foundation that is applicable to various design domains beyond the built environment (Leitner 2015). This approach assumes that a solution to a recurring design problem—such as creating a pleasant interior and developing a socially inclusive business model—can be generalised and serve as a generic solution for that sort of problem over and over again, whenever and in whichever context it occurs. These generic solutions can be adapted to different contexts—such as private and business interiors and non-profit and commercial business models—and combined with other solutions to address more complex problems and to allow for more individual designs (Alexander et al. 1977; Leitner 2015). Considering how patterns can be combined, how they interact and influence each other, and how they can change and evolve over time is what distinguishes a pattern *language* from a simple list of patterns (Alexander 1979; Alexander et al. 1977).

This chapter follows the Alexandrian approach of interpreting patterns as "problem-solution combinations" (Leitner 2015) and develops a theoretical framework for future research that is required to develop a "sustainable business model pattern language." The notion of pattern has long been used in fields such as architecture, organisation and software development, interaction design, and education to identify, classify, and document best practices (see, e.g., the various pattern languages developed by Takashi Iba and his team).[2] We suggest that it is time for a systematic approach to identifying, classifying, and documenting the available knowledge about SBMs as solutions to the recurring challenges of moving towards corporate sustainability. A pattern-theoretical approach seems to be well-suited for this endeavour as it combines an established theoretical foundation with rich examples from which we can learn, such as Alexander's pattern language (Alexander 1979; Alexander et al. 1977), as well as some guidance for the development of a pattern language while leaving sufficient room for our own interpretation of an appropriate and useful language for SBM patterns.

This chapter is *not* proposing such a language, but compiling some of the required theoretical and conceptual ingredients to do so in future research projects. It is also an open invitation to the SBM community to join our endeavour, which so far includes explorations of SBM patterns (Carroux 2017; Lüdeke-Freund et al. 2018a) and circular economy business model patterns (Lüdeke-Freund et al. 2018b), as well as studies of food waste prevention business model patterns (Ohnesorge 2017) and stakeholder relationship patterns (Froese 2017).

Based on these experiences, we discuss the following issues in this chapter: why the development of an SBM pattern language is needed (Sect. 2); some theoretical and conceptual issues that have to be considered (Sect. 3); different methods to identify and develop business model patterns (Sect. 4); how patterns can be used to extend business model innovation tools (Sect. 5); and finally, the most important issues we have to consider as we embark on the journey of developing a full SBM pattern language (Sect. 5).

2 Why Is an SBM Pattern Language Needed?

What are the reasons to engage in the effort of developing an SBM pattern language? There are many reasons, such as the need to consolidate the available knowledge about SBMs, to provide a means to support creative processes, to compare and transfer solutions to ecological and social problems that were developed in different contexts, and so on. We think that two reasons are particularly important: first, to promote the *convergence and consolidation* of the rich but dispersed knowledge about business-model-based solutions to ecological, social, and economic problems, instead of adding further and sometimes rivalling SBM classifications; and second, to create *knowledge for action*, where action takes the meaning of designing more sustainable organisations.

While we acknowledge the value of variety and redundancy with regard to SBM classifications, we think that it is time to explore whether there is the potential to develop a *shared language* that can be used to document, communicate, and apply the various SBM patterns that are nowadays available and that will be available in the future. The development of such a language would not be possible without the variety and redundancy in the experiences and accounts of researchers, business men, designers, and many more. But properly speaking about and applying SBMs requires a language consisting of words (patterns) and rules how to use these words to create sentences and finally whole stories—just as with Alexander's observation that people design their environment by using shared pattern languages (see the quote at the beginning of the chapter). We build on Alexander's pattern theory and philosophy to create the outline of a research agenda to develop a consolidated and useful SBM pattern language (Alexander 1979; Alexander et al. 1977).

The first reason to develop an SBM pattern language, *striving for convergence and consolidation*, is related to the recent proliferation of different perspectives on SBMs, which are mostly efforts to classify different SBMs (e.g., Beltramello et al. 2013; Bisgaard et al. 2012; Clinton and Whisnant 2014). As noted elsewhere in relation to business models (e.g., Massa et al. 2017; Zott et al. 2011), early efforts of many emerging lines of inquiry are dedicated to making sense of the field by defining and classifying its main objects/phenomena of inquiry (here, business models). Defining the objects/phenomena of inquiry is needed not only to sketch the boundaries of the field itself, but also to allow a fruitful dialogue with other researchers (cf. Lüdeke-Freund and Dembek 2017). Definitions, in this sense, represent points of departure rather than points of arrival, or to put it differently, instances that allow starting a conversation rather than terminating it. Related to this, classifying the objects/phenomena domain of inquiry is often a natural step when one starts to recognise that the domain of inquiry is not homogenous, but rather that there are several manifestations (or types) of the same phenomenon or object.

The early SBM literature is characterised by efforts to define the SBM construct (e.g., Abdelkafi and Täuscher 2016; Joyce and Paquin 2016; Stubbs and Cocklin 2008; Upward and Jones 2016) as well as to make sense of it by developing classification schemes. We found a number of publications, each attempting to make sense of the SBM phenomenon by describing types—for example, Beltramello et al. (2013) and Bisgaard et al. (2012), who propose nine and eight green business models, respectively, or Clinton and Whisnant (2014), who identified 20 business models addressing diverse ecological and social issues. A critical assessment of these contributions reveals that they are certainly valuable and in some cases even pioneering the field of SBM classification. But taken together they seem to offer a number of perspectives that are not only partly divergent but also difficult to reconcile (see our review and consolidation of 14 classifications in Lüdeke-Freund et al. 2018a). We need a unifying perspective if we are to unlock the potential of SBM research and practice. In other words, the first reason for developing an SBM pattern language is that we need a unifying, systematic, and methodically solid classification scheme (ibid.).

The second reason why an SBM language is needed relates to a question that is maybe a bit unconventional from the perspective of traditional academic knowledge creation: How to design more sustainable organisations? To approach answers to this question, we have to understand the challenges of designing more sustainable organisations and how to overcome these challenges through well-crafted interventions (cf. Parrish 2010). In this sense, an SBM pattern language is concerned with *developing knowledge for action*, which means knowledge that can guide action in practice (as complementary to more "normal" academic efforts to advance theoretical knowledge to improve understanding and predictions). A more elaborate answer to this question requires exploring the meaning of the term "design." According to the perspective of design sciences, organisations are man-made social "artifacts" that are distinguishable from natural objects and phenomena that occur independently of human activity (Simon 1996). The term design thus is used to depict the idea that organisations are created purposefully. In a way not dissimilar to the perspective of engineering, applying a design perspective to the challenge of creating more sustainable organisations means to posit that organisations are the product of conscious human decisions and efforts and can therefore be "designed" in various ways. An SBM pattern language would be a means to support this design challenge.

In his seminal book *The Sciences of the Artificial*, Herbert Simon (1969/1996) proposes that the design of artifacts requires three main elements: (i) a specification of the purpose of design, (ii) guiding criteria for design, and (iii) an understanding of the environment surrounding the design. The purpose of design specifies the goals to be reached. Using an engineering example, the project "designing a bridge" requires specifying the purpose of the project (e.g., to connect two villages across a river). Criteria for design represent the required body of knowledge (e.g., material science and construction science) that supports engineers in designing a bridge according to the project's goal and purpose. A specification of the environment means to understand the environmental conditions and constraints the design project faces (e.g., an analysis of the geology of the terrain to determine the shape and size of the bridge). Similarly, an SBM pattern language, understood as a design tool, should support its users in considering or even formulating the goals and purposes of more sustainable organisations, offer guiding criteria for such an endeavour, and create awareness for the environmental conditions under which more sustainable organisations are designed.

Therefore, our initial set of 45 patterns to support sustainability-oriented business model innovation describes patterns in a way that allows users to consider these aspects (Lüdeke-Freund et al. 2018a). For example, the pattern "differential pricing," originally taken from Clinton and Whisnant (2014), is described along three dimensions (a more detailed pattern example is given below):

- *Context (as a starting point to describe environmental conditions)*: Base of the Pyramid (BoP) and low-income groups in both developed and developing countries are often excluded from consumption due to price barriers.
- *Problem (can be used to specify the purpose of an SBM)*: Customers might need the same product, but have different payment thresholds. Hence, some customers are either unwilling or unable to pay as much as others for the same product.
- *Solution (providing criteria for business model design; here, a pricing model)*: Charging groups with higher payment thresholds higher prices to subsidise those groups that cannot afford to pay as much.

An SBM pattern language is needed as it would provide a valuable "tool box" that would consolidate the rich and growing knowledge of a whole research and practice community and turn it into knowledge for action. It would offer a set of solutions to recurrent problems that can inspire and guide entrepreneurs and managers in designing more sustainable organisations, for example, in terms of more ecologically benign production processes or more socially inclusive pricing models. Such a language would also contribute to creating stronger ties between management and entrepreneurship science on the one hand and the perspective of design science on the other hand. Establishing such ties is important, particularly if we are to create knowledge for action that is meant to offer guidance for the development of more sustainable organisations in practice (cf. Joyce 2016; Upward and Jones 2016). We will use our ongoing pattern projects as a starting point for this endeavour (Carroux 2017; Froese 2017; Lüdeke-Freund et al. 2018b; Lüdeke-Freund et al. 2018a; Ohnesorge 2017).

3 What Are Theoretical and Conceptual Elements of an SBM Pattern Language?

Moving from single patterns to a full-pattern language requires the development of different theoretical and conceptual elements that finally allow constructing a language. These elements include an understanding of the meaning of the notion of language in relation to business models, formats for the description of business model patterns (i.e., a notation), and a systematisation of the connections between the different patterns.

3.1 Approach to the Meaning of "Business Model Pattern Language"

As the actual goal of research on SBM patterns is the development of a new pattern language, the meaning of "language" in relation to business models has to be clarified. Just as a language consists of words that can be used across domains and rules how to use and combine these words, a pattern language consists of patterns that can be used in different situations and contexts as well as guidelines on how to use and combine these patterns. The seminal work *A Pattern Language* by Christopher Alexander et al. (1977), as well as Leitner's (2015) concise summary of major parts of Alexander's oeuvre, can be used as starting points. *A Pattern Language* contains not only 253 patterns describing design options for towns, buildings, and construction but also an introduction to the concept of pattern language and its most essential conceptual features. Deeper insights into Alexander's pattern theory and philosophy are provided in his book *The Timeless Way of Building* (1979).

3.1.1 An "Alexandrian" Interpretation of Business Model Patterns

The basic unit of a pattern language are entities called "patterns," which are defined by Alexander et al. (1977, p. x) as follows: "Each pattern describes a problem which occurs over and over again in our environment, and then describes the core of the solution to that problem, in such a way that you can use this solution a million times over, without ever doing it the same way twice." This definition points to at least three characteristic features: First, a pattern describes a *problem-solution combination* and thus contains a statement about a problem that is perceived as important and a statement about a potential solution to that problem; second, it is a *recurring problem*; and third, there is a *generic and adaptable solution* to that problem.

Table 2.1 Business model pattern definitions

Authors	General business model pattern definition
Abdelkafi et al. (2013, p. 14)	"The relationship between a certain context or environment, a recurring problem and the core of its solution."
Osterwalder and Pigneur (2009, p. 55)	"Business models with similar characteristics, similar arrangements of business model Building Blocks, or similar behaviors."
Gassmann et al. (2014, p. 17)	"A business model [pattern] is a specific configuration of the four main business model dimensions who-what-how-why that has proven successful."
Amshoff et al. (2015, p. 3)	"Reusing solutions that are documented generally and abstractly in order to make them accessible and applicable to others."

Source: Adapted from Ohnesorge (2017)

Patterns are also discussed and used by business model scholars and for business model innovation in practice (see exemplary definitions in Table 2.1). Early publications, for example, on e-business models (cf. Alt and Zimmermann 2001), as well as more recent works, for example, the patterns database by Remane et al. (2017), deal with the variety of business models that occur in different domains and often try to structure and make use of this variety. Remane et al. (2017, p. 2; building on Abdelkafi et al. 2013) define business model patterns as "proven solutions to recurring problems during business model design." Transferring the concept of pattern to business models, we see that it is about problem-solution combinations that are proposed to support business model developers and innovators in accomplishing their design tasks.

Remane et al. (2017) also show that different types of patterns can be distinguished. They separate *complete pattern frameworks* depicting whole business models (e.g., Business Model Canvas) from *prototypical patterns*, which are industry-specific problem-solution combinations, and *solution patterns*, which address single or several components of a business model. It is important to consider that patterns do not always describe complete business models (e.g., all nine building blocks of the Business Model Canvas), but also refer to single components or partial models (e.g., customer segments or financial models). Taking freemium business models as an example (e.g., Gassmann et al. 2014), which offer basic products or services for free along with premium versions that require a payment, shows that, for example, pricing models can be used to denote the most characteristic features of whole business models.

This relation between partial and complete business model patterns points to another important feature of a pattern language. Patterns occur on different scales (e.g., regions, towns, or buildings as in the case of Alexander et al.'s (1977) pattern language) and patterns can, or *should*, be used in combination. The implications of this aspect of a pattern language for the development and use of SBM patterns will be discussed below.

3.1.2 Using the "Alexandrian form" to Describe Business Model Patterns

An efficient way of describing patterns is the so-called Alexandrian form (Falconer 1999; Leitner 2015), which is a template-like structure that supports the development of an encyclopaedic description of the patterns contained in a pattern language. Alexander et al. (1977, pp. x–xi) use the following format to describe each of their 253 patterns.

It starts with a *picture* of an archetypal example, followed by a brief introduction to set the *context* for the pattern. The context is described in terms of larger patterns that are supported or completed by the pattern in question. This is followed by a *headline* that summarises the essential problem addressed by the pattern in one or two sentences. Then, the longest section of each pattern description is the *body of the problem* which "describes the empirical background of the pattern, the evidence for its validity, the range of different ways the pattern can be manifested in a building, and so on" (Alexander et al. 1977, p. xi). After the problem description comes the "heart of the pattern" (ibid.), which is the *solution*. "This solution is always stated in the form of an instruction—so that you know exactly what you need to do, to build the pattern." (ibid.) The main body of the pattern closes with a *diagram* showing the main components of the solution. Finally, *references to smaller patterns* that are needed to embellish and fill out the pattern are given.

Table 2.2 shows an example of the Alexandrian form. It contains the pattern "House Cluster" described in *A Pattern Language* (Alexander et al. 1977, pp. 197–203).

Table 2.2 Pattern example "House Cluster"

Pattern aspect	Pattern description[a,b]
Name	House Cluster (37)
Context description and related larger patterns	"… the fundamental unit of organization within the neighborhood—*Identifiable Neighborhood (14)*—is the cluster of a dozen houses. By varying the density and composition of different clusters, this pattern may also help to generate *Density Rings (29), Household Mix (35),* and *Degrees of Publicness (36).*"
Problem statement	"People will not feel comfortable in their houses unless a group of houses forms a cluster, with the public land between them jointly owned by all the householders."
Examples and explanations	"When houses are arranged on streets, and the streets owned by the town, there is no way in which the land immediately outside the houses can reflect the needs of families and individuals living in those houses […]. This pattern is based on the idea that the cluster of land and homes immediately around one's own home is of special importance […]. The clusters seem to work best if they have between 8 and 12 houses each […]. In all cases common land which is shared by the cluster is an essential ingredient. It acts as a focus and physically knits the group together. This common land can be as small as a path or as large as a green. On the other hand, care must be taken not to make the clusters too tight or self-contained, so that they exclude the larger community or seem too constricting and claustrophobic. There needs to be some open endedness and overlapping among clusters […]."
Solution statement	"Arrange houses to form very rough, but identifiable clusters of 8 to 12 households around some common land and paths. Arrange the clusters so that anyone can walk through them, without feeling like a trespasser."
Related smaller patterns	"Use this pattern as it is for low densities, up to about 15 houses per acre; at higher densities, modify the cluster with the additional structure given by *Row Houses (38)* or *Housing Hill (39)*. Always provide common land between the houses—*Common Land (67)* and a shared common workshop—*Home Workshop (57).*"

Source: Adapted from Alexander et al. (1977)
[a]Numbers in parentheses refer to the pattern index used in *A Pattern Language*
[b]The original pictures showing an archetypal example and a solution sketch were omitted here, but can be found online at http://www.patternlanguage.com

Table 2.3 shows an exemplary pattern from our review of 45 SBM patterns, described according to the Alexandrian form (taken from Carroux 2017). The pattern "Product-Oriented Service" (found in Tukker 2004) explains how product offerings can be augmented with complementary services, and how such product-oriented services can help to market new and ecologically improved products (e.g., e-mobiles). The solution illustration uses a slightly extended version of the "Business Model Canvas," including ecological and social costs and benefits (Osterwalder and Pigneur 2009). Other SBM frameworks such as the "Business Innovation Kit" (Breuer 2013), "Triple Layered Business Model Canvas" (Joyce and Paquin 2016), or the "Strongly Sustainable Business Model Ontology" (Upward and Jones 2016) can also be used to describe SBM patterns (and are assumingly better suited to do so).

Regardless of the framework used to illustrate SBM patterns in terms of their business model components, it is important to understand that a complete SBM pattern description requires more than a canvas-like or box-and-arrow illustration. It needs an informative name, a context

Table 2.3 SBM pattern example "Product-Oriented Service"

Pattern aspect	Pattern description[a,b]
Name	Product-Oriented Service (9.2)
Context description and related patterns	Many companies follow green or eco-design strategies and thus try to implement *Hybrid Models/Gap-Exploiter Models (3.1)*, processes, and products that *Maximise Material Productivity and Energy Efficiency (3.2)*, or ecologically driven *Product Design (3.3)*. This often involves new products and/or new ways of using products (e.g., following regular maintenance schedules or using electric power instead of liquid fuels). The *Product-Oriented Service (9.2)* pattern offers an approach to value proposition design that can increase the attractiveness of new and/or more complex but ecologically superior products (Bohnsack and Pinkse 2017).
Problem statement	New or complex products are often less attractive for potential users and thus require additional support and services, such as maintenance or updates, to convince users to switch from old and ecologically inefficient products to new and more eco-friendly versions.

(*continued*)

Table 2.3 (continued)

Pattern aspect	Pattern description[a,b]
Examples and explanations	The value proposition of the product-oriented service business model is characterised by offering additional services for eco-friendlier versions of established and/or complex products and technologies. This can increase their attractiveness for potential users. Tesla sells e-mobiles as products owned by individual customers. The company also offers the charging infrastructure, where the revenue model is currently changing from free to paid charging. Further services include over-the-air software updates that add new features and functionality to the cars. By augmenting the core product with these and further services can make it easier to switch from traditional cars to e-mobiles. This business model pattern is still geared towards product sales, but the sales can result in social and environmental benefits, such as an increase in material and energy efficiency as well as less risk for customers.
Solution statement	Offer services that are convenience-increasing for the users of a new and/or complex eco-friendly product. Use this tactic to increase the willingness of potential users to buy the product.
Solution illustration	*Business Model Canvas:* **Key Partners** — **Key Activities**: Activities relating to the product-related services **Key Resources** — **Value Proposition**: Offer additional services for battery-powered electric vehicles, including the charging infrastructure and software updates **Customer Relationships** — **Channels** — **Customer Segments**: Potential and current EV-Buyers **Cost Structure**: Costs associated with product-related services **Revenue Streams**: Revenue from sales of products and rendering of product-related services **Social & Environmental Costs**: N/A **Social & Environmental Benefits**: Increase efficiency, less risk for customers and other related social and environmental benefits
Further related patterns	New product-service combinations according to the *Product-Oriented Service (9.2)* pattern can be supported by alternative pricing patterns such as *Differential Pricing (1.1)*, *Freemium (1.2)*, or a *Subscription Model (1.4)*.

Source: Adapted from Carroux (2017)
[a]Numbers in parentheses refer to the pattern index used in Lüdeke-Freund et al. (2018a)
[b]"Business Model Canvas" based on Osterwalder and Pigneur (2009)

description, a problem and solution statement, and an extensive problem and solution description including examples, as well as references to related patterns. The requirement of cross-references between patterns points to a requirement that is crucial for the development of a pattern language, namely an understanding of the relationships between patterns.

3.1.3 Connections Between Patterns as a Precondition for a Pattern Language

Identifying and systematising the connections between different business model patterns is a necessary conceptual requirement for a full-pattern language. However, according to our reading of the business model literature, little has been said about how business model patterns connect to each other and how these connections form a versatile system that is more than just a simple pattern list. The Alexandrian form's requirement to identify larger patterns that include the pattern in question (e.g., a house pattern that includes a roof pattern) as well as smaller patterns that can be used to embellish it (e.g., a vault pattern that can be used to embellish the roof pattern) asks the language designer to systematically structure the different connections between the patterns contained in a language. This is to grasp "the collection of … patterns as a whole, as a language, within which you can create an infinite variety of combinations" (Alexander et al. 1977, p. xi)—combinations that allow users of the language to create sentences and whole stories.

In *A Pattern Language*, the patterns are ordered in a hierarchical manner, from large structures (regions and towns) down to details of construction (such as floor surfaces and wall textures). Alexander et al. (1977) refer to this hierarchy and related linearity as a simplification of the language's structure, which, as they acknowledge, is in fact more like a network. This simplified hierarchical order allows using smaller patterns to embellish larger patterns, and larger patterns to take up smaller patterns (as in the house, roof, and vault example above). This way of using the language is based on the different connections between the patterns. Alexander et al. (1977) provide different examples of how the language works and which role the connections between certain larger and smaller patterns play: "In short, no pattern is an isolated entity. Each pattern can exist in the world, only to the extent that is supported by other patterns: the larger patterns in which it is embedded, the patterns of the same size that surround it, and the smaller patterns which are embedded in it." (Alexander et al. 1977, p. xiii)

The following Fig. 2.1 illustrates how the idea of pattern connections can be applied to business model patterns. Referring again to the aforementioned example of the "Product-Oriented Service" pattern, we can imagine the left pattern in the middle row to be the "Product-Oriented Service" pattern. This pattern is embellished, for example, by a pricing and a production pattern (lowest row). It is furthermore complemented by a business infrastructure and a customer relationship pattern (middle row). The complete business model, for example, to market e-mobiles based on the augmented "Product-Oriented Service" pattern, results on a higher level where all smaller patterns are integrated into a whole new model (at the centre of the highest row), which is also supported by other patterns (e.g., a banking pattern that offers complementary financial services to customers and an additional circular economy pattern that offers

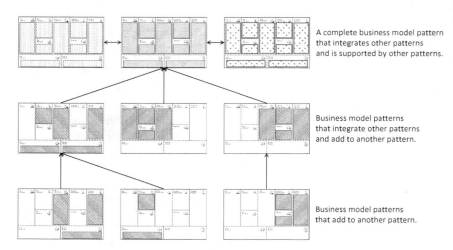

Fig. 2.1 Illustration of connections between business model patterns (Source: own illustration; "Business Model Canvas" based on Osterwalder and Pigneur 2009)

refurbishment and upgrades). On this level, the different sentences created with the business model pattern language merge into a completely new story.

Although our review of 45 SBM patterns seems to be the most complete list of patterns dealing with ecological, social, and economic issues (Carroux 2017; Lüdeke-Freund et al. 2018a), and although more patterns were identified and developed in further studies (Froese 2017; Lüdeke-Freund et al. 2018b; Ohnesorge 2017), we did not yet create a system of connections between these patterns. Following Joyce's (2016) approach, a first step would be to define the primary classification criterion to identify and systematise such connections. Is it about connecting SBM patterns in a way that leads to complete business model designs, that is, addressing every business model component? Or is it about connecting patterns in a way that ensures that ecological, social, and economic issues are always addressed together? It could also make sense to apply both criteria simultaneously. However, defining this aspect of a future SBM pattern language requires additional research.

3.2 Definition of "Sustainable Business Model Pattern"

The purpose of using business model patterns is to support organisations in creating, delivering, and capturing value (cf. Remane et al. 2017). Developing an SBM pattern language requires an extended understanding of this purpose. Research on SBMs has resulted in different approaches to defining this purpose in a more stakeholder-inclusive manner and with an emphasis on sustainable value creation (e.g., Boons and Lüdeke-Freund 2013). Accordingly, Schaltegger et al. (2016) define an SBM, or "business model for sustainability," as follows: "A business model for sustainability helps describing, analyzing, managing, and communicating (i) a company's sustainable value proposition to its customers and all other stakeholders, (ii) how it creates and delivers this value, and (iii) how it captures economic value while maintaining or regenerating natural, social, and economic capital beyond its organisational boundaries" (Schaltegger et al. 2016, p. 6).

Based on these considerations we propose the following definition for an SBM pattern (Lüdeke-Freund et al. 2018a): A *sustainable business model pattern* describes an ecological, social, and/or economic problem that arises when an organisation aims to create value, and it describes the core of a solution to this problem that can be repeatedly applied in a multitude of ways, situations, contexts, and domains. An SBM pattern also describes the design principles, value-creating activities, and their arrangements that are required to provide a useful problem-solution combination.

We furthermore propose three basic guiding criteria that should be considered to increase the likelihood of designing truly sustainable organisations:

- An SBM pattern, or a combination of SBM patterns, is incomplete as long as not all dimensions—ecological, social, and economic—are considered (building on Alexander et al.'s (1977) notion of complete patterns).
- An SBM pattern, or a combination of SBM patterns, should enable organisations to reduce forms of ecological, social, and/or economic value destruction in absolute terms (which could be considered as contributions to weak sustainability) or to increase forms of ecological, social, and/or economic value creation in absolute terms (which could be considered as contributions to strong sustainability) (cf. Bocken et al. 2013; Upward and Jones 2016; Yang et al. 2017).
- An SBM pattern, or a combination of SBM patterns, is incomplete as long as not all core aspects of a business model are considered—for example, defined as value proposition, value delivery, value capture, and value creation (cf. Joyce 2016).

This set of guiding criteria is not complete and should be extended and refined with those developed by, for instance, Upward and Jones (2016) and Breuer et al. (2018). Any endeavour dedicated to developing an SBM pattern language will have to develop such criteria, which resonate to a certain degree with Alexander's normative criteria of creating lively and liveable environments for people (Alexander 1979; Alexander et al. 1977).

4 How Can Sustainable Business Model Patterns Be Developed?

Developing a full SBM pattern language requires identifying and systematically describing existing patterns. Overall, developing pattern collections is a classification task that requires solid and well-justified methods to identify and finally classify relevant patterns. Once this task has been accomplished, further steps can be taken to develop a full language according to the theoretical and conceptual considerations discussed in the preceding section.

4.1 Identifying, Describing, and Classifying Patterns

The classification of business models is an important issue, but it is hardly studied from a methodological point of view. For example, Lambert (2015, p. 50) finds that several business model classifications are proposed, such as typologies of e-businesses or revenue models, but that these are often "proposed with little or no justification or explanation." That is, the underlying philosophies and criteria of classifications remain unclear, but these are crucial to define the actual purpose and quality of classifications.

In general, a classification "involves the ordering of objects into groups or classes on the basis of their similarity" (Lambert 2015, p. 50). It is an important way of organising knowledge since "ordering of objects into classes provides meaning to reality" and "is a necessary step in understanding a research area" (ibid.). While biological classifications, for example of insects or mammals, come to mind, we also find classifications in sociology (e.g., social milieus), economics (e.g., industries), or business and management research (e.g., organisational forms). Lambert (2015, p. 51) makes a clear point for classifications: "Classifications make it possible to study and make generalizations about discrete, homogeneous groups of objects and, ultimately, propose mid-range theories […]." Such mid-range theories are important to explain, for instance, why certain business models are more vulnerable to changing market conditions than others, or why some business models contribute to the solution of ecological or social problems while others do not. To contribute to theory development, any set of business model patterns must therefore be systematically described, and, first and foremost, its underlying classification must be methodologically rigorous and well justified.

Classifications can be based on the so-called essentialist philosophy (Rich 1992). Essentialism builds on the theoretical proposition that objects possess some essential traits and that these are necessary and sufficient to categorise objects. Essentialist classifications are derived *a priori* in a conceptual manner. They are called typologies (containing types). Smith (2002, p. 381) explains that "the key characteristic of a typology is that its dimensions represent concepts rather than empirical cases. The dimensions are based on the notion of an ideal type, a mental construct that deliberately accentuates certain characteristics and not necessarily something that is found in empirical reality." Classifications can also be grounded in the so-called empiricist philosophy and result from empirical observations. Such classifications are referred to as taxonomies (containing taxa). Rich (1992, p. 761) adds that "the typology is an invention of individual creativity, [and] the taxonomy is an empirical tool."

Different methods can be used to develop business model pattern typologies and taxonomies, depending on the point of departure and the purpose of the intended classification. We briefly summarise the methods that were so far applied in our pattern studies.

4.2 Case Study-Based Approaches

Froese (2017) and Ohnesorge (2017) developed a case-based approach to identify stakeholder relationship patterns and food waste prevention patterns, respectively. The aim of Froese's study (2017) was to identify and describe the stakeholder relationship patterns of so-called post-growth pioneers, that is, companies that aim to sustain without being dependent on growing business activities. A comparative multiple-case study approach was developed, including interviews with nine post-growth SMEs from Germany. Semi-structured interviews and further materials such as company websites were used as primary and secondary data sources, allowing for data triangulation. The data was analysed within cases and then compared across cases and with the extant literature on post-growth businesses and stakeholder theory, enabling syntheses and generalisations as a basis for theory building (Eisenhardt 1989; Miles and Huberman 1994; Yin 2013). Froese (2017) used a modified version of the Alexandrian form containing pattern title, a description of the situation (context and social or stakeholder problem), the social value objective, the value creation and delivery approach, and the value outcome. This pattern template was derived from the social layer of Joyce and Paquin's (2016) "Triple Layered Business Model Canvas." Using the aforementioned data sources and this stakeholder relationship pattern template allowed identifying and describing seven new patterns (for further details see Froese 2017):

- Value-guided focusing
- Relational engagement for sustainable business
- Forging relations on socialisation and service
- Collaboration as an efficient team
- Building communities for social change
- Paving the way for new solutions
- Getting in touch with society

Ohnesorge (2017) developed a multiple-case study approach that followed the principles of qualitative research, applying analytic induction logic, as defined by Gioia et al. (2013). The aim of the study was to identify business model patterns that are applied by organisations that try to prevent food waste. Semi-structured interviews were conducted with four different organisations; additional secondary data sources were also used. Ohnesorge (2017), too, used a modified version of the Alexandrian form including pattern name, problem statement, context description, purpose of the pattern, solution statement, context resulting from the application of the pattern, examples and explanations, a business model sketch, and related patterns. This form was partially inspired by Falconer's (1999) business pattern template. The traditional "Business Model Canvas" was used to illustrate the patterns. Six new patterns were identified in the context of food waste prevention (for further details see Ohnesorge 2017):

- Access to untapped resources
- Community building
- Cross-financing education
- Green jump-start
- Participative pricing
- Value-based collaboration

These two studies proved that new patterns can be identified through case studies. Reviewing and classifying existing patterns described in the literature represents another approach to developing pattern collections. The following two examples go beyond the identification of patterns as they also develop new classification systems.

4.3 Literature-Based Approaches

4.3.1 Morphological Analysis

Lüdeke-Freund et al. (2018b) reviewed several circular economy business model frameworks found in the academic and practitioner literature (in total 12 studies from 2010 to 2016). Their review shows that some circular economy business models are frequently discussed, while some are framework-specific and some use a different wording to refer to similar models. The identified business models were described in detail along the business model elements proposed by the "Business Model Canvas." The initial set of 37 circular economy business models was reduced to 26 by merging doublets and similar models. A morphological analysis was applied to these 26 models, which included defining the major dimensions of the circular economy business models (value proposition, value delivery, value capture, and value creation) and identifying the various characteristics of these dimensions. Based on this morphological analysis, a broad range of design options for circular economy business models were identified and a typology of six major patterns was proposed (for further details see Lüdeke-Freund et al. 2018b):

* Repair and maintenance
* Reuse and redistribution
* Refurbishment and remanufacturing
* Recycling
* Cascading and repurposing
* Organic feedstock

4.3.2 Delphi Survey and Card Sorting

Another review-based approach was developed by Carroux (2017) and Lüdeke-Freund et al. (2018a). Their SBM pattern taxonomy was created by applying a five-step research approach consisting of (i) identifying and reviewing relevant literature, (ii) extracting SBM patterns from the literature, (iii) developing initial pattern groups, (iv) creating SBM pattern groups using the "Modified Delphi Card Sorting" method (Paul 2008), and finally (v) associating the SBM patterns and groups to sustainable value creation. Ten international experts participated in the Modified Delphi Card Sorting exercise, which served as a consensus-building process to classify 45 business model patterns into meaningful groups, and additionally evaluated the patterns' potential to contribute to sustainable value creation. The resulting taxonomy identifies six major categories: patterns to support ecological effectiveness, social effectiveness, economic effectiveness, eco-efficiency, socio-efficiency, and integrative value creation. The following 11 thematic pattern groups are contained within these categories (for further details see Lüdeke-Freund et al. 2018a):

* Pricing & revenue
* Financing
* Eco-design
* Closing-the-loop
* Supply chain
* Giving
* Access provision

- Social mission
- Service & performance
- Cooperative
- Community platform

We suggest that this taxonomy of 11 thematic groups, which contain 45 SBM patterns, can serve as the basis for a new pattern language that can be used by scholars and practitioners from various disciplines and industries to study and advance SBMs. This SBM pattern taxonomy, and future SBM pattern language, can be used, for example, to extend the existing business model innovation tools.

5 How Can Patterns Motivate Sustainable Business Model Innovation?

Business model patterns are already used in practice. In the following, two business model innovation tools are introduced that make use of patterns. The first tool uses printed facilitations cards and thus represents an analogue approach. It includes card sets representing a comprehensive collection of revenue and pricing patterns. The second tool is an online version of the "Business Model Canvas" (Osterwalder and Pigneur 2009), which makes use of different supporting algorithms and business model pattern packs. Both tools make use of pattern lists rather than languages. These could be further developed into full languages and thus more systematic and versatile instruments to support business model innovation.

5.1 Card-Based Facilitation Method: The Business Innovation Kit and Its Revenue and Pricing Patterns

The Business Innovation Kit (BIK) supports start-up teams, innovators, moderators, and learners in the development of values-based business models. It helps in exploring viable revenue models, walking through the customer journey, elaborating on each customer touchpoint, and pursuing normative orientations like dedication to sustainability or values of privacy (Breuer 2013; Breuer and Lüdeke-Freund 2018). Participants interact in a playful manner, without external assistance. From the outset, the BIK was designed for an ideal situation of face-to-face interaction in mixed, multidisciplinary groups, allowing for fast and highly responsive live interaction among participants, fostering creativity, instant decision-making, and informal probing of mutual commitments. Printed cardboard cards, a flexible "playground," and templates that are available in digital and paper format facilitate direct collaboration (Fig. 2.2). The BIK combines a didactic concept for the implementation of workshops with playful elements (gamification with elements such as puzzles, challenges, and competitions) and a dedicated orientation towards the values of customers, companies, and employees, with an orientation towards sustainability (as an example see the workshop described in Breuer and Lüdeke-Freund 2017b).

Participants gather around the playground, on a table or mapped onto the walls, and follow the BIK's basic rules while they pursue a joint course

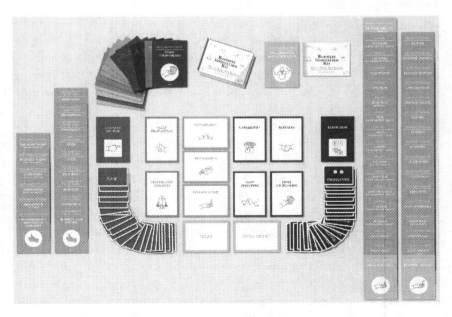

Fig. 2.2 The BIK "playground" and facilitation cards

of actions and perform exercises described on the cards. Initially, the clarification of shared values, visions, and the main purpose of the project creates the common ground and reference point for the development of new business models (Breuer and Lüdeke-Freund 2017a). Case cards present exemplary business model patterns and allow the participants to familiarise themselves with the minimal set of eight business model components. These are the value proposition, stakeholders, touchpoints, distribution, revenues, capabilities, partners, and cost structure (details in Breuer 2013). Structured brain-writing exercises are triggered through generative questions. First individually, then as a group, participants answer questions like "Who is affected positively or negatively by your business?" All ideas are collected in an idea pool. Within a refinement exercise the best ideas are selected, and some are used as an anchor for creating alternative business model ideas. Typically, two to five alternative models are created. Towards the end of a session, so-called challenger cards present short scenarios to consider and prepare for, and not only to challenge assumptions but also trigger entertaining comments and reflections. For instance, responding to a potential omission of their most important distribution channel or to an open-source or zero emission offering of a competitor may foster reasoning about dependencies of the developed business models and their embeddedness in wider ecosystems. Advanced knowledge is conveyed, for example by using additional cards proposing drivers for business cases for sustainability or the differentiation of revenue models and customer journeys (Breuer and Lüdeke-Freund 2018).

A set of cards is available to elaborate on alternative revenue model patterns (Fig. 2.3). They ensure that the scope of potential revenue models pertaining to the business in question is covered. Currently, these cards cover 30 patterns of popular revenue methods as well as pricing schemes. These patterns have been extracted and complied based on a review of scientific and consulting literature on new (especially digitally enabled) revenue models. Each is described on one card with a succinct description, key characteristics, and examples from different industries. A simple matrix overview allows for a quick check of the most interesting combinations of revenue methods and pricing schemes. Once relevant combinations are identified, single patterns or pattern combinations can be used as heuristics to explore how the emerging business model can be

Research on Sustainable Business Model Patterns: Status quo...

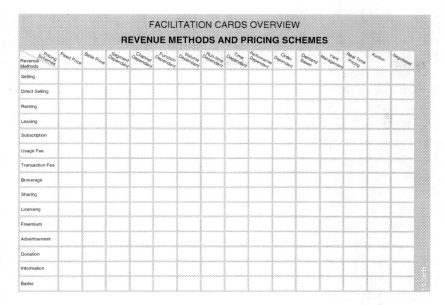

Fig. 2.3 Possible pattern combinations of revenue methods and pricing schemes

redesigned by applying the pattern(s). Using pattern combinations is well in line with Alexander et al.'s (1977, p. xiii) proposition that "no pattern is an isolated entity" and that "[e]ach pattern can exist in the world, only to the extent that is supported by other patterns."

An example: In a recent project, we explored new business models for digital services of a large car manufacturer. We identified a set of new offerings based on a review of customer values and trends such as the differentiation of car-sharing options and increasing degrees of autonomous driving. For each potentially new offering, an exploration of alternative business and revenue models was prepared (beyond the traditional fixed price-per-feature sales), and different participants filled out the playground template with their initial ideas for each business model component (UXBerlin 2018). Preselected revenue model patterns were used in the live workshop to leverage revenue models from adjacent industries. For instance, the pattern of performance-dependent pricing was used, which is known from aircraft engine manufacturers that price turbines based on flying hours (e.g., "power-by-the-hour" offered by Rolls-Royce). Thinking through the characteristics of the pattern and the kind of solution it provides then triggered a fruitful discussion of business and revenue models that shift the burden of maintenance from the customer to the turbine manufacturer or a service provider, while tapping the potential environmental benefits of product-service-systems (Tukker 2015), which themselves represent a specific type of SBM patterns. This example shows that using patterns and pattern combinations in a business modelling exercise can lead to the creation of new and more complete patterns. Again, this resonates well with Alexander et al.'s (1977) and Alexander's (1979) pattern theory.

Different card sets such as example cards, revenue patterns, customer journey cards with patterns for each customer touchpoint, sustainability driver, and maturity cards can be flexibly combined to explore, elaborate on, evaluate, and critically discuss different patterns and pattern combinations to support the development of partial and whole business models. Playful elements such as challenging the underlying model assumptions or thinking through awkward combinations of patterns and business model components also encourage self-directed and cooperative learning. Patterns can help sustainable business modellers to think and work in a networked and cooperative manner.

5.2 Digital Business Modelling Using Patterns: The Smart Business Modeler

In the context of company workshops, start-up accelerators, and graduate education, the team of the Smart Business Modeler noticed that founders of start-ups were often looking for a "business buddy," companies were asking for structured guidance in their business modelling processes, and students were at times limited in their imagination when it came to business model innovation. While offline workshops or accelerators are great ways to offer this kind of support, these are often punctuated initiatives. The Smart Business Modeler team saw an opportunity to provide online guidance based on continuous intelligence augmentation (IA) that includes learning, building, transforming, and sharing business model designs (Fig. 2.4).

Research on Sustainable Business Model Patterns: Status quo...

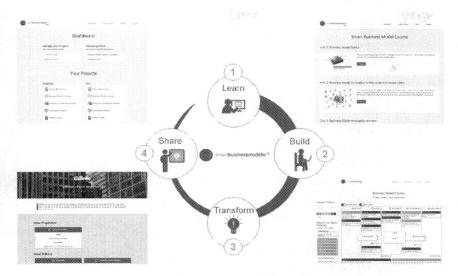

Fig. 2.4 Value proposition of the Smart Business Modeler

In that sense, the Smart Business Modeler was created due to a lack of tools for online business modelling. Since the failure to create a sound business model is a "top 20 reason" for start-ups to fail (CB Insights 2018) and the lack of experience in new business models accounts for 16% of disrupted industries (KPMG 2015), the core idea of the Smart Business Modeler is to combine business modelling playbooks in combination with pattern packs. Playbooks offer a guided step-by-step approach and are particularly useful for start-ups or other users that have a great idea but lack a "business buddy." The pattern databases are very useful for users such as companies to avoid cognitive biases and be aware of current market trends. Current online business model tools leave users often in their existing frame of mind and at the "post-it stage." By giving a set of playbooks and pattern packs that include more than 250+ patterns, an intuitive user interface and tested user experience, as well as IA tools such as wizards, pre-fill logics, and recommendations, the Smart Business Modeler can spur lateral thinking, push implementation, and create business models that create and capture more value.

The Smart Business Modeler has been used by companies (e.g., Grundfos), accelerators (MIT Design X), and universities in undergraduate, graduate, and executive programmes (e.g., Católica-Lisbon or Tunis Business School). The main features used were the online courses on business modelling, the IA-based business model canvas as well as extensive and adaptable pattern databases that allow creating innovative business models tailored to target customers and key stakeholders. Furthermore, it offers the possibility to create closed communities, for instance for company-internal innovation programmes, workshops, or even degree courses, which can use the tool to communicate, comment on, and rate business model designs. It can also be a rich source for research; for instance, it allows linking anonymised educational and professional backgrounds from LinkedIn to business model innovation creation processes.

After free registration to the Smart Business Modeler, single users or entire teams can create unlimited amounts of projects. The tool offers online courses, an internal message board, and a comprehensive pattern library that provides inspiration and ideas for the development and configuration of business models. These can be created by using the IA-enabled business model canvas which supports fast drag-and-drop business modelling, and further functionalities such as instant knowledge through info boxes and a customised one-page website that allows sharing a business model with interested parties (Fig. 2.5).

Currently, the pattern library contains six business model pattern packs, including a circular economy (Lüdeke-Freund et al. 2018b) and a sustainability pattern pack (Lüdeke-Freund et al. 2018a). These patterns can be directly applied to the canvas via drag-and-drop. The IA function then proposes certain business model elements that can be designed according to the pattern (e.g., the "cradle-to-cradle" pattern in the circular economy pack proposes to modify the value proposition, key activities, key resources, and revenue stream elements).

The pattern library and its pattern packs are not a static archive, but a dynamically growing and adaptable repository of best practices in terms of complete and partial business model designs. This feature resonates with Alexander et al.'s (1977) idea of a living language that evolves over time. However, the packs are not full languages in an Alexandrian sense as relationships and interactions between the different patterns and pattern packs are not yet considered, which is important for the emergence

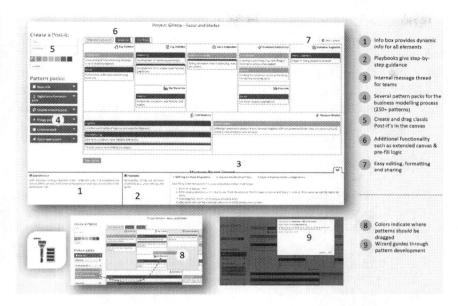

Fig. 2.5 IA-enabled business modelling with the Smart Business Modeler

of the networked structures of a language (ibid.). A research agenda to develop an SBM pattern language could build on this pattern library and develop it further into a full-pattern language.

6 Concluding Remarks and Issues for Future Research

The value and potential of business model patterns has been discussed by different authors, such as Girotra and Netessine (2013) or Remane et al. (2017). The latter state that "the importance of the concept is underlined by the finding that 90% of all business model innovations are a recombination of existing business model patterns … Therefore, by drawing upon aspects that have already been proven to be successful for other companies and industries, the use of business model patterns provides an efficient way to undertake business model innovation …" (Remane et al. 2017, p. 2).

Unfolding these advantages of business model patterns to help overcome the challenges of designing more sustainable organisations requires the development of a full SBM pattern language. While current research offers first insights into SBM patterns, these are mostly limited to pattern lists and do not provide full-pattern languages in an Alexandrian sense. Therefore, future research has to address several theoretical, conceptual, and methodical issues to move towards a full SBM pattern language. Some of these issues were discussed in this chapter. A future research agenda should consider at least these points:

- How to consolidate the available knowledge on SBM patterns, and how to convert it into "knowledge for action"?
- What kind of template or Alexandrian form is best suited to describe and archive SBM patterns?
- How to identify and systematise the various connections between different SBM patterns to create an overarching structure?
- How to define normative guiding criteria to increase the likelihood of effective contributions to sustainable organisational design?
- Which methods are best suited to develop SBM classifications, both typologies and taxonomies?
- How to test the effectiveness of SBM patterns as an additional element of business model innovation tools?

These questions are an open innovation to SBM scholars and practitioners to join our endeavour. Our initial studies on SBM patterns presented in this chapter may serve as a starting point.

Notes

1. Also referred to as "business models for sustainability" (e.g., Wells 2013). Both terms are used interchangeably in this chapter.
2. Since 2002, the Iba Lab at Keio University & CreativeShift Lab created 67 pattern languages including 1610 patterns; see http://web.sfc.keio.ac.jp/~iba/languages.html (as of April 2018).

References

Abdelkafi, N., and K. Täuscher. 2016. Business Models for Sustainability from a System Dynamics Perspective. *Organization & Environment* 29 (1): 74–96.

Abdelkafi, N., S. Makhotin, and T. Posselt. 2013. Business Model Innovations for Electric Mobility—What Can Be Learned from Existing Business Model Patterns? *International Journal of Innovation Management* 17(1): Art. 1340003.

Alexander, C. 1979. *The Timeless Way of Building.* Cambridge, MA: Oxford University Press.

Alexander, C., S. Ishikawa, M. Silverstein, M. Jacobson, I. Fiksdahl-King, and S. Angel. 1977. *A Pattern Language: Towns, Buildings, Construction.* Cambridge, MA: Oxford University Press.

Alt, R., and H.-D. Zimmermann. 2001. Preface: Introduction to Special Section—Business Models. *EM—Electronic Markets* 11 (1): 3–9.

Amshoff, B., C. Dülme, J. Echterfeld, and J. Gausemeier. 2015. Business Model Patterns for Disruptive Technologies. *International Journal of Innovation Management* 19 (3): Art. No. 1540002.

Beltramello, A., L. Haie-Fayle, and D. Pilat. 2013. *Why New Business Models Matter for Green Growth.* Paris: OECD Publishing.

Bisgaard, T., K. Henriksen, and M. Bjerre. 2012. *Green Business Model Innovation—Conceptualisation, Next Practice and Policy.* Oslo: Nordic Innovation.

Bocken, N., S. Short, P. Rana, and S. Evans. 2013. A Value Mapping Tool for Sustainable Business Modelling. *Corporate Governance: The International Journal of Business in Society* 13 (5): 482–497.

———. 2014. A Literature and Practice Review to Develop Sustainable Business Model Archetypes. *Journal of Cleaner Production* 65: 42–56.

Bohnsack, R., and J. Pinkse. 2017. Value Propositions for Disruptive Technologies: Reconfiguration Tactics in the Case of Electric Vehicles. *California Management Review* 59 (4): 79–96.

Bohnsack, R., J. Pinkse, and A. Kolk. 2014. Business Models for Sustainable Technologies: Exploring Business Model Evolution in the Case of Electric Vehicles. *Research Policy* 43 (2): 284–300.

Boons, F., and F. Lüdeke-Freund. 2013. Business Models for Sustainable Innovation: State-of-the-art and Steps Towards a Research Agenda. *Journal of Cleaner Production* 45: 9–19.

Breuer, H. 2013. Lean Venturing: Learning to Create New Business Through Exploration, Elaboration, Evaluation, Experimentation, and Evolution.

International Journal of Innovation Management 17 (3): Article 1340013 (22 pp.).

Breuer, H., K. Fichter, F. Lüdeke-Freund, and I. Tiemann. 2018. Sustainability-Oriented Business Model Development: Principles, Criteria, and Tools. *International Journal of Entrepreneurial Venturing* 10 (2): 256–286.

Breuer, H., and F. Lüdeke-Freund. 2017a. *Values-Based Innovation Management: Innovating by What We Care About*. Houndmills: Palgrave Macmillan.

Breuer, H., and F.Lüdeke-Freund.2017b. Values-Based Network and Business Model Innovation. *International Journal of Innovation Management* 21 (3): Article 1750028 (35 pp.).

———. 2018. Values-Based Business Model Innovation—A Toolkit. In *Sustainable Business Models: Principles, Promise, and Practice*, ed. L.Moratis, F.Melissen, and S.Idowu. Springer, in print.

Carroux, S.2017. *Patterns for Sustainable Business Model Innovation. Creating a Pattern Taxonomy for Business Model Innovation in the Sustainability Context*. Master thesis, University of Hamburg, Hamburg.

CB Insights. 2018. *The Top 20 Reasons Startups Fail*. Accessed April 26, 2018. https://www.cbinsights.com/research/startup-failure-reasons-top/.

Clinton, L., and R. Whisnant. 2014. *Model Behavior—20 Business Model Innovations for Sustainability*. London: Sustainability.

Eisenhardt, K. 1989. Building Theories from Case Study Research. *The Academy of Management Review* 14 (4): 532–550.

Falconer, J. 1999. The Business Pattern: A New Tool for Organizational Knowledge Capture and Reuse. *Proceedings of the Annual Meeting-American Society for Information Science* 36: 313–330.

Froese, T.2017. *Time for New Relationships: Stakeholder Relationship Patterns of Post-Growth Businesses*. Master thesis, University of Hamburg, Hamburg.

Gassmann, O., K. Frankenberger, and M. Csik. 2014. *The Business Model Navigator: 55 Models That Will Revolutionise Your Business*. Pearson Education Limited.

Gioia, D., K. Corley, and A. Hamilton. 2013. Seeking Qualitative Rigor in Inductive Research: Notes on the Gioia Methodology. *Organizational Research Methods* 16 (1): 15–31.

Girotra, K., and S. Netessine. 2013. OM Forum—Business Model Innovation for Sustainability. *Manufacturing & Service Operations Management* 15 (4): 537–544.

Joyce, A. 2016. *A Proposal for a Design Approach to More Sustainable Business Models: Tools, Process and Outcomes to Envision the Future of an Organization*. Doctoral dissertation, Concordia University, Montreal.

Joyce, A., and R.L. Paquin. 2016. The Triple Layered Business Model Canvas: A Tool to Design More Sustainable Business Models. *Journal of Cleaner Production* 135: 1474–1486.

KPMG. 2015. *5 Insights & Predictions on Disruptive Tech from KPMG's 2015 Global Innovation Survey*. Accessed April 28, 2018. https://www.forbes.com/sites/louiscolumbus/2015/11/08/5-insights-predictions-on-disruptive-tech-from-kpmgs-2015-global-innovation-survey/#224de63a3cbb.

Lambert, S. 2015. The Importance of Classification to Business Model Research. *Journal of Business Models* 3 (1): 49–61.

Leitner, H. 2015. *Pattern Theory—Introduction and Perspectives on the Tracks of Christopher Alexander*. Graz: HLS.

Lüdeke-Freund, F., and K. Dembek. 2017. Sustainable Business Model Research and Practice: Emerging Field or Passing Fancy? *Journal of Cleaner Production* 168: 1668–1678.

Lüdeke-Freund, F., S. Carroux, A. Joyce, L. Massa, and H. Breuer. 2018a. The sustainable business model pattern taxonomy—45 patterns to support sustainability-oriented business model innovation. *Sustainable Production and Consumption*. Online first 26 June 2018.

Lüdeke-Freund, F., S.Gold, and N.Bocken. 2018b. A Review and Typology of Circular Economy Business Model Patterns. *Journal of Industrial Ecology*, in print. Online first 25 April 2018.

Massa, L., C. Tucci, and A. Afuah. 2017. A Critical Assessment of Business Model Research. *Academy of Management Annals* 11 (1): 73–104.

Miles, M., and A. Huberman. 1994. Cross-case Displays: Exploring and Describing. In *Qualitative Data Analysis: An Expanded Sourcebook*. Thousand Oaks: Sage.

Ohnesorge, M.2017. *Thinking Outside the Bin—Sustainable Business Model Patterns for Food Waste Prevention*. Master thesis, University of Hamburg, Hamburg.

Osterwalder, A., and Y. Pigneur. 2009. *Business Model Generation: A Handbook for Visionaries, Game Changers, and Challengers*. Amsterdam: Self-published.

Parrish, B. 2010. Sustainability-driven Entrepreneurship: Principles of Organization Design. *Journal of Business Venturing* 25 (5): 510–523.

Paul, C. 2008. A Modified Delphi Approach to a New Card Sorting Methodology. *Journal of Usability Studies* 4 (1): 7–30.

Rauter, R., J. Jonker, and R.J. Baumgartner. 2017. Going One's Own Way: Drivers in Developing Business Models for Sustainability. *Journal of Cleaner Production* 140: 144–154.

Remane, G., A. Hanelt, J. Tesch, and L.M. Kolbe. 2017. The Business Model Pattern Database—A Tool for Systematic Business Model Innovation. *International Journal of Innovation Management* 21 (1): Article 1750004.

Rich, P. 1992. The Organizational Taxonomy: Definition and Design. *Academy of Management Review* 17 (4): 758–781.

Schaltegger, S., E.G. Hansen, and F. Lüdeke-Freund. 2016. Business Models for Sustainability: Origins, Present Research, and Future Avenues. *Organization & Environment* 29 (1): 3–10.

Simon, H. 1969/1996. *The Sciences of the Artificial*. 3rd ed. Cambridge, MA: The MIT Press.

Smith, K. 2002. Typologies, Taxonomies, and the Benefits of Policy Classification. *Policy Studies Journal* 30 (3): 379–395.

Stubbs, W., and C. Cocklin. 2008. Conceptualizing a 'Sustainability Business Model. *Organization & Environment* 21 (2): 103–127.

Tukker, A. 2004. Eight Types of Product–Service System: Eight Ways to Sustainability? Experiences from SusProNet. *Business Strategy and the Environment* 13 (4): 246–260.

———. 2015. Product Services for a Resource-Efficient and Circular Economy—A Review. *Journal of Cleaner Production* 97: 76–91.

Upward, A., and P. Jones. 2016. An Ontology for Strongly Sustainable Business Models: Defining an Enterprise Framework Compatible with Natural and Social Science. *Organization & Environment* 29 (1): 97–123.

UXBerlin. 2018. *Refinement for Business Modelling (Template)*. Accessed April 26, 2018. http://www.uxberlin.com/wp-content/uploads/2018/02/Values-Based_Business_Modelling_UXBerlin.pdf.

Wells, P. 2013. *Business Models for Sustainability*. Cheltenham: Edward Elgar Publishing.

Wirtz, B.W., A. Pistoia, S. Ullrich, and V. Göttel. 2016. Business Models: Origin, Development and Future Research Perspectives. *Long Range Planning* 49 (1): 36–54.

Yang, M., S. Evans, D. Vladimirova, and P. Rana. 2017. Value Uncaptured Perspective for Sustainable Business Model Innovation. *Journal of Cleaner Production* 140: 1794–1804.

Yin, R. 2013. *Case Study Research: Design and Methods*. 5th ed. Thousand Oaks: Sage.

Zott, C., R. Amit, and L. Massa. 2011. The Business Model: Recent Developments and Future Research. *Journal of Management* 37 (4): 1019–1042.

3

Designing Sustainable Business Models: Exploring IoT-Enabled Strategies to Drive Sustainable Consumption

Nancy Bocken, Emilia Ingemarsdotter, and Diana Gonzalez

1 Introduction

Product service systems (PSS) are combinations of 'tangible products and intangible services designed and combined so that they are jointly capable of fulfilling specific customer needs' (Tukker 2004, p. 246). Some PSS are more product oriented (e.g. advice, additional warrantee, or servicing), others more use oriented (e.g. leasing, renting, sharing), and again others more result oriented (e.g. pay per unit of service or for a functional result) (Tukker 2004). PSS are often positioned as a means to deliver sustainability benefits across the product life cycle (Mont and Tukker 2006). The shift toward a 'service economy' could contribute to dematerialization or 'a reduction in the materials intensity of economic activities' (Heiskanen and Jalas 2000,

---

N. Bocken (✉) • E. Ingemarsdotter • D. Gonzalez
Industrial Design Engineering, Delft University of Technology,
Delft, The Netherlands
e-mail: N.M.P.Bocken@tudelft.nl; E.K.Ingemarsdotter@tudelft.nl

p. 5). It could help reduce total product life cycle impact, including material selection as an input to product design, manufacturing, distribution, product/service use phases as well as product reuse and recovery strategies (Aurich et al. 2006; Bocken and Allwood 2012). Potential product life cycle sustainability advantages of PSS over direct product sales relate to breaking the link between profit and production volumes, reducing resource consumption and material use, motivating inclusion of through-life and end-of-life issues (e.g. repair and remanufacturing), stimulating enhanced efficiency in use, and encouraging design for product longevity (Bocken et al. 2014). However, in order to achieve desirable sustainability results, these elements will need to be built into the PSS. Particularly, environmental impact from the use phase is often not addressed (Mont 2004). This calls for more design efforts to take into account environmental considerations in the development of PSS offerings.

In the field of sustainable design, tools and methods have been developed to help product designers stimulate sustainable consumption patterns as part of products and services (Tang 2010; Bhamra et al. 2011). Strategies range from purely informative (e.g. eco-information) to more holistic product design approaches (e.g. eco-steer or clever eco-design) (Tang 2010). While knowledge is available about the range of options, Bhamra et al. (2011) argue that behavior-changing devices need to be tested and prototyped, and that ethical considerations related to Design for Sustainable Behavior strategies need to be explored in greater depth. For example, users may reject 'intelligent products' when they are unable to switch off certain controlling functionality (Wever et al. 2008). Thus, new business models incorporating such strategies need to be experimented with and validated with real customers (Ries 2011).

New opportunities to design for sustainable consumption arise as more and more products are being augmented with sensors and communications technology. Such 'smart products' can make sense of their local situation and interact with human users (Kortuem et al. 2010). Together, these products make up the emerging 'Internet of Things' (IoT). The IoT has been defined as 'a conceptual framework that leverages on the availability of heterogeneous devices and interconnection solutions, as well as augmented physical objects providing a shared information base on global scale, to support the design of applications involving at the same virtual level both people and representations of objects' (Atzori et al. 2016, p. 137). While abstract, the definition tells us that the IoT provides new design possibilities based on interconnectivity between humans and products. In 'smart PSS', designers have new opportunities to develop individualized interactions and experiences based on data collected about the user (Valencia Cardona et al. 2015). Smartness of products can support changes toward sustainable behavior by creating decisions for users that may not be apparent, natural, or habitual to them or proposing more accurate features according to the context and moment of use. Also, their ability to collect real-time data enables immediate feedback to the user and supports awareness creation. Hence, smart PSS has the potential to influence user behavior for sustainability, but more research is needed about how to design and implement such PSS. Moreover, the IoT has been described as a third wave of IT-driven transformation in business that could fundamentally change companies and competition (Porter and Heppelmann 2014). Hence, the IoT can be regarded as a trend that needs to be understood also in the context of sustainable business models.

This research connects the fields of sustainable business models, design for sustainable behavior, and IoT, investigating the potential for smart products to interact with PSS users in a way that stimulates and supports sustainable behavior and improved environmental performance in the use phase. Examples of consumer-oriented PSS offerings are explored in terms of design strategies and IoT capabilities applied. We explore the following research question: *How can IoT strategies be used to design appropriate PSS solutions that encourage sustainable consumption?*

2   Literature Background

The literature background provides an overview of research on sustainable business models, design for sustainable behavior, and smart products. In Sect. 2.4, we use this background to develop a framework to support the design of sustainable business models.

2.1 Sustainable Business Models

Sustainable business models and PSS can help gain a competitive advantage while reducing environmental impact and contributing positively to society (Boons and Lüdeke-Freund 2013). In brief, business models describe the way business is done. Typically, they are depicted as comprising of three main parts: a 'value proposition' (product/service offering), 'value creation and delivery' (how value is created and delivered to the customer), and 'value captured' (how value to the customer and other forms of value are captured) (Teece 2010; Bocken and Short 2016). While the popularity of sustainable and circular business models is on the rise in academia, with an increasing number of publications, a lot of this work remains conceptual and there is insufficient evidence on the potential positive effects of such new business models. Sustainable business model success depends on business viability, customer satisfaction as well as environmental soundness (Mont 2004). To achieve greater sustainability benefits, sustainable business models need to be set up in the right way (e.g. to stimulate sustainable consumption). More research is needed to 'design' sustainable business models to achieve the desired positive effects (Tukker 2004; Mont and Tukker 2006).

Some business models may be more appropriate to achieve positive sustainability effects than others. It appears that the vision of a company and its owners/shareholders is an important starting point and driver for sustainability (Bocken et al. 2016; Kraaijenhagen et al. 2016; Leising et al. 2017). This vision may be articulated, using the idea of a 'sustainable value proposition', as a pledge (in absolute values) made by a company about its environmental or societal ambitions (Manninen et al. 2018). Outdoor sports equipment and clothing producer Patagonia and furniture manufacturer Vitsœ have visions that incorporate the idea of 'sufficiency', that is, to moderate consumption levels (Bocken and Short 2016). Through its Common Threads Initiative, Patagonia (2011) pledges to make products that last and that are reparable and recyclable. The company also asks customers to make a pledge to only buy what is necessary and look after clothing through maintenance and repair. Both Patagonia and Vitsœ pursue a product-oriented approach with high service levels (e.g. maintenance, repair, warrantees) (Bocken and Short 2016). On the servitized end of the product-service business model spectrum, Tukker (2004) argues that renting, sharing, and pooling can lead to environmental gains as goods are used more intensively and (in the case of pooling) consumables in the use phase are providing benefits for several persons at the same time. Finally, function-oriented PSS models could have the highest potential for environmental performance, because they focus on the end result (e.g. clean clothing, fresh air) (Tukker 2004).

To achieve significant 'system-level impact', often seen as a key feature of sustainable business models (Stubbs and Cocklin 2008; Bocken et al. 2013, 2014), total consumption volumes would need to be reduced in addition to reducing the impact per unit of service or functional result. In a 'pay per use' contract, where customers only pay when they use the product or access the service (e.g. launderettes or car sharing paid for by the hour or kilometer driven), users may be more conscious about their behavior and reduce their usage (e.g. wash or drive less) (Tukker 2004; Bocken et al. 2017). In contrast, in leasing contracts with a fixed monthly fee, there may be little incentive to engage in eco-efficient driving and optimizing fuel efficiency and routing (Backers and Tietge 2017), because the user does not pay for fuel or maintenance. Studies have argued that user behavior can even become less responsible when a product is not owned, leading to, for example, higher fuel consumption and increased product wear (e.g. Fischer et al. 2015). 'Rented and leased products may be handled more carelessly, especially if the contract includes free maintenance or replacement' (Klapwijk et al. 2006, p. 248). Hence, while service-oriented models hold promise, the impact depends on the type of model and how it has been 'set up' to drive sustainable consumption.

Hence, although sustainable business models hold promise to deliver sustainability benefits, the interplay between benefits and possible adverse effects needs to be more widely understood. Table 3.1 provides an overview of potential environmental benefits, as well as possible adverse effects related to four types of PSS: leasing, renting-sharing, pay-per-use, and functional result (as first categorized by Tukker 2004).

Table 3.1 Different PSS and potential impacts

Business model	PSS example	Examples of potential environmental benefits	Examples of potential adverse effects
Leasing	Car leasing	Service providers are incentivized to continually improve design for optimized cost over total life cycle and for multiple life cycles (Tukker 2004; Bocken et al. 2014). Service providers are responsible for maintenance, repair, and control: • Incentive for long product life • Responsibility for maintenance, care, and control might lead to resource efficiency improvements (e.g. reduced energy in use phase)	Products such as cars are typically not designed for intensive use and are replaced often due to wear and tear (Mont 2004). Lack of responsibility from the user and control over actual behavior. For example, a 10% increase in environmental impact was identified in car leasing contracts despite a 'cleaner fleet', for example, due to lack of skills in 'eco-driving, lack of route optimization, and not charging electric cars regularly (Backers and Tietge 2017)
Renting/Sharing	Car and tool sharing (Mont 2004)	Potential environmental benefits of leasing, plus: More intensive use. Use of the product may be discouraged (e.g. cost per km and/or hour in addition to other contract cost) Shared cars are estimated to be lighter and more fuel efficient than the average car (the Netherlands example mentioned in Mont 2004). Sharing may reduce the number of cars on the roads by 44% and distances driven by 30–60% (Mont 2004) • For example, Zipcar (car sharing) estimates that it takes six personally owned vehicles off the road and that 40% of users sold their car or did not buy a new one (Bocken 2017).	People use shared products more intensively, so products would need to be designed for quality, durability, and shared usage (Mont 2004; OnePlanetCrowd 2018). Running costs (e.g. fuel) are not included, so there is little incentive to use the product (e.g. drive) carefully. Similarly, in the case of product sharing (e.g. Peerby; OnePlanetCrowd 2018) there is no financial transaction between users, and sharing happens based on the basis of trust, which could lead to product misuse. The traveling done using a car-sharing service might substitute public transport or bike rides, rather than the use of a personal car (Boons and Bocken 2017).

(continued)

Table 3.1 (continued)

Business model	PSS example	Examples of potential environmental benefits	Examples of potential adverse effects
Pay-per-use	Washing machine/ Copier machines	Potential environmental benefits of leasing, plus: More conscious use—pay per use might reduce total usage. For example, the 'pay per wash' model offered by HOMIE seems to lead to more sustainable consumption (Bocken et al. 2017) and document management systems can reduce paper use significantly (e.g. 80% in the case of Vodafone; Environmental Paper Network 2018)	Copiers at work: An employee in an office, the user of a copier machine, is often not the one paying for copying. Therefore, the pay per use model does not directly incentivize the user to copy less. • True cost will need to communicated, alternative technology made available, and nudges need to be present to reduce usage (Bocken et al. 2017; Environmental Paper Network 2018)
Functional result	Selling m^3 of fresh air in offices (Bocken et al. 2018) Pay per lux/the service of light rather than lamps (Philips Lighting Holding B.V. 2017)	Potential environmental benefits of leasing, plus: Paying for an *outcome* or *result*, rather than a product could incentivize service providers to be energy and cost efficient and deliver quality and durability and long-lasting products. • For example, Philips Lighting Holding B.V. (2017) estimates that its new lights last 75% longer and use 50% less energy than former ones. • Volkswagen partnered with Philips Lightning on 'connected LED lighting', through an access based business model, enabling the company to save 80% on energy consumption (Nobre and Tavares 2017)	Over dimensioning because of being afraid to not meet contract promises. • For example, the extra resources required due to the new IoT infrastructure might outweigh the resource efficiency benefits due to over-specification (Lelah et al. 2011). • Sometimes difficult to set up the contract so that it is clear what needs to be delivered (Tukker 2004).

Source: Developed from Tukker (2004)

2.2 Design Strategies for Sustainable Behavior

In the field of design, key authors have investigated potential strategies to influence consumer behavior as a strategy to improve a product's sustainability performance. This section reviews design strategies focused on sustainable consumption.

Consumer behavior is not easy to analyze or influence because it is found to be formed by attitudes, intentions, ability to influence, and actual actions (Ajzen 1991). It is a construct of internal factors such as personality and external factors (e.g. economic, societal), behavior patterns, and behavior-change incentives (Kollmus and Aygeman 2002; Bocken 2017). Strategies for sustainable behavior can range from informative and guiding strategies (e.g. making the user aware of his or her resource use) to more 'forceful' (e.g. product bans) and embedding strategies (e.g. most sustainable behavior is the default) (Bocken and Allwood 2012). The softer approaches may only give information to the user about the 'best behavior' (e.g. wash at 30°C is better for the environment). Strategies 'in the middle' may involve nudging that steer people in the right direction through changing the choice infrastructure, to make the 'most sustainable' choice easiest (e.g. making the staircase more prominent than the elevator in order to encourage people to take the stairs) (Thaler and Sunstein 2008). Also, when people need to opt out and they are by default 'in' (e.g. in the case of being a donor), the uptake will be much larger (Thaler and Sunstein 2008). The more forceful approaches would include product bans and phasing out the worst products from a range as what happened with low-energy-label home appliances (SDC 2006).

In the field of Sustainable Design, authors have built on these notions to develop sustainable design product/service design strategies that influence the consumer at different levels (e.g. Bhamra et al. 2008, 2011; Tang 2010; Wever et al. 2008). On the one hand, products could be guiding behavior. Eco-feedback includes sending messages to remind the user about positive behavior (e.g. a message recommending to switch off a device entirely; Wever et al. 2008) or comparing behavior with that of neighbors. An eco-spur goes a level further by incentivizing sustainable energy use by providing incentives and rewards to the user and providing options or features that make the use more sustainable (e.g. money saved through energy savings are donated to a good cause; Baldassarre et al. 2017). At the most extreme end, there is 'forced behavior' (Wever et al. 2008) where the user cannot change settings. For instance, it might not be possible to drive faster or wash at a higher temperature because these options are unavailable or blocked to the user, or, in the case of a smart product, the user would not be able to change the setting as the smart function decides on the 'best option'. Table 3.2 shows an overview of potential design interactions at a product/service level based on the framework Design for Sustainable Behaviour as presented by Tang (2010) and Bhamra et al. (2011). An additional strategy not captured in the table relates to 'functionality matching' (Wever et al. 2008). This refers to the notion that sustainable consumption is more likely to happen if service or product features match with the user's desired features. In this way, redundant functionalities can be avoided and the inclusion of effective functions facilitated (Wever et al. 2008).

2.3 Capabilities of Smart Products

The IoT is an overarching term referring to the interconnections of digitally augmented physical objects (Atzori et al. 2016). A 'smart object' can be defined to have the ability to sense, interact, and communicate with their environment (Kortuem et al. 2010). Data recorded by smart products, about product use and performance, can support a more service-based business model (Lightfoot et al. 2011). The IoT has also been acknowledged for its ability to improve energy efficiency in buildings (e.g. Pan et al. 2015). Information about how a unique item has been used during its life can inform maintenance actions by predicting and preventing failure. This is already done in, for example, airplane jet engines and wind farms (Kwon et al. 2016). Moreover, product-in-use data can be used to reduce risks in reuse and remanufacturing by estimating actual remaining lifetimes and assessing the quality of used products (e.g. Ondemir and Gupta 2014). Given their interactive nature, smart products can potentially also guide and/or steer users toward more sustainable behavior.

Table 3.2 Design interventions and strategies for sustainable behavior

Control	Spectrum	Design intervention			
		Lilley et al. (2005) and Lilley (2009)	Lockton et al. (2008)	Wever et al. (2008)	Tang (2010) and Bhamra et al. (2011)
User	Informing	*Eco-feedback* Users are informed about their consumption or impact. The design 'Provides tangible aural, visual or tactile signs as reminders to inform users of resource use'.	*Persuasion and feedback* Users are in a friendly way invited to change his or her behavior through information about consumption. It might include social comparison.	*Eco-feedback* The user is informed in order to encourage reflection. This means that judgment is left to user's criteria on what to do with the received information.	*Eco-information* Consumables are made visible, understandable, and accessible in order to inspire consumers to reflect upon their use of resources. *Eco-choice* The consumers are encouraged to think about their use behavior and to take responsibility of their actions through providing consumers with options. *Eco-feedback* Users are clearly informed about what they are doing and to facilitate consumers to make environmentally and socially responsible decisions through offering real-time feedback.

(*continued*)

Table 3.2 (continued)

Control	Spectrum	Design intervention			
		Lilley et al. (2005) and Lilley (2009)	Lockton et al. (2008)	Wever et al. (2008)	Tang (2010) and Bhamra et al. (2011)
Product	Steering	*Scripts and behavior steering*	*Affordances and constraints*	*Scripting*	*Eco-spur*
		Without determining their actions, users are guided to do what the designer intended through the design of constraints or affordances.	Affordances or constraints are used to lead, guide, or limit user's actions to follow certain behavior. It might include, defaults, limits and targets, and physical constrains.	The design leads to sustainable use by creating obstacles for unsustainable use or making behavior so easy that the user does not think about it, thus enabling the desired behavior.	Users are inspired to explore more sustainable usage through providing rewordings to 'prompt' good behavior or penalties to 'punish' unsustainable usage.
					Eco-steer
					Users are facilitated to adopt more environmentally or social desirable use habits through the prescriptions and/or constraints of use embedded in the product design.

(*continued*)

Table 3.2 (continued)

Control	Spectrum	Design intervention			
		Lilley et al. (2005) and Lilley (2009)	Lockton et al. (2008)	Wever et al. (2008)	Tang (2010) and Bhamra et al. (2011)
Product	Embedding	*Intelligent products and systems*	*Context based*	*Forced functionality*	*Eco-technology*
		Also called persuasive technology. Some decisions are taken by the product itself, which is assumed to be 'intelligent' to mitigate control or block unsustainable user behavior.	This strategy combines the two above-mentioned strategies. Each one is triggered according to user's behavior at a specific time. This strategy is dependent on Smart Products, which adapt the features, affordances or constrains according to information input or environment conditions.	Intelligent products are designed that adapt to changing circumstances or strong obstacles to prevent unsustainable behavior.	Use habits are restrained and the users are persuaded or their behavior controlled automatically by design combined with advanced technology.
					Clever design
					The product is design so that users automatically act environmentally or socially sustainably, without raising awareness.

In previous research, the capabilities of 'smart, connected' products have been broadly categorized into monitoring, control, optimization, and autonomy (Porter and Heppelmann 2014). The IoT capability of *monitoring* gives insights into the use of the product. This can be provided as feedback to the user, who can then choose to act upon that information or not. Using data, a product can alert its users, or maintenance providers, to changes in circumstances or performance (Porter and Heppelmann 2014). Through the capability of *control*, smart products can allow users to control their own systems remotely, or let the service providers and/or the system itself exercise control without user involvement (Porter and Heppelman 2014). For example, users can switch off the heating remotely when not at home, or the system can switch off itself when it notices that no one is present. *Optimization* is about 'goal-based improvements' using algorithms which learn from historical user behavior (Porter and Heppelman 2014). Real-time monitoring of product conditions can also allow firms to optimize services by performing preventative maintenance when failure is imminent (Porter and Heppelman 2014). *Autonomous* products combine monitoring, control, and optimization capabilities to achieve a level of autonomy. Such products can interpret data, 'self-diagnose', and act accordingly (Porter and Heppelman 2014). In this chapter, we use the abovementioned categorization of four main IoT capabilities (summarized in Table 3.3) in order to analyze how IoT-enabled strategies for sustainable consumer behavior could be implemented in PSS. We aim to explore to what extent IoT capabilities are leveraged in current PSS offerings, taking this categorization as a starting point.

2.4 Framework: How IoT Capabilities Can Support PSS Design to Encourage Sustainable Behavior

In this section, a framework is developed to analyze real-world PSS cases. The framework is developed based on literature that categorizes IoT capabilities and sustainable behavior design strategies.

In Sect. 2.2, it was found that eco-design strategies can be roughly divided into guiding, steering, and embedding. The design for sustain-

Table 3.3 Overview of IoT capabilities suitable for sustainable PSS

IoT capability	Description
Monitoring	Sensors and external data sources enable the comprehensive monitoring of: • the product's condition • the external environment • the product's operation and usage Monitoring also enables alerts and notifications of changes
Control	Software embedded in the product or in the product cloud enables: • Control of product functions • Personalization of the user experience
Optimization	Monitoring and control capabilities enable algorithms that optimize product operation and use in order to: • Enhance product performance • Allow predictive diagnostics, service, and repair
Autonomy	Combining monitoring, control, and optimization allows: • Autonomous product operation • Self-coordination of operation with other products and systems • Autonomous product enhancement and personalization • Self-diagnosis and service

Source: Porter and Heppelmann (2014)

able behavior strategies by Tang (2010) and Bhamra et al. (2011) was found to be most complete and is used in our framework in Table 3.4. In Sect. 2.3, we identified four main IoT capabilities: monitoring, control, optimization, and autonomy (Porter and Heppelmann 2014). The user's control over these capabilities varies from full in monitoring to limited in autonomy where the product takes decisions on behalf of the user. Similarly, the sustainable behavior design strategies state a variation in the user's control from full when providing feedback and limited when the functionality is forced by smart products. In this way, IoT capabilities and design strategies can be related. It should be noted that there may be several essential 'non-IoT related strategies' that can drive sustainable consumption in the business model. This line is added in Table 3.4 for completeness. The framework in Table 3.4 was designed to support the design of sustainable business models using IoT and sustainable behavior strategies, and is used in Sect. 3 to explore strategies implemented in existing business cases.

3   Methods

This paper addresses the following question: How can IoT strategies be used to design appropriate PSS solutions that encourage sustainable consumption?

To evaluate this question, we look into two sectors in which new PSS have been developed, and consumer behavior is an important factor contributing to product life cycle impacts:

1. Washing machines and the potential to stimulate sustainable behavior
2. Car-sharing services to stimulate sustainable car usage

We use a case study approach with snapshot cases to apply and test the framework in Table 3.4. Abbreviated case study reviews or snapshots can be used to describe and provide an evidence base for cross-case analysis of findings in the form of abbreviated vignettes (Yin 2009). For each of the

Table 3.4 Framework to support PSS design to encourage sustainable behavior using IoT strategies

Level of control is with		User ←—————→ Product						
		Sustainable design strategies							
		Eco-info	Eco-choice	Eco-feedback	Eco-spur	Eco-steer	Eco-technology	Clever design
		Guiding			Steering		Embedded	
User / Product	IoT Strategies	Monitoring						
		Control						
		Optimization						
		Autonomy						
	Other (non-IoT strategies)							

Source: Developed from Porter and Heppelmann (2014), Tang (2010) and Bhamra et al. (2011)

Table 3.5 Cases reviewed for study

Sector	Snapshot case	Geographical scope	Business model (as offered in March 2018)
Washing machines	HOMIE	The Netherlands	Pay per use—pay per wash
Washing machines	Bundles	The Netherlands	Monthly subscriptions
Washing machines	Miele	International	Pay per product (conventional product sales)
Washing machines	Whirlpool	International	Pay per product (conventional product sales)
Car sharing	Zipcar	International	Monthly subscription plus pay per use rates or no monthly subscription with higher pay per use rates
Car sharing	Car2Go	International	Pay per use—rent by the minute, hour, or day
Car sharing	Greenwheels	The Netherlands	Monthly subscription plus hourly and daily rates

two areas—car sharing and washing machines—illustrative cases are used to demonstrate the variety of strategies. We do this in order to sketch the potential for using IoT and sustainable design strategies to encourage sustainable behavior in PSS design and to identify gaps in the actual application of such strategies.

Desk-based research for the case companies in Table 3.5 was conducted. Data were sourced from publically available sources, such as company websites, press releases, and reports. The key selection criteria included the need to pursue a PSS-type business model and/or to use IoT capabilities. Table 3.5 provides an overview of the cases and their currently pursued business models.

4 Cases

4.1 Washing Machines

This section describes HOMIE, Bundles, Miele, and Whirlpool as examples of cases that are applying IoT in varying ways. It also discusses links to sustainability.

HOMIE offers a pay per use service (homiepayperuse.com) for home appliances. It is a spin-off from TU Delft, the Netherlands, founded in 2016. Inspired by shared appliances such as launderettes, but realizing that most people want the convenience of their own appliance at home, the founders wanted to minimize the environmental impact of home appliances. By introducing pay per use (i.e. pay per wash), high-quality appliances that can be easily repaired, maintained, and potentially remanufactured can be offered on an affordable basis, and sustainable behavior can be stimulated as paying per use may help reduce total product usage. By monitoring user behavior, the company gives tailored advice to improve laundry behavior (Bocken et al. 2017). It also uses the embedded strategy of only offering high-quality and energy-efficient washing machines. However, this does not rely on an IoT capability. Currently the service does not employ any strategies related to control or optimization, for example, to facilitate for the user to run the machine outside of peak hours in electricity demand from the grid.

Bundles was founded in 2014 based on the premise that the use of sustainable appliances can be cheaper than the ownership of low-quality disposable appliances (throw-away appliances) if we start using it in a smarter way and was inspired by visionary thinkers, such as Walter Stahel (Performance Economy) and Ellen MacArthur (Circular Economy) (www.bundles.nl). It developed a subscription model that originally focused on selling packages of washing cycles (bundles) instead of washing machines (Achterberg et al. 2016). The customer can either pay for a higher monthly subscription or opt for a lower one plus paying per wash. By attaching a tracking device to their washing machines the company is able to maintain ownership of the machines while monitoring their usage (Achterberg et al. 2016). Statistics gathered from the machine are displayed on the Wash-App, which provides the customer with insights into the overall cost of doing their laundry, including energy, water, and detergent consumption, which reduces the costs for the customer, but could also help extend the life of the machine (Achterberg et al. 2016).

Miele is 'an independent family-owned company since its establishment in 1899 and is equally committed to its owners, employees, customers, suppliers, the environment and society' (Miele 2018a). It focuses on manufacturing domestic appliances as well as machines for use in commercial operations and medical. Its vision is to be the world's most trusted and desirable premium brand and therefore sets 'high standards for durability, performance, ease of use, energy efficiency, design and service' (Miele 2018a). Ninety-three percent of the washing machines it sold in 2015/2016 were categorized in the top energy class A+++, while two years before, this figure was only 63%. Miele also focuses on durability: 'using valuable resources efficiently is about more than saving water and energy [it] also means being gentle on the dishes and clothes that you wash in our appliances—so that they last longer and require less frequent replacement. The shorter programme durations in our washing machines extend the life of textiles' (Miele 2018b). Miele pursues various strategies to embed IoT in its devices and save energy, for example, through Miele@Home and SmartStart (Miele 2018c) (Table 3.6). The former is about remotely controlling the appliance and the latter is about starting the appliance automatically at the time when energy cost and impact are lowest.

The *Whirlpool* smart washing machine (Whirlpool 2018) is an interesting case in terms of eco-interactions: by using its interface and an app as main interaction channels, it has implemented various connectivity levels as well as sustainable behavior strategies. At the embedding level, smart grid and Eco-Boost connections enabled with NEST—itself an IoT business starting with its smart thermostat in 2011 (www.nest.com)—are innovative solutions to facilitate sustainable decisions by providing automated decision-making. In this case, NEST works as an autonomous trigger of a sustainable action when automatically running the machine in Eco-Boost mode when there are no people at home. This example also shows that one single feature can include multiple strategies for sustainable behavior, as smart grids which provide feedback on energy price, can make recommendations to steer behavior and works autonomously if activated. Remote control is also offered to activate Eco-Boost. There is also an auto-dispensing option to optimize dosages (Whirlpool 2018).

Through these cases, it was found that IoT strategies are used in various ways in washing machines, but are not always optimally used for different business model strategies. For example, paying per use could be integrated with smart settings: a pay per use system could use differential

Table 3.6 Washing machines snapshot case summary

Level of control is with			Sustainable design strategies					
			Eco-info	Eco-choice	Eco-feedback	Eco-spur	Eco-steer	Eco-technology	Clever design
			Guiding			Steering		Embedded	
User → Product	IoT Strategies	Monitoring	Monthly feedback on consumption. Personal and Social comparison (HOMIE). Wash app to inform about sustainable behavior (Bundles) Feedback in cycle time and stage. Smart grid interface shows energy consumption and advice on possible improvements with an energy adviser and rate revealer. (Whirlpool)			Economic incentive in the business model to wash less (HOMIE, Bundles). Tailored suggestions plus goal setting based on user date (e.g. advice to wash at lower temperatures and use the eco-button (HOMIE)			
		Control				Remote control, start, delay, and pause cycles. Choose the cycle, activate Eco-Boost (lowers water and temperature, and increases tumbling time) and fresh air (used align with smart grid) (Whirlpool) Miele@Home app allows users to control devices remotely and start them e.g. at times when energy cost are lowest. (Miele)			
		Optimization				Repair support, in case of failure the machine diagnoses itself. (Whirlpool)			
		Autonomy				Miele SmartStart automatically starts devices when energy cost are lowest (produced by own solar panels or electricity provider)		Autonomously connected with NEST to wash in Eco-Boost if no one is at home. Smart delay runs the machine when energy is cheaper. Detergent and softener auto-dispense (Whirlpool)	
	Other (non-IoT strategies)							Offering high-quality energy efficient devices (all cases)	

and lower pricing according to the most optimum time of the day and setting to do the laundry to reduce energy use and could automatically charge more when the user wants to override these optimum settings to choose less energy-efficient options. Indeed, some of the washing machines can autonomously decide on an optimal time to run in order to save energy costs. We found no examples of making the eco-function (i.e. the most environmentally sustainable option) the default choice. A potential feature related to IoT is the optimization of dosages and even detergent compositions (perhaps mixing different elements). This could be done based on each unique wash (load, type of textile), thereby ensuring that the appropriate amount and type of detergent is used. Some washing machines regulate the amount of water used based on the weight of the laundry. However, similar functions could be developed that also reduce energy and detergent use.

4.2 Car Sharing

This section describes Zipcar, Car2Go, and Greenwheels as examples of car sharing that are applying IoT in varying ways with potential positive sustainability impacts.

Zipcar is 'the world's largest car sharing and car club service' (http://www.zipcar.com/). The user pays a monthly subscription plus a fee or only a usage fee depending on the payment model chosen. This business model requires monitoring of the hours that the cars have been used as well as the kilometers driven. However, the Zipcar model does not incentivize driving less or more eco-efficiently, that is, to minimize the fuel use per kilometer driven. Here, an embedded strategy could be to only offer cars that score high on environmental performance. In the case of Zipcar, the user in some areas can opt for a more sustainable type of car, for example, an electric car, but it is not a default. The choice of more sustainable car models does not relate directly to an IoT capability. However, if the car was programmed to only let the user drive in an optimally eco-efficient manner, then that would score as an embedded design strategy using the capability of optimization. Finally, after 180 miles of driving, you have to start paying 0.45 per mile, which may help reduce total mileage driven (Zipcar 2018).

Car2Go is a car-sharing service available in 26 cities and 8 countries worldwide for its 3.1 million members. Users are charged per minute, hour, or day of use (Car2Go 2018). Cars are available in designated spots of the city and users can check their availability in a real-time map in the app, the service offers one-way travels, so cars do not have to be returned to the starting point (https://www.car2go.com/US). Offered cars are exclusively from two manufacturers: Smart and Mercedes-Benz. Car2Go has approximately 14,000 cars of which 1400 are electric ones at the time of writing (Car2Go 2018).

As in the Zipcar example, car monitoring is essential for the service offer. Interestingly, in this case one-way journeys enable different use dynamics that rely on real-time data collection for car localization. Remote control of the car is available to open the car, which facilitates access to the service. Offering only electric cars in some cities (Amsterdam, Stuttgart, Madrid) restricts user options to the most environment-friendly ones. However, there is no specific feedback on the impact of using these instead of gasoline cars.

Greenwheels is a car-sharing pay-as-you-go service. Users can rent one of their 1700 cars in the Netherlands through the app or by using an 'OV-chipkaart' (public transportation card). The payment is defined according to the selected monthly plan, as well as the kilometers traveled and the time the car was used. There are also options for day, week, or weekend renting. According to their environmental measurements, the sharing model has reduced car use by 18% by incentivizing other means of transportation as well as more optimal routes; also each car is used by about 21 people. These changes have led to an average reduction of 230–320 kg CO_2 emissions per user per year (Greenwheels 2018). The service deeply relies on car monitoring to establish which cars are available and how many kilometers have been driven. Also, remote control is embedded in the app as a strategy to facilitate access to the service and speed up the booking process, which even though is not directly related with sustainable behavior could potentially increase consumer acceptance of such a service. However, there is no offer of particular environmental friendlier cars such as electric or hybrid cars. Users are informed about kilometers driven and time consumed, but there is no feedback on the environmental impact of this.

In the car-sharing examples, IoT appears to be used mainly to 'make the system work' (e.g. locating cars, allowing users to book and access cars remotely) and not so much yet to stimulate sustainable consumption, whereas this business model could have the potential to do so (e.g. Table 3.1). There is potential for IoT strategies to keep cars at their most optimal mechanical conditions by reporting on car spare parts condition and performance, to prevent malfunctioning parts. Also, there is an

Table 3.7 Car-sharing snapshot case summary

		User ←――――――→ Product						
Level of control is with		Sustainable design strategies						
		Eco-info	Eco-choice	Eco-feedback	Eco-spur	Eco-steer	Eco-technology	Clever design
		Guiding			Steering		Embedded	
User → Product	IoT Strategies	**Monitoring**	User receives information about number of hours and kilometers they have driven (all) Monitors usage of carsby users (all)						
		Control	Ability to filter for 'sustainable' cars (Zipcar)						
		Optimization							
		Autonomy							
	Other (non-IoT strategies)				Economic incentive in pricing structure (Zipcar) Offering only electric cars (Car2go)			

opportunity for autonomous cars connected to real-time navigation apps to automatically choose the most optimal in relation to the current traffic situation. Advice on driving behavior could also be provided through optimization strategies. While some of these technologies exist, ranging from algorithms (Fügenschuh et al. 2018) to simple apps (Toyota glass of water app to reduce fuel usage by 10%; Chambers 2010), it appears that the car-sharing companies reviewed have not really adopted these yet, while there should be an economic incentive to reduce energy usage for the service provider (Tukker 2004). It could be the case that the upfront cost of 'more sustainable' cars is too prohibiting so that the service providers go for cheaper options instead. Nevertheless, Table 3.7 shows that there are many underexplored strategies in this sector.

5 Discussion

In this section, we discuss the following findings: the limited strategic use of IoT as well as the opportunity to use IoT more strategically to stimulate sustainable behavior, and some avenues for future work.

The cases of white goods and car sharing indicate that the uptake of IoT in general, and to stimulate sustainable consumption in particular, is still rather limited. The focus seems to be on 'guiding' strategies facilitated by monitoring. Little use is made of 'sustainable defaults' or of autonomous decision-making. The use of IoT at this stage seems to be more focused on practical applications (e.g. remote activation of appliances) without a clear proposition to the customer, rather than a strategic and holistic strategy making the most of such technology. Also, whereas there is opportunity for optimization, a lot of choices are left to the consumer. This may be in line with ideas of Wever et al. (2008), who argue that too much control may annoy users. Also, it links to the work by Bhamra et al. (2008, 2011) and Bocken et al. (2017), who argue that new options need to be trialed, together with users, in order to find out which options would gain the biggest traction and would most effectively drive sustainable consumption.

Some of the businesses and strategies could benefit from a clearer 'environmental value proposition' (Manninen et al. 2018) or environmental ambition and appropriate strategy to ensure that IoT gets used more profoundly as part of the business model. Whereas some have a more holistic strategy (e.g. HOMIE through its direct focus on driving sustainable consumption), many of the reviewed companies seem to 'assume' that a service business model will drive sustainable consumption, first of all, by reducing the number of products (e.g. cars) per user, such as in the case of car sharing, and second of all, by creating a higher consciousness about actual usage when paying for a service per hour (see e.g. Chase 2012) or per use (Tukker 2004; Bocken et al. 2017).

In summary, IoT has the potential to improve sustainability performance in the use phase of PSS. However, service providers as well as product-oriented businesses do not take full advantage of the IoT capabilities, such as optimization and autonomy. By using design strategies for sustainable behavior, some of the adverse effects in Table 3.1 could also be mitigated. For example, the design of the product could be optimized for energy efficiency and settings could be controlled so that the user always uses the best available option from an environmental perspective. Furthermore, if running costs (e.g. fuel) are not included in the cost, it will be more difficult to incentivize customers to use products in a better way. Again, automation and optimization could help here. While autonomously operating devices such as cars are still subject to intense debate around safety in particular, there may be great benefits from an environmental perspective (e.g. optimization routes and driving in the most fuel-efficient way). A well-designed connected PSS has the potential to enable more balanced and complete implementation of sustainability practices.

Finally, the systematic testing between different types of IoT strategies was out of scope for this study. Future research could also identify additional IoT capabilities that play a role for sustainable behavior strategies. Moreover, IoT capabilities can be used to leverage a diverse set of sustainable strategies, also outside the use phase. In particular, IoT has gained attention for contributing to 'circular strategies' such as reuse, remanufacturing, and recycling. Future research could expand the exploration of the most effective use of IoT and additional sustainable design strategies to design and develop the most sustainable forms of novel business models.

6 Conclusion

This paper addresses the following question: How can IoT strategies be used to design appropriate PSS solutions that encourage sustainable consumption?

Based on literature in the fields of sustainable design strategies and IoT capabilities we developed the 'Framework to support PSS design to encourage sustainable behavior using IoT strategies' (Table 3.4). This was applied to real-world company cases in two sectors: white goods and car sharing. It was found that the companies investigated do not yet use IoT in a strategic way. The potential to use IoT to drive sustainable consumption as part of new and existing business models remains rather underexplored. Holistic strategies are envisaged that combine monitoring, control, optimization, and autonomy. Also, the full suite of options, ranging from guiding to steering and embedding strategies could be trialed with users to achieve the greatest sustainability effects.

This research has some limitations. The research is limited by the number of cases reviewed and types of industries covered. It is likely that particular startups or large business in specific geographical contexts are in fact developing and trialing some new IoT strategies. Nevertheless, despite the fact that this study may not provide a 'complete' picture, we did identify a general tendency toward the lack of an integrated approach of using IoT strategies to their full potential in new sustainable business models to drive sustainable consumption.

Future research could include action-oriented research to trial and experiment with different types of sustainable business models to explore what the most effective strategies are to drive sustainable behavior.

Acknowledgements This work was funded by the Circular European Economy Innovative Training Network, Circ€uit, an action funded by the European Commission under the Horizon 2020 Marie Skłodowska Curie Action 2016 (Grant Agreement number 721909).

References

Atzori, L., A. Iera, and G. Morabito. 2016. Understanding the Internet of Things: Definition, Potentials, and Societal Role of a Fast-Evolving Paradigm. *Ad Hoc Networks* 56: 122–140. Elsevier B.V. https://doi.org/10.1016/j.adhoc.2016.12.004.

Aurich, J.C., C. Fuchs, and C. Wagenknecht. 2006. Life Cycle Oriented Design of Technical Product-Service Systems. *Journal of Cleaner Production* 14 (17): 1480–1494.

Backers, K., and U. Tietge. 2017. Cleaner Car Contracts Benchmark 2017. Overview of Vehicle Fleets and Efficiency Benchmark. Cleaner Car Contracts and ICCT, April 2017. Accessed February 20, 2018. https://www.natuurenmilieu.nl/wp-content/uploads/2017/05/CCC_benchmark_overview_2017_170501v2-003.pdf.

Bhamra, T., D. Lilley, and T. Tang. 2008. Sustainable Use: Changing Consumer Behavior Through Product Design. In *Proceedings of Changing the Change: Design Visions, Proposals and Tools*, Turin, Italy.

———. 2011. Design for Sustainable Behavior: Using Products to Change Consumer Behavior. *Design Journal* 14 (4): 427–445.

Bocken, N.M.P., and J.M. Allwood. 2012. Strategies to Reduce the Carbon Footprint of Consumer Goods by Influencing Stakeholders. *Journal of Cleaner Production* 35: 118–129.

Bocken, N.M.P., C.A. Bom, and H. Lemstra.2017. Business-Led Sustainable Consumption Strategies: The Case of HOMIE. In *18th ERSCP Conference*, Greece, 1–5 October 2017.

Boons, F., and N. Bocken.2017. Business Models and the Sharing Economy: An Ecosystem Perspective. In *Product Lifetimes and the Environment (PLATE)*, 8–10 November 2017.

Car2Go. 2018. Factsheets. Accessed March 22, 2018. https://brandhub.car2go.com/web/6570a0eb69e15b2f/factsheets/.

Chambers, N.2010. New Toyota MPG Initiative: "Drive Like You've Got a Glass of Water on Your Dash". *Popular Mechanics*. Accessed April 4, 2018. https://www.popularmechanics.com/cars/a5996/new-toyota-mpg-initiative/.

Chase, R. 2012. How Technology Enables the Shared Economy. http://www.greenbiz.com/video/2012/05/02/how-technology-enables-shared-economy.

Environmental Paper Network. 2018. Case Studies. Accessed February 20, 2018. http://www.environmentalpaper.eu/projects/about-shrinkpaper/case-studies/.

Fischer, Susanne, Henning Wilts Meghan O'Brien, Steger Sören, Schepelmann Philipp, Jordan Nino David, and Rademacher Bettina. 2015. Waste Prevention in a "Leasing Society". *International Journal of Waste Resources* 5: 170. https://doi.org/10.4172/2252-5211.1000170.

Fügenschuh, Armin, Henning Homfeld, Marc Johann, Hanno Schülldorf, and Anke Stieber. 2018. Use of Optimization Tools for Routing in Rail Freight Transport. In *Handbook of Optimization in the Railway Industry*, 161–179. Cham: Springer.

Greenwheels. 2018. About Greenwheels. Accessed March 22, 2018. https://www.greenwheels.com/nl/nl-en/private/about-greenwheels.

Heiskanen, E., and M. Jalas.2000. Dematerialization Through Services—A Review and Evaluation of the Debate. The Finnish Environment 436 Ministry of the Environment Environmental Protection Department, Helsinki.

Klapwijk, R., M. Knot, J. Quist, and P.J. Vergragt. 2006. Using Design Orienting Scenarios to Analyze the Interaction between Technology, Behavior and Environment in the SusHouse Project. In *User Behavior and Technology Development*, 241–252. Dordrecht: Springer.

Kortuem, G., F. Kawsar, V. Sundramoorthy, and D. Fitton. 2010. Smart Objects as Building Blocks for the Internet of Things. *IEEE Internet Computing* 14 (1): 44–51. https://doi.org/10.1109/MIC.2009.143.

Kraaijenhagen, C., C.VanOppen, and N.Bocken. 2016. *Circular Business. Collaborate & Circulate.* Circular Collaboration, Amersfoort, The Netherlands. https://circularcollaboration.com/.

Kwon, D., M.R. Hodkiewicz, J. Fan, T. Shibutani, and M.G. Pecht. 2016. IoT-Based Prognostics and Systems Health Management for Industrial Applications. *IEEE Access* 4: 3659–3670. https://doi.org/10.1109/ACCESS.2016.2587754.

Leising, E., J. Quist, and N. Bocken. 2017. Circular Supply Chain Collaboration in the Built Environment: A Conceptual Framework and Three Cases from the Netherlands. *Journal of Cleaner Production* 176: 976–989.

Lelah, A., F. Mathieux, and D. Brissaud. 2011. Contributions to Eco-design of Machine-to-Machine Product Service Systems: The Example of Waste Glass Collection. *Journal of Cleaner Production* 19: 1033–1044.

Lightfoot, H.W., T. Baines, and P. Smart. 2011. Examining the Information and Communication Technologies Enabling Servitized Manufacture. *Proceedings of the Institution of Mechanical Engineers, Part B: Journal of Engineering Manufacture* 225 (10): 1964–1968. https://doi.org/10.1177/0954405411399019.

Lilley, D. 2009. Design for Sustainable Behavior: Strategies and Perceptions. *Design Studies* 30 (6): 704–720. https://doi.org/10.1016/j.destud.2009.05.001.

Lilley, D., V.A. Lo house, and T.A. Bhamra. 2005. Towards Instinctive Sustainable Product Use. In *2nd International Conference in Sustainability, Creating the Culture*, 2–4 November, Aberdeen Exhibition & Conference Centre, Aberdeen.

Lockton, D., D. Harrison, and N. Stanton. 2008. Making the User More Efficient: Design for Sustainable Behavior. *International Journal of Sustainable Engineering* 1 (1): 3–8.

Manninen, K., S. Koskela, R. Antikainen, N. Bocken, H. Dahlbo, and A. Aminoff. 2018. Do Circular Economy Business Models Capture Intended Environmental Value Propositions? *Journal of Cleaner Production* 171: 413–422.

Miele. 2018a. Philosophy. Accessed March 22, 2018. https://www.miele.com/en/com/philosophy-2095.htm.

———. 2018b. Sustainability. Accessed March 22, 2018. https://www.miele.com/en/com/4782.htm.

———. 2018c. Freedom at Home. Accessed March 22, 2018. https://www.miele.co.uk/brand/smarthome-28350.htm.

Mont, O. 2004. Reducing Life-Cycle Environmental Impacts Through Systems of Joint Use. *Greener Management International* (45): 63–77. https://doi.org/10.9774/GLEAF.3062.2004.sp.00006.

Nobre, G.C., and E. Tavares. 2017. Scientific Literature Analysis on Big Data and Internet of Things Applications on Circular Economy: A Bibliometric Study. *Scientometrics* 111 (1): 463–492.

Ondemir, O., and S.M. Gupta. 2014. Quality Management in Product Recovery Using the Internet of Things: An Optimization Approach. *Computers in Industry* 65 (3): 491–504. https://doi.org/10.1016/j.compind.2013.11.006.

Patagonia. 2011. Introducing the Common Threads Initiative—Reduce, Repair, Reuse, Recycle, Reimagine. Accessed March 1, 2018. https://www.patagonia.com/blog/2011/09/introducing-the-common-threads-initiative/.

Philips Lighting Holding B.V.2017. Case Study. Schiphol Airport Maakt Verantwoorde Keuze Voor Circulaire Verlichting, May 2017.

Ries, E. 2011. *The Lean Startup: How Today's Entrepreneurs Use Continuous Innovation to Create Radically Successful Businesses*. London: Penguin Books.

Sustainable Development Commission (SDC). 2006. *I Will If You Will: Towards Sustainable Consumption*. ISBN: 1 899581 84 7.

Tang, T. 2010. *Towards Sustainable Use: Design Behavior Intervention to Reduce Household Environment Impact*. Loughborough: Loughborough University.

Thaler, R.H., and C.R. Sunstein. 2008. *Nudge: Improving Decisions About Health, Wealth, and Happiness*. New Haven, CT: Yale University Press.

Tukker, A. 2004. Eight Types of Product-Service System: Eight Ways to Sustainability? Experiences from Suspronet. *Business Strategy and the Environment* 13 (4): 246–260. https://doi.org/10.1002/bse.414.

Valencia Cardona, A.M., Ruth Mugge, Jan P.L. Schoormans, and Hendrik N.J. Schifferstein. 2015. The Design of Smart Product-Service Systems (PSSs): An Exploration of Design Characteristics. *International Journal of Design* 9 (1): 13–28.

Wever, Renee, Jasper Van Kuijk, and Casper Boks. 2008. User-Centred Design for Sustainable Behaviour. *International Journal of Sustainable Engineering* 1 (1): 9–20.

Whirlpool. 2018. Connected Appliances. Accessed March 22, 2018. https://www.whirlpool.com/home-innovations/connected-appliances.html.

Zipcar. 2018. Miles Included. Accessed March 22, 2018. https://support.zipcar.com/hc/en-us/articles/220623207-Miles-Included.

4

Sustainability Goal Setting with a Value-Focused Thinking Approach

Kaisa Manninen and Janne Huiskonen

1 Introduction

Today, when sustainability is proclaimed as the next frontier in innovation, almost all organizations accept the concept (Silvestri and Gulati 2015). Firms are concerned with sustainability issues and want to contribute to it with their actions (Palmer and Flanagan 2016). Organizational change toward sustainability can be approached from an organizational or institutional level of analysis. In the former, the leaders of the organization are important players in the journey toward sustainability. The institutional perspective is very different and considers the contextual circumstances that enable, push, or inhibit organizations

---

K. Manninen (✉) • J. Huiskonen
Industrial Engineering and Management, Lappeenranta University of Technology, Lappeenranta, Finland
e-mail: Kaisa.Manninen@lut.fi; Janne.Huiskonen@lut.fi

from moving from one state to another. The role of managers in the change process is seen as secondary (Greenwood et al. 2015). In this chapter, we concentrate on the organizational perspective, because one viewpoint is that sustainability is often not in the core of an organization, but apart from the strategy. Organizations that truly embrace sustainability should move it to their core (Silvestri and Gulati 2015). Thus, sustainability initiatives and claims should be aligned with the organization's identity (Glynn et al. 2015). The organizational identity is influenced strongly by the values of the owners and top managers who together form the basis for corporate responsibility (Bansal and Song 2017; Kaldschmidt 2011) and have an effect on how the organization makes sustainability decisions.

Maximizing profit has been the predominant logic in doing business. However, sustainability has increased its importance, but it is difficult to analyze to what extent sustainability is only a means to achieve profit, to what extent they have equal weight, and in which cases sustainability may have even greater importance than profit. Therefore, it is important to capture the rationale in sustainability management practices (Schaltegger and Hörisch 2017). Understanding the fundamental objectives of the firm can help to provide purpose and meaning for the business and thus clarify the question of rationale.

We approach the problem of profit versus sustainability from ethical and scientific perspectives of sustainability. The aim is, first, to understand how the values of decision makers affect the sustainability objectives of the firm and, second, how sustainability science can assist decision makers by providing a factual basis of sustainability in decision-making situations, and thus contribute to sustainability management.

To understand the values of decision makers and their impact, we propose two approaches. The Value-Focused Thinking (VFT) approach (Alencar et al. 2017; Keeney 1992, 1994, 1996) is used to examine and reveal the sustainability objectives of the firm and to understand the values of decision makers behind the objectives. In addition, the values and objectives are analyzed by applying the concepts of the alternative objective functions for the firm (Lankoski and Smith 2017) in order to understand the relationship of profit and sustainability in the decision-making context.

We suggest that to assess the consequences of sustainability-related decisions better, a factual basis is needed, and sustainability science offers a proper perspective for that. Sustainability science helps decision makers to understand how the firm can contribute to a more transformational change with its sustainability objectives. Decision makers can then reassess their objectives and purpose in doing business, and decide whether the objectives truly represent their firm's identity, that is, what the firm wants to be and what kind of external image it gives to its stakeholders (Silvestri and Gulati 2015). Our study provides a framework to support the sustainability management of a company by combining the values of decision makers, the sustainability objectives of the firm, and a scientific perspective of sustainability to foster sustainable development.

2 Understanding the Purpose of Doing Business

Organizations need a multidimensional view of performance (Bansal and Song 2017), and in many companies the objective of business is already something different than only profit (Lankoski and Smith 2017). For example, according to the institutional logic, great companies create frameworks that use societal value and human values as decision-making criteria instead of extracting more economic value. These companies believe that corporations have a purpose, and they meet stakeholders' needs in many ways. However, all companies need capital to carry out business activities and sustain themselves. Profit is not the sole end, but a way to ensure that returns will continue (Kanter 2011). Sustainable organizations must make profit to exist, but they do not just exist to make profit (Stubbs and Cocklin 2008). Social welfare is an implicit objective and a firm is defined around its purpose and values (Kanter 2011; Lankoski and Smith 2017). The purpose of a sustainable company can be defined as a concrete goal or objective that reaches beyond profit maximization, that is, environmental and social outcomes (Henderson and Van den Steen 2015; Stubbs and Cocklin 2008). At the same time profit is a "means" to achieve sustainable outcomes (Stubbs and Cocklin 2008). A firm does not have to have only one objective or purpose for doing business, but it can contain, for example, both profit and social welfare. In the situation of many purposes, the relationship between different objective variables has to be specified clearly (Lankoski and Smith 2017).

Lankoski and Smith (2017) define different relationship types between profit and social welfare (Table 4.1). An alternative objective function is an equation specifying which output the firm aims to maximize or minimize, with which variables as inputs, and under which constraints. The relationship types are based on three analytical dimensions: (1) whether the two variables are considered as process characteristics or end objectives, (2) whether preferences between the two variables are lexicographic or compensating, and (3) whether the relationship between the two variables is mutually supportive or mutually conflicting. The first two dimensions are decision issues, meaning that managers or owners can decide how they want to conceive the relationship between the two variables in their firm. The third dimension is, by contrast, an empirical question that determines whether certain approaches to combining profit and social welfare are in fact possible in the real world. Ten different alternative objective functions for firms can be identified on the basis of the different relationships (Table 4.1). One of the functions excludes and nine include social welfare, meaning that social welfare can be (1) entirely absent from

Table 4.1 Relationships between the variables of profit and social welfare

Relationships between the variables of profit and social welfare	
None	Only one variable is maximized and there is no place for the other variable.
Instrumental	One variable (the instrumental variable) is a means to achieve the other variable (the end objective).
Constrained	One variable (the objective) is maximized so that the value of the other variable (the constrained) stays within a preset range.
Complementary	Both variables are mutually supportive end objectives. Both variables may be equally regarded as end objectives at the same time, and both may be maximized at the same time.
Hierarchical	One variable has priority over the other, as in lexicographic ordering. The more important objective is satisfied first, after which the less important objective is satisfied to the extent possible without affecting the outcome of the first objective.
Weighted	An approach to integrate multiple objectives with weighting. The objective given priority varies from one decision-making situation to another according to preset criteria.

Source: Lankoski and Smith (2017)

the objective function, (2) a process characteristic, (3) one of the end objectives, (4) the only end objective, adjusted by profit as a process characteristic, and (5) the only variable in the objective function.

The alternative objective functions provide a basis for considering organizational purpose also from the sustainability point of view. The alternative objective functions extend the discussion of different logics to do business and provides a framework to aid organizational change toward sustainability. The term sustainability is defined in closer detail below, but in this context, it includes the economic, environmental, and social perspectives of business in general. We apply the alternative objective functions to explore different logics to do business from the perspective of profit and sustainability (Fig. 4.1). In our viewpoint, the conventional financial logic represents the extreme of the relationship type "None". Sustainability logic has received increased attention, but in many cases it still appears as an instrumental logic to do business, where environmental and social actions are means to achieve profit (Gao and Bansal 2013). The integrated logic presented by Gao and Bansal (2013) is close to the relationship type "Complementary" presented by Lankoski and Smith (2017). The

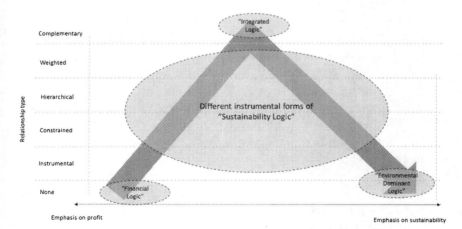

Fig. 4.1 The relationship types of profit and sustainability (reproduced from Lankoski and Smith 2017) combined with the "Financial Logic", "Integrated Logic" (Gao and Bansal 2013), "Environmental Dominant Logic" (Montabon et al. 2016), and "Sustainability Logic" (e.g., Gao and Bansal 2013; Greenwood et al. 2015)

Environmentally Dominant Logic by Montabon et al. (2016) is an opposite of financial logic, and represents a situation where priority is given to the environment, then to the society, and last to profit. In its extreme form, environmental and social welfare are maximized and there is no place for profit in it. However, as Lankoski and Smith (2017) state, this does not prevent a well-managed firm from making profit, but profit is the result rather than the driver in the process of value creation. Therefore, we see that when it is not the case of social enterprises but companies doing business, the company needs some capital to carry out business activities and sustain themselves (Kanter 2011).

One of the challenges in building truly sustainable organizations is that although firms' strategies increasingly integrate sustainability (Palmer and Flanagan 2016), and different logics to do business can be identified (Fig. 4.1), it often requires a significant shift in the identity of the firm, as well as in its core structure and processes (Henderson et al. 2015). The organizational identity defines "what the organization is" and "what it stands for" (Silvestri and Gulati 2015). By understanding the different alternative purposes for business, the company can reflect them toward their identity. According to Lankoski and Smith (2017), managers or owners can decide how they regard the relationship between profit and sustainability in their firm. The personal values of managers influence their strategic decisions (Kaldschmidt 2011), and thus sustainability-related decisions are likely affected by the decision makers' values. However, sustainability is a complex issue, and decision makers have often difficulties to see the effects of their decisions in a larger, systemic-level context. The scientific perspective can offer a factual perspective to solve this problem. However, decision makers still have to clarify to what extent they base their decisions on values and to what extent on facts.

3 Combining Values and Scientific Viewpoints in Sustainability Decision-Making

Managerial values play an important role in all decisions and especially in strategic decision-making, because they are embedded in the organizational values. Therefore, sustainability-supporting values of leaders and managers are a key to making strategic decisions that support the successful balance of economic, environmental, and social goals (Kaldschmidt 2011).

Values form the basis of the ethical standpoint of the firm's decision makers, and therefore, business ethics can be understood to be the ideas about conduct that are generally accepted among the members of a group that operates within a company. In other words, values guide individual employees' judgment and action in situations that are not governed by laws or other institutionalized elements (Pearce 2013). From the research perspective, business ethics evaluates humanistic values in management and gives meanings to it. However, factual data from science is needed to discover the causes and effects of decisions. Therefore, it is useful to understand how ethics and science are manifested in corporate sustainability discussion. On the basis of historical roots, ethics can be linked to corporate responsibility, whereas the background of sustainability is in natural sciences (Bansal and Song 2017). However, in many companies corporate responsibility and sustainability are synonyms (Bansal and Song 2017; Markman et al. 2016). The separation of the concepts clarifies the discussion when considering and making decisions about sustainability management.

Applying perspectives from both corporate responsibility and sustainability increases understanding of how to set better and effective sustainability objectives. First, corporate responsibility represents the ethical standpoint of the company. Corporate responsibility combines the values and beliefs of the decision makers at the individual level, but also presents why and how the company commits to sustainability at the organizational level. Second, sustainability-related decisions can be justified by factual data from the scientific perspective of sustainability (Bansal and Song 2017). Finally, sustainability management operationalizes corporate responsibility and sustainability science at the organizational level by including formulation, implementation, and evaluation of environmental and socioeconomic sustainability-related decisions and actions (Starik and Kanashiro 2013) (Fig. 4.2).

3.1 Values for Sustainability Decisions

The values of decision makers are formed in part by the organization they work for. By exploring decision makers' values, we can recognize how the organization understands sustainability and what is its orientation toward

Fig. 4.2 Corporate responsibility and sustainability science perspectives to support sustainability management at the organizational level

it, whether sustainability is at the periphery or at the core of the organization's identity (Silvestri and Gulati 2015).

According to den Ouden (2012), from the psychological perspective, values define what people strive for (human values) and how they influence their behavior (motivational values). At the organizational level, the purpose and objectives are based on the core values of the firm, and provide motivation for its management and employees to contribute to the creation of value (den Ouden 2012). Kaldschmidt (2011) studied in her dissertation the intersection of personal values, corporate sustainability, and how leaders' personal values influence the strategy process and its outcomes in terms of the formulation of competitive sustainability strategies. She utilized Schwartz' theory of basic human values, which is based on the idea that values guide individuals and are grounded in what they see as desirable. Fundamentally, they have different motivational aspects, as in the definition by den Ouden (2012). Kaldschmidt (2011) presents five main features of Schwartz' theory that all conceptions of values have (Schwartz 2006; Schwartz and Bilsky 1987; Schwartz 1992 in Kaldschmidt (2011)):

1. *Values are beliefs.* These beliefs are tied to emotion and not to objective ideas.
2. *Values are a motivational construct.* That is, they refer to desirable goals that are worth striving for.
3. *Values transcend specific situations.* The abstract nature of values distinguishes them from norms and attitudes, which refer to more specific actions, objects or situations.

4. *Values guide selection or evaluation (of actions, policies, people, and events).* This way, values can be understood as standards or criteria.
5. *Values are ordered by relative importance to one another.* Individuals hold values in ordered systems that include priorities. The hierarchical nature of values also differentiates them from attitudes and norms.

Kaldschmidt (2011) studied which personal values of leaders need to be prioritized in order to make strategic decisions that support the sustainable development and performance of a firm. She found a connection between the certain personal values profiles of leaders and the sustainability strategy of a firm. She also stated that for sustainable business practices to be reality and not just greenwashing, more is needed than just putting up a values statement that includes social and environmental responsibility.

In-depth understanding of the decision makers' sustainability-related values can provide a useful insight into the core values of an organization and its purpose to do business. Referring to the main features of Schwartz' theory of basic human values, sustainability—related values could be interpreted as guiding principles for decision makers toward desirable, trans-situational economic, environmental, and social goals, varying in importance (Schwartz 2007). Although we concentrate on the understanding of human values, it is notable that the sustainability value concept can be approached also from sociological and ecological perspectives. Then it is not a matter of human values, but seeing that the society and nature are a value in themselves (den Ouden 2012). For that perspective, that is, to understand the absolute value of the society and nature, science can offer factual data to support decision-making (Bansal and Song 2017).

3.2   Scientific Viewpoints to Sustainability

Earlier studies have brought out concerns about the effects of sustainability management. Although companies are willing to impact sustainability issues, and sustainability actions are taken in several companies, ecological analyses indicate worsening or even alarming conditions (Dyllick and Muff 2016; O'Neill and McElroy 2017; Whiteman et al. 2013). One reason for this is that companies' sustainability goals and the progress toward them are commonly assessed on the basis of comparisons (1) relative to a baseline year (e.g., the last reporting period), (2) relative to the current best practice (e.g., best performers in an industry), or (3) relative to the company's own targets (e.g., to reduce CO_2 emissions by 20% by 2020). These kinds of benchmarks can lead to situations where incremental, and in absolute terms even ineffective improvements are seen as progress toward sustainability (Kurucz et al. 2017). In addition, to use these kinds of benchmarks as a measure of sustainability progress, setting goals only based on, for example, the level of best practice of the industry, may lead to ineffective actions, and in the worst case, the goals are not linked to the overall strategic objectives of the company at all. Another reason for ineffective results of sustainability management is that the sustainability strategy is not linked to macro-ecological processes and boundary conditions. In other words, the scientific viewpoint of sustainability is ignored (Whiteman et al. 2013).

The Triple Bottom Line (TBL) has been a dominant concept to describe sustainability (Montabon et al. 2016). It incorporates three performance dimensions—social, environmental, and financial—and represents thus in an optimal situation the ideology of "Integrated Logic" (Gao and Bansal 2013) to do business (see Sect. 2). However, in reality, social and environmental aspects are often instruments to improve economic performance (Montabon et al. 2016), representing the left side of Fig. 4.1, where the emphasis is on profit. This results from a technocentric (a.k.a. anthropocentric (Purser et al. 1995)) worldview about sustainability, which requires increases in production and consumption, economic growth, and valuation and utilization of natural resources. In addition, the technocentric approach views man's role as one of control over nature (Landrum and Ohsowski 2017).

The concern for a technocentric bias in the field of organizational science concerning social issues in management or relations between business and the natural environment was already highlighted in the 1990s. It was stated that *"if researchers and managers are to move toward an 'ecocentric' paradigm, they need more than a popular understanding of ecology. Indeed, there is a need to clearly differentiate anthropocentric from ecocentric approaches to environmental issues*" (Purser et al. 1995, p. 1055). The same criticism was raised 20 years later when Starik and Kanashiro (2013, p. 9) argued that "*...one or more new theories of sustainability management may be needed in the management literature...most other organization/management theories that have been used in sustainability research do not either explicitly or implicitly recognize the obvious (or near-obvious) fact that all human organizations are embedded within the natural environment, and that, all of those which have human managers and other employees, also contain the natural environment inside of their respective biophysical bodies*".

Recent research supports the ecocentric worldview in sustainability (Whiteman et al. 2013), which recognizes that economic growth is bounded by environmental limits, natural resources need to be preserved to support life, and all activity must remain within ecological limits (Landrum and Ohsowski 2017). This is a systemic perspective toward sustainability, including natural and social systems. The systemic approach makes sustainability a complex issue to understand at the organizational level. Therefore, sustainability science can provide material for micro-level organizational implementation of sustainability, as individual companies are a part of larger social systems (Bansal and Song 2017).

When discussing sustainability, it is almost necessary to bring out the term sustainable development. Probably the best-known description for the term is the definition by the Brundtland Commission: "*Sustainable development is development that meets the needs of the present without compromising the ability of future generations to meet their own need*" (Broman et al. 2012, p. 21). Shortly, it means the transition from the current, unsustainable society to a sustainable society (Broman et al. 2012). The report of the Commission took a systemic perspective, arguing that the world's complex challenges could be solved only by systematic collective endeavors, and the collapse of natural systems would erode the sustainability of organizational systems, as all physical resources are ultimately drawn from the earth. Furthermore, poor social conditions could catalyze organizational dissent. Therefore, the systems scholars assumed that corporate actions were inherently connected to the social and natural systems (Bansal and Song 2017).

3.3 Value Profiles for Clarifying a Company's Sustainability Strategy

Significant changes are needed in the transition toward a sustainable society in order to realize sustainable development (Broman et al. 2012). In the two sections above, we discussed, first, values of decision makers, which form the base for corporate responsibility and how the firm commits to sustainability and, second, the scientific perspective of sustainability, which can support decision makers to take a more systemic approach in sustainability-related decision-making.

When there is a strong cohesion of sustainability-oriented values among decision makers, strategic and operational sustainability-related decisions will be more likely made consensually (Kaldschmidt 2011). Further, it could be interpreted that if the values of decision makers are consensually aligned with the scientific perspective of sustainability complying with sustainability principles, an effective sustainability strategy will be likely to be implemented. Therefore, in order to truly foster sustainable development, the values of decision makers and the scientific perspectives of sustainability in sustainability management have to be combined.

The levels of management can be divided into three parts: (1) normative management, which defines the basic management philosophy and the company's identity, (2) strategic management, which defines long-term strategic goals, and (3) operational management, which defines how the organization can reach its goals (Baumgartner 2014). When applying the management levels to sustainability management, our approach provides input mainly to the normative and strategic management levels (Fig. 4.3).

We see consistency between the organizational purposes to do business (based on the relationship types by Lankoski and Smith (2017)) and the viewpoints on sustainability (Fig. 4.4). We express this consistency as alternative *value profiles, representing the organizational purpose to create environmental, social and economic output in different relationships*. The points along the arrow are manifestations of different value profiles, where the beginning of the arrow (left corner) represents a *profit-dominant profile*

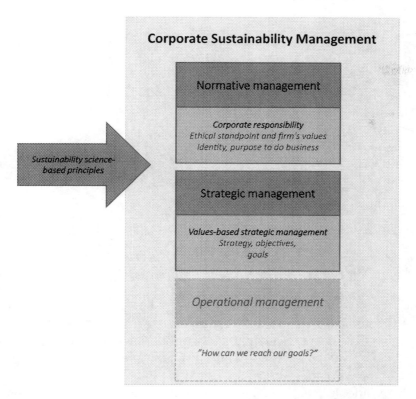

Fig. 4.3 Sustainability management levels (based on Baumgartner (2014) supported by sustainability science-based principles)

and the right head of the arrow a *sustainability-dominant profile*. The top of the arrow represents an *integrated profile*. Our interpretation is that when a company is moving from the profit-dominant profile toward the sustainability-dominant profile (from left to right), the instrumental role of the environmental and social perspectives of sustainability changes to having a role of absolute value. In other words, the purpose to do business changes from a financial logic to a more sustainability-dominant logic and an ecocentric worldview to do business. Alignment of organizational values with (the requirements of) the respective value profile is important if a company plans to change its position in the value continuum. In accordance with our earlier assumption, in order to reach the right corner,

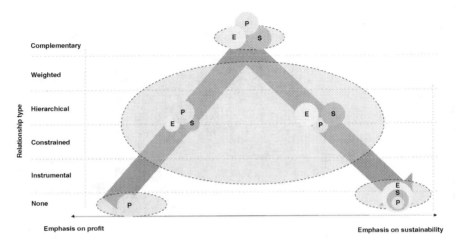

Fig. 4.4 Possible value profiles of a company (based on the range of alternative objective functions by Lankoski and Smith (2017))

the values of decision makers should be aligned with the ecocentric worldview of sustainability. However, the philosophy of the ecocentric worldview has to be operationalized in order to be able to carry out business in accordance with ecocentric sustainability principles. The operationalization of the ecocentric worldview is discussed in Sect. 4.2.

By positioning itself to some point along the arrow, the firm can identify who they are and who they want to be. In other words, the firm can consider its purpose beyond profits (Henderson and Van den Steen 2015). This is done at the normative management level, and it defines the basis for strategic management. Strategic management is a process of planning, implementing, and evaluating company-wide decision-making, enabling an organization to achieve its long-term objectives (Baumgartner 2014). In other words, normative management clarifies the strategic sustainability goal setting and makes sustainability-related goal setting more transparent, so that the decisions are based on the values the firm wants to follow. In addition, this approach supports the operational management level, where the sustainability strategy is implemented (Baumgartner 2014). Normative management provides a basis for the early phases of sustainable business model innovation and facilitates developing value propositions that are in line with the fundamental values of the firm.

4 Framework of Values-Driven Sustainability Management

In the sections above, we stated that effective sustainability management requires combining the ethical and scientific perspectives of sustainability. The values of decision makers are in an important role in strategic sustainability decision-making. In order to foster sustainable development effectively, the values of the decision makers have to be aligned with the scientific principles of sustainability. In practice, this will help the decision makers to set concrete sustainability objectives and goals and put them into action.

In order to help decision makers to consider their values and combine the scientific perspective of sustainability to them, we present a framework of Values-Driven Sustainability Management (VDSM) (Fig. 4.5). The framework includes existing approaches that can be used as tools to combine ethical and scientific perspectives in practice. We have modified the approaches in order to create a comprehensive framework for VDSM. The alternative objective functions approach used in phase 2 was described in Sect. 2 above, as it introduces the discussion of a firm's

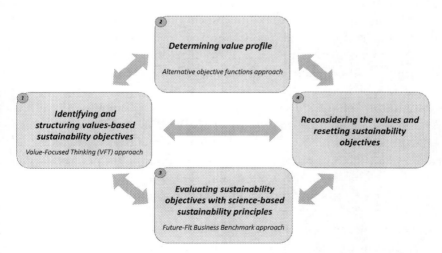

Fig. 4.5 Framework for effective Values-Driven Sustainability Management

purpose to do business. The applied approaches used in phases 1 and 3 are described in Sects. 4.1 (Value-Focused Thinking) and 4.2 (Future-Fit Business Benchmark), as they are more concrete methods to be utilized. Section 4.3 describes the fourth phase of the framework.

The framework consists of four iterative phases and specific approaches. In the first phase, the VFT approach (Sect. 1 in Chap. 4) is utilized to identify and structure values-based sustainability objectives. The starting point is the firm's sustainability objectives in a certain decision context. The aim is to structure the means-ends network of the objectives, where the ends represent the fundamental objectives, and the means help to achieve the ends. With the help of the means-end network, the fundamental objectives of the firm can be identified, and it can be recognized how the sustainability objectives are positioned in this network. The objectives are grouped depending on how they represent the environmental, social, or economic dimensions of sustainability. This phase helps to clarify the question of whether sustainability is the fundamental purpose of the firm's business or whether sustainability is just an opportunity to improve some of the firm's competitive factors.

In the second phase, the alternative objective functions approach is used to identify the value profile (Fig. 4.4 and Sect. 2) of the company. The objective network, structured in the first phase, is reflected against the relationship types of profit and sustainability, and it is analyzed what the emphasis of the objectives is from the profit-sustainability perspectives. With the help of this phase, the management philosophy can be determined, and it can be identified how well it represents the ecocentric worldview.

In the third phase, the scientific perspective of sustainability is involved. We suggest using the Future-Fit Business Benchmark (Sect. 4.2), which relies on the ecocentric worldview and uses science-based environmental and social system conditions as a basis to define the business principles for sustainable business (Kurucz et al. 2017). The aim of this phase is to present the scientific perspective for sustainable business to decision makers, so that they can reassess their values and purpose to do business against this perspective.

In the fourth phase, the decision makers can reconsider their values and possibly restructure their own sustainability objectives, based on the analysis done in the earlier phases (Sect. 4.3).

4.1 Value-Focused Thinking Approach for Identifying and Structuring Objectives

In Sect. 3.1 we stated that decision makers' values are formed in part by the organization they work for and on the basis of the company's identity. Further, the company's identity affects how the company is oriented toward sustainability-related decisions. Decision-making is often based on choices between alternatives, and the decision maker concentrates first on the alternatives to solve a problem or achieve a goal, and after that addresses the objectives or criteria to evaluate the alternatives. This kind of a decision-making approach is called alternative-focused thinking (Keeney 1992, 1996). However, the time and effort spent in relation to decision-making is used best when thought is given to values. This will generate viable alternatives that are in accordance with the values of the decision makers involved. The VFT methodology seems to be advantageous compared to other traditional methods applied in decision-making in the context of sustainability (Alencar et al. 2017). It differs from the alternative-focused paradigm by the following features (Keeney 1992, 1996):

- The values are made explicit by identifying and structuring the values appropriate for the decision situation qualitatively.
- The articulation of values in decision situations comes before other activities.
- The articulated values are used explicitly to create alternatives and to identify decision opportunities.

We propose that applying the first two phases of VFT in the sustainability-related decision situation (Fig. 4.6) helps to examine and reveal the sustainability objectives of the firm and to understand the values of the decision makers behind the objectives. An objective is a statement of something that one desires to achieve, and it is characterized by three features: a decision context, an object, and a direction to preference. A fundamental objective characterizes an essential reason for interest in the decision context. The means objective is of interest in the decision context because of its implications for the degree to which another (more fundamental) objective can be achieved (Keeney 1992).

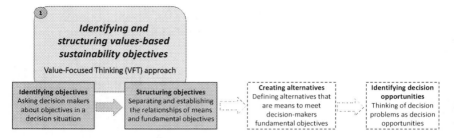

Fig. 4.6 Connection of the Value-Focused Thinking (VFT) approach (Keeney 1992, 1996) and the Values-Driven Sustainability Management Framework. The values of decision makers are identified and structured based on the techniques of the VFT. The phases of the VFT presented with dotted lines are excluded

Sustainability objectives can vary depending on the decision context, but a company might also have sets of broader and general strategic sustainability objectives which guide the decision-making. However, the first aim is to define the fundamental sustainability objectives in a certain decision context by asking, for example, what the decision maker wants to achieve in this decision context. At this stage, the objectives are not prioritized. The outcome is a list of all kinds of sustainability objectives. The next step is to structure the list and convert possible alternatives, constraints, and criteria into objectives, and after that to separate the means and fundamental objectives and establish their relationships by examining the reasons for each. This step involves linking objectives through means-ends relationships and specifying fundamental objectives. Separating ends objectives from specific means objectives should lead to at least one fundamental sustainability objective in a given decision situation (Keeney 1996). After the structuring phase, the means-ends network and the identified fundamental objectives can be utilized in the next phases of the framework.

Alencar et al. (2017) utilized the VFT approach to study the implementation of sustainability in a built environment. They structured objectives based on the values of the actors involved in civil construction. The aim was to provide actions that can be implemented during the design and construction phases and that may bring positive impacts to a sustainable building. This example shows that VFT can be applied successfully in the sustainability context. Therefore, we state that the VFT approach deepens the understanding of sustainability objectives set by decision makers. Sustainability objectives are linked to the values of decision makers, and further decisions come thus closer to the decision makers. The approach can also reveal new perspectives and change the attitudes of decision makers toward sustainability.

4.2 Future-Fit Business Benchmark for Evaluating Objectives

The international discussion about sustainable development started primarily by the Brundtland Commission's definition of sustainable development, and after that numerous definitions, frameworks, models, and initiatives have been developed to help make our societies more sustainable (Baumgartner 2011). The Sustainable Development Goals (SDGs) provide strong guidance in terms of the impacts and outcomes that companies and other stakeholders should strive to deliver. Companies want to focus more on impacts with their sustainability goals, and SDGs provide both structure and ambition for companies to consider their goal setting (O'Neill and McElroy 2017). However, to avoid incremental and ineffective improvements in sustainability and to motivate for real change, companies need a reference to a desired future state, which they can use as a benchmark to assess their sustainability progress (Kurucz et al. 2017).

There are several approaches aimed at operationalizing the idea and concepts of sustainable development. The approaches can be divided, for example, to *strategic planning processes* and approaches offering *more concrete goals*. The Framework for Strategic Sustainable Development (FSSD) is an example of a strategic planning process framework. In addition to the process framework, it contains principles that define sustainability (Broman and Robèrt 2017). The context-based goals offer more concrete goals aimed at allocating specific science- and/or ethics-based thresholds for companies (Bertels and Dobson 2017; O'Neill and McElroy 2017). An example of context-based goals is the Science-Based Targets approach, in which a company can adopt a target to reduce greenhouse gas emissions, which is in line with the level of decarbonization required to keep the global temperature increase below 2°C compared to pre-industrial temperatures (Science

Based Targets 2018). Another example of more concrete goals is the Future-Fit Business Benchmark (FFBB), which is a science-based, co-created, and openly available framework intended to introduce a new generation of sustainability metrics (Future-Fit Foundation 2017). Compared to the context-based goals, the FFBB defines the minimum acceptable level of environmental and social performance, which all organizations should strive at. The philosophy of the FFBB is that we must change the way we do business, and only then will we be able to achieve the SDGs (Future-Fit Foundation 2017; Kurucz et al. 2017).

We propose applying the FFBB to provide a factual scientific perspective for VDSM (phase 3 in Fig. 4.5). To our knowledge, the FFBB presents the most comprehensive attempt aimed at operationalizing science-based environmental and social system conditions to the organizational level. The FFBB builds on the strategic sustainability paradigm that highlights the nested dependencies of nature, society, and economy, that is, the ecocentric worldview. Shortly, the FFBB is a framework for performance assessment, including goals describing what a truly sustainable organization would look like, that is, what an assessment of such a business would reveal in the best case (Kurucz et al. 2017). Reflecting on Fig. 4.4, the FFBB represents the sustainability dominant logic to us.

The FFBB is based on sustainability principles of FSSD (also called system conditions), which offer clear guidance to what to aim for by defining what must *not* happen. From the business perspective, the system conditions offer a solid, science-based foundation for identifying what every company must do, as well as what any company may do beyond that (Broman and Robèrt 2017; Future-Fit Business Benchmark 2017; Kurucz et al. 2017). The system conditions are based on studies of ecological and social systems and dialogues with natural and social scientists (Broman and Robèrt 2017). In the FFBB, every business is defined to be just one actor in a complex and dynamic value web, influencing and influenced by a wide range of other social systems. The value web is segmented into suppliers, operations, products, and the society. The value web serves as the basis for determining the extent to which a company should be held responsible for system condition breaches, and the degree to which a company may seek to have a positive impact. The company is responsibly and wholly accountable for impacts within its direct control, but also from the systems perspective mutually accountable for certain impacts out of its direct control (Future-Fit Business Benchmark 2017).

In theory, every company could set sustainability goals based on the system conditions, but in practice, only most progressive companies are likely to invest in the effort required to find out how to do this. In addition, without clear guidance to what the destination is, companies would frame their ambitions and assess their progress in completely different ways. This can lead to incremental and even ineffective improvements in sustainability, as mentioned in Sect. 3.2. Therefore, the FFBB provides 23 Break-Even Goals (Table 4.2), which are formulated so that they give business leaders a clear destination to aim for. The goals are grouped in four areas: fostering well-being, respecting nature, optimizing resources, and strengthening the society. The goals are defined so that:

- Each goal is expressed as a single sentence, whose meaning can be grasped by business leaders, investors, and other key stakeholders without lengthy explanations.
- Each goal represents the minimum level of performance to aim for in one part of the value web (e.g., products, operations) and relates to one issue (e.g., wages, waste).
- All goals together identify the social and environmental break-even point that every company must reach.

For companies to be able to monitor their performance and prioritize where action is needed most, each goal is supported by both progress and supplementary indicators. The Break-Even Goals present the requirements of what *every* company *should* do.

In addition to the Break-Even Goals, the FFBB includes instructions for positive pursuits of what *any* company *may* do. The positive pursuits mean actions a company takes *to enable* others in the value web to reach the break-even point (Future-Fit Business Benchmark 2017). However, we concentrate only on the Break-Even Goals, and the positive pursuits are excluded from our framework (Fig. 4.7).

Table 4.2 Future-Fit Break-Even Goals (Future-Fit Business Benchmark 2017)

Future-Fit Business…	…must reach these Break-Even Goals	Where in the value web this applies			
		Suppliers	Operations	Products	Society
Fosters well-being	Community health is safeguarded	1	x		
	Employee health is safeguarded	1	x		
	Employees are paid at least a living wage	1	x		
	Employees are subject to fair employment terms	1	x		
	Employees are not subject to discrimination	1	x		
	Employee concerns are actively solicited, impartially judged and transparently addressed	1	x		
	Product communications are honest, ethical, and promote responsible use			x	
	Customer health is safeguarded			x	
	Products do not harm people or the environment			x	
Respects nature	Energy comes from renewable sources	1	x		
	Water use is environmentally responsible and socially equitable	1	x		
	Natural resources are managed to respect the welfare of ecosystems, people, and animals	1	x		
	Operational emissions do not harm people or the environment	1	x		
	Operations emit no greenhouse gases	1	x		
	Operations do not encroach on ecosystems or communities	1	x		
	Products emit no greenhouse gases			x	
Optimizes resources	Operational waste is eliminated	1	x		
	Products can be repurposed			x	

(continued)

Table 4.2 (continued)

Future-Fit Business…	…must reach these Break-Even Goals	Where in the value web this applies			
		Suppliers	Operations	Products	Society
Strengthens society	Procurement safeguards the pursuit of future-fitness	1	x		
	Business is conducted ethically				x
	The right tax is paid in the right place at the right time				x
	Lobbying and corporate influence safeguard the pursuit of future-fitness				x
	Financial assets safeguard the pursuit of future-fitness				x

1—Companies must strive to improve the operational future-fitness of their supply chains over time: such supplier impacts are captured indirectly by the goal *Procurement safeguards the pursuit of future-fitness*

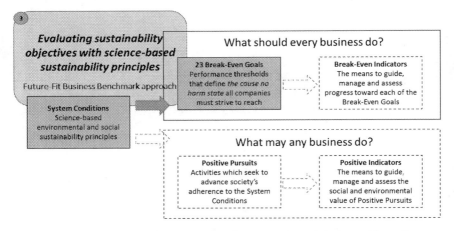

Fig. 4.7 The connection of Future-Fit Business Benchmark (adapted from Future-Fit Foundation 2017) and the Values-Driven Sustainability Management Framework. The System Conditions and 23 Break-Even Goals are used as a basis to correlate sustainability objectives with science-based sustainability principles. The phases of the FFBB with dotted lines are excluded from the study

4.3 Reconsidering the Values and Resetting Sustainability Objectives

In the fourth phase of the framework, no specific approach is utilized. At this phase, the decision makers are aware of their values on the one hand and scientific sustainability principles on the other, and can reconsider their values and possibly reset the sustainability objectives. The overall aim is that when decision makers go through all the phases of the framework, the values-based sustainability objectives are made transparent and the decision makers can recognize the gap between their objectives and the requirements of the sustainable development principles operationalized in the FFBB. The VFT approach has probably given some material to consider values-based alternatives to fill this gap. Recognizing the gap and analyzing their values help decision makers to determine the sustainability strategy of the company and to form a basis for values-based sustainability goal setting that will truly foster sustainable development.

5 Discussion and Conclusion

In this chapter, we have argued that strategic sustainability decision-making requires understanding both the values of decision makers and facts from sustainability science. The values form the basis for the normative level of sustainability management, and sustainability science offers facts for setting the sustainability strategy. We have presented a framework of VDSM that combines these perspectives. The presented framework enables companies to rethink the purpose of doing business, as well as the way to do business. In addition, it provides phases which help decision makers to analyze their values and sustainability objectives in order to set values-based sustainability goals that comply with sustainability principles, thus truly fostering sustainable development. In the following sections, we present a few viewpoints of the framework in sustainability goal setting, and how the use of the framework supports operational sustainability management.

5.1 Implications on Sustainability Goal Setting

The values of decision makers and facts from sustainability science provide a basis for a company's sustainability strategy, but the company still needs to make the strategy visible by determining long-term goals. The goals are related to the objectives firms want to reach, and concretize and make the objectives measurable. The goals are either achieved or not, and they can motivate for greater achievement of objectives (Keeney 1992). The framework can be utilized in sustainability goal setting in the following ways.

First, when the values are made transparent and the fundamental objectives are identified, there is a possibility that the analysis reveals something that the decision makers did not expect. It may seem, for example, that with the current identity and management philosophy, it is impossible to reach the goals proposed by the FFBB, although the decision makers would be willing to try that. According to Lankoski and Smith (2017), it is a decision issue, how the decision makers want to conceive the relationship between two variables (in this case profit and sustainability). Therefore, they can choose to restructure their objective network, so that the emphasis on sustainability will increase and thus the FFBB goals will be more likely to be achieved.

Second, the framework helps companies to extend their outlook on the strategic objectives. One aim of the VFT approach is that it helps to create alternatives and to identify decision opportunities. Therefore, the decision makers can find new ways to influence sustainable development and rethink their objectives. In addition, a company may find out that a certain sustainability objective actually has an effect on some more fundamental objective or on a larger context. In this case, the role of sustainability goals is more instrumental and a means to achieve something else, but that else can be also other than profit.

Third, the scientific perspective of sustainability helps companies to focus on essential issues and avoid greenwashing. When the values and science are combined, the decision makers can focus on those sustainability issues that are most important for them. This will increase their motivation, and the focus area can be later enlarged to involve other sustainability aspects as well.

Finally, the time perspective is emphasized when setting sustainability goals. For example, the realization of the 23 Break-Even Goals of the FFBB is a several years' process for many companies. In addition, a company that wants to act in a sustainable manner, and in the best case has a strong sustainability-dominant profile (Fig. 4.4), needs profit to survive (Kanter 2011; Stubbs and Cocklin 2008). This means that a company probably cannot comply with the philosophy behind the sustainability-dominant profile in the short-term decisions every time. Although the ecocentric worldview is the overall management philosophy, decision makers are sometimes forced to make decisions where the instrumental role of sustainability is emphasized in order to ensure the company's future survival through profit making. Therefore, future research is needed to find out how a company with a sustainability-dominant profile can put its sustainability strategy into practice and solve the possible contradictions between profit and sustainability logics in decision-making.

5.2 Implications on the Operational Level of Sustainability Management

When looking at the operational level of sustainability management, the research on sustainable business models has increased in recent years. However, a major barrier to sustainable business model innovation and design is the lack of a structuring systems perspective that includes an operational definition of sustainability and strategic guidelines for how an organization can support the sustainable development of the society while strengthening its own competitiveness (França et al. 2017). The comprehensive FSSD offers a process for strategic planning and includes sustainability principles. However, the framework of the FFBB can facilitate companies to set more concrete sustainability goals, because the FFBB gives a clear required state toward all companies must strive (Kurucz et al. 2017). In addition, when the values of decision makers are taken into account, there is greater possibility that the goals are tried to be reached. In other words, the idea of sustainable management is already included deeply in the normative management level (Baumgartner 2014). In the best case, this will increase the innovations and the development of new sustainable business models, because new alternatives to reach the goals must be invented.

References

Alencar, M.H., L. Priori Jr., and L.H. Alencar. 2017. Structuring Objectives Based on Value-Focused Thinking Methodology: Creating Alternatives for Sustainability in the Built Environment. *Journal of Cleaner Production* 156: 62–73.

Bansal, P., and H. Song. 2017. Similar But Not the Same: Differentiating Corporate Sustainability from Corporate Responsibility. *Academy of Management Annals* 11: 105–149.

Baumgartner, R.J. 2011. Critical Perspectives of Sustainable Development Research and Practice. *Journal of Cleaner Production* 19: 783–786.

———. 2014. Managing Corporate Sustainability and CSR: A Conceptual Framework Combining Values, Strategies and Instruments Contributing to

Sustainable Development. *Corporate Social Responsibility and Environmental Management* 21: 258–271.

Bertels, S., and R. Dobson. 2017. The Road to Context: Contextualising Your Strategy and Goals. A Guide. Embedding Project.

Broman, G.I., and K. Robèrt. 2017. A Framework for Strategic Sustainable Development. *Journal of Cleaner Production* 140: 17–31.

Broman, G., K. Robèrt, G. Basile, S. Byggeth, T. Connell, D. Cook, H. Haraldsson, et al. 2012. *Sustainability Handbook. Planning Strategically towards Sustainability.* Studentlitteratur AB: Lund.

den Ouden, E. 2012. *Innovation Design: Creating Value for People, Organizations and Society.* London: Springer.

Dyllick, T., and K. Muff. 2016. Clarifying the Meaning of Sustainable Business. *Organization & Environment* 29: 156–174.

França, C.L., G. Broman, K. Robèrt, G. Basile, and L. Trygg. 2017. An Approach to Business Model Innovation and Design for Strategic Sustainable Development. *Journal of Cleaner Production* 140: 155–166.

Future-Fit Business Benchmark. 2017. Future-Fit Business Benchmark. Methodology Guide. Release 2.

Future-Fit Foundation. 2017. Future-Fit Business Benchmark. Request for Comments. Changes and Additions Proposed for Release 2.

Gao, J., and P. Bansal. 2013. Instrumental and Integrative Logics in Business Sustainability. *Journal of Business Ethics* 112: 241–255.

Glynn, M.A., C. Lockwood, and R. Raffaelli. 2015. Staying the Same While Changing: Organizational Identity in the Face of Environmental Challenges. In *Leading Sustainable Change: An Organizational Perspective*, ed. R. Henderson, R. Gulati, and M. Tushman, 143–170. Oxford: Oxford University Press.

Greenwood, R., P. Devereaux Jennings, and B. Hining. 2015. Sustainability and Organizational Change: An Institutional Perspective. In *Leading Sustainable Change—An Organizational Perspective*, ed. R. Henderson, R. Gulati, and M. Tushman, 323–355. Oxford: Oxford University Press.

Henderson, R., R. Gulati, and M. Tushman. 2015. Leading Sustainable Change—An Introduction. In *Leading Sustainable Change—An Organizational Perspective*, ed. R. Henderson, R. Gulati, and M. Tushman, 3–21. Oxford: Oxford University Press.

Henderson, R., and E. Van den Steen. 2015. Why Do Firms Have "Purpose"? The Firm's Role as a Carrier of Identity and Reputation. *American Economic Review* 105: 326–330.

Kaldschmidt, S. 2011. *The Values of Sustainability: The Influence of Leaders' Personal Values on Sustainability Strategies.* Dissertation of the University of St. Gallen School of Management, Economics, Law, Social Sciences and International Affairs. Dissertation No. 3906.

Kanter, R.M. 2011. How Great Companies Think Differently. *Harvard Business Review* 89: 66–78.

Keeney, R.L. 1992. *Value-Focused Thinking: A Path to Creative Decision Making.* Cambridge, MA: Harvard University Press.

———. 1994. Using Values in Operations Research. *Operations Research* 42: 793–813.

———. 1996. Value-Focused Thinking: Identifying Decision Opportunities and Creating Alternatives. *European Journal of Operational Research* 92: 537–549.

Kurucz, E.C., B.A. Colbert, F. Lüdeke-Freund, A. Upward, and B. Willard. 2017. Relational Leadership for Strategic Sustainability: Practices and Capabilities to Advance the Design and Assessment of Sustainable Business Models. *Journal of Cleaner Production* 140: 189–204.

Landrum, N.E., and B. Ohsowski. 2017. Identifying Worldviews on Corporate Sustainability: A Content Analysis of Corporate Sustainability Reports. *Business Strategy and the Environment* 27: 128–151.

Lankoski, L., and N.C. Smith. 2017. Alternative Objective Functions for Firms. *Organization & Environment* 1–21. First Published 1 September 2017.

Markman, G.D., M. Russo, G.T. Lumpkin, P.D.D. Jennings, and J. Mair. 2016. Entrepreneurship as a Platform for Pursuing Multiple Goals: A Special Issue on Sustainability, Ethics, and Entrepreneurship. *Journal of Management Studies* 53: 673–694.

Montabon, F., M. Pagell, and Z. Wu. 2016. Making Sustainability Sustainable. *Journal of Supply Chain Management* 52: 11–27.

O'Neill, R., and S. McElroy. 2017. Targeting Value: Setting, Tracking & Integrating High-Impact Sustainability Goals. *SustainAbility.*

Palmer, T.B., and D.J. Flanagan. 2016. The Sustainable Company: Looking at Goals for People, Planet and Profits. *Journal of Business Strategy* 37: 28–38.

Pearce, J.A. 2013. Using Social Identity Theory to Predict Managers' Emphases on Ethical and Legal Values in Judging Business Issues. *Journal of Business Ethics* 112: 497–514.

Purser, R.E., C. Park, and A. Montuori. 1995. Limits to Anthropocentrism: Toward an Ecocentric Organization Paradigm? *The Academy of Management Review* 20: 1053–1089.

Schaltegger, S., and J. Hörisch. 2017. In Search of the Dominant Rationale in Sustainability Management: Legitimacy- or Profit-Seeking? *Journal of Business Ethics* 145: 259–276.

Schwartz, S.H. 1992. Universals in the Content and Structure of Values: Theoretical Advances and Empirical Tests in 20 Countries. In *Advances in Experimental Social Psychology*, 1–65. Elsevier Science & Technology.

———. 2006. A Theory of Cultural Value Orientations: Explication and Applications. *Comparative Sociology* 5: 137–182.

———. 2007. Value Orientations: Measurement, Antecedents and Consequences Across Nations. In *Measuring Attitudes Cross-Nationally: Lessons from the European Social Survey*. London: SAGE Publications.

Schwartz, S.H., and W. Bilsky. 1987. Toward A Universal Psychological Structure of Human Values. *Journal of Personality and Social Psychology* 53: 550–562.

Science Based Targets. 2018. Science Based Targets. Accessed February 12, 2018. http://sciencebasedtargets.org/contact-us/.

Silvestri, L., and R. Gulati. 2015. From Periphery to Core: A Process Model from Embracing Sustainability. In *Leading Sustainable Change: An Organizational Perspective*, ed. R. Henderson and R. Gulati, 81–110. Oxford University Press.

Starik, M., and P. Kanashiro. 2013. Toward a Theory of Sustainability Management: Uncovering and Integrating the Nearly Obvious. *Organization & Environment* 26: 7–30.

Stubbs, W., and C. Cocklin. 2008. Conceptualizing a "Sustainability Business Model". *Organization & Environment* 21: 103–127.

Whiteman, G., B. Walker, and P. Perego. 2013. Planetary Boundaries: Ecological Foundations for Corporate Sustainability. *Journal of Management Studies* 50: 307–336.

5

Sustainable Business Model Ideation and Development of Early Ideas for Sustainable Business Models: Analyzing a New Tool Facilitating the Ideation Process

Ulla A. Saari, Leena Aarikka-Stenroos, Leena Köppä, Jörg Langwaldt, Stina Boedeker, and Saku J. Mäkinen

---

U. A. Saari (✉) • L. Aarikka-Stenroos
Center for Innovation and Technology Research (CITER), Laboratory of Industrial and Information Management, Tampere University of Technology, Tampere, Finland
e-mail: ulla.saari@tut.fi; leena.aarikka-stenroos@tut.fi

L. Köppä
Innovation Services/Y-kampus, Tampere University of Technology, Tampere, Finland
e-mail: leena.koppa@tut.fi

J. Langwaldt
Research Services, Tampere University of Technology, Tampere, Finland
e-mail: jorg.langwaldt@tut.fi

S. Boedeker
Funding Services, University of Tampere, Tampere, Finland
e-mail: Stina.Boedeker@uta.fi

© The Author(s) 2019
A. Aagaard (ed.), *Sustainable Business Models*, Palgrave Studies in Sustainable Business In Association with Future Earth, https://doi.org/10.1007/978-3-319-93275-0_5

1 Introduction

With the requirements for more sustainable innovations and businesses, in the future, research and business teams will need to create new, innovative ideas that are innately sustainable solutions instead of merely adding superficial sustainability fixes to current non-sustainable solutions (Bocken et al. 2014). How to facilitate sustainable business model (SBM) development is a contemporary challenge in the fields of, for example, business and product management. SBM creation is inherently multidisciplinary and requires input from various different kinds of stakeholders.

To increase and extend the toolkit in the field of sustainable business, this chapter introduces a novel tool that facilitates the ideation process of SBMs. We have developed and validated a tool called the Impact Canvas˚ tool (IC tool) that enables cooperation in multidisciplinary teams. The IC tool has a registered trademark. The general version of the tool template is included in the Appendix and can be used under a Creative Commons Attribution-ShareAlike 4.0 International License. The IC tool has been used in workshops in the university and business environment since 2015; and based on user feedback, it can be considered a user-friendly and practical tool for research and business teams developing ideas in the early ideation phase. The IC tool has been designed for teams that are developing new, innovative and sustainable research and business ideas and business models. With its visual user interface, the IC tool supports creativity among and communication between team members with different backgrounds. The IC tool supports the formation of teams comprising people from different disciplines, both from academia and business, which enables the development of ideas from scratch without restricting boundaries or guidelines from existing organizations. The IC

S. J. Mäkinen
Laboratory of Industrial and Information Management, Tampere University of Technology, Tampere, Finland
e-mail: saku.makinen@tut.fi

tool helps team members share their knowledge and together develop new, innovative research and business ideas with a clear vision of the impact of the solution. The ideation of sustainable research and business ideas must consider a wider perspective than the economic viability of the idea; in addition, environmental and social perspectives need to be incorporated into the idea. The wider perspective must also be supported by the tool used in the ideation process, which should help team members to create a common strategic business vision.

The first section of this chapter describes on a general level the situation and challenges that teams may face when developing early ideas for sustainable business ideas and models. The second section discusses the literature on the use of tools for creating and developing innovative ideas and sustainable business. In the third section, the background, the development team, and iteration cycles of the IC tool are described. Then, the requirements for interdisciplinary communication and tools supporting multidisciplinary teams are discussed. The IC tool has been tested by various development teams in association with workshops arranged by the authors, and the results are presented. The final section of this chapter describes the future development plans for the tool so that it can better support the needs of multidisciplinary teams innovating new sustainable ideas and business models that account for the social, environmental, and economic challenges in the world.

2 The Development of Early Ideas into Sustainable Business Ideas and Models

We start by discussing the particular methods and tools that can be applied when developing sustainable business ideas. Research has elaborated teaching and training practices, interaction methods (e.g., between industry and university), learning methods, and the use of tools (Doganova and Eyquem-Renault 2009; Hixson and Paretti 2014; John et al. 2016). There are a set of well-known tools used for business modeling, such as the Business Model Canvas (BMC) (Osterwalder and Pigneur

2010), to increase innovative business ideas and entrepreneurial activities in society. There is even an extended version of the BMC with a triple-layered approach (cf. triple-layered business model canvas by Joyce and Paquin 2016) that can help yield a more holistic view of existing business models in organizations. This canvas, however, was developed for business modeling and therefore does not necessarily help in the early ideation phase. When working with the BMC, the team concentrates on practical business development by formulating actual business strategies with offerings, customer needs, infrastructure, and finances (Osterwalder and Pigneur 2010). The BMC does not examine the challenges that exist in the very early-phase development of ideas aimed at rendering research or innovative ideas into business ideas, nor does the BMC consider sustainability aspects from societal and environmental perspectives.

The development of sustainable business ideas is not a simple and straightforward process, especially when there is uncertainty about novel technologies and possible future markets do not yet exist for the solution (Kokshagina et al. 2016). The exploration phase of ideas in the early ideation phase may require a tool that can help the team to develop their ideas more effectively (Kokshagina et al. 2016; Heising 2012). The methods used to develop business ideas and technical solutions for novel markets are important in the early phases of the ideation, and there has been a call for studies on creative design methodology, especially for innovations based on scientific findings (Gillier and Piat 2011). In order for research findings to have a positive and sustainable impact for society and the environment, the developers of both research and business ideas must share a vision that is meaningful and long-lasting (Sarewitz 2016). In the early ideation phase, special attention should be paid to the vision statement of the business (cf. Reid and de Brentani 2012).

2.1 Different Perspectives from Multiple Stakeholders Are Required in the Development of Sustainable Business Models

SBMs include a triple bottom-line approach and account for the interests of multiple kinds of stakeholders representing society and the environment.

The vision and purpose of a team or organization that aims to develop sustainable business or research ideas needs to be considered from the triple bottom-line dimensions, that is, *social, environmental,* and *economic* perspectives, and sustainable organizations are those that pursue economic profit alongside the fulfillment of the other two dimensions (Stubbs and Cocklin 2008). SBMs aim at driving and implementing innovation for sustainability, and they embed sustainability in the business strategy and processes of companies (Bocken et al. 2014). When working on developing an SBM, it is crucial to engage and collaborate with stakeholders, and sustainable organizations are those that understand that in order to be successful, they must consider their stakeholders (Stubbs and Cocklin 2008). Teams working on new ideas need to make an effort to always increase societal and environmental benefits in addition to the economic gain achieved by the business (Bocken et al. 2014). Business model innovations for sustainability have been defined by Bocken et al. (2014) as:

Innovations that create significant positive and/or significantly reduced negative impacts for the environment and/or society, through changes in the way the organisation and its value-network create, deliver value and capture value (i.e. create economic value) or change their value propositions.

The development of sustainable business ideas and models based on academic research findings can still be challenging for researchers, entrepreneurs, and businesspeople in the early idea development phase. Especially, the societal and environmental impacts of novel business ideas should be considered from many perspectives: academically from several disciplines and, in the business environment, from many types of stakeholders. Business and customer value cannot be created by companies independently; instead, collaboration with various stakeholders has become more critical for companies (Bocken et al. 2014), and many organizations are already listening to their stakeholders and trying to take their views into account in their development initiatives (Rauter et al. 2017).

Universities and companies are expected to deliver new, more sustainable solutions to the markets. Research results should also have a societal impact and solve real problems in the world (Sarewitz 2016). The current demand for more sustainable businesses and technologies on the markets has also placed higher expectations on researchers and businesses to cooperate more closely and bring forth positive results for investments in research projects (Edler and James 2015; McNie et al. 2016).

2.2 The Important Role of Teamwork in the Development of Sustainable Business Models

Organizations are formed by teams that play an important role in the ideation and development of business and research initiatives for the organization (DeChurch and Mesmer-Magnus 2010), and complex societal and environmental problems require sustainable solutions that must be developed by multidisciplinary teams. Teams are increasingly working on the development of solutions for global problems and ideas for new innovations to ensure the competitiveness of the organization, and this requires a multidisciplinary approach in the team (Kay et al. 2018).

In multidisciplinary teams, however, challenges can arise when they need to cooperate, as the team members may have different perspectives and backgrounds for solving problems and creating new solutions, and it may be hard for the team to communicate as a result (Cronin and Weingart 2007). Teams developing sustainable solutions and business ideas are often multidisciplinary, and in many organizations teams consist of members from different functions and departments; in this sense, the approach can even be called transdisciplinary (Kay et al. 2018). Multidisciplinary teams working on sustainability-related topics have been shown to be strongly committed to their team mission in university contexts, especially teams consisting of university students; working in a multidisciplinary team has been demonstrated to offer a beneficial way to develop new skillsets and experiences among students (Kay et al. 2018).

The early ideation phase is critical for the outcome of the innovation process and business development, and it can be considered part of the market-visioning phase in which new business opportunities are sought

(Markides 2006). When creating a business vision, the team must be motivated and possess understanding and knowledge for analyzing a business opportunity and for elaborating a business solution for the markets, which requires several iterations to produce the solutions to the key questions (O'Connor and Veryzer 2001). In the New Product Development (NPD) process, the personal competencies of the individual team members to communicate and network is critical for the formulation of a market vision that enables the launch of a sustainable business solution on the markets (Reid and de Brentani 2012). The business and market vision needs to be strategically clear so that it can guide the innovation process in the correct direction (Reid and de Brentani 2012), which requires a methodological approach for the teamwork.

2.3 Introducing a Novel Tool Designed Particularly for Early Idea Development: The Impact Canvas

The IC tool is an early-phase idea-testing tool that enables the involvement of many stakeholders and enables cross-boundary collaboration for ideation and innovation, both of which are increasingly needed (Reypens et al. 2016; Aarikka-Stenroos et al. 2017). The IC tool has been developed with the aim to enable ideation and business idea development by involving many stakeholders and accounting for various perspectives, which often emerge in the very early stages of the development of a business idea and business model. When working with the IC tool, researchers and business people can together form a start-up team and cover the most critical factors for a business opportunity, that is, formulate a business vision, collect initial customer requirements, analyze possible competition on the markets, and look for initial resourcing sources, thus developing an initial idea for a sustainable business solution that has a place on the markets (Impact Canvas® tool 2016; Aarikka-Stenroos et al. 2016).

To both ensure and emphasize the use of the IC tool in an interactive way, it features a built-in iteration. We discovered that the iteration potential and aspect were important features for the involvement of different stakeholders as well as their perspectives. The tangible benefit of

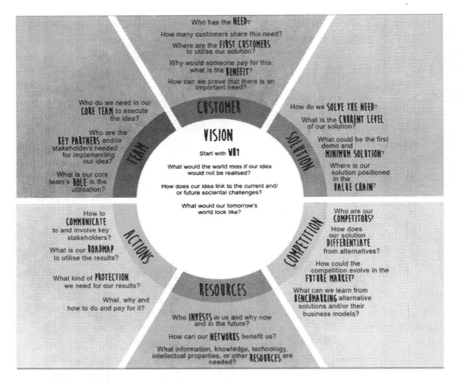

Fig. 5.1 Impact Canvas tool and a built-in iteration with Status—Target—Test and Do for each section of the canvas

the built-in iteration arises from the fact that our tool poses questions not only with an interactive tone, but also with a visual reminder for the interaction on the canvas itself. The user is more or less obliged to think and implement testing and/or actions per every section of the canvas. We have used both the questions on each of the content elements and the label of "Status—Target—Test and Do" for enabling the visible, even tangible, iteration (Fig. 5.1).

The interactive tone in the content elements of the canvas can be seen in the sections and questions below.

- *Vision*: How does our idea link to current and/or future societal challenges?
- *Customer*: All the questions have a tone that determines the interaction; for example, Why would someone pay for this: What is the need? How can we prove that there is an important need?
- *Solution*: Where is our solution positioned in the value chain?
- *Competition*: What can we learn from benchmarking the alternative solutions and/or their business models?
- *Resources*: Who invests in us and why—now and in the future? How can our networks benefit us?
- *Actions*: How do we communicate with and involve key stakeholders?
- *Team*: Who are the key partners and/or stakeholders needed for implementing our idea?

3 Tools Approach for Creating and Developing Innovative and Sustainable Business Ideas

In this section, we discuss how a tool can assist a team in the early ideation phase. We particularly address tools that enable the development of novel sustainable (business) ideas. The role of such tools is discussed in the field of business development as well as in innovation management and entrepreneurship. Next, we discuss in more detail what the different literature streams have said thus far about such tools.

First, in the field of business development and start-ups, there are tools for identifying and developing new businesses and business ideas. Such tools focus on the structured design and development of business. The most established tool in this field is the Business Model Canvas (BMC) developed by Osterwalder (e.g., Osterwalder and Pigneur 2010; Osterwalder et al. 2014), which was created to design, analyze, and define value propositions and key principles of business by the focal firm. The BMC is a visual template comprising sections describing a firm's or product's value proposition, customers, finances, and infrastructure for developing new or describing prevailing business models. As a tool, the BMC can also be applied as a large outline so that team members can cooperatively sketch, iterate, and discuss the elements of the business model or as a web-based software format. As a tool, it can be used to foster understanding, learning, discussion, creativity, and analysis.

There are many other canvas tools that can facilitate business development, such as the Lean Canvas and the Value Proposition Canvas. The Lean Canvas is particularly designed for startups (Maurya 2012). The Value Proposition Canvas focuses more on value creation and business ideas that can be derived from the value creation potential. These canvasses serve as tools that highlight the most important elements of business, but they also enable the presentation of the most critical elements in a simple and communicative form. For example, Eppler et al. (2011) conducted a study whereby the team processes of managers innovating business models were compared. The teams utilized different kinds of artifacts (business model templates, physical sketched objects, or PowerPoint templates). They found that using a template tool significantly improved perceived collaboration but decreased perceived creativity, which is an indication that tools can have a distinctive impact on collaborative teamwork in particular for business model development.

Second, as ideation is part of creative thinking and is thereby helpful, one literature stream has examined tools that aim to increase creativity. The widely cited work by Shneiderman (2007) underlines that research on and the development of creativity support tools concentrate on tasks that aid discovery in sciences, exploration in design, innovation in engineering, and imagination in arts. The focus of studies in the field of tools for supporting collaborative creativity has been on digitalized tools (Warr and O'Neill 2007; Shneiderman 2007), not on canvas-like tools. This field, however, increases our understanding of how diverse canvases, templates, and devices can serve as Individual, Group, and Social Creativity Support Tools. Shneiderman (2007) suggested, based on his work, that creativity support tools should be user-friendly for novices, yet provide ambitious functionality for experts.

Creativity brings forth innovation; so accordingly, there is also a set of studies that have discussed the role and contribution of tools for innovation. This approach highlights practical tools and methods that drive new ideas to emerge and lead to innovation (Markman and Wood 2009; O'Brien 2010; Hidalgo and Albors 2008). Such tools can address the development of a design or product, creativity in general, or business or market intelligence (see full review in Hidalgo and Albors 2008). When tools are used to drive innovation, they can motivate participants and support collaboration for open innovation, thereby enabling very diverse actors to join in (Antikainen et al. 2010).

Third, ideation and communication should happen in collaboration between different stakeholders. Antikainen et al. (2010) stressed that it is fundamental for tools and toolkits to support communication between different stakeholders. Information gaps can arise from the asymmetrical distribution of information in a team, and therefore it is important that the tool enables knowledge representation and that team members can communicate with others who have different backgrounds and levels of knowledge. Antikainen and colleagues argued that tools should make the differences between collaborating team members and stakeholders transparent and help team members to transform their varying contributions into a format or language that the whole team understands.

Fourth, one stream has discussed tools as boundary objects that enable communication over boundaries, different actors, and stakeholders—the relevant aspect for sustainable business. For example, a widely cited work by Carlile (2002) noted, based on extensive observations, that there are different boundary objects, such as drawings, prototypes, and process maps, that in cross-functional settings are useful for communication and knowledge transformation. Here, canvas tools can be conceptualized as boundary objects that enable discussions over boundaries. Carlile (2002) identified three characteristics of such boundary object tools that make them useful in joint problem solving and ideation.

A boundary object comprises a common language for individuals to share their knowledge. A useful boundary object offers a practical way for individuals to define and learn how their views differ while allowing them to specify their knowledge and concerns as concretely as possible with regard to the problem at hand. A boundary object offers a standardized model, method, and map that together enable diverse stakeholders and actors to specify their specialized concerns. This feature of boundary objects typically pushes a cross-functional team to address critical values and priorities, as well as their consequences for individuals. Here, the concreteness of the tool is the key, as Carlile (2002) put it:

For example, a 'process model' is certainly less concrete than a physical part, but when it is used to represent and learn about the sources of a design 'bottleneck' in a complex product development process, its particular 'concrete' means suit the nature of the problem faced. Of course, once this specifying and learning of differences and dependencies has taken place, we are often left with negative consequences that must be resolved.

Furthermore, an effective boundary object enables individuals to jointly build upon their knowledge. If negative aspects are identified, then the individuals should have the opportunity to change, negotiate, or modify the boundary object. In agreement with these characteristics of an effective boundary object, according to Carlile (2002), "*individuals must be able to draw on, alter, or manipulate the content of a boundary object to apply what they know and transform the current knowledge used at the boundary. Further, the knowledge transformed and created through the use of objects, models, and maps can then be used to enhance the content of shared repositories and the use of standardized forms and methods.*" Here, summing briefly, diverse tools, such as canvases, models, and maps, support transforming and archiving knowledge among multiple actors. A boundary object can represent individual team members' knowledge, helping them learn about the differences in the team as well as dependencies, thereby cooperatively converting knowledge toward solving the challenges and problems introduced in the team. Canvases can serve as boundary objects that function as "integrating devices" (Lawrence and Lorsch 1969)—not only tools, but also methods and standardized forms for formulating and learning about the differences and dependencies identified in the team. Applying this approach, the canvas can facilitate a process of building on common knowledge as team members learn, discuss, and modify their current knowledge base and create novel knowledge to solve the identified issues (see also Teece et al. 1999).

A boundary object also facilitates communication between various stakeholders representing different professions. This is relevant, as contemporary professional work (science, business, and technology design) is heterogeneous insofar as it involves multiple actors representing different professional cultures (Engeström et al. 1995; Akkerman and Bakker 2011), and therefore learning is not only about being or becoming an expert in a particular expertise domain, but also about cooperating across boundaries. The term *boundary crossing* refers to how professionals may need to enter into an unfamiliar territory and *"face the challenge of negotiating and combining ingredients from different contexts to achieve hybrid situations"* (Engeström et al. 1995, p. 319; see Akkerman and Bakker 2011). Here, the concept of boundary object evokes how canvases as tools can bridge overlapping practices in different fields and disciplines. Developing new innovative business ideas, communicating them to others, and elaborating the ideas further are not easy tasks, particularly for professionals with no background in innovation or business.

Fifth, canvases can also be considered as tools for education and for learning business perspectives. Several studies in the field of innovation education and coaching have considered business model tools as "innovation devices" (Doganova and Eyquem-Renault 2009) and "tools that support innovation" (Hixson and Paretti 2014; John et al. 2016), which are therefore beneficial for education. Here the focus has been on diverse teaching models and learning processes (e.g., Fayolle and Gailly 2008). A recent study by Harms (2015) examined self-regulated learning and team learning in a lean start-up environment. All these studies emphasized that innovation and entrepreneurship education and coaching can apply diverse tools and methods that enable both individual and team-based learning and facilitate dynamic iteration. These studies, however, focused on the use of tools, and did not therefore provide any theoretical or practical insights into how new tools and canvases are generated for SBM development.

4 Background and Development of the Impact Canvas® Tool

To respond to the need for a novel tool to assist multidisciplinary teams in the early ideation phase, practitioners at the Tampere University of Technology (TUT), University of Tampere (UTA), and Tampere University of Applied Sciences (TAMK) jointly developed an ideation tool, the IC (Aarikka-Stenroos et al. 2016). The IC tool has been designed for testing and developing ideas in the very early phases of research and business idea development.

At best, business and research aim for impacts on society and economy. Professionals challenged with ever shorter innovation cycles must accelerate ideation and engage with users already in the early idea development phase. The need for speed and societal solutions are the demands business developers must satisfy to ensure timely impact of their ideas. The need for speed to reduce time-to-market calls for pivoting and fail-fast testing of ideas against the actual needs of real customers. The development of solutions for societal challenges requires knowledge generation by interdisciplinary teams. Likewise, need-driven or use-driven research embarks from a user perspective. The resource-demanding process of getting ideas to the user requires a clear vision and a diverse team.

At the Research and Innovation Services of the University of Tampere and Tampere University of Technology, professionals advising pre-start-up and research teams on impact development acted on the need for novel tools to structure ideation. There was a clear need to increase open dialogue within teams and increase the expected impact of ideas. To this end, these peers met during November 2014 in a workshop to review and discuss the tools they used to facilitate the identification and description of the expected impact of research ideas during the research funding acquisition phase. As an outcome of the meeting, three advisors decided to team up and develop a new tool differing extensively from existing checklists aimed to ensure impact.

The development team set out to design a tool to visualize the ideation process, raise awareness of customers' needs, and foster collaborative idea development. One team member made the others aware of the BMC, a visual chart comprising elements describing a firm's or product's value proposition, infrastructure, customers, and finances. During the workshop, a first version of the new tool was sketched, including five elements, that is, four fields enclosing one element in the center. Already at this stage of the tool development, the center element included the question "Why?" The four outer elements included as topics: Current versus foreseen framework changes, Transfer of results, Customer, Team, and Stakeholders. In the beginning, this new tool was referred to as Exploitation/Impact/Utilization Canvas.

In 2015, the initial team of three advisors continued the unfunded voluntary tool development and invited peers to join the effort. The next important contribution was the integration of the NABC (Need, Approach, Benefit, and Competition) model promoted by Tekes, the national innovation funding agency in Finland, to effectively present a solution to others. Thus, in January 2015, the design of the canvas was altered to include the NABC model and six elements around the central element "Why?" In March 2015, the idea to gamify the canvas was sparked and the elements' content was continuously refined. The team developed game rules to guide users of the tool and to generate a playful user experience. In May, the six outer elements were color coded. Tests of the gamified canvas during summer and early autumn 2015 indicated that the framework of the game did not increase usability. The game's demand of having a start and an end did not support the team's aim for lean iterations. The given questions in the canvas were sufficiently self-guiding such that game rules would not be required. Emphasis was kept on promoting sharing between different groups developing their business or research ideas with the canvas. In autumn 2015, the tool's layout was refined to its current form, and later the name "Impact Canvas" was added to the canvas. In November 2015, after abandoning its gamified use, the tool was supplemented with a brief usage instruction and a selected example of supporting tools, like the Blue Ocean Canvas. The IC was repeatedly tested with different groups, and its content was continuously refined.

During 2016 and 2017, development and commercialization of the tool was financially supported by two national co-funded projects. In relation to the national projects, peers from the Tampere University of Applied Science joined the development team. Feedback collected during tests added to the collaborative, iterative development of most suitable wording for different target groups. In February 2016, the usage instruction was omitted altogether while keeping a supplementary right-hand explanatory field. In the next version, even the explanatory field was omitted. The IC was disseminated in various national and international events as well as online. The online pdf-version includes fill-in text boxes. In May 2016, "Status-Target-to-do" notes were added to the six outer elements to enhance lean iteration. In March 2017, the development team decided to share the tool under a Creative Commons Attribution-ShareAlike 4.0 International License. The "Impact Canvas" is protected as a European trademark. In late 2017, a version of the IC including only keywords was tested, and the idea resulted in further reduction of the text on the canvas and the highlighting of keywords.

Development of the new tool through a collaborative, iterative process by a diverse group of practitioners lasted three years and resulted in an acknowledged tool for early ideation, testing, and development of ideas. The tool has been designed to visualize the ideation process, raise awareness of customers' needs, and foster collaborative idea development. The tool development and testing has been studied, and the results have been published (cf. Aarikka-Stenroos et al. 2016; Saari et al. 2017) (Fig. 5.2).

The IC is visual, self-explanatory, easily approachable, and adaptable to suit diverse user communities. These features make it distinctive from other business model tools. The focus lies on the impact of the business solution in society and on the environment while also addressing customer needs in detail. It is suitable for existing businesses as well as pre-start-ups and research teams.

The IC satisfies the need of coaches and professionals for flexible tools to facilitate ideation toward responsible solutions matching real needs of customers and society. From the beginning of the development, the tool centered around the question "WHY" and "VISION" to motivate the user(s) to reflect on underlying motives and ambitions. The two aspects aim at an open dialogue, especially in diverse teams, to better communicate why they do what they do. The IC aims to trigger discussions and collaborative learning between users.

The organization of the content elements is open in the sense that the user can select where to start. The tool is oriented toward testing and follow-up actions (Status—Target—Test and Do) and enables a circular, iterative process. Open questions foster collaborative working and deeper reflection on the idea. The tool does not require a minimum set of proven facts and figures to start with and uses common terminologies to minimize barriers toward its usage. The IC in its current format is an easy-to-use tool in the earliest phases of idea development by teams with representatives with different backgrounds in different disciplines; this has been proven from

Sustainable Business Model Ideation and Development of Early... 135

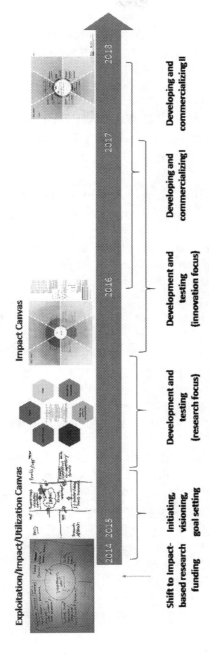

Fig. 5.2 The development timeline and iteration cycles of the Impact Canvas tool

the results of several tests among researchers, research facilitators, research grant applicants, and students (Aarikka-Stenroos et al. 2016), as well as among senior researchers and professors who also have experience in the industry and business (Saari et al. 2017).

5 Means to Facilitate Communication Over Boundaries in Multidisciplinary Teams for SBM

The IC tool benefits multidisciplinary teams that need to communicate, explore, and develop innovative and viable business ideas and models based on the different knowledge backgrounds of the individual team members. Each content element of the tool offers an important aspect that needs to be explored and developed in the ideation phase. The vision statement is surrounded on the template by six elements: customer, solution, competition, resources, actions, and team. Together, the content elements form a holistic basis for further action planning to implement the research or business idea. In addition to being a tool, the IC is also a boundary object that facilitates communication between team members and thus helps to explore different perspectives based on the different backgrounds of the multidisciplinary team. As the tool template includes guiding questions tailored based on the background and disciplines of the team members, the threshold to start using the tool is very low.

The visual content elements and layout of the IC tool facilitate the discussion and exploration of different kinds of innovative research and business ideas that can help to create an SBM in a later phase. The different content elements help the development team members cover the essential requirements and topics for developing a new research or business idea. The content elements are interconnected and can be discussed in whatever order is most suitable for the team. The vision element of the IC tool is the focal point that guides the team to consider their strategy and drivers for business development, the impact on society, and the environment as well. The formulation of a vision statement helps the team members to consider sustainability and share more comprehensive strategies that also account for the impact of the research or business idea on the environment and society at large. The following guiding questions for the vision element have been used in the general version of the IC tool: Why do we exist?; What would the world miss if our idea was not realized?; How does our idea link to current and/or future societal challenges?; What would our tomorrow's world look like?; What is the value of this research from the industry point of view?

When scientists apply for research funding, they encounter substantial funding programs, such as the EU Horizon2020 framework program (2014-2020), which identifies societal challenges and calls for multidisciplinary projects to solve them. Multidisciplinary projects funded by EU framework programs need to spend time defining the key concepts of the research project (e.g., computer sciences, language studies, psychology, cognition science, engineering, and marketing). Multidisciplinary projects rehearse interdisciplinary communication in these situations. The ones that take part in proposal preparation must come to an understanding of the shared research plan. In the kick-off meeting and during the first year, the multidisciplinary teams need to learn to understand and even speak a common language. When members of the same consortium collaborate, they can detect the parts and terms they need to clarify together.

Some of the issues in the general version of the tool were caused by the terminology, and some of the terms were modified for another field of science. When working in a multidisciplinary team, the general version of the IC tool is used. The decisive requirement for an interdisciplinary tool is "Are the researchers willing to make an effort to develop interdisciplinary communication in order to build multidisciplinary projects?" The ones who want to compete for H2020 funding or find creative ideas are those most likely to be willing, especially when multidisciplinarity becomes one of the evaluation criteria for the funding applications. The ones who feel safe and unthreatened by other disciplines may act as pioneers and break through the unproductive silos between disciplines, thereby building an academic ecosystem wherein all parts of the system are necessary and interdisciplinary communication is a benefit. Multidisciplinarity is the avenue to both innovation and originality.

6 Feedback from the Users of the Impact Canvas Tool

The concept of the IC tool resulted from several development iterations, during which we collected feedback from workshops where the tool was introduced and utilized for teamwork. As a result of the iterations and further development of the IC tool based on user feedback, it has been found to, for example, support teamwork and boost the creativity of individuals in the team. The benefits of using the IC tool in the early ideation phase also include the following: It allows multidisciplinary teams to collaborate by sharing their knowledge and developing upon a common basis for their ideas; the tool offers a structured approach for proceeding through the required areas for developing a business or research idea further in practice; and the tool guides the team to form a strategic vision that accounts for a broader perspective on their idea, including the social and environmental sustainability perspectives in addition to the economic perspective.

6.1 Method and Data

The IC tool has been introduced by some of the IC tool development team members in workshops with participants from different fields and with different levels of education and business experience. After the workshops, the participants were asked to fill in a survey on their perceptions and experiences of using the tool for the first time.

Several training sessions were held on the IC tool at different universities and during some conferences in 2017. Feedback was collected and analyzed from training sessions held at different Finnish universities, the Brunel University London, the EARMA conference (European Association of Research Managers and Administrators), and a workshop for research support staff at universities in Denmark and Germany. In addition, the tool has been used for student project work and workshops with industry representatives on circular economy facilitated by coaches from the Tampere University of Technology.

The training sessions on the use of the IC tool were arranged in a similar fashion by the same group of trainers at all the locations. None of the participants had earlier been in contact with the tool, as it was still novel. After the IC tool was introduced to the participants, they had the opportunity to try it out and develop an idea in a group. The instructors offered support in the use of the guiding content elements on the IC when developing the idea. After the training, the participants shared their ideas and experiences on the use of the tool with the rest of the group. In the survey distributed immediately after the session, the participants were asked to evaluate their experience of the tool, concentrating on usability, content elements in general, collaborative and motivational aspects, as well as the look and feel of the tool. The responses were given on a five-point Likert scale (ranging from strongly disagree = 1 to strongly agree = 5).

The analyzed sample included 110 respondents to the first version of the survey and 24 respondents to the second version. The respondents were mostly from Finland (43%); however, we also received feedback from Germany (10%) and other European countries (27%), while some respondents did not list their country of origin (14%). From the respondents, 60% were female, 33% male, and 7% did not respond to this question. The respondents represented the following age groups: 25% were 18-24 years (representing the students involved in the workshops), 12% were 25-34 years (representing younger researchers and company representatives), 29% were 35-44 years (representing more senior researchers and company representatives), 26% were 45-54 years, 4% were over 55 years, and 4% of the respondents did not report their age.

There were experienced academic researchers among the respondents, with doctoral degrees and a minimum of 10 years of experience from research work (n = 46). These participants had various roles, for example, research coordinator, advisor, researcher manager or director, and professor.

Most of the experienced researchers had worked in academia (85%), but some respondents had worked in companies in the private sector, either as employees (15%) or entrepreneurs (11%). In addition, a large number of respondents were experienced research advisors and coaches, who represent a demanding user group.

6.2 Results from the Surveys

Based on the surveys conducted after the workshops, it was first verified that the visual presentation of the tool was appealing to the workshop participants. The use of different colors to differentiate the content elements also helped the users visually differentiate various aspects of the idea that needed to be developed. Based on the feedback, we verified that the majority of the users thought the "The Impact Canvas is aesthetically pleasing" and "The layout of the Impact Canvas is logical and can be quickly understood." Next, the development team wanted to ensure that the tool was user-friendly and could be used immediately by the teams after a short introduction. Based on the feedback from the users, we verified that most of the users thought the "The Impact Canvas is easy to use" and that "The guiding questions on the Impact Canvas are easy to understand."

To ensure that the IC tool truly enabled users to explore innovative ideas in the very early stages of their development, we collected feedback from the participants at idea development workshops regarding this aspect. The majority of the respondents thought that "The Impact Canvas serves its purpose very well and helps with the early idea development." In addition, the development team wanted the tool to help users collaborate with other team members with varying backgrounds. To ensure that the IC tool indeed helped in this respect, we asked the users to explain whether "The Impact Canvas helps me to involve my team members in the idea development."

In the survey, the workshop participants were also asked how the tool helped them to individually contribute to the teamwork. The responses to the statements, "The tool boosts their creativity on an individual level," "The impact Canvas inspires me to work on an idea," and "The Impact

Canvas boosts my creativity" indicated that on the individual level, the participants for the most part felt that the tool helped them get inspired and create ideas in the team (Table 5.1).

Neither the level of education nor the age of the respondents had a significant influence on the way the respondents perceived the usefulness of the tool, as there were no significant differences when comparing the means with the ANOVA method (analysis of variance). The only question on which these two factors had an impact was the question about how well the "The Impact Canvas helps to discuss an idea with others outside my team." Those respondents with a master's degree (mean = 4.04; $n = 27$) or a doctoral degree (mean = 3.96; $n = 46$) evaluated this statement significantly higher. Also, the over 3544 age group (mean = 4.19; $n = 32$) scored this statement higher.

As the feedback from the first survey version focusing on the initial use and perceptions of the tool was so positive, we wanted to focus next on the actual content elements of the tool. The feedback survey was modified in the next phase so that it concentrated more on collecting respondents' views on the actual content elements and the guiding questions in

Table 5.1 Results from the first version of the feedback survey focusing on testing the user-friendliness and usefulness of the tool in multidisciplinary teams

Survey statement	Mean	SD
The Impact Canvas is aesthetically pleasing	3.77	0.860
The layout of the Impact Canvas is logical and can be quickly understood	3.76	0.860
The Impact Canvas is easy to use	3.78	0.759
The guiding questions on the Impact Canvas are easy to understand	3.73	0.744
The Impact Canvas serves its purpose very well and helps with the early idea development	3.83	0.848
The Impact Canvas helps me to involve my team members in the idea development	3.87	0.743
The impact Canvas inspires me to work on an idea	3.82	0.747
The Impact Canvas boosts my creativity	3.68	0.834
The Impact Canvas improves my understanding of the required elements to develop an idea into a realistic plan for a business or a project	3.84	0.711

SD, standard deviation
Response scale: strongly disagree = 1 to strongly agree = 5

each individual item. Feedback was collected from two different workshops for this part. One workshop was held in Finland, and it focused on developing business ideas for the circular economy. The other workshop was held in Denmark for research funding experts and applicants, in which the use of the IC tool for developing research and business ideas was explored.

Based on the second survey, we received further confirmation that the content elements and guiding questions within them also gave the users a good overview of the required perspectives that need to be considered in the early ideation development phase. The respondents considered that the individual content elements and their guiding questions helped in the teamwork (Table 5.2).

The results from the second survey completed at two workshops give a strong indication that the tool has elements and guiding questions that are meaningful to the users. As the number of respondents was

Table 5.2 Results from the second version of the feedback survey focusing on the content elements

Survey statement	Mean	SD
I think that idea and business development tools (e.g., Impact Canvas, Business Model Canvas) are very useful and help to discuss topics in groups.	4.08	0.929
The VISION element and its guiding questions were important for the overall discussion.	4.00	0.722
The CUSTOMER element and its guiding questions were important for the overall discussion.	3.96	0.751
The SOLUTION element and its guiding questions were important for the overall discussion.	4.21	0.588
The TEAM element and its guiding questions were important for the overall discussion.	3.79	0.588
The COMPETITION element and its guiding questions were important for the overall discussion.	3.96	0.624
The RESOURCES element and its guiding questions were important for the overall discussion.	3.92	0.717
The ACTIONS element and its guiding questions were important for the overall discussion.	3.96	0.690

SD, standard deviation
Response scale: strongly disagree = 1 to strongly agree = 5

very small for the second feedback survey, we will need to continue collecting more feedback on the content elements as the IC tool is developed further.

7 Future Development of the Tool: The Impact Canvas® Tool as a Platform

Next we discuss how the IC tool will be further developed so that it can better serve in sustainable business idea and model development. The IC tool works as a stand-alone model and forms a cooperation platform that enables a great variety of activities to be built upon it. The aim is to facilitate the best possible benefit from these prospects for multiple different kinds of usage in the future. The tool and the platform can be used for developing different kinds of ideas, ranging from business to research funding, as well as in various kinds of situations. For instance, an idea can be a research, business, or service idea or concept, and it can be utilized in an early phase of the development when, for example, looking for the most suitable utilization path. The tool can be applied by different teams and people on their own. The tool can be used with support from a coach or a facilitator. Furthermore, the tool can be applied as a platform and the basis for coaching programs for separate teams with facilitated collaboration and mutual learning.

We, the development team members of the IC tool,[1] have been and will be actively developing and testing different ways to utilize the tool in its current format as a template as well as a platform for teamwork. The vision is to create a platform that:

- is adaptable to different kinds of coaching and conceptualizing sessions,
- can be modified for special use cases,
- enables self-learning and lean experimenting of different kinds of ideas.

In early 2017, we initiated a coaching and conceptualizing concept that is adaptable to different contexts. This way, the execution possibilities of the Impact Canvas˘ tool were broadened. The concept is based on the seven aspects of the IC tool and includes a carefully considered package of facilitation methods, coaching tools, and processes. The concept and the coaching methods are flexible for different kinds of business environments and research contexts. The concept also includes intensive working sessions facilitated by coaches for developing ideas. This enables the processing of an idea with a variety of perspectives that can help to clarify the larger picture and context of an idea on a wider scale. Intensive and facilitated work with an idea from a variety of perspectives makes it possible to test the assumptions of the development team quickly and efficiently. This can, and usually will, generate re-thinking and re-framing of an idea rapidly and with minimal resources.

The IC tool is useful as it creates a common language and understanding in the development team for different aspects of the impact of the idea. The tool permits the development of ideas with a flexible and iterative process, which is the most important part of our concept. When the IC tool is used in ideation workshops, it ties the sessions together and can be used as a platform and as an iteration tool. The challenge and mission for the team is to trust the ideation process, which is also enhanced with coaching and facilitating methods and tools provided by the IC tool development team.

One example of the adaptability of the IC tool to different contexts is the collaboration the development team has had with a national research program that supports research ideas from life science and health technology. The program is designed to support research ideas from these fields in their very early phases, when both commercial and scientific applications for research findings are being developed. In spring 2018, the team started a coaching program arranged for nine research teams from the research fields of life science and health technology. Most of the people in these teams are researchers from Finnish universities. Some of the teams also have members from companies and business developers from these special fields. Intensive workshops will be arranged for these teams to develop the impact aspect of their research ideas and results. The concept will be implemented in the form of workshops and homework for the teams between the coaching sessions. As the participants are researchers mainly from the same field, they already have a common language and lexicon for the relevant theoretical and technological point of views. Our tool and the concept, however, also create a common language and understanding gradually in the process, even though the team members would not have a similar background. The collaboration and sharing of ideas and information is implemented step by step with discussions, sharing of ideas, and getting to know the other participants. The underlying way of working is to develop ideas with a creative mindset that concentrates on lean thinking, doing, and experimenting.

The IC tool can be modified to serve different kinds of needs from various kinds of user groups and disciplines. The tool is a platform and represents a philosophy upon which different modifications, applications, and trials can be built. The development team has tested the platform and its philosophy by tailoring the guiding questions in the different content elements of the tool for specific situations and special targets. The tailoring of the tool was done, for example, in autumn 2017 for the specific needs for the stakeholder workshop sessions in a circular economy project. In addition, at the University of Tampere, the IC tool was modified to coach researchers from Social Sciences and Humanities and Medical Sciences. Afterward, a modified version was created and tested for the Social Sciences and Humanities (IC SSH). Thereafter, a combination of the two versions was used to create a version for the Medical Sciences (IC MED).

Another example of the modification of the tool according to the target group is the development of the discussion and networking method for collaboration between researchers and industry and business representatives. The tailored questions for this particular purpose have been modified by our team of two experts and coaches, one from business and industry collaboration services and the other from innovation and entrepreneurship services. The collaboration has ensured that the needed special requirements have been considered. The target user group will be researchers who are interacting with industry and business people. The specified target is to clarify the value of their research from the industry point of view.

In early 2018, a team of two experts with different knowledge bases made a simplified version of the IC tool with the same content elements but fewer questions per section. This version of the tool is intended for networking between researchers and business representatives and will still be tested. The IC tool has been simplified as there is a limited time frame for the facilitated networking. The testing will be completed in a lean manner at an event called TechBites, which is organized in collaboration with the university and the business sector of the city of Tampere. The working method in the event includes two interconnected parts. The first session is called Pitch and Catch, where the researchers have a chance to present their case briefly, that is, pitch, to the participants of the event. The participants will then choose two of the pitchers they want to talk to further. The pitches have been designed especially for the purpose of clarifying and creating interaction, and they have been created with the help of the framework of the specially tailored IC tool. The second part of the TechBites event is a facilitated networking session called the Science Playground. In this phase, the focus is on networking and team building. The IC tool is used for this, and the participants can ask questions or make suggestions on the different content elements of the tool for a further meeting. We believe that the methods and tools used in such idea development sessions can be developed even further so that the collaboration event is inspiring, relaxed, and fun despite the differing backgrounds of the participants and stakeholders.

The idea of lean process thinking and doing is utilized in both our concepts and teamwork. The development team's aim is to develop our activities in the same way as we coach and facilitate the ideation processes of our customers and users. Self-learning and coaching are key concepts for our way of working. The lean way of developing ideas and testing them with users and customers as soon as possible has been the approach in our development work since the beginning. We have developed new aspects and features to be included in the tool in close interaction with our customers, users, and networks, and the development work will continue.

The IC tool is one example of a tool that can support early-phase ideation and SBM. It supports learning, sharing, peer-to-peer discussions, and dialogue that together comprise the backbone of team activities, help to develop new ideas, and account for different perspectives when developing sustainable business ideas and sustainable business models.

Notes

1. The development team includes Leena Köppä (TUT, team leader), Langwaldt Jörg (TUT), Ulla Saari (TUT), Leena Aarikka-Stenroos (TUT), Marja Hyypiä (TUT), Stina Boedeker (UTA), Riitta Kivimäki (UTA), Anne Tuhkunen (UTA), Tiina Koskiranta (TAMK), Leena Eerola (TAMK), and Marika Vuorenmaa (TAMK).

References

Aarikka-Stenroos, L., S. Boedeker, L. Köppä, and J. Langwaldt. 2016. How to Develop a New Innovation Education Tool: A Case Study. In *The ISPIM Innovation Summit*, Kuala Lumpur, Malaysia 2016.

Aarikka-Stenroos, L., E. Jaakkola, D. Harrison, and T. Mäkitalo-Keinonen. 2017. How to Manage Innovation Processes in Extensive Networks: A Longitudinal Study. *Industrial Marketing Management* 67: 88–105.

Akkerman, S.F., and A. Bakker. 2011. Boundary Crossing and Boundary Objects. *Review of Educational Research* 81 (2): 132–169.

Antikainen, M., M. Mäkipää, and M. Ahonen. 2010. Motivating and Supporting Collaboration in Open Innovation. *European Journal of Innovation Management* 13 (1): 100–119.

Bocken, N.M., S.W. Short, P. Rana, and S. Evans. 2014. A Literature and Practice Review to Develop Sustainable Business Model Archetypes. *Journal of Cleaner Production* 65: 42–56.

Carlile, P.R. 2002. A Pragmatic View of Knowledge and Boundaries: Boundary Objects in New Product Development. *Organization Science* 13 (4): 442–455.

Cronin, M., and L. Weingart. 2007. Representational Gaps, Information Processing, and Conflict in Functionally Diverse Teams. *Academy of Management Review* 32 (3): 761–773.

DeChurch, L.A., and J.R. Mesmer-Magnus. 2010. Measuring Shared Team Mental Models: A Meta-analysis. *Group Dynamics: Theory, Research, and Practice* 14 (1): 1–14.

Doganova, L., and M. Eyquem-Renault. 2009. What Do Business Models Do?: Innovation Devices in Technology Entrepreneurship. *Research Policy* 38 (10): 1559–1570.

Edler, J., and A.D. James. 2015. Understanding the Emergence of New Science and Technology Policies: Policy Entrepreneurship, Agenda Setting and the Development of the European Framework Programme. *Research Policy* 44 (6): 1252–1265.

Engeström, Y., R. Engeström, and M. Kärkkäinen. 1995. Polycontextuality and Boundary Crossing in Expert Cognition: Learning and Problem Solving in Complex Work Activities. *Learning and Instruction* 5 (4): 319–336.

Eppler, M.J., F. Hoffmann, and S. Bresciani. 2011. New Business Models Through Collaborative Idea Generation. *International Journal of Innovation Management* 15 (6): 1323–1341.

Fayolle, A., and B. Gailly. 2008. From Craft to Science: Teaching Models and Learning Processes in Entrepreneurship Education. *Journal of European Industrial Training* 32 (7): 569–593.

Gillier, T., and G. Piat. 2011. Exploring Over: The Presumed Identity of Emerging Technology. *Creativity and Innovation Management* 20 (4): 238–252.

Harms, R. 2015. Self-regulated Learning, Team Learning and Project Performance in Entrepreneurship Education: Learning in a Lean Startup Environment. *Technological Forecasting and Social Change* 100: 21–28.

Heising, W. 2012. The Integration of Ideation and Project Portfolio Management—A Key Factor for Sustainable Success. *International Journal of Project Management* 30 (5): 582–595.

Hidalgo, A., and J. Albors. 2008. Innovation Management Techniques and Tools: A Review from Theory and Practice. *R&D Management* 38 (2): 113–127.

Hixson, C., and M.C. Paretti. 2014. Texts as Tools to Support Innovation: Using the Business Model Canvas to Teach Engineering Entrepreneurs About Audiences. In *IEEE International Professional Communication Conference (IPCC)*, October 2014, IEEE, pp. 17.

Impact Canvas® tool. 2016. http://y-kampus.fi/en/y-tools/impact-canvas/

John, P.K., S. Gregor, and R. Sun. 2016. A Research Engagement Canvas to Facilitate University-Industry Collaboration. In *ISPIM Innovation Symposium* (p. 1), June 2016, The International Society for Professional Innovation Management (ISPIM).

Joyce, A., and R.L. Paquin. 2016. The Triple Layered Business Model Canvas: A Tool to Design More Sustainable Business Models. *Journal of Cleaner Production* 135: 1474–1486.

Kay, M.J., S.A. Kay, and A.R. Tuininga. 2018. Green Teams: A Collaborative Training Model. *Journal of Cleaner Production* 176: 909–919.

Kokshagina, O., P. Le Masson, B. Weil, and P. Cogez. 2016. Portfolio Management in Double Unknown Situations: Technological Platforms and the Role of Cross-Application Managers. *Creativity and Innovation Management* 25 (2): 270–291.

Lawrence, P. R. and Lorsch, J. W., 1969. *Developing Organizations: Diagnosis and Action.* Mass.: Addison-Wesley.

Markides, C. 2006. Disruptive Innovation: In Need of Better Theory. *Journal of Product Innovation Management* 23 (1): 19–25.

Markman, A.B., and K.L. Wood, eds. 2009. *Tools for Innovation: The Science Behind the Practical Methods That Drive New Ideas.* Oxford: Oxford University Press.

Maurya, A. 2012. *Running Lean: Iterate from Plan A to a Plan That Works.* O'Reilly Media Inc.

McNie, E.C., A. Parris, and D. Sarewitz. 2016. Improving the Public Value of Science: A Typology to Inform Discussion, Design and Implementation of Research. *Research Policy* 45 (4): 884–895.

O'Brien, E., ed. 2010. *Knowledge Management for Process, Organizational and Marketing Innovation: Tools and Methods.* IGI Global.

O'Connor, G.C., and R.W. Veryzer. 2001. The Nature of Market Visioning for Technology-Based Radical Innovation. *Journal of Product Innovation Management* 18 (4): 231–246.

Osterwalder, A., and Y. Pigneur. 2010. *Business Model Generation: A Handbook for Visionaries, Game Changers, and Challengers.* Wiley.

Osterwalder, A., Y. Pigneur, G. Bernarda, and A. Smith. 2014. *Value Proposition De-sign: How to Create Products and Services Customers Want.* Wiley.

Rauter, R., J. Jonker, and R.J. Baumgartner. 2017. Going One's Own Way: Drivers in Developing Business Models for Sustainability. *Journal of Cleaner Production* 140: 144–154.

Reid, S.E., and U. de Brentani. 2012. Market Vision and the Front End of NPD for Radical Innovation: The Impact on Moderating Effects. *Journal of Product Innovation Management* 29 (S1): 124–139.

Reypens, C., A. Lievens, and V. Blazevic. 2016. Leveraging Value in Multi-stakeholder Innovation Networks: A Process Framework for Value Co-creation and Capture. *Industrial Marketing Management* 56: 40–50.

Saari, U., L. Aarikka-Stenroos, S. Boedeker, L. Köppä, and J. Langwaldt. 2017. Assessing the Usefulness of an Early Idea Development Tool Among Experienced Researchers. *CERN IdeaSquare Journal of Experimental Innovation* 1 (2): 3.

Sarewitz, D. 2016. Saving Science. *The New Atlantis* 49: 4–40.

Shneiderman, B. 2007. Creativity Support Tools: Accelerating Discovery and Innovation. *Communications of the ACM* 50 (12): 20–32.

Stubbs, W., and C. Cocklin. 2008. Conceptualizing a "Sustainability Business Model". *Organization and Environment* 21 (2): 103–127.

Teece, D.J., G. Pisano, and A. Shuen. 1999. Dynamic Capabilities and Strategic Management. in M.H. Zack (Ed.), *Knowledge and Strategy* (pp. 77–115). Boston: Butterworth Heinemann.

Warr, A., and E. O'Neill. 2007. Tools to Support Collaborative Creativity. In *Tools to Support Collaborative Creativity Workshop Held as Part of Creativity and Cognition Conference*, June 2007.

6

Business Models for Multiple Value Creation: Exploring Strategic Changes in Organisations Enabling to Address Societal Challenges

Jan Jonker and Niels Faber

1   Introduction

We live in a society in transition. Institutional configurations that have carefully been crafted over past decades are currently being scrutinised. This envisaged transition demands new methods of organising—new societal deals at an individual and a collective level—and also abandoning the ways of working and organising with which we have become familiar. What worked in the past may no longer be relevant in the present and the future. This reorientation departs from the notion that the primary reason to organise is and always has been to create forms of value.

Everywhere around us, initiatives addressing sustainability become apparent; however, the factual impact of these remains minimal. A more radical shift is required, and the alternative approach must become obvious. In order to achieve this, the role of organisations—more particularly,

J. Jonker (✉) • N. Faber
Nijmegen School of Management, Radboud University,
Nijmegen, The Netherlands
e-mail: n.faber@fm.ru.nl

the way we organise—requires revision. Only then will solutions emerge that could contribute to the present wicked societal, economic, and social problems. Self-organising initiatives and networks suddenly appear in various societal domains that reveal human desires and abilities more than ever before. Whether we label these as self-sustainability, self-organisation, or participatory society, these initiatives challenge current relationships between the societal actors, citizens, businesses, and governments. This change in the division of roles results in an increasing demand upon citizens' abilities to organise matters themselves. They will have to actively take responsibility for their own well-being, health, food, and much more. Individuals will need to solve the problems in their own environment themselves as much as possible. When they do so, the consequence is a substantial redesign and rebuild of society.

A societal transition may succeed if it is connected to transactions. Our society builds on a continuous flow of transactions, large and small, 24/7. Some transactions have a short-term impact; others carry their effects over longer periods. Transactions determine how people relate to each other. A transaction means intentional exchange with the idea of reciprocally creating value. This, however, encompasses more; specifically, a transaction also incorporates transactional properties: a certain interaction between people that itself is of value. Transactions take shape on the basis of communication and the logic of emotion (e.g., Habermas 1981).

Sustainability is not about better; it is about different. It concerns systemic change, adopting new ways of working, creating, and sharing the things that are of value. Organising differently necessitates a new generation of transaction models, namely, those that enable reciprocal value creation between people that are in balance with the (natural) environment. Searching for alternative transaction models implies that we relate differently in the realm of organisations; instead of vertically in hierarchies, relationships are formed horizontally in networks. This has a rather crucial impact on how parties relate to each other in terms of governance and control and the way coordination unfolds. The exploration of such new forms of organising is currently emerging throughout Western societies leading to amorph concepts such as the sharing and collaborative economy (Botsman and Rogers 2011; Sundararajan 2016).

1.1 Societal Challenges

Underlying these transitions, we observe a range of societal challenges. Current societal arrangements cannot appropriately address the changing needs of society and will unavoidably and increasingly lead to negative impacts on both society and the habitat if continued as currently arranged. A repository of current societal challenges reflecting this need for transition has been made by the United Nations and has led to the identification of the Sustainable Development Goals (SDGs; United Nations 2015). The SDGs are considered to be wicked problems, and the debate regarding them can be summarised as a discussion on sustainability (WCED 1987) that, over time, has fanned out into three separate debates on (a) sustainification, (b) circularity, and (c) inclusivity and the ways they are related to each other. For clarity, it increasingly amounts to a 'radical' process of sustainification which is explained as the process in which various actors (governments, businesses, and citizens) collectively engage in realising far reaching, impactful goals regarding sustainability (Ellen MacArthur Foundation 2012; UNEP 2011; European Commission 2018).

1.2 Wicked Problems

Taking a comprehensive perspective on today's society reveals that the societal challenges are to be considered as placeholders for an increasing number of wicked problems (Churchman 1967; Rittel and Webber 1973). Wicked problems are complex and interlinked issues for which no single solution exists. Even stronger, aiming for a solution in one area leads to a series of new problems in related areas. Problems of a wicked nature seem to be characteristic for our times, be they in food, politics, health, energy, asylum seekers, and so on (Faber and Jonker 2015). This implies that problems of a wicked type may no longer be solved by single disciplines, by one government or one nation, or within one specific geo-region. Conditions that might lead to solving the specified issue are incomplete and contradictory, and the requirements under which solutions are created might appear to change over time. Instead, interdisciplinarity seems to be inevitable. Given the increasing interrelated nature and complexity of the problems, we contend that addressing them can only be successful when solutions simultaneously create an array of values for different constituents. This need for multiple value creation calls for rebalancing the dominant unilateral focus on single (primarily financial) value creation.

1.3 Criticising Value Creation

In the past two centuries, the way that value creation has been organised has become increasingly the prerogative of organisations. These are rational-functional structures designed towards a single end be it manufacturing products, delivery of services, or a combination of both (e.g., Product Service Systems; Tukker 2004). This has led to organisational designs enabling value creation from an inside-out perspective. While the fulcrum of this way of organising seems to be efficiency, it does not simultaneously take into account the negative impacts on the short or long term. In recent years, organisations have attempted, at best, to alleviate these impacts through so-called CSR programmes of a different and often auto-referential nature. While this has certainly led to increasing awareness, we must conclude that this has not resulted in a direction that has sufficient impact on the nature of the current fundamental questions (United Nations 2015). Consequently, organisations have functioned exclusively by targeting money as the core and only means of value exchange. The dominant transaction model that has been established deliberately and legally excludes and externalises a wide array of costs, particularly ecological and social. As a consequence, various values are not taken into consideration in the actual cost-benefit analyses. Hence, a limited and poor transaction model that only considers forms of value creation that can be monetised became omnipresent. Things of value that cannot be monetised do not matter and thus do not contribute to the business results.

1.4 The Role of Organisations and Organising

Organisations are our most utilised 'institutions' and, in Western societies at least, we cannot live without them. The organisation is a deliberately created social artefact (Simon 1969) that thrives on 'blending' relationships into a nexus of contacts and contracts: social, economic, emotional, environmental, and so on. Organising (and managing) depends on how you conceptualise an organisation and how this is strategised and deployed in policies, plans, and actions. Stakeholders (both old and new) are the 'building blocks' in this nexus of relationships and contracts. Companies have always known stakeholders. What has changed is the number of stakeholders and the nature of their role(s) and manifestations (that is, whether they are considered as friends or foes). Organisations manage their responsibilities to their social (stakeholders) and natural environments through the strategies and operational practices that they deploy to achieve their goals. '[S]takeholder theory merely recapitulates [...] standard business assumptions [...] it rests on the idea that value is created when entrepreneurs [...] put together a deal that simultaneously, and over time, satisfies [...] groups of stakeholders who play a critical role in the ongoing process of the business. Of course, any entrepreneur knows this as second nature. Business is just creating value for stakeholders' (McVea and Freeman 2005, pp. 57–58).

We use the products and services of those organisations for all types of purposes, both for those that are commercial and for the 'common good'. Every day, we make thousands of decisions in organisations. With these decisions, we permanently construct and reconstruct those organisations. The continuous flux of decisions and activities are directly linked to shaping our society. In this way, ordinary everyday organisational decisions significantly influence sustainability issues, although we might not always be aware of it. The connection between our human existence and organisations is such that we cannot even properly function without everything that is organised through our own actions and, simultaneously, which actions materialise around us. Indeed, we as human beings can only act since we are surrounded by a thoroughly organised environment, which we refer to as the 'organisational ecology' of 'interdependent organisations'. It is here that we must also make swift progress with issues of sustainability.

Organisations were developed centuries ago to help create different forms of collective values—the common good as well as the private good. Organising is not a goal in itself. Rather, it is a means of realising for and with each other that which is of value. In this context, there are three commonly accepted collective values: social, economic, and ecological.

Sustainability can be interpreted as a general (umbrella) value within which the above-mentioned common values are embedded. It is not something that needs to be inherently included when organising.

In this context, the observation that organisations themselves are evolving and thus subject to change appears to be appropriate. In this change, their role(s), the way(s) they are structured, their place in the value chain, and the societal expectations all become a factor. As a consequence, we increasingly observe organisations actively searching for ways to address societal challenges. The combination of societal challenges and wicked problems requires a different approach to organising that leads to multiple values for multi-actors. This is beyond the quest to address sustainability but, instead, about simultaneously organising social, ecological, and other values (Gleeson-White 2014). This tendency is expressed in a variety of loosely coupled experiments in a broad variety of domains. Regarding organisational structure, experiments take shape around concepts such as horizontal and vertical organising (Brafman and Beckstrom 2006; Laloux and Wilber 2014). In networks, we observe the use of blockchain technology (Faber and Jonker 2018). In governance, we see how the organisation is replaced by cities as the focal entity. Gradually, an organisational landscape emerges in which classical functional organisations are blended with digital and social networks, and the requirements of the value they should deliver is hybridised—requesting to organise more than just one dominant value. In this way, the landscape is shifting towards one that is able to deal with wicked problems.

2 Concerning the Nature of Business Models

Value creation is the central idea of a business model. In essence, a business model describes the way in which value creation is organised between parties (at a certain time, in a certain context, and given the available means). It is common to describe a business model from a perspective where the organisation is the focal point and using three basic building blocks in their construction. The first is the logic of value creation leading to a value proposition: what added value, financially and socially or ecologically as well, is created and for whom? The second building block is the way in which this value proposition is organised. This relates to both activities within the individual organisation as well as activities in cooperation with value chains or network partners. The underlying rationale for this perspective is that parties work together on the basis of competences in order to create a certain product or service. We emphasise that an organised value proposition has tangible and intangible properties almost by definition, giving way to a whole range of so-called product service systems (Tukker 2004; Tukker and Tischner 2006). The third building block concerns one or more revenue models where the costs related to the organisation of the business model are joined with the revenues generated from selling the value proposition. Traditionally, the focus here is on financial profitability. Part of this focus is not to include a number of costs (e.g., social or ecological) in the cost price calculation because these are considered to be externalities (Buchanan and Stubblebine 1962) and hence irrelevant from the business perspective.

These three basic building blocks combined represent a conventional description of a business model. Additionally, the three blocks are configured on the basis of a strategy providing a specific, economic-rational logic to operate in a dedicated, empirical context (De Wit and Meyer 2014; Mintzberg 1987; Mintzberg et al. 1998). Business models are, by definition, value creating configurations of building blocks connected through diverse strategic logics. Although we depart here from a limited number of building blocks, these can vary depending on a multitude of factors. Considering the context, constituents involved, assets and resources available, and assumed needs and expectations of clients and other parties that are involved, the logic and the number of building blocks that comprise a business model is changing. It is of no wonder that typologies of business models abound.

3   A Changing View on Business Models: Strategic Directions

In order to address societal challenges, a change in conventional business model thinking is imminent. This change is inspired by, amongst others, Bidmon and Knab (2018), Schaltegger et al. (2016) but is also fuelled by societal challenges such as the SDGs. It is noteworthy that the change originates simultaneously from academia and practice and thus the relevance of intended changes do reflect a genuine need. These changes of business models, therefore, surpass what is commonly known as business model innovation (e.g., Girotra and Netessine 2014). This particular stream of literature concentrates on the innovation of business models that are inherently organisation-centric and cannot be considered as more than re-configurations of existing revenue models that operate on the premise of cost-benefit analyses.

The quest to create multiple values for multiple actors collaborating in a value cycle over time requires a reconceptualisation of the concept of business models. We observe three movements that should be embedded:

1. The aim to move from single to multiple values creating logic;
2. The move from an organisation-centric supply-chain approach to organising value cycles;
3. Move from a single-actor (clients) perspective to addressing the pluralistic needs of multiple actors (community).

Beginning with the principle that a business model should provide an actionable (value-creating) perspective for the constituents that are involved and enable them to address wicked problems, we contend that the use of conventional business models is no longer appropriate. This follows from the observation that conventional business models are shaped around organisation-centric logics ultimately leading to a cost-benefit analysis. These business models thrive on the premise that they do not have to incorporate certain costs that are designated as 'externalities', be it in the short or long term. Consequently, the actual cost-benefit analysis never reflects the true price of the value that is created. In effect, this approach forms the stepping stone to systemic economic arrangements where prices are artificially kept low for the sake of monetary economic growth. Consider, for example, the actual price of T-shirts, hamburgers, or coffee and what the impact would be if the true costs would be incorporated in the price tags. This critique fuels the need to evaluate and reconsider the building blocks and the logic of value creation underpinning conventional business models.

Considering the ambition to come to sustainable and circular business models, value creation must be founded on three encompassing alternative principles that provide strategic direction:

1. *Lifespan extension*: Using or re-using (raw) materials as carefully and as long as possible where waste is raw material and renewability of (raw) materials comes first;
2. *Servitisation*: The service (functionality) replaces the product and, as a result, manufacturers retain responsibility for and an interest in the development of long-lasting (raw) materials of products throughout their life cycle;
3. *Decomposition/debonding*: The components of which a product consists (so the components of a car, house, highway, etc.) or the substances comprising materials may be disassembled or debonded again—and with ease—and be used as part of a (raw) material or part of a product.

The meaning of value creation changes when applying these principles, leading to a way of working that aims not only to value creation through transformation that is supported by forms of servitisation but to preserve, restore, or revitalise value(s). This leads to a twofold revision of the logic of value creation. First, it becomes an inter-organisational task between various constituents who are involved over time. Second, the aim of value creation broadens in scope giving way to a concept referred to as multi-value creation. That means that more than one value is addressed simultaneously in the process of organising. This subsequently leads to a widening scope with respect to cost-benefit analysis. Non-monetisable values are incorporated into accounting practices. Not only financial return matters, but issues such as social capital, ecological capital, or intellectual capital are also placed on balance sheets, and their developments are reflected in profit and loss statements. A vivid example addressing these changes in accounting can be found, among others, in the practices of Social Return on Investment (SROI; Millar and Hall 2013), the Reporting 3.0 initiative (Reporting 3.0 n.d.), and the more conceptual multi-capital approaches for integrated reporting (Gleeson-White 2014; Porritt 2007). Consequently, a breed of business models emerges based on the above-mentioned movement and principles. We observe, among others, extended product service models, models based on closed loops, models initiated by communities of people, models explicitly addressing public matters (e.g., electricity, care, or food), and models explicitly addressing societal challenges such as poverty, illiteracy, or access to clean drinking water and sanitation. These models adopt different strategic perspectives either explicitly or implicitly. Hence, it becomes relevant to explore the array of emerging strategic perspectives.

3.1 Strategic Perspectives

Strategies are the actionable perspectives that organisations apply to realise and guide their activities. These core activities involve physical activities used for the reuse or transformation of materials (redesign, repair, refurbish, remanufacture, redesignate, recycle, convert, and substitute). Strategies may be purely technical in nature (meaning that they directly correspond to the activities involved) but also concern organisational perspectives on activities or a combination of both. If a move is made towards sustainification, circularity, and inclusivity, then we may assume that this is reflected in strategic choices. We identify six distinct strategies.

1. *Servitisation*: not surprisingly, this is the first of the six strategies. It concerns the process in which the function of a product is sold as a service and ownership of the product (e.g., washing machine, central heating, car, and lawn mower) remains with the original manufacturer. This mainly involves durable consumption goods. This strategy may consequently lead to dematerialisation, which is actually a situation in which someone pays for access to a product's functions but does not obtain ownership. This challenges current revenue models and ownership conventions.
2. *Lifespan extension*: this strategy also reappears. The aim is the pursuit of extending the use of a product (or its parts) for as long as possible, preferably in its original state. This may concern, for instance, office furniture that finds its way to second or third users but also a second

life for vehicles and refurbishment of electronic devices of all sorts. An important challenge of this strategy is to assure the responsibility even in the event that a product has moved to a foreign market. An organisation may achieve this assurance, for instance, by doing that by itself or by involving subsequent supply-chain partners. The consequence of this strategy is that the same product or part can be the object of multiple transactions over its lifespan. Once again, this represents quite a challenge regarding revenue models.

3. *Recycling*: this strategy addresses the partial or complete recovery of raw materials, components, or products with a preservation of value. We distinguish four types of recycling strategy: (a) mechanical, (b) manual, (c) thermal, and (d) chemical. While the conventional connotation is derived from mechanical and manual recycling, a practice steadily emerges that demonstrates the efficacy of chemical recycling in closed loops, aiming for a sustainable solution. It is noteworthy that this may lead to low-value (e.g., old mattresses become insulation material, clothing is turned into low-end carpets) versus high-value recycling (e.g., plastic is sorted in such ways that recycling leads to pure monomer streams of materials). As such, high-value recycling is the prelude to a conversion strategy.

4. *Conversion*: the core of this strategy is the transformation of material remains (such as old tires), emissions (such as carbon-dioxide), and remaining value (such as energy surpluses) in new (basic) products. In other words, this strategy operates at the level of raw materials. This means, for instance, that old tires are transformed into carbon blocks, carbon-dioxide is turned into methane gas, electricity is converted to hydrogen, or fermentation of sewage waste is used for energy. Conversion enables a strategic perspective on closed material loops. Under the premise that it includes both use and design, it contributes to the ultimate aim of the circular economy, specifically, value preservation of raw materials. We observe a lack of conceptualisation regarding determining the impact on sustainification of conversion processes and consequences for the underpinning revenue models.

5. *Substitution*: this strategy concerns the replacement of raw materials by others with particular emphasis on the application of bio-based materials (e.g., stalks of plants for cellulose in paper, grass from road

verges for concrete filler or paper, and hemp for textiles). It is important here to focus on those bio-based materials that do not negatively impact sustainability, which is not the case by definition. For instance, if corn is cultivated with the aim to turn it into bio-diesels, the arable land surface that is required is such that it cannibalises on the production of food. The same can be observed with palm-oil which involves severe deforestation of primeval forests, including loss of biodiversity. While interest to stimulate substitution is growing, the underpinning revenue models remain problematic as long as there is not a true-price-level playing field. This implies that full costs should be incorporated in corresponding conventional revenue models.

6. *Eco-efficiency*: this strategy has been around for quite a while since it was launched by the World Business Council for Sustainable Development in 1992 (Schmidheiny and Business Council for Sustainable Development 1992; Ehrenfeld 2008). It implies the reduction of the use of raw materials, energy, travelling distances, pollution through toxins, use of land, and so on. For a long period of time, this has been considered to be a first step on the way to sustainability. An advantage of this strategy is that it enables clear calculations. Fewer kilometres being travelled directly translates into lower costs for fuel, lower carbon-dioxide emissions, and less maintenance. This approach fits perfectly with conventional business models and requires no changes of existing accountancy practices. Not surprisingly, this has become a popular strategic approach. Yet its pitfall is that even a modest action in this respect can be used without any repercussions to sell 'green' which leads to 'greenwashing' (e.g., Blome et al. 2017).

In practice, we often observe a combination of these strategies which results in a business model that is suited for a specific business in its particular context. This entails the selection of a primary strategy that best fits the value creation objectives. Often, a secondary strategy is selected as the supporting strategy. As a result, most companies work with an amalgamation of various strategic perspectives (see, for instance, Mintzberg et al. 1998; Treacy and Wiersema 1993).

4   A Changing View on Organising Business Models: A Multi-actor Perspective

The overall aim to sustainify, organise circularity, and strive for social inclusivity stimulates a new generation of organising business models that facilitates working with closed loops, collective value creation, and sharing created value. This is contrary to the existing generation of how business models are currently organised; these are entirely based on the linear design of our current economy and thus follow the logic of input-through-put-output. What matters is the production of volume and the speed at which this is realised. Conventional business models offer only minimal accountability with regard to the origins of (raw) materials (and the conditions under which they are procured), the design of composites, and the ecological and social consequences that the extraction of raw materials entails. These are externalised within the limits of a legal framework. The consequence of the changing perspective based on the outlined strategic approaches to value creation invigorates a reconsideration of how value creation is organised by constituents involved in the life cycle. We take the stance that impactful sustainification, either in value chains or closed loops, and a simultaneous realisation of social inclusion is, by definition, the result of a collective inter-organisational effort. To come about this implies a reconsideration of the underlying organisational model.

This implies a transition from a dominant organisation-centric organisational model that has flourished for the past two centuries. While this model is certainly not abandoned, it is complemented by various configurations of network models. These models take different shapes and are fuelled by rapidly emerging developments such as the Internet of Things (IoT) and Internet of Services (IoS). These two developments lead to three distinct organisational concepts enabling the involvement of multiple actors. We make a distinction in (a) organising in a hub and spoke model (also known as Spider Web model versus the Starfish Model; Brafman and Beckstrom 2006), (b) organising in a Mesh Network (also known as the Beehive Model; Benyus 2002), and (c) organising in circles or loops (also known as the Butterfly Model; Ellen MacArthur Foundation 2012, 2013, 2014). In the section below, we briefly typify these organisational models and demonstrate how they lead to alternative concepts for value creation.

4.1 Starfish Model

The hub and spoke, or Spider Web model, is not new in the debate on organisational concepts (Brafman and Beckstrom 2006; Marshall 1890). However, thus far, it has primarily been discussed from an intra-organisational perspective. Originally, the hub is one of the two components in the hub-spoke network model (e.g., O'Kelly 2008). In organisations, its function is that of both a connection between parts of the organisation as well as a relay between the various parts it connects. For instance, in logistics, the hub is often a central depot where packages are gathered that potentially originated from all outskirts of the network and where packages for delivery are sent out. More generically and from an inter-organisational perspective, the hub connects various parts of a single organisation and relays goods and information between different departments or locations. As such, Mintzberg and Van der Heijden (1999) typify hubs as centres of coordination.

From a multi-actor perspective, hubs are considered as collaborative constructs between various constituents. Brafman and Beckstrom (2006) label these types of hubs as the Starfish model. The Starfish model is characterised by a relationship that evolves between peers. Furthermore, this organisational model features built-in organisational redundancy. This implies that, if a part of the organisation has become defunct, other parts have the capacity to take over the lost functionality. This contrasts with the original Spider Web model in which the spider is perceived as the hierarchical superior position in the web (Brafman and Beckstrom 2006). In the event that the Spider is defect, in principle, the entire organisation might cease functioning. What further sets the Starfish model apart is that its constituents concern a variety of entities. These can be organisations but can also be civilians or governmental and non-governmental organisations that are participating. The perspective on hubs presented in this context goes beyond the inter-organisational or even intra-organisational perspective that has been discussed in the literature (ibid.).

Hubs vary in their forms and sizes from regional networks to networks at the level of city neighbourhoods. They take shape around the function they aim to fulfil; a function that follows from societal challenges that need to be resolved of which the constituents have a shared understanding. Hubs emerge because none of the constituents is individually able to address the topic or needs that are created from the topic or concern. The need requires collective, coordinated action. Fulfilling the need exceeds the capabilities and competencies of the individual constituents. Needs that hubs typically address range from fulfilling societal needs such as energy, health care, and waste management to city-based gardening or action-based learning to school dropouts. The hub, as the centrepiece of this form of organising, takes the role of coordinator of actions of its constituents. While hubs are positioned in the centre of a network of activities, they do not, by definition, correspond to a single organisation. The coordinating role may be simultaneously fulfilled by constituents from diverse organisations.

Additionally, various motives are distinguishable around which hubs take shape. For instance, hubs have been observed that emerge around a guiding principle or design such as the circular economy (e.g., Wirth 2014; Park et al. 2010; Winkler 2011) or an open-source principle (e.g., Birtchnell and Urry 2013). Other hubs develop from a shared desire to create a (societal) difference, taking a specific theme (e.g., transition impact), function (e.g., creating mobility), or technology (e.g., 3D printing) as a starting point. A common denominator is the strive to address societal challenges whereby hubs focus on both social and material issues. Value creation in network configurations involving hubs is realised through the coordinated actions of its constituents. The values that are thus created are values that they share (e.g., Porritt 2007).

4.2 Beehive Model

The Beehive model originated in the context of information and communication technology. In this 'world', the 'mesh' concept refers to so-called rich interconnections among devices or nodes (Toh 2001). 'Rich' means that devices principally can connect to any other device that is in the neighbourhood. 'A mesh network is a local network topology in which the infrastructure nodes (i.e., bridges, switches, and other infrastructure devices) connect directly, dynamically, and non-hierarchically to as many other nodes as possible and cooperate with one another to efficiently route data from/to clients' (Wikipedia 2018). A mesh network consists of clients, routers and gateways. Clients are often laptops, cell phones, and other wireless devices while the mesh routers forward traffic to and from the gateways which may, but need not, be connected to the Internet. A mesh network is reliable and offers redundancy in the access to capacity. This model of organising can also be found in nature, for example, how bees organise their colony.

Bees live in hives making use of a functional way of organising. Each colony consists of three types of bees, each with a distinct task. The queen lays eggs, the male drones fertilise them, and the female workers—representing the majority of a colony—gather food and care for the breeding system. Bees evolve in their short life spans to do various tasks. While aging, workers take other tasks upon themselves. At the beginning of their lives, they feed the larvae; next, they operate as the hive air conditioner, using their wings to ventilate; subsequently, they take care of cleaning the hive; finally, they participate in the gathering of food outside of the hive. The way a beehive is organised resembles the working of a mesh network. Similarly, there is redundancy throughout the population of bees in the hive, tasks are interchangeable within the colony, and there is no specific central coordinating mechanism that rules them. The fulcrum of value creation in a beehive is the routine of breeding bees and, as such, keep the colony alive during the relatively short season. In order to feed the new breed and survive winter, honey is gathered and stockpiled. Since the queen is the nucleus in this process, she is maximally pampered and courted. The essence is survival of the colony and, consequently, the queen. In both the mesh ICT network and the way of organising of a beehive, there is no hierarchical functional way of organising in place. Since maintaining the system's functionality is quintessential, tasks are interchangeable similar to nodes or bees.

4.3 Butterfly Model

The Butterfly Model is based on the notion of 'loops'. A loop is a circular organisational approach in which the fulfilment of needs and expectations is realised through a series of interlinked activities. Loops come in different shapes and sizes and are grounded on an industrial as well as a biological foundation.[1] The industrial foundation begins from the premise of using ores and minerals as the basis of industrial materials. The biological foundation is based on the assumption that materials are repeatedly subject to conversion and substitution since they are decomposed and reduced. The result is a new 'raw' material, forming the building blocks for biological life. This subsequently offers ample ground for the next cycle of bio-based materials. The concept of loops contrasts with the classical linear model of fulfilment where materials are put to use in a take-make-waste approach with a deliberate beginning and end. In this approach, materials are deliberately subject to the principal of obsolescence (London 1932; Stevens 1960).

The assumption for the Butterfly Model is that these two 'streams' should be addressed simultaneously. The closed-loop model has emerged from the discipline of industrial ecology (also known as industrial symbiosis) in which the functioning of ecosystems has been used as an exemplar for industrial processes and systems. This is also known under the headers of biomimicry (Benyus 2002), the blue-economy (Pauli 2010, 2016, 2017), and cradle-to-cradle (McDonough and Braungart 2002). In essence, the open-loop model is based on a non-direct feedback approach in which, consequently, the output of the system is neither measured nor fed-back into the loop.

We take the stance that both loop approaches are quintessential in organising a different economic system. When combining several of these loops, a system emerges with certain properties. This leads to an array of loops creating a systems approach in which open and closed loops are intertwined. This is a premise based on addressing sustainification, circularity, and inclusivity. The closed-loop model enables having control over the (raw) materials, their use during the life cycle, the transformation, and the quality. However, not all materials maintain their original state. Just consider, for instance, vegetables, petrol, and cement. These materials are transformed in the process of being used and do not return to their initial state. The implication is that such materials cannot be used in a closed loop. Instead, the open loop provides structure to incorporate, classify, and redistribute materials from different provenances. As such, an open loop forms a platform that enables asset management. Since both types of loops are often in use in a complementary way in the actual economic system, the consequence is that sustainification, circularity, and inclusivity should be embedded in both types. This gives way to a 'family' of activities commonly known as the RE's.

1. *Redesign*: Here, the key question is if the components comprising a product (so a car, house, or a polymer, etc.) can be salvaged with ease meaning it can be taken apart and altered without too much loss of material and 'costs' (energy, labour, etc.). This calls for new ways of design.
2. *Repair*: the key is to maintain and reuse existing products with limited modification and possible upgrade with the aim of lifetime extension;
3. *Refurbish*: the key is to upgrade and update products and spare-parts with the aim to create a second life and afford the possibility to put them on the market 'as new';
4. *Remanufacture*: concerns the re-fabrication of an entire product with the reuse of second-hand materials and parts;
5. *Repurpose*: products, parts, and possibly raw materials are used in different applications;
6. *Recycle*: reclaiming (raw) materials with their reuse in mind. This means that materials are salvaged preferably with a high value, making them as good as new;

Besides this conventional typology, we add two more activities, namely:

7. *Conversion*: concerns the transformation of material and waste in new materials. For example, carbon-dioxide converted into methane or electricity that is used to make hydrogen;
8. *Substitution*: strive towards the replacement of conventional raw materials by sustainable or bio-based materials. Think, for instance, about tomato foliage as a substitute for cellulose for paper production or using citrus peels to extract fragrances and aromatics.

In the Butterfly Model, value creation takes shape in the eight activities distributed across closed and open loops as well as bio-based and industrial materials. The activities are not exclusive to one specific loop or material but may apply to both. This implies that the concept of value creation can have different connotations depending on the loop and the available material. This raises the question if the historically emerged connotation of value creation—primarily based upon the notion of industrial transformation—is still applicable in these organisational models regarding the focus on sustainability, circularity, and inclusivity. For example, conversion can occur with bio-based material in both a closed and an open loop. Furthermore, the idea of loops necessitates a broader range of constituents over time. This is reinforced by the observation that the distinction between materials and the operations inflicted on these implies the involvement of distinct specialists, technologies, and knowledge.

4.4 A Different Approach to Organising Value Creation

The presented organisational models (Starfish Model, Beehive Model, Butterfly Model) provide a series of alternatives for the dominant design of the linear organisational model. This is relevant since the ambition to organise with a different set of values in mind requires fundamentally different models of organising. The past has abundantly shown that the linear model thrives on an organisation-centric approach aiming at efficiency and achieving this through the externalisation of social and ecological aspects that are stipulated in legal frameworks. Furthermore, the linear model leads to strategic behaviour based on functional specialisation. If the aim is to create a series of new, sustainable business models while considering social challenges and changing expectations from society towards companies, these organisational models offer a rich and promising breeding ground for developing a new series of business models.

5 A Brief Typology of Emerging Business Model Archetypes

Elaborating on these organisational models, we conceptualise three business model archetypes. These archetypes are elaborated and illustrated by giving some examples. We refrain from providing a more conceptual analysis in this contribution given the fact that such an analysis would require empirical research that is more thorough. Here, we introduce the following archetypes based upon a distinct perspective on value creation:

1. *Sustanification*, based on asset management;
2. *Inclusivity*, based on community management;
3. *Circularity*, based on industrial and bio-based material management.

The three archetypes originate from different perspectives on value creation and lead to the alternative construction of business models.

The leading principle of the first archetype of business models is to make use of the existing functionality of assets as much as possible and thus make use of their idle capacity. The central assumption here is that products are underused and thus have so-called idle capacity. In applying the concept of servitisation (Tukker 2004), this idle capacity is used efficiently by providing access to the surplus of functionality to a broader audience. An implication of servitisation is that the ownership of products does not change but remains with the producer or service delivery agent. The underlying idea is that this will afford the opportunity for this entity to maintain the functionality of the product and make sure its life expectancy is prolonged, preferably at low costs, eventually leading to a decrease in the need of resources. Good examples are the following companies: Floow2 (Netherlands), BlaBlaCar (France), and VéloLib (France).

The perspective of inclusivity focuses in particular on the social aspects of value creation, taking the creation of a community as the pivot-point. Core to the community-based business models is the notion that value creation is realised because a community addresses one or more wicked problems that impact their daily lives. A community specifically emerges around the current issue(s). Considering the support of the IoT and the IoS and given the observed trend that an increasing number of people in society lead the undertaking of such an endeavour, it becomes almost common to establish an energy co-operative, a shared mobility platform, or a direct food-distribution hub. This leads to a redefinition and reconfiguration of the roles of citizens, businesses, and governments in the assurance of the commons (Ostrom 2014). Examples of this type of business model are: Bedzed (United Kingdom), Samsø Island energy generation (Denmark), or the co-operative Windpark Nijmegen (Netherlands).

The perspective of circularity finds its origin in the performance of assets (Stahel 1982). Over time and under the influence of many authors (among others, McDonough and Braungart 2002; Pauli 2010; Ellen MacArthur Foundation 2012), this evolved into the ambition to aim for value preservation of materials. It implies not only a closed loop of materials but also a corresponding design enabling the longevity and quality preservation of materials being applied with minimum leakage and loss. We take the stance that, most probably, this is not the end of the 'value' journey specifically for this business model archetype. Eloquent examples of the circularity archetype are Pooling Partners (Netherlands), Roof2Roof (Netherlands), Interface (United States of America), Willemen Groep (Belgium), and Umicore (Belgium). In the near future and considering the growing call upon organisations to engage in societal challenges, we may expect that a focus on preservation is insufficient and will probably be extended towards restorative and regenerative forms for value creation.

6 On the Changing Nature of Value Creation in the Economy

An economy in transition is changing and expanding the perspective on value creation. First and foremost, the transition we are currently witnessing encompasses a broadening view on the matter, going from single towards multiple value creation. As already indicated, McVea and Freeman (2005) provide the theoretical foundation for the concept of value creation. Considering this, multiple value creation implies the generation of values for multiple constituents occurs in parallel. While value creation is not new to business strategy, *multiple* value creation *is* relatively new to the business arena. However, it appears as if the ideas behind it have been around for quite a while. In 1960, Frederick already touched on the premise of multiple value creation: 'Social responsibility in the final analysis implies a public posture toward society's economic and human resources and a willingness to see that those resources are used for broad social ends and not simply for the narrowly circumscribed interests of private persons and firms' (Frederick 1960, p. 60). The use of resources must create value for a number of stakeholders, not just those at the end of the line. Frederick maintains that business has been charged with this responsibility because, in essence, it has been given the keys to drive the economy and must, therefore, concern itself not just with its destination but with that of its passengers as well. Seemingly a man ahead of his time, Frederick (1960) holds that, rather than hoping that the need or pressure to pursue profit or individual interests will disappear, institutional solutions should be sought that can steer these efforts in other social directions as well. This change will not occur naturally but will require the 'constant tinkering with institutional mechanisms of society' (Frederick 1960, p. 61).

Elbing (1970) echoes and elaborates on Frederick's perspective and contends that the function of business is not purely economic and cannot adequately be analysed as such. According to Elbing, it is the responsibility of society and stakeholders to measure an organisation's success not only in economic but also in social terms: 'In recognition of the network of social consequences of business activity we can no longer measure the influence of business solely in terms of economic well-being and national wealth. The ultimate purpose of business, as of any institution in society, is to be "socially profitable". The firm must be appraised, then, in terms of its total contribution to society, not merely its economic contribution' (Elbing 1970, p. 83).

Emerson et al. (2004) introduce another term, 'blended value', that means essentially the same thing, though they emphasise the collaboration between organisations to a greater degree. They define blended value as value that is 'generated from the combined interplay between the component parts of economic, social and environmental performance. All firms…create Blended Value—the only issue up for debate is the degree to which they maximize the component elements of value…' (Emerson et al. 2004, p. 13). This implies that distinct types of value cannot be separated based on the type of business—profit, non-profit, investment—but that types of business models are faced with their own obstacles in optimising these values during performance. This gives way to the introduction of the concept of multiple value creation.

Multiple value creation and blended value are fairly new terms to the vernacular of academia and business. However, the ideas that gave rise to their contemporary interpretation are not new. They can be traced to intellectual thought concerning value creation, business ethics, human values, responsibility, and so on. What has happened is that all of these ideas have been combined to essentially form the basis for a concept that has been developed in response to the societal challenges and wicked problems. Against this background, we postulate that multiple value creation needs to evolve and should be elaborated into a dimension that runs from—and encapsulates—value creation via value preservation to value restoration.

1. *Value creation* in the linear economy is realised through the transformation of materials in which sustainability is realised through (re)design (amongst others, through modularity, standardisation), eco-efficiency, life-cycle analysis, and servitisation (Product Service Systems / Product as a Service).
2. *Value preservation*, seen as the key of the circular economy, operates through organising various types of loops in which value is created through recycling, conversion, and substitution of materials.
3. *Value restoration* reveals two different streams, specifically, restorative and regenerative forms of value creation, that take shape around the idea that businesses contribute more to the societal challenges than sustanification of ongoing practices or the preservation of materials.

We argue that the above provided overview offers grounds for a tentative typology of five different economies: (a) a depletion economy, (b) a sustainified economy, (c) a circular economy, (d) a restorative economy, and finally, (e) regenerative economy. Since the first three economies are already addressed in the previous text, we limit ourselves to a brief description of the latter two. In a restorative economy (adopted from Hawken 2010), success and viability is determined by the ability to integrate with or replicate cyclical ecological systems in its means of production and distribution. In such an economy, restoring the environment and making money would be the same process. The regenerative economy is an economic system that works to regenerate capital assets (Lovins 2013). A capital asset is an asset that provides goods and/or services that are required for or contribute to human well-being. Ultimately, it addresses a transition about seeing the world in a different way—a shift to an ecological world view in which nature provides the foundations for a model. In the regenerative process that defines thriving, living systems must define the economic system itself. This tentative typology shows that the debate on sustanification and circularity needs to be broadened beyond the dominant economic design. Current efforts based on eco-efficiency, sustainification through life-cycle analysis, and designing in terms of circularity are, in the end, still not addressing economic fundamentals.

7 Discussion and Conclusions

Facing a multitude of societal challenges, including the quest for a sustainable development, a circular economy, and inclusiveness of people, the transition of society is set in motion. Actors throughout society, including businesses, encounter a plethora of wicked problems when addressing the challenges raised by this transition. Fundamental to these wicked problems is that they entail a wide variety of distinct, yet intertwined, values. This calls for a wider approach to value creation beyond the contemporary perspective that societal actors are used to applying regarding this topic. With value creation being key in business models, one might assume that businesses could tackle such wicked problems with ease. However, this is not the case due to two main shortcomings. First, thus far, business models have only provided piecemeal improvements and patching solutions to societal challenges. We have shown that this is instigated chiefly because of a misalignment between the characteristics of the wicked problems and the logics that drive value creation in conventional business models. Second, conventional business models are inherently organisation-centric while the wicked problems we face demand collaboration between a variety of constituents throughout society. Both shortcomings fuel the rise of a new generation of business models; business models that are specifically pieced together to address one or more of the wicked problems comprising the societal challenges.

We have presented three distinct archetypes of business models that address societal challenges yet operate differently. Servitisation business models focus on sustainification and aim to make more efficient and effective use of available assets. Value creation is realised through alleviating the need for resources. Social inclusivity resides in the middle of community-based business models. It aims to create a wide array of social values. Finally, circular business models fundamentally question current product designs and the ways that materials are used to produce these. These models strive for the preservation of materials and avoiding system leakages. In this archetype, value creation equals value preservation. Together, the three archetypes take their specific place in and give shape to the transition of society.

The outlined societal transition sets the stage for intertwined economic and the businesses challenges. We have addressed only a small number of the implications for businesses and business models being part of this transition such as how a new generation of business models deals with value creation considering identified societal challenges. These changes open a debate on the place that business models assume on a continuum ranging from depletion via eco-efficiency (or sustainification) and circularity (focusing on value preservation) towards value restoration and regeneration economies. The nature of business models that capture the two latter forms of value creation remains unaddressed in this contribution. We can only assume that an ongoing and intriguing debate is ahead.

Notes

1. The distinction between industrial and bio-based material is not entirely correct. What is meant here is that a distinction is made between materials that are man-made from ores and minerals, denoted as industrial, and materials that are composites of materials with a biological origin. Both types of materials are essentially synthesised by humans, possibly on an industrial scale.

References

Benyus, Janine M. 2002. *Biomimicry: Innovation Inspired by Nature*. New York: Harper Perennial.

Bidmon, Christina M., and Sebastian F. Knab. 2018. The Three Roles of Business Models in Societal Transitions: New Linkages Between Business Model and Transition Research. *Journal of Cleaner Production* 178 (Mar.): 903–916. https://doi.org/10.1016/j.jclepro.2017.12.198.

Birtchnell, Thomas, and John Urry. 2013. Fabricating Futures and the Movement of Objects. *Mobilities* 8 (3): 388–405. https://doi.org/10.1080/17450101.2012.745697.

Blome, Constantin, Kai Foerstl, and Martin Schleper. 2017. Antecedents of Green Supplier Championing and Greenwashing: An Empirical Study on Leadership and Ethical Incentives. *Journal of Cleaner Production* 152 (May): 339–350. https://doi.org/10.1016/j.jclepro.2017.03.052.

Botsman, Rachel, and Roo Rogers. 2011. *What's Mine is Yours: How Collaborative Consumption is Changing the Way We Live*. London: Collins.

Brafman, Ori, and Rod Beckstrom. 2006. *The Starfish and the Spider: The Unstoppable Power of Leaderless Organizations*. New York: Portfolio/Penguin Group.

Buchanan, James M., and Wm. Craig Stubblebine. 1962. Externality. *Economica* 29 (116): 371–384. https://doi.org/10.2307/2551386.

Churchman, C. West. 1967. Wicked Problems. *Management Science* 14 (4): B-141–B-241.

Ehrenfeld, John R. 2008. Eco-efficiency: Philosophy, Theory, and Tools. *Journal of Industrial Ecology* 9 (4): 6–8. https://doi.org/10.1162/108819805775248070.

Elbing, Alvar O. 1970. The Value Issue of Business: The Responsibility of the Businessman. *The Academy of Management Journal* 13 (1): 79–89. https://doi.org/10.2307/254927.

Ellen MacArthur Foundation. 2012. Towards the Circular Economy Vol. 1: Economic and Business Rationale for an Accelerated Transition. Cowes, UK: Ellen MacArthur Foundation. https://www.ellenmacarthurfoundation.org/assets/downloads/publications/Ellen-MacArthur-Foundation-Towards-the-Circular-Economy-vol.1.pdf.

———. 2013. Towards the Circular Economy Vol. 2: Opportunities for the Consumer Goods Sector. Cowes, UK: Ellen Mac Arthur Foundation. https://www.ellenmacarthurfoundation.org/assets/downloads/publications/TCE_Report-2013.pdf.

———. 2014. *Towards the Circular Economy Vol. 3: Accelerating the Scale-Up across Global Supply-Chains*. Cowes, UK: Ellen Mac Arthur Foundation. https://www.ellenmacarthurfoundation.org/assets/downloads/publications/Towards-the-circular-economy-volume-3.pdf.

Emerson, Jed, Sheila Bonini, and Kim Brehm. 2004. The Blended Value Map. www.blendedvalue.org; http://www.blendedvalue.org/wp-content/uploads/2004/02/pdf-bv-map.pdf.

European Commission. 2018. *Action Plan: Financing Sustainable Growth*. European Commission. https://www.duurzaambedrijfsleven.nl/download/ec-action-plan-financing-sustainable-growth.pdf.

Faber, N.R., and J. Jonker. 2015. A Hub Is a Hub, Not a Network: Towards a Typology of Hubs Framed as a Transferor for Sustainable Development. *Global Cleaner Production and Sustainable Consumption Conference*, Sitges, Spain.

Faber, Niels, and Jan Jonker. 2018. At Your Service: How Can Blockchain Be Used to Address Societal Challenges? In *Implication of the Blockchain*, ed. Horst Treiblmaier and Roman Beck. London: Palgrave Macmillan.

Frederick, William C. 1960. The Growing Concern over Business Responsibility. *California Management Review* 2 (4): 54–61. https://doi.org/10.2307/41165405.

Girotra, Karan, and Serguei Netessine. 2014. Four Paths to Business Model Innovation. *Harvard Business Review* 92 (7–8): 96–103.

Gleeson-White, Jane. 2014. *Six Capitals: The Revolution Capitalism Has to Have—Or Can Accountants Save the Planet?* Sydney: Allen & Unwin.

Habermas, Jürgen. 1981. *Theory of Communicative Action, Volume One: Reason and the Rationalization of Society*. Translated by Thomas A. McCarthy. Vol. 1., 2 vols. Boston, MA: Beacon Press.

Hawken, Paul. 2010. *The Ecology of Commerce Revised Edition: A Declaration of Sustainability*. Rev. ed. New York: Harper Business.

Laloux, Frederic, and Ken Wilber. 2014. *Reinventing Organizations*. 1st ed. Brussels: Nelson Parker.

London, Bernard. 1932. *Ending the Depression Through Planned Obsolescence*. New York, N.Y: n.p.

Lovins, Hunter. 2013. The Business Case for Sustainability. *Natural Capitalism Solutions* (blog), October 15, 2013. https://natcapsolutions.org/15-oct-2013-tinley-park-il-illinois-green-business-association-igba-summit/.

Marshall, Alfred. 1890. *Principles of Economics*. London: Macmillan.

McDonough, W., and M. Braungart. 2002. *Cradle to Cradle: Remaking the Way We Make Things*. New York: North Point Press.

McVea, John F., and R. Edward Freeman. 2005. A Names-and-Faces Approach to Stakeholder Management: How Focusing on Stakeholders as Individuals Can Bring Ethics and Entrepreneurial Strategy Together. *Journal of Management Inquiry* 14 (1): 57–69. https://doi.org/10.1177/1056492 604270799.

Millar, Ross, and Kelly Hall. 2013. Social Return on Investment (SROI) and Performance Measurement. *Public Management Review* 15 (6): 923–941. https://doi.org/10.1080/14719037.2012.698857.

Mintzberg, Henry. 1987. The Strategy Concept I: Five Ps for Strategy. *California Management Review* 30 (1): 11–24.

Mintzberg, Henry, and Ludo Van der Heyden. 1999. Organigraphs: Drawing How Companies Really Work. *Harvard Business Review* 77 (5): 87–94.

Mintzberg, Henry, Bruce Ahlstrand, and Joseph Lampel. 1998. *Strategy Safari—A Guided Tour Through the Wilds of Strategic Management*. New York: The Free Press.

O'Kelly, Morton E. 2008. A Geographer's Analysis of Hub-and-Spoke Networks. In *Transport: Critical Essays in Human Geography*, ed. Susan Hanson and Mei-po Kwan, 335–350. Aldershot and Burlington, VT: Ashgate.

Ostrom, Elinor. 2014. Do Institutions for Collective Action Evolve? *Journal of Bioeconomics* 16 (1): 3–30. https://doi.org/10.1007/s10818-013-9154-8.

Park, Jacob, Joseph Sarkis, and Zhaohui Wu. 2010. Creating Integrated Business and Environmental Value within the Context of China's Circular Economy and Ecological Modernization. *Journal of Cleaner Production* 18 (15): 1494–1501. https://doi.org/10.1016/j.jclepro.2010.06.001.

Pauli, Gunter. 2010. *Blue Economy-10 Years, 100 Innovations, 100 Million Jobs*. Taos, NM: Paradigm Publications.

———. 2016. *The Blue Economy: 200 Projects Implemented US$ 4 Billion Invested 3 Million Jobs Created*. New Delhi: Academic Foundation.

———. 2017. *The Blue Economy 3.0: The Marriage of Science, Innovation and Entrepreneurship Creates a New Business Model That Transforms Society*. XLIBRIS.

Porritt, Jonathan. 2007. *Capitalism as If the World Matters*. London: Routledge.

Reporting 3.0. n.d. REPORTING 3.0. *REPORTING 3.0*. Accessed April 19, 2018. https://reporting3.org/.

Rittel, Horst W.J., and Melvin M. Webber. 1973. Dilemmas in a General Theory of Planning. *Policy Sciences* 4 (2): 155–169. https://doi.org/10.1007/BF01405730.

Schaltegger, Stefan, Erik G. Hansen, and Florian Lüdeke-Freund. 2016. Business Models for Sustainability, Business Models for Sustainability: Origins, Present Research, and Future Avenues, Origins, Present Research, and Future Avenues. *Organization & Environment* 29 (1): 3–10. https://doi.org/10.1177/1086026615599806.

Schmidheiny, Stephan, and Business Council for Sustainable Development. 1992. *Changing Course: A Global Business Perspective on Development and the Environment*. English Language ed. Cambridge, MA: The MIT Press.

Simon, Herbert A. 1969. *The Sciences of the Artificial*. Cambridge, MA: The MIT Press.

Stahel, Walter R. 1982. The Product-Life Factor. In *Inquiry into the Nature of Sustainable Societies: The Role of the Private Sector*, ed. Susan Grinton Orr, 72–104. HARC.

Stevens, Brooks. 1960. Planned Obsolescence. *The Rotarian*, February.

Sundararajan, Arun. 2016. *The Sharing Economy: The End of Employment and the Rise of Crowd-Based Capitalism*. Cambridge, MA: MIT Press.

Toh, Chai K. 2001. *Ad Hoc Mobile Wireless Networks: Protocols and Systems*. 1st ed. Upper Saddle River, NJ: Prentice Hall.

Treacy, Michael, and Fred Wiersema. 1993. Customer Intimacy and Other Value Disciplines. *Harvard Business Review* 71 (Jan.–Feb.): 84–93.

Tukker, Arnold. 2004. Eight Types of Product–service System: Eight Ways to Sustainability? Experiences from SusProNet. *Business Strategy and the Environment* 13 (4): 246–260. https://doi.org/10.1002/bse.414.

Tukker, Arnold, and Ursula Tischner. 2006. Product-Services as a Research Field: Past, Present and Future. Reflections from a Decade of Research. *Journal of Cleaner Production* 14 (17): 1552–1556. https://doi.org/10.1016/j.jclepro.2006.01.022.

UNEP, ed. 2011. *Decoupling Natural Resource Use and Environmental Impacts from Economic Growth*. Kenya: UNEP.

United Nations. 2015. Sustainable Development Goals—United Nations. *United Nations Sustainable Development* (blog), 2015. http://www.un.org/sustainabledevelopment/sustainable-development-goals/.

WCED. 1987. *Our Common Future*. New York: Oxford United Press.

Wikipedia. 2018. Mesh Networking. *Wikipedia*. https://en.wikipedia.org/w/index.php?title=Mesh_networking&oldid=832237349.

Winkler, H. 2011. Closed-Loop Production Systems—A Sustainable Supply Chain Approach. *CIRP Journal of Manufacturing Science and Technology, Production Networks Sustainability* 4 (3): 243–246. https://doi.org/10.1016/j.cirpj.2011.05.001.

Wirth, Steffen. 2014. Communities Matter: Institutional Preconditions for Community Renewable Energy. *Energy Policy* 70 (July): 236–246. https://doi.org/10.1016/j.enpol.2014.03.021.

Wit, Bob de, and Ron Meyer. 2014. *Strategy*. Andover.

7

Managing Innovation for Circular Industrial Systems

Sofia Ritzén

Economic growth stands today in direct relation to resource consumption, few businesses grow without an increased consumption of material and energy. This is in terms directly related to a number of the largest challenges we are causing for meeting a sustainable development: depletion of resources in itself and the ecological and social harmful impacts such as acidification, ecosystem disturbances on land and in the sea, the greenhouse gas effect, and unfair resource distribution with poverty as an effect. The concept of circular economy has attracted a much greater interest as a solution for meeting these challenges and the concept contests the strict relation between economic growth and resource consumption. The increasing interest in circular economy is seen by the emergence of a number of new organizations focusing on it. The positioning of established well-reputed consultancy firms, the efforts of lobby organizations, the establishment of research projects in academia and not least the

---

S. Ritzén (✉)
Integrated Product Development, Department of Machine Design, KTH Royal Institute of Technology, Stockholm, Sweden
e-mail: ritzen@kth.se

efforts taken by national agencies worldwide in national strategies and societal development programs signal that it is gaining great attention. In addition, there is a great interest in circular economy also in the corporate world, probably driven by the model promising proactive measures for sustainable development combined with continued business competitiveness. Similar reasons are likely for any kind of organization or stakeholder putting forward circular economy, it is a proactive strategy for mitigating the severe problems that our overconsumption of natural resources is causing and it is solution oriented. As circular economy has become a strong component of national and global strategies for a sustainable development and with the increasing interest in the corporate world it is motivated to develop a more profound understanding of the concept. There is a need to go from the somewhat abstract and often too ideological description of the concept that meets various stakeholders in many contexts and to define critical measures for a transition to a circular economy. Such measures relate both to an understanding of the critical parameters of a circular system and identifying critical actions for an organization.

This chapter will give a description of what the concept of circular economy is and it will illustrate the complexity of the concept and the challenges connected to a transformation to circular economy. How the unsustainable resource consumption that we see today drives a concept such as the circular economy forward will be outlined and the complexity of the concept will be reflected upon. An attempt to identify the critical resource efficiency parameters and the business parameters these relate to will be described, outlining a framework for a manufacturing firm to become inspired from in their transition to a circular economy. Two illustrations from industry will complement this more abstract reflection on the circular economy, not only underlining its complexity but also highlighting the opportunities it affords. In addition, possible insecurities in relation to the actual sustainability aspects of the concept will be highlighted, and the claim will be made that the circular economy is about integrating sustainable development and business development and that this drives the need to develop a capability in industrial organizations not only to innovate new product service systems for a sustainable development but also to new business models. Therefore, the final part of this chapter will outline a few, though highly critical issues for innovation capabilities that are supportive, or even necessary, for a circular economy transition in industry.

1 Defining the Concept Circular Economy

One meaning of *economy* is that it is the careful management of available resources (Oxford Dictionaries 2018). Following on from this, a circular economy is the management of closed flows of resources, meaning that resources are kept at their highest value as long as possible and where ingoing resources as well as waste, emissions, and energy leakage are minimized. Ingoing resources are circulated in order to be used over and over again. Closing resource flows, creating material loops, require a proactive design of product service systems so that physical goods last for a long time; products and components are reused, maintained, repaired, refurbished, remanufactured; and materials are recycled. A circular economy is in contrast to a linear model, where physical goods are produced, used, and wasted. The fundamental core of a circular economy is the closing of resource flows, however, to make it a desirable, feasible, and viable concept, it must be related to the business model of the organizations delivering the physical goods. Reusing, maintaining, repairing, refurbishing, remanufacturing, and recycling must be a competitive business. Defining the business model is consequently the other fundamental part of the core of the circular economy.

In current economic systems, at least in industrialized market economies, the dominant logic of a manufacturing company is that it delivers its product in exchange for money. In a circular economy this logic has to be changed, emphasizing the need to focus on value delivery instead of product delivery. The detachment of economic growth from consumption of natural resources requires larger shifts in the society than that manufacturing firms detach their business from delivering physical goods, which is also a statement by Kirchherr et al. (2017). They make an interesting analysis of how circular economy has been conceptualized so far and find that the concept of circular economy is still many times oversimplified. The critical systemic shift is often neglected in studies on circular economy and it is oversimplified when recycling activities are seen as turning an organization into a circular economy. They also see that many scholars do not relate the concept to sustainable development and that others do not relate the concept to the profitability of organizations, though both of these aspects are, as described above, the very core of a circular economy. Variations in the definition of circular economy are perhaps not a great problem, as different conceptualization might be purposeful depending on the context; however, the definition of circular economy by Kirchherr et al. (2017) is well worth referring to:

> A circular economy describes an economic system that is based on business models which replace the 'end-of-life' concept with reducing, alternatively reusing, recycling and recovering materials in production/distribution and consumption processes, thus operating at the micro level (products, companies, consumers), meso level (eco-industrial parks) and macro level (city, region, nation and beyond), with the aim to accomplish sustainable development, which implies creating environmental quality, economic prosperity and social equity, to the benefit of current and future generations. (Kirchherr et al. 2017, p. 229)

It is especially valuable, and relevant, as a definition since it stresses that it relates to both production and consumption processes. Circular economy will shift locus of product innovation and necessarily increase the co-creation by producers and consumers as a consequence of the integration of technology innovation and business model innovation. Furthermore, they, among a few, stress in their definition that circular economy should aim for sustainability with regard to all the three dimensions of economy, ecology, and social welfare for current and future generation, also stressing the need to include a time perspective. In addition, they relate to several system levels, miso, meso, and macro, underlining the necessity to go between a whole system and its parts and simultaneously make changes at different levels. The circular economy is not merely on management of resources in one specific product service system but really relate to the whole innovation ecosystem of value deliveries and to every stakeholder in society. In regard to this it is important to outline all the aspects that must be considered for a transition to a circular economy and all the perspectives that need to be adopted.

An example of a product service system that has, at least in several countries, reached a certain stage of a circular economy is cans for beverages. They are produced in aluminum, glass, or polyethylene (PET) and in the countries referred to here, cans are collected after use. Glass bottles are cleaned and used again for approximately 20 times until they are worn out (and lost on the way often ending up in deposit) when the material goes back to recycling. Aluminum cans are recycled and new cans can be produced, in the same way as PET bottles. The collection system is accomplished by a refund system, when buying a can a fee is added to the price, which is given back to the customer on return of the can at specific collection sites. The refund is paid out by a store or the like selling beverages. It builds on a strong enough incentive from customers to keep their cans and return them and on the fact that the bottles or cans collected hold enough value that the recycling organization that runs facilities for refunding can be financed by the producing companies buying back the resource. The rate of take back and recycling is also increased by the fact that the value of cans is so high that collection in public areas becomes attractive. The can example is limited in that it partly refers to a product service system where material is recycled and when reused, as for glass bottles, no specific requirements need to be put on the product in order for it to be reusable. The reused bottle is also used for the same function as the original and adoptions are merely concerned with the fact that bottles are inspected on arrival and cleaned before reuse. Yet a limitation with this example is that the market is within national borders. However, the example illustrates the need of multiple actors to jointly define the system, a governmental organization providing the refund function, retail companies to deal with fees and refunds, and producers to bring in supply from different sources, that is, numerous private and public stakeholders are involved. In Sweden as an example the refund is 5–10% or the beverage price—in countries where resources such as glass bottles are more precious a bottle can have a much higher price than the beverage in itself, which in addition illustrates the importance of incentives and user involvement in realizing a circular system.

High technology products are more resource intensive than products in the beverage example. Few products are adapted to a circular economy even if certain raw materials hold such a high value that they are recycled at high rates and by their nature are efficient to recycle as not being degradable. A product, for example, an electric handheld tool is composed of hundreds of components of several different metals and plastics. Material suppliers and sub-suppliers are numerous for the manufacturing firm, each in their hand with numerous customers to satisfy. The complexity of the system is increasing in relation to the different materials used, number of components, variety of technologies, number of markets, and variety in customers and their specific needs and expectations. If the handheld tool is considered in relation to closing material flows, issues connected to supply of basic materials, supply of components, maintainability and serviceability during primary product life, reusability of products, possibility of secondary product lives, take-back systems and incentives of customers to be involved in closing material flows need to be clearly addressed. Keeping track of products, components, and materials is an additional issue that requires conscious data management. Most of these issues mirror the network of different actors in the value chain, often requiring new relationships and new roles in the network.

Quite a common approach in the circular economy literature has been to identify and analyze barriers to a circular economy. It has its justification for finding possible measures for a transition to circular economy, motivated by how innovation is preferably conducted: finding the real problems and needs before developing solutions. Several taxonomies including different categories of barriers are to be found in the literature (e.g., Shi et al. 2008; Kok et al. 2013; Kügler 2016; Andersson Torstensson 2016; Ghisellini et al. 2016; de Jesus and Mendonca 2018). To summarize, these categories are identified and described:

- structural and operational (relating to organization, formal routines, decision-making, control mechanism, and processes within the organization as well as along the value chain);
- financial (relating to the business relevance for a commercial company as well as for the circular economy as a societal shift);
- technological (relating to the actions needed to close material loops in direct relation to developing and producing the product service system but also to use and after-use actions);

- regulatory (relating to local, regional, and national regulation both hindering and supporting closing material loops);
- attitudinal (relating to the change inertia from peoples' unwillingness and inability to change in organizations and the need to see things in new ways).

In the example given above on an electrical handheld tool, the barriers that are created with the changes needed throughout the life cycle of the product relate to all these categories. The organization is functionally structured, frequently with the outcome of less collaboration between, for example, manufacturing and marketing, or between design and sales, which is critical for developing product service systems that become attractive on the market. Goals and measures in the company are most likely not set to support use of less products but they have a business logic whereby selling more physical goods is always better. Suppliers are not given the requirements that come with a circular system and customers are unaware of how circular systems could affect them, both in increased values and in requirements of active changes in their use of the product. Systems for take-back and increased reuse of physical goods do not exist and are not actively supported by the society. Sustainability is not seen as a strategic business matter but one typically organized in a support function ensuring that regulations for manufacturing are met. Though these examples of barriers are somewhat simplified, the intention is to illustrate how complex the change toward a circular economy is.

The research on circular economy mirrors the multiple aspects and perspectives of circular economy, through different points of departure in research projects and through different theoretical assumptions and based on different fields of literature (Merli et al. 2018). Circular economy is, for example, dealt with focusing manufacturing (e.g., Rashid et al. 2013), design concepts (e.g., den Hollander et al. 2017), regulatory measures (e.g., Ranta et al. 2018), policy (e.g., McDowall et al. 2017), and supply chain (e.g., Genovese et al. 2017), beside numerous conceptual publications focus in the concept in general (e.g., Ghisellini et al. 2016; Geissdoerfer et al. 2017; Homrich et al. 2018). Less is published with an innovation management perspective, which is remarkable as the capabilities of orienting between the complex dependencies in circular systems and within the rich networks of actors that circular systems will require, strongly relate to innovation capabilities within firms. In addition, the new innovations that closing material flows will require are often radically new and will break up market logics and supply chains in disruptive ways, putting further emphasis on managing innovation.

2 The Resource Parameters of Circular Economy

Value delivery is in a majority of cases created with some kind of physical goods. Value is often delivered through or by a product and frequently a product is experienced as *the* value. In a successful business, value is exchanged between different parties, and a business is frequently equal to money and physical goods shifting owners. Also, in a pure service business, goods are involved in one way or another, and material as well as energy is consumed even if not directly through deliveries of products. Resource flow is, therefore, relevant to consider in any business matter. From a sustainability perspective resource flow is not only relevant to consider, it is fundamental. Environmental impacts occur during every life phase of a product, from the extraction of natural resources, the production of materials and products, the use of the products, and when the product has reached its end-of-life. The environmental problems that we see today are directly connected to our resource consumption. We overconsume resources making them scarce and more and more difficult to extract, with increased costs both from a monetary and environmental perspective. And the resource consumption results in emissions to land, water, and air. The resource consumption does not only represent ecological unsustainable development, but also social unsustainable development. Resources are unequally distributed between developed and underdeveloped countries, between rich and poor people, and raw material extraction is often connected to an unfair treatment of people characterized by human inequalities through unsafe and unhealthy work environments. In our society, the social effects might not be as obvious, although, the uneven resource usage distribution is a major unsustainability issue. There are numerous figures to be found on resource consumption, all revealing an increase in material consumption and an uneven distribution over the world. One investigation shows, for instance, that the consumption per capita in Europe for the year 2000 was 36 tons, while the consumption in the United States was 68 tons, in Africa 15 tons, and in Asia 14 tons (SERI/Global 2000 2009). Sweden is an interesting case, as real poverty by definition is non-existent in this country now, but the country has a population leaving large environmental footprint. Sustainable development requires a paradigmatic change in how resources are used, which is a driving force for better understanding the connection between resource flows and business or value transitions. A great challenge is to understand how to share resources and to develop the way of living, and consuming, in well-developed countries so that reduced resource usage is not experienced as a retrograde development and loss of welfare.

One of the first researchers addressing circular economy as a critical approach to a sustainable development was Walter Stahel (Stahel 1982) who wrote about the spiral loop system, addressing the need to keep products in use as long as possible, and requiring actions, such as repairing, reusing, reconditioning, and recycling. The idea of referring to a number of R's has been used numerous times since then with various interpretations of the necessary R's. Nußholz (2017) investigates circular economy from the perspective of the product life cycle and resource efficiency and defines actions for increasing resource efficiency at each main stage of a life cycle. These actions are somewhat overlapping, for example, reducing the demand for new material during material extraction could have the same reducing effect as increasing life span during the use phase, which is not a problem. More remarkable is that energy consumption or transports are not included despite being so critical for the life cycle assessments of products and services. However, the life cycle perspective is critical and complements many sources on circular economy, especially in relation to the parameters of resource efficiency that a manufacturing firm has to consider. The actions prescribed in the circular economy literature are often a mixture of resource efficiency increasing actions, business models on a conceptual level, or measures required for defining circular systems. Analyzing a number of general sources on circular

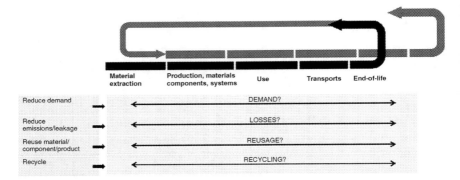

Fig. 7.1 The critical resource efficiency parameters in relation to the life cycle perspective of a physical product

economy, including the various R-descriptions inspired by Nußholz (2017) stressing the life cycle perspective, it is here stressed that the resource parameters that need to be addressed in developing circular systems could be limited to demand, losses, reuse, and recycling, as also described Fig. 7.1.

3 The Business Parameters of Circular Economy

A business can be said to be the creation of a value that is economically appropriated by the company delivering the value and that meets a need or solves a customer's problem. When the cost of the creation and the delivery of the value is less than what the customer pays for it, a successful business exists. A business *model* is the conceptual logic of how the firm creates and appropriates this economic value (Linder and Williander 2017). A business model can also be said to be the device that operationalizes the strategies of a company and clarifies how goals for the business in hand might be reached. A business model comprises a number of components, differing in their number and level of analysis in different sources, as outlined by Richardson (2008), who also synthesizes these into the three main elements: value proposition, value creation and delivery, and value capture. The well-known business model canvas, created by Osterwalder and Pigneur (2010), contains nine elements that are organized into these three major components. Business Model Innovation is the renewal of these components or elements: it is the process of devising and realizing a novel way to create an appropriate economic value (McGrath 2010). The typical innovation process within an industrial company is in general occupied with technological changes, most often with an effect on one of the elements in the business model. However, often innovation is less related to changes in structures for securing the income of sales of goods and services, that is, the revenue models in capturing the value. A sustainable development has often put the focus on changing physical goods, technologies, materials, components, and so on. However, the business model and particularly the revenue model is typically not innovated to the same extent. Sustainable business models put the focus on this and the circular economy model clearly emphasizes the need to consider both technology and business.

Transiting into a circular economy requires changes to the firms involved as earlier described in Resource Parameter section above. The majority of the changes are to a large extent primarily dealing with resource consumption restrictions. Few studies outline business models at less than a conceptual level, and ways to reach a sustainable business model are also only schematically described. Several procedures for action do not differ between resource efficiency increasing actions and conceptual business models, for example, reuse or recycle is defined in the same scope as sharing platforms. The Ellen MacArthur Foundation defines actions for policymakers, in their toolkit RESOLVE (Ellen McArthur Foundation 2015). This prescribes critical measures for increasing resource efficiency such as shifting to renewable energy sources and materials, removing waste, and recycling materials. It also defines what could be seen as conceptual business models as sharing assets, reusing products, and dematerialization. Accenture (2014) which as a consultancy firm has a pragmatic approach to managing for change, expresses five business models for a circular industrial system at a conceptual level with some focused on resource efficiency and some rather on revenue models or new ways of owning products. Schulte (2013) defines circular business models from a resource efficiency perspective, without a clear reflection of the actual value proposed for customers. The lack of definitions of the actual elements of a business model is, hence, a common theme in the present literature.

An exemption and a valuable contribution is made by Lieder and Rashid (2016) that in particular addresses three different revenue models: sell, rent, and pay per functional unit. They clearly express this particular element in a business model for circular systems. The circular economy approaches for defining circular business models, for which examples are given in Fig. 7.2, can be summarized in a logical chain of measures. Maximizing material and energy efficiency and/or minimizing material and energy losses require that products, components, and materials are cycled within the societal system where products are used. This in turn requires that new solutions for selling and buying products are defined; that is, the value transfer has to be developed. Finally, developing value transfer requires an active effort in actually identifying the values for actors involved in the system. In Lodsgård and Aagaard (2017), value-in-exchange refers to producers and value-in-use to consumers, which might clarify the fact that value is different for producers and consumers, although a win-win balance is required. For new solutions on selling and

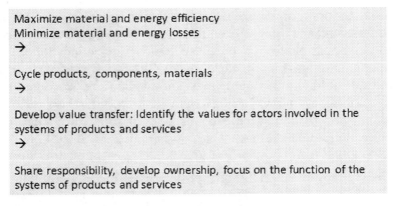

Fig. 7.2 Logical chain of actions, necessary steps for closing material loops while finding new business models

buying, there are variations in how ownership and responsibilities are distributed over the product life cycle and this requires a focus on the function instead of on physical goods. A focus on function stresses the need to look at the combination of products and services and how this combination brings value to customers while decreasing resource consumption. Figure 7.2 illustrates the steps in a logical chain of actions, derived from the extant literature on circular economy.

Within the area of product service system, preceding the more recent development of circular economy with a narrower focus on product development, there is a dominant idea that, by adding services to a value delivery, that is, defining a system of products *and* services, the ecological and social impact will decrease as we will consume fewer resources. Tukker (2004) suggested considering a continuum of product service systems (PSS) from a pure product to a pure service and developed eight archetypes of PSS models. He categorized these into product-oriented, use-oriented, and result-oriented models along a continuum. These categories have different implications for the value creation, value delivery, and value capture as outlined in Fig. 7.3 (referring to Tukker's original analysis where these three parts were expressed). The continuum from pure products to pure services is here seen to be a valuable contribution in developing new circular business models.

	Product oriented	Use oriented	Result oriented
Value creation	Provider takes responsibility for the **deliverables and contracted services**.	Provider is responsible for the **usability** of the product or service.	Provider is responsible for **delivering performance**.
Value delivery	Provider **sells and services** the product-sale and service (e.g. maintenance or recycling).	Provider **assures the usability** of the physical product along with service.	Provider actually **delivers performance** and are **liable for quality** of performance.
Value capture	Customer **pays for physical product** and for the performed services.	Customer can make **continuous payments over time** (e.g., leasing).	Customer **payments are based on outcome units**; that is, they pay for the result.

Fig. 7.3 Value creation, delivery, and capture will be different with different orientations in developing product service systems (after Tukker 2004)

While circular business models are in the making, in real life and in the literature, the area of sustainable business models has grown over the years and provides a valuable contribution to understanding both the parameters of circular economy and the innovation of circular business models. A number of sources are tuning into a definition of sustainable business models that complement traditional business models that are anchored in the view that commercial companies are only engaged in economically profitable values (e.g., Osterwalder et al. 2005; Teece 2010). In contrast, sustainable business models depart from this perspective and emphasize the fact that value is created for numerous stakeholders, not the least for our nature. Schaltegger et al. (2016) state that a *sustainable value* cannot be created for customers without considering the value to other stakeholders. A sustainable business model is in many ways disruptive to a traditional business model as the concept of values is considerably changed integrating values from an economic, ecological, and social perspective. It emphasizes the need to understand the roles of different actors in developing circular systems and it puts further emphasis on what was described above, that responsibility and/or ownership is a critical parameter in this development.

A circular economy will, hence, change the logic of the product life cycle and create new actors as well as making existing actors further develop their roles. Service provider could possibly find new roles as intermediators between manufacturing firms and customers (as stressed by Heyes et al. 2018), for example, for repair and service and data management. Another example is waste management firms that could develop into resource management firms, which is also already seen in more offensive firms today. In addition, the relation between manufacturing firms and customers, between producer and consumer will change and ownership of physical goods is a critical issue that needs to be better understood. For instance, we need a better understanding of the pricing models to be used, that is, what specific actors are willing to pay for what specific value. A major question is to understand how also sustainability values are paid for as the reduced ecological and social impacts might not be part of the proposition that the customer typically considers as a main value.

4 Combining Resource Efficiency Parameters and Critical Business Model Parameters

Joyce and Paquin (2016) suggested a triple-layered business model canvas prescribing that for each element in the canvas a model for economic, ecological, and social values is produced (three aspects horizontally) and that for each element a consideration of the combination of these is made (three aspects vertically). Inspired by this and with the business model canvas in mind, the resource efficiency parameters are suggested to be used as criteria for analyzing each element in the canvas, as illustrated in Fig. 7.4. In the figure, a suggestion of checkpoints for developing a new business model is also made, with the intention to make the relation between the resource efficiency parameters and the canvas elements more concrete.

Still, this approach to defining a circular business model mainly challenges the business model of the producer, at least as in a traditional role of being in charge of the resources used in the delivery to customers. Concluding from the reflection on circular business model parameters

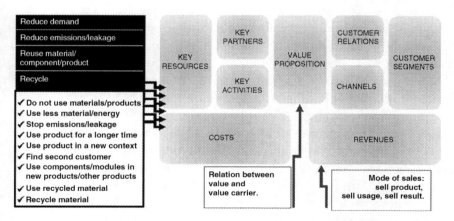

Fig. 7.4 A number of resource efficiency parameters should inspire each element in a business model, and specifically the value proposition and the revenue model must be carefully considered to secure a business aligned to closing material loops

above, the value proposition as well as the revenue model should be even more carefully considered when defining a circular economy business model. Critical parameters to consider when analyzing and defining these two elements in the business model are also illustrated in Fig. 7.4. The relation between value and value carrier refers to how value that the customer is willing to pay for relates to whether it is delivered with a product or with a service. In a similar vein, sales mode relates to whether the customer is willing to pay for the product or for the function. The variation from fully product focused to fully function focused is strongly connected to value proposition and models for owning with private and individual ownership at one extreme and societal sharing at the other. Value for customers also has to be connected to the many issues of ecological and social sustainable development as users indeed could perceive such values and be willing to pay for them.

5 Empirical Illustrations

In order to address some of the complexity and many challenges that the circular economy entails, two illustrations from practice are given. The illustrations are based on empirical research conducted in the past two years, in large mature firms from manufacturing industry. These companies represent the full complexity of the issues that need to be considered for a transition to a circular economy, with products as the core in the value delivery to customers, advanced technologies for production and in products, and value chains with numerous actors both downstream and upstream. Still, there are a few differences between the illustrations, that have also led the selection of these specific cases. One of the companies has taken a firm decision to develop a circular product service system offered to customers. It is driven by top management understanding that the company has to align to a sustainable development and that in the future their competitiveness will only be secured if they lead a development to highly increased resource efficiency. This illustration intends to specifically illustrate what has been characteristic for a project where the intention is to develop and implement a circular system. The second illustration is more typical of a manufacturing firm of today. They have made no decision to

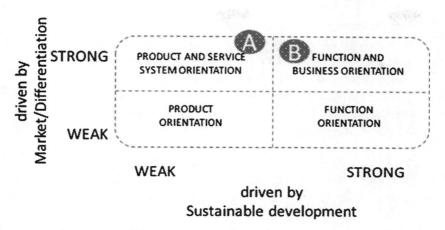

Fig. 7.5 Different driving forces push for different innovation

develop circular systems. Still sustainability is seen as a top priority strategy for the company and they have made several changes during the last year that are perfectly in line with the things that an outspoken aim to close material loops would entail. Both of these companies are driven by securing competitiveness in the future, but differ in how far they stress the aim to align to a sustainable development, which Fig. 7.5 describes. The four field diagram describes the aim of innovation in industrial companies based on research of both relating to products service systems and circular economy, addressing that different driving forces: more or less business driven and more or less driven by ambitions to align to a sustainable development will give different innovation orientations.

5.1 From Product to System, Challenging the Current Business Logic

A is an established and mature industrial company. The company has embraced key sustainability targets as part of their strategy, following the Paris agreement. The products the company has delivered have changed a number of times during its history, and its ability to innovate the product portfolio, supported by an efficient production, has created a competitive organization. Today, the business is focused on different types of outdoor powered products. The products are of very high quality, technologically advanced, at the forefront of development and appeal to a high-end customer segment in terms of high professionalism with customers and high-performance demands. The products are changing profile, partly due to an increased portfolio of battery driven products relating to the company's ambition in sustainable development. Also, their digital service portfolio drives sustainable use of products and fleets by optimizing their customers operations.

The empirical research underlying this illustration focused partly on understanding the perception of circular economy in the organization, its role and relevance for the company given its position in the value chain as well as what barriers could be identified for a transition in a circular economy. Interviews were held with individuals from a number of functions in the company, such as sustainability, manufacturing, purchasing, R&D, and product management. The overall analysis of the barriers reveals no actual surprises and they relate to the categories also found in the literature. Financial barriers are addressed, relating to a yet limited understanding of the profitability and business case in the circular economy. However, given the company's role in the value chain and the industry dynamics (see below), it is not a surprise that valid business cases with financial variables on product level end-to-end were not found. However, examples of business cases exist but in a more narrow scope relating to the company's sustainability targets.

Structural barriers concern both internal aspects with yet some unclear responsibilities on lower level in areas like R&D and Business Development to drive development toward the relevant scope in the circular economy. On Group Management level it is clear where responsibility lies, and Group coordination is managed from a function frequently measuring progress and taking action against set sustainability targets. It is fair to say that although strategic initiatives are ongoing with the supplier base more work needs to be done to sort out modus operandi in-between. It is highly unlikely that the strategy will direct, nor the value chain will allow, the company to enter the business of recycling. Therefore, the barrier of infrastructure was only briefly reflected upon from the company's perspective end-to-end. It is important to state that in this industry the used market of products is small and material recycling is handled by specialist companies. Therefore, there is no business logic for the company in a foreseeable future to take back products or components after end of life. Materials are recycled mainly as customers scrap their end-of-life products at the recycling firms.

Interestingly, we found barriers that must be categorized as more attitudinal: a lack of interest in following new trends and a certain resistance to becoming involved in issues not directly a matter of the current business or technology. These barriers were perceived of as barriers at an individual level, however, are most likely also related to a certain risk aversion and view of sustainability issues in parts of the organization. Also, it is of relevance to note that, among the respondents in this investigation, none were particularly involved in developing the business model or the revenue model.

The investigation of barriers to circular economy was probed from the outside; there was an interest from within to understand what it could mean and to identify barriers: as of now, the company has clear sustainability targets and a strategic direction but not for the greater scope, end-to-end, in the circular economy. Within scope, the company drives change initiatives firmly.

Extending the perception and experience of "value from products" to "value from products and services" is an ongoing trend in many manufacturing firms, including company A as mentioned earlier. The products A delivers have been developed for greater performance, to be more economical in operation, more ergonomic in use, and so on. Fleet services are a key ability available to help the operators monitor progress and machine parameters to be preventive in maintenance as well as sustainable in operations. The company is increasing the service content in its value deliveries, hereby exploring new opportunities with digital technology also relating to the business model, for example, uptime. This is a development that is in line with a circular economy, because it means a break between resource utilization and the value the company delivers; the business model gets a different logic than with traditional product delivery. However, it is not an obvious change to implement because it requires new ways of working within the company and that certain basic assumptions are questioned. An employee within the company expresses the idea that "the product DNA in the organization has to be challenged." New ways of working include how to understand the customer's needs and how to interact with the customer to define the right requirements for innovation within the organization. You must also work more actively with business model innovation, especially to understand how to create a revenue model for the new values that are being provided. A consequence to capture the opportunities for increased service and new technology is increased integration between different sections of the company, such as sales, marketing, product management, technology and product development, and service development.

With increased digital content in the value deliveries, the company has piloted, in experimental ways, new ways of doing business. In addition to the Fleet service example, Company A tested a new business model based on the rental economy offering sustainable, environmental friendly products. Instead of selling products to customers, customers rented a product with all bookings and payments made online. Most of the lessons learned by the company, both in terms of which new business opportunities are created and what challenges are faced are relevant to a transformation toward the role and relevance the company seek in the value chain in a circular economy.

However, since the life cycle of the products is not taken into account, there are probably further opportunities for innovation in a wider scope of the circular economy.

5.2 From Linear to Circular—Co-creation of Business Models

B is also a company with a long history, being a large and mature company within hygiene products. They have for a long time been part of an even larger organization that recently split into raw material production and B, developing and producing products for health and hygiene management both for professionals and consumers. They have a large number of brands approaching different markets offering solutions for hygiene and health care. Their profile is to deliver advanced and high-quality products and they have a strong position on the market with production and distribution all over the world. In contrast to A the products that B delivers are consumed while used. Also, B was early on involved in proactively assessing the environmental performance of products and the resource consumption perspective has in recent decades been at the top of the agenda of the company. Sustainability and issues related to a sustainable development has a strong position in the company.

The empirical survey in B took a slightly different angle, since within the last few years, B has run a circular economy project. In B, there is a classic organizational structure such as in A, with manufacturing, R&D, purchase, sales, sustainability, and so on. Innovation is also being carried out in the department of global brand development, where projects also aim for longer term results and at least partly for breakthrough products. Innovation teams of two to five people are assigned to work on specific themes or problems and projects are categorized at different levels: breakthrough, next generation, upgrade, and cost save. Team members always represent both technology/products and market. A steering committee is assigned to each team with representatives from the department representing different expertise relevant to the specific project. In 2015, a team of one person from technology and one from market was assigned to develop post-consumer waste management and sustainable solutions. The insight behind the setup of the team was and is the increased importance to create value after use.

The work in the innovation team has so far resulted in a new solution including tissue usage for personal hygiene in connection to public spaces or in large organizations. The core value in the new solution is to recycle the tissue in order to reduce monetary costs for the tissue products and increase the environmental performance of these products, and the long-term business is that if raw materials are not put into closed loops, customers will use other suppliers. By-products such as waste collectors are complementing the new service, and new solutions for handling the waste from washroom to mill are needed to a certain extent. This also leads to some changes in behavior, especially for cleaners of washrooms. The actual recycling process is not, however, a problem per se or in need of being changed, but the collection and keeping it separated from other paper is. Recycling of wet resistant papers means a different processing than the one for other paper categories, such as newspapers and cartoons.

Consequently, the innovation has mainly been in services, and the greatest need has been on developing the business model that makes it possible to economically take back the waste and turn it into the resource that it actually is for the mill.

The innovation team was strongly committed to their assignment and complemented each other well in competence (engineering and market). They perceived a perfect timing for the project as circular economy had become a topic on several different agendas. As B joined an international corporate network on circular economy (CE100, Ellen McArthur Foundation) they had good support both from peers and experts and could find partners to pilot their innovation with. Early on, they started to collaborate closely with potential customers, who on their side were strongly driven by developing their organizations and activities toward a sustainable development. It was also a critical measure to team up with colleagues at sales departments close to potential customers and at the mills delivering the tissue products. Collaboration efforts also successively included cleaning companies and waste management companies. In parallel to the innovation activities targeted at the new circular product and service system regulations and labeling were investigated. This project was at a certain time lifted out from the formal innovation funnel as goals and measures were difficult to apply in this breakthrough project; also, the steering committee was changed so as to include top management who could secure a long-term perspective and allow a certain risk taking. The innovation work could be characterized as two parallel streams of finding business opportunities together with customers, a proactive and forward-looking work, and of identifying and overcoming barriers due to regulations or routines on the market as well as due inertia to change within the own organization.

Developing the revenue model has required the largest innovation effort, and currently two different models are being applied and assessed, one business model where company B is the full-service provider and a second one where the recycling partner/waste management partner owns the service agreement with the end customer. A key in finding a revenue model, besides the obvious need to find mutual value exchange, has been to ease the contract management for the large final customers involved. To be specific, it is the revenue model, the monetary transactions for the actors in this innovation system, that is the most explicit barrier to overcome for taking this project to a broad scale implemented and established business, from where it is now, a successful pilot including real businesses with important customers. Of greatest importance for success with this innovation effort has been the close collaboration with customers and acting in the network of different internal departments and partners in the supply chain. The innovation team members themselves stress that working closely with pilot customers has been critical, and together with them adapting a learning attitude where an openness to what is known and what is not known is allowed. This builds trust that is so critical in any collaboration. It also relates to communication: to inform and open up for dialogues about this specific case in a way that clearly advocates the possible values in new systems is important, both toward customers along the value chain, but also for acceptance within the own organization.

6 Managerial Implications for Organizations Involved in the Transformation into a Circular Economy

Transforming into a circular economy demands a large number of changes with several managerial implications. Co-creation with both customers and suppliers is essential. This means integrated innovation work in an innovation ecosystem, although also an integration between different disciplines and competences within a firm. The work performed in collaboration between different actors and different functions should be manifested in the innovation of new business models, which is an innovation focus that is often foreseen in manufacturing firms. These aspects are elaborated on in this section, leading to a final reflection on measures both at a strategic level and at a more operational level: setting formal processes and controls as well as organizing in radical innovation teams, experimenting, and communicating.

7 Innovation Ecosystem—No Company Is an Island in Sustainable Development

The changes needed to transit to a circular economy include every actor in a value chain, relating to the different phases of a product life cycle: raw material extraction, manufacturing of materials, components, systems, transports, use, and end of life. In a circular economy, new players also become important, as service providers (e.g., for retake and remanufacturing), actors supporting or making new revenue models feasible (e.g., for financing) and it most likely gives customers new roles in the business ecosystem. This could mean changes in behavior due to closing material loops, but also due to new forms of ownership. In addition, actors as policy makers, governments at local, regional, and national levels and certification bodies are crucial for driving or supporting a transition toward circular economy. From the manufacturing company perspective, taking a key role in managing these networks is of vital importance, and there are no shortcuts from, with endurance, building relations with different actors. The illustrations in this chapter point to a key action in building relations, to as quickly as possible making a joint effort with potential customers. The innovation process should become a co-creation of value with customers and finding the possible lead users or innovators among customers is highly recommended. In relation to circular economy, lead users are most likely customers who include the ecological and social aspects of sustainable development in the value proposition they find attractive. As in any innovation, customers and users are not always the same actor, and co-creation might sometimes need to be extended to the final user in order to develop a sustainable business model.

8 Innovating the Business Model for Circular Systems

Each actor in the business ecosystem needs to re-consider all critical elements of their business models; specifically, the value proposition and the revenue model have to be considered. This does not mean that the value creation or delivery to customer is of any less importance for developing circular product and service systems, although several of the elements in these parts are directly linked to the resource efficiency parameters in circular economy and also often directly related to the innovation of technology and products, which are actions more grounded in most industrial organizations. Considering the elements of a business model in relation to every system life cycle phase and considering multiple lives of product service systems is important. The synthesis of which parameters actually play a role both from the resource efficiency perspective and from the business model perspective can assist in these considerations, as outlined in Fig. 7.1. Especially important in the creation of value propositions is investigating the value carrier (product/service) and how important this is for different customers and the different modes of ownership. Considering the range from selling products to selling functions and from fully individual ownership to shared ownership is a constructive measure for questioning traditional revenue models that might be obstructive with a circular economy. One of the key capabilities in developing circular systems hence relates to continuously creating desirable and feasible sustainable business models. This is also supported by the illustrations given here; being able to describe and communicate internally and with customers the business case of closing material loops is fundamental to success in a transition toward circular economy. Also, other empirical investigations reveal that there is a lack of integration between product development and business development, pointing to a critical issue for a sustainable development: to put every aspect of a sustainable development on a strategic level of a firm.

9 Strategy and Experiments

Putting sustainability on the strategic level of a firm is also putting the need to be more radical in innovation on the agenda. Many of the changes needed for a circular economy will require radical changes in technology, products, and business. And, if there is a strategy in a company to align to a sustainable development, a number of strategy levers need to be analyzed and developed. Formal processes and routines, organizational structures, management controls and attitudes to working with sustainability issues are crucial issues to consider.

Formal processes might not be tailored for work in cross-disciplinary teams. This is seen in innovation in common and relates strongly to also circular economy as a value proposition and value capture needs to be re-designed in collaboration between different functions within a company as well as together with customers and users. Formal streamlined processes are often adjusted to take small steps in innovation, and an exploitation of knowledge within the firm is made for incremental innovations in the product service system. For a circular economy, more of exploration is needed, seeking knowledge outside the organization, creating cognitive conflicts, where different perspectives and experiences meet. These differences are also to be found within an organization, though they might need to challenge ordinary ways of working. The illustration of the innovation team in B clearly addresses this point as the combination of technology and market was a key factor in their success, together with an organizing of their innovation work separated from ordinary processes and routines in steering the project. Also, goals and measures need to be challenged when managing radical innovation. In the case of circular economy, where new modes of value transfer are needed and value carriers (products or services) must be considered, traditional goals relating to sales volumes of physical goods becomes obvious to challenge.

Yet another issue that relates strongly to managing for radical innovation is experimentation. Both illustrations show pilot projects from these large organizations where critical steps toward a circular economy have been taken: co-creating fully circular systems in a network of actors with customers as main partners in this, and designing and implementing new modes for selling and delivering products to customers. It is clear in both cases that experimenting and piloting is taking them forward, which does not mean that these are experiments that are made without clearly set goals and a strict agenda to succeed in business development. A link between these experiments and success is then also the storytelling within companies and together with customers.

References

Accenture. 2014. Circular Advantage, Innovative Business Models and Technologies to Create Value in a World without Limits to Growth. *Accenture Strategy*. https://www.accenture.com/t20150523T053139.

Andersson Torstensson, L. 2016. *Internal Barriers for Moving Towards Circularity—An Industrial Perspective*. Master thesis, MMK 2016:151 MCE 336, KTH, Stockholm, Sweden.

de Jesus, A., and S. Mendonca. 2018. Lost in Transition? Drivers and Barriers in the Eco-innovation Road to the Circular Economy. *Ecological Economics* 145: 75–89.

den Hollander, M.C., C.A. Bakker, and E.J. Hultink. 2017. Product Design in a Circular Economy: Development of a Typology of Key Concepts and Terms. *Journal of Industrial Ecology* 21 (3): 517–525.

Ellen McArthur Foundation. 2015. Delivering the Circular Economy—A Toolkit for Policymakers. *Report RESOLVE*, 2015.

Geissdoerfer, M., P. Savaget, N.M.P. Bocken, and E.J. Hultink. 2017. The Circular Economy—A New Sustainability Paradigm? *Journal of Cleaner Production* 143: 757–768.

Genovese, A., A.A. Acquaye, A. Figueroa, and S.C.L. Koh. 2017. Sustainable Supply Chain Management and the Transition Towards a Circular Economy: Evidence and Some Applications. *Omega* 66 (Part B): 344–357.

Ghisellini, P., C. Cialani, and S. Ulgiati. 2016. A Review of Circular Economy: The Expected Transition to a Balanced Interplay of Environmental and Economic Systems. *Journal of Cleaner Production* 114: 11–32.

Heyes, G., M. Sharmina, J.M.F. Mendozam, A. Gallego-Schmid, and A. Azapagic. 2018. Developing and Implementing Circular Economy Business Models in Service-Oriented Technology Companies. *Journal of Cleaner Production* 177: 621–632.

Homrich, A.S., G. Galvao, L. Gamboa Abadia, and M.M. Carvalho. 2018. The Circular Economy Umbrella: Trends and Gaps on Integrating Pathways. *Journal of Cleaner Production* 175: 525–543.

Joyce, A., and R.L. Paquin. 2016. The Triple Layered Business Model Canvas: A Tool to Design More Sustainable Business Models. *Journal of Cleaner Production* 135: 1474–1486.

Kirchherr, J., D. Reike, and M. Hekkert. 2017. Conceptualizing the Circular Economy: An Analysis of 114 Definitions. *Resources, Conservation and Recycling* 127: 221–232.

Kok, L., G. Wurpel, and A.t.P.o.t.C.E. Wolde. 2013. *Unleashing the Power of the Circular Economy*. Amsterdam: IMSA for Circle Economy.

Kügler, M. 2016. *Barriers and Drivers Towards Circular Economy Within Industrial Manufacturers*. Master thesis report, Technishe Universität Munchen, Münich, Germany.

Lieder, M., and A. Rashid. 2016. Towards Circular Economy Implementation: A Comprehensive Review in Context of Manufacturing Industry. *Journal of Cleaner Production* 115: 36–51.

Linder, M., and M. Williander. 2017. Circular Business Model Innovation: Inherent Uncertainties. *Business strategy and the Environment* 26: 182–196.

Lodsgård, L., and A. Aagaard. 2017. Creating Value Through CSR Across Company Functions and NGO Collaborations—A Scandinavian Cross-industry Case Study. *Scandinavian Journal of Management* 33: 162–174.

McDowall, W., et al. 2017. Circular Economy Policies in China and Europe. *Journal of Industrial Ecology* 21: 651–661.

McGrath, R. 2010. Business Models: A Discovery Driven Approach. *Long Range Planning* 43: 247–261.

Merli, R., M. Preziosi, and A. Acampora. 2018. How do Scholars Approach the Circular Economy? A Systematic Literature Review. *Journal of Cleaner Production* 178: 703–722.

Nußholz, J. 2017. Circular Business Models: Defining a Concept and Framing an Emerging Research Field. *Sustainability* 9: 1810.

Osterwalder, A., and Y. Pigneur. 2010. *Business Model Canvas*. Hoboken, NJ and Canada: John Wiley and Sons.

Osterwalder, A., Y. Pigneur, and C.-L. Tucci. 2005. Clarifying Business Models: Origins, Present, and Future of the Concept. *Communications of the Association for Information Systems*, 16.

Oxford Dictionaries. 2018. Accessed March 6, 2018. https://en.oxforddictionaries.com/definition/economy.

Ranta, V., L. Aarikka-Stenroos, P. Ritala, and S.J. Mäkinen. 2018. Exploring Institutional Drivers and Barriers of the Circular Economy; A Cross-regional Comparison of Chine, the US and Europe. *Resources, Conservation and Recycling*. https://doi.org/10.1016/j.resconrec.2017.08.017.

Rashid, A., F.M.A. Asif, P. Krajnik, and C.M. Nicolescu. 2013. Resource Conservative Manufacturing: An Essential Change in Business and Technology Paradigm for Sustainable Manufacturing. *Journal of Cleaner Production* 57: 166–177.

Richardson, J. 2008. The Business Model: An Integrative Framework for Strategy Execution. *Strategic Change* 17: 133–144.

Schaltegger, S., E.G. Hansen, and F. Lüdeke-Freund. 2016. Business Models for Sustainability: Origins, Present Research, and Future Avenues. *Organization and environment* 29 (1): 3–10.

Schulte, U.G. 2013. New Business Models for a Radical Change in Resource Efficiency. *Environmental Innovation and Societal Transitions* 9: 43–47.

SERI/Global 2000. 2009. Overconsumption? Our Use of the World's Natural Resources, Sustainable Europe Research Institute (SERI) and Global 2000 (Friends of the Earth Austria).

Shi, H., S.Z. Peng, Y. Liu, and P. Zhong. 2008. Barriers to the Implementation of Cleaner Production in Chinese SMEs. Government, Industry and Expert Stakeholders' Perspectives. *Journal of Cleaner Production* 16: 842–852.

Stahel, R.W. 1982. The Product-Life Factor. In *NARC, Hrsg. An Inquiry into the Nature of Sustainable Societies: The Role of the Private Sector*. Mitchell Prize Papers, 72–96.

Teece, D.J. 2010. Business Models, Business Strategy and Innovation. *Long Range Planning* 43 (2–3): 172–194.

Tukker, A. 2004. Eight Types of Product Service System: Eight Ways to Sustainability? Experiences from SUSPRONET. *Business Strategy and the Environment* 13: 246–260.

8

Leveraging Sustainable Business Model Innovation Through Business-NGO Collaboration

Annabeth Aagaard and Lise Lodsgård

1 Introduction

A company's ability to innovate in the domain of sustainability represents a necessary business capability, whether through small incremental steps or radical, disruptive innovations (Adams et al. 2012). As a consequence, business model innovation (BMI) is emerging as a potential mechanism to integrate sustainability into business (Schaltegger et al. 2012; Jolink and Niesten 2015). However, adopting the existing business model frameworks into sustainability is not viable, as emphasized by Adams et al. (2012), who underline that sustainable business models (SBMs) and sustainable business model innovation (SBMI) requires more integrated thinking and the

A. Aagaard (✉)
Aarhus University, Herning, Denmark
e-mail: aaa@btech.au.dk

L. Lodsgård
BTECH, Centre for Business Development, Aarhus University,
Aarhus, Denmark
e-mail: lilo@btech.au.dk

reconfiguration of several business aspects, such as capabilities, stakeholder relationships, knowledge management, leadership, and culture. This has led to an extensive supply of SBM typologies and definitions.

Although there is a growing body of literature discussing sustainability and sustainable development on the political and society level (Dryzek 2005), the operationalization of the concept in relation to business is still rather weak, as stressed by a number of researchers (e.g., Bansal 2005; Stubbs and Cocklin 2008; Zink et al. 2008; Carroll and Shabana 2010). Thus, the emphasis of this chapter is to explore this gap in research to understand and operationalize SBMs into corporate practices and performances in creating new business opportunities on the corporate level (Holling 2001; Newman 2005).

2 Sustainable Business Models and Sustainable Business Model Innovations

With the growing theoretical and empirical interest in SBMs, more and more definitions and frameworks are emerging in identification and mapping of the concept and its different characteristics (Aagaard 2016). Stubbs and Cocklin (2008) assert that SBMs use both a systems and a firm-level perspective, build on the triple bottom line approach to define the firm's purpose and measure performance, include a wide range of stakeholders, and consider the environment and society as stakeholders. Lüdeke-Freund (2010) describes SBM as a business model that creates competitive advantage through superior customer value and contributes to a sustainable development of the company and society.

However, throughout the chapter we will apply the following definition of SBM innovation in our elaboration of the topic: "Innovations that create significant positive and/or significantly reduced negative impacts for the environment and/or society, through changes in the way the organisation and its value-network create, deliver value and capture value or change their value propositions" (Bocken et al. 2014, p. 44).

In mapping the typologies of SBM, we have identified a number of different typologies describing new business logics that benefit both business and society. These typologies include sustainability business models (Birkin et al. 2009), community development business models (Stubbs and Cocklin 2008), social business models (Yunus et al. 2010), triple bottom line business models (Osterwalder and Pigneur 2005), green business models (Sommer 2012), inclusive business models (Michelini and Fiorentino 2012), and the triple-layered business models (Joyce and Paquin 2016). The objective of this chapter is not to choose one typology over another, but to explore the breadth of the concept and how it is facilitated through business- non-government organization (NGO) collaborations.

In identification of SBMI, Schaltegger et al. (2012) propose three different categorizations: defensive, accommodative, and proactive business model innovations. The defensive strategies (adjustment) are explained as incremental business model adjustments to protect current business models focusing on risk and cost reduction often driven by the need for compliance. The accommodative strategies (improvement, integration) are modifications of internal processes and include some consideration of environmental or social objectives (e.g., environmental protection). The proactive strategies (full integration) concern the redesign of the core business logic of the firm for sustainable development. In addition, Bocken et al. (2014) introduce eight different SBM archetypes to describe groupings of mechanisms and solutions that contribute to the design of business models for sustainability. The archetypes are (1) Maximize material and energy efficiency, (2) Create value from "waste," (3) Substitute with renewables and natural processes, (4) Deliver functionality rather than ownership, (5) Adopt a stewardship role, (6) Encourage sufficiency, (7) Repurpose the business for society/environment, and (8) Develop scale-up solutions. In the selected case examples, more or less all of the above categorizations will be presented, as business-NGO collaboration is applied across very different contexts and with different objectives, as explored in the next section.

In our review of the existing studies on SBM and SBMI, it appears that the studies are structured into intra-organizational, inter-organizational, and societal levels (Boons and Lüdeke-Freund 2013). In this chapter, we have primarily addressed the inter-organizational collaborations between private businesses and NGOs in mapping the objectives of different types of SBM through these collaborations. The literature review also revealed that SMBI in practice tends to be ad hoc and neither systematic nor systemic (Stubbs and Cocklin 2008). This challenges our inherent need as academics to map and identify innovation processes and stresses the need for further research in the empirical SMBI processes and their managerial and organizational implications. In our investigation of SBMs facilitated through business-NGO collaboration, we have identified and observed a similar ad hoc and "trial-and-error" approach in establishing SBMs through these types of collaborations (Aagaard 2016; Lodsgård and Aagaard 2017).

In our assessment and operationalization of SBM and SBMI in this chapter, we emphasize the value created, delivered, and captured through the specific SBM to the customer, the business, and society (Aagaard and Ritzén 2018). From a traditional economic perspective, value is defined as value derived from value-in-use and value-in-exchange. This means that value-in-use relates to the customers'/end-users' subjective perception of the value of a product or service, and value-in-exchange refers to the transformation of value into monetary achievement of the company (Bowman and Ambrosini 2000; Makadok 2001). Consequently, the business and its shareholders are able to capture a certain amount of exchange value determined by the competitive position and bargaining power of the customers (Bowman and Ambrosini 2000; Makadok and Coff 2002).

Thus, from the economic perspective, value capture refers to economic value gains and is tightly related to value measures and financial performance in the business logic. Through the elaborated multi-level perspective developed by Lepak et al. (2007), the classic company-centric understanding of value-in-use and value-in-exchange is extended into a holistic approach, which also captures the individual, business/organizational, and societal levels. This implies that value-in-use is extended from customer perceptions as target users into a broader context, where target users are found among multiple actors on the individual, organizational, and societal levels, and value beyond pure economic gains may therefore be captured on more levels as well (Lepak et al. 2007). In the context of SBM through business-NGO collaborations, more scholars reframe the value construct, extending the one-dimensional shareholder logic of profit maximization to more stakeholders and levels of attention (Upward and Jones 2016; Pedersen et al. 2016; Schaltegger et al. 2016).

3 Business-NGO Collaborations

In the rise of global awareness of sustainability issues, companies are met with increasing public pressure and have to deal with the risks of, for example, poor PR and boycott of products. One of the main drivers for companies to collaborate with NGOs in designing SBMs is therefore also to reduce these risks (Pedersen et al. 2011) and to improve the company's image and reputation, while shaping the industry standards, avoiding confrontations (Pedersen and Pedersen 2013), and maintaining and increasing legitimacy (Heap 2000; Yaziji and Doh 2009). Thus, collaborations with NGOs enable businesses to stay ahead of future sustainable issues and troubles (Yaziji and Doh 2009). Consequently, NGOs possess an extremely valuable but intangible resource in terms of legitimacy, which is required and requested by many companies in the context of developing a sustainable business and business model.

Since business-NGO collaborations rarely succeed by chance, more researchers have emphasized not only the drivers and benefits but also the challenges that invariably arise when such "odd couples" (Rivara-Santos and Rufin 2010) as "suits and roots" (Bowen et al. 2010) with different mindsets and values meet in common awareness in order to collaborate and create new SBMs together. More researchers have recognized the dynamics of trust as the most significant collaborative mechanism in generating a positive collaborative outcome (Ring and Van de Ven 1992; Morgan and Hunt 1994; Sarkar et al. 1997; Gulati 1998; Koza and Lewin 1998; Inkpen 2000; Ozman 2009). Trust is defined by Barney and Hansen (1994) as "the mutual confidence that no party to an exchange will exploit another's vulnerabilities." Following this definition, it could be argued that trust is present in a given collaboration when partners have positive expectations that the another partner is honest and reliable and when no partner behaves in opportunistic ways although it is possible because the other partner is in a vulnerable position, dependent on the other partner's resources or legitimacy (Madhok 1995; Aulakh et al. 1997). In the literature on inter-organizational collaborations, we have identified a number of relational dynamics and aspects related to trust, including:

1. Collaborative history and longitudinal aspects (Ring and Van de Ven 1994; Gulati 1995)
2. Familiarity, common sense making and cultural similarity (Gulati 1995; Johnson et al. 1997; Sarkar et al. 1997; Mandell and Steelman 2003; Leung and White 2006)
3. Vulnerability in resource contribution (resource dependence) and power distribution (Inkpen and Currall 1997; Johnson et al. 1997; Zaher and Harris 2006)

These dynamics and aspects seem to influence the degree and development of opportunism, commitment, common sense making, conflicts, and misunderstandings, and thereby the level of trust in between partners. Chesbrough et al. (2006) underline that in the developing world context, a coherent, locally relevant SBM is critical in meeting the goal of developing profitable, sustainable markets. They further emphasize that the successful implementation is highly correlated with the extent to which program managers thought through their implementation of their business model customized to the local conditions (p. 52). The social and ethical dimensions are especially relevant in the case of new, emerging low-income markets, where the world's poorest people, "the bottom of the pyramid" (BOP), are considered new customers (Charter and Clark 2007).

In providing a theoretical overview and discussion of SBM through business-NGO collaborations, mapping dominant institutional orientations, governance mechanisms, and managerial challenges across different institutional contexts, the academic literature was screened through databases using the following keywords and terms: collaboration between commercial actors and NGOs, partnerships and social alliances between business and NGOs, cross-sector social-oriented partnerships, and inter-sector partnership. As a result of the literature review, we identified four archetypes of SBM, and through the theoretical analysis of four case examples based on document studies of secondary data and interview sessions with business and NGO representatives we identify some of the significant characteristics and challenges within each of the archetypes.

As such, the cases do not capture the entire range of characteristics and challenges in creating SBM through business-NGO collaborations, which would require a multiple case study, as intended for further research. However, the cases serve as an empirical illustration of SBM within different institutional logics and collaborative contexts, their characteristics, and key considerations that management of both NGOs and businesses must take into account in terms of governance mechanisms and managerial challenges.

In exploration of business-NGO collaborations, we apply one of the cornerstone contributions on the topic, the collaborative continuum, by Austin (2000). The collaboration continuum contains different degrees of integration and interaction between partners, including three stages:

1. *The philanthropic stage*, which is characterized by simple resource exchanges, typically through one-way donations toward the NGO in terms of either financial, material, or volunteer resources and an "arm's length" approach to the collaboration.
2. *The transactional stage*, where collaborations move from unilateral resource exchange toward bilateral resource exchange of more complementary resources through activities such as sponsorship, cause-related marketing, events, information campaigns, and NGO-initiated codes of conduct (Austin 2000). These types of collaborations are very similar to normative regulations, symbolic actions, and so on, applied by companies in order to gain third-party endorsement through their Corporate Social Responsibility (CSR) (Matten and Moon 2008; Angus-Leppan et al. 2010).
3. *The integrative stage*, which is characterized by addressing more complex problems with a rather high level of knowledge exchange and a broader scope of common activities, for example, market development and innovative improvement in existing practices and products where capabilities and resources are put into play in new ways to create common value (Austin 2000; Austin and Seitanidi 2012). This last stage is characterized as strategic partnerships and highlighted as the most promising collaborative form in creating innovation (Jamali et al. 2011).

Recently, Austin and Seitanidi (2012) developed the original collaborative continuum by adding a fourth transformational stage. This stage of business-NGO collaborations builds on the integrative stage by migrating the collaboration to higher levels of convergence and is characterized by large-scale disruptive social innovations improving the living conditions for the beneficiaries at the community and society level. Finally, Austin (2003) argues that when the level of organizational integration increases, it may develop into jointly governed entities very similar to equity partnerships and joint ventures in the hierarchy end of the collaborative continuum of inter-organizational collaborations.

The four stages of business-NGO collaborations by Austin and Seitanidi's (2012) study, which this chapter builds on, are presented in Fig. 8.1.

The collaborative continuum was not developed with the purpose of studying SBMs. However, the continuum emphasizes the different characteristics and purposes of various forms of collaborations between businesses and NGOs, which we need to take into account when trying to understand how companies can leverage SBMs and sustainable value creation through collaborations with NGOs. As such, this chapter focuses on the company angle as to how value is created for the business side through these collaborations. Exploring value creation from the perspective of NGOs is also an interesting research path to pursue. However, this

NATURE OF RELATIONSHIP	Stage I Philanthropic >	Stage II Transactional >	Stage III Integrative >	Stage IV Transformational
• Level of Engagement	Low ←			→ High
• Importance to Mission	Peripheral ←			→ Central
• Magnitude of Resources	Small ←			→ Big
• Type of resources	Money ←		→ Core Competencies	
• Scope of Activities	Narrow ←			→ Broad
• Interaction Level	Infrequent ←			→ Intensive
• Trust	Modest ←			→ Deep
• Internal change	Minimal ←			→ Great
• Managerial Complexity	Simple ←			→ Complex
• Strategic Value	Minor ←			→ Major
• Co-creation of value	Sole			→ Conjoined
• Synergistic value	Occasional ←			→ Predominant
• Innovation	Seldom ←			→ Frequent
• External system change	Rare ←			→ Common

Fig. 8.1 The collaborative continuum of business-NGO collaborations. Source: Austin and Seitanidi (2012, p. 736)

is not the objective of this chapter or study. As more and more companies are pursuing SBMs, we need to develop a better understanding of the characteristics, drivers, and potential challenges of the different collaborative forms for companies to best select, combine, and manage these collaborations with NGOs individually and in combination. It is important to note, when applying the collaborative continuum in this study of SBMs, that these collaborative types are not to be considered stationary or "pure" types, as in practice they will develop and overlap as new sustainable issues or circumstances arise, as emphasized by Austin and Seitanidi (2012). As many organizations engage in multiple collaborations with several partners on a continuous basis, it is only fair to assume that businesses may also engage in a number of SBMs through different business-NGO collaborations with different NGOs at the same time. Another interesting question is therefore related to the longitudinal aspects of how to manage and optimize across different business-NGO collaborations and across different contexts, projects, and over time; however, this is outside the scope of this chapter.

4 Different Types of SMBs Through Business-NGO Collaborations

In combining the collaborative continuum and levels of interaction with the value creation and value capture of the SBM, we have conceptualized four archetypal scenarios identifying drivers and challenges in creating SBMs through business-NGO collaborations. Thus, collaborative activities and case examples emphasizing cause-related marketing and common communication campaigns we identify as "marketing-focused sustainable business models." The collaborative activities and case examples stressing NGO-initiated standards, codes of conduct, stewardship councils, and so on, we identify as "regulative sustainable business models." And collaborative activities and case examples addressing emerging markets at the BOP (developing countries) and development of fair trade engagements we identify as "inclusive sustainable business models." And finally, collaborative activities and examples regarding different types of welfare innovation at the community level we label "social investment business models." The four different archetypes of SBMs through business-NGO collaborations are explained individually in the next subsections.

4.1 SBM Archetype 1: Marketing-Focused Sustainable Business Models

Within this archetype of business-NGO collaborations, a growing body of literature examines these collaborations from a marketing perspective in studies of traditional philanthropy and cause-related marketing, where donations are tied to sustainable consumer choices (Austin 2003; Wymer and Samu 2003). Recently, cause-related marketing has become extremely popular as one of the fastest-emerging segments in corporate marketing (Austin 2000, 2003; Wymer and Samu 2003). A shift took place when former conventional checkbook philanthropy moved from corporate charity budgets to marketing budgets linking products with sustainable causes (Austin 2003; Vogel 2005). Additionally, NGOs have become more businesslike and have changed their philanthropic funding strategies into more marketing-driven strategies (Dees 1998; Millar et al. 2004; Saunders and Borland 2013).

The majority of research within this field of research uncovers the drivers related to the business case in terms of sales increase, consumer awareness, product differentiation, increased reputation, public relations, and so on. Especially within an Anglo-Saxon institutional context, the positive impacts of third-part endorsement and legitimacy on consumer purchase decisions are well documented (Austin 2003; Basil and Herr 2003; Novak and Clarke 2003; Millar et al. 2004). As such, these collaborations are mostly characterized by external legitimacy drivers and by symbolic transactional value creation rather than integrative or transformative value creation in terms of Austin and Seitanidi's (2012) collaborative continuum.

4.1.1 A Case Example of Marketing-Focused SBM

A recent example of these joint marketing campaigns is Coca-Cola and the World Wildlife Fond's (WWF) cooperation to save the polar bear in the Arctic, where Coca-Cola uses its huge marketing muscle and communication skills to raise awareness of the problem. Similarly, as part of the campaign, Coca-Cola uses an image of a polar bear mother and her cubs on the Coca-Cola cans. Thus, it can be argued that the Coca-Cola product has added a symbolic and ethical element of sustainable innovation. Despite the significant benefits outlined above in terms of economic and branding values, more researchers point to the importance of managerial challenges, such as risk of over-commercialization, dangerous donations, negative attitudes toward company brand, and "greenwashing" (Basil and Herr 2003; García et al. 2003; Saunders and Borland 2013). It is not always easy for partners to predict possible consumer and stakeholder response (Austin 2003).

A huge managerial challenge within these collaborations is therefore to ensure a proper fit between missions, brands, market segments, products and sustainable causes and to ensure it is adapted among key stakeholders (Austin 2003; Basil and Herr 2003; Wymer and Samu 2003). Related to the dimensions of trust outlined previously, it seems that the power balance in these marketing-focused SBMs may be more to the benefit of the business partner, including risk that the NGO's credibility will be jeopardized and their freedom to publicly express criticism will be limited and thereby their position to gain future funding will be damaged (Wymer and Samu 2003; Millar et al. 2004).

There is also some evidence that these collaborations are challenged by goal conflicts because the business partner wants more ambitious goals than the NGO partner because it will bring them in a more beneficial situation of external communication (Adderly and Mellor 2014). Furthermore, some critics emphasize that companies in general spend more resources on advertising and image building from a company-centric perspective than they do building awareness of the sustainable cause (Wymer and Samu 2003). Moreover, these partnerships are typically short-term contracts running for 1–2 years, which is why business partners constantly search for more "marketable" causes (Wymer and Samu 2003; Saunders and Borland 2013). This may prevent these collaborations from becoming vehicles fostering continuous innovative improvement, continual learning, and migrating to the next level of integrative and transformative collaboration.

4.2 SBM Archetype 2: Regulative Sustainable Business Models

Regulative SMB through business-NGO collaborations typically emerge from environmental or social codes of conduct and standards and from stewardship councils (e.g., the Marine Stewardship Council, MSC, and the Forest Stewardship Council, FSC) initiated or led by NGOs in order to move businesses toward more sustainable innovations and practices in products, production methods, supply chain, consumption, and so on (Heap 2000; Kong et al. 2002; Spar and La Mure 2003; Doh and Guay 2004; Potts and Haward 2006; Arenas et al. 2009; Kourula 2010).

There is some evidence that these innovative regulations push companies to comply in an attempt to gain legitimacy, third-party endorsement, ethical credibility, protection of corporate brand and interests at the industry level, and so on (Spar and La Mure 2003; Waddock 2008; Peloza and Falkenberg 2009; Perez-Batres et al. 2012). To support this argument, since the FSC was initiated by Greenpeace, WWF, Nepenthes, and a huge part of the forest industry in the early 1990s, 28,303 companies worldwide have earned FSC certificates and the right to use the FSC logo on their products. Similarly, since the WWF and Unilever initiated the MSC in 1999, 34,000 companies worldwide have earned MSC certification. These insights lead to an understanding of business-NGO collaborations within this archetype as enablers for environmental and social regulative innovations at an industrial level rather than single strategies from a business-centric perspective. In this respect, more researchers argue that these collaborations typically move from dyadic partner relations at the company level toward more complex multi-party alliances and co-governance involving a wide range of partners at the industry level (Stafford et al. 2000; Doh and Guay 2004; Peloza and Falkenberg 2009).

4.2.1 A Case Example of Regulative SBM

One example that illustrates the potentials and driving mechanisms of these NGO led regulative SBMs is the case of Greenpeace and the

German refrigerator company Foron. Prior to the collaboration, Greenpeace created a notable pressure and campaigned against the entire refrigerator industry in order to motivate companies to apply to their newly developed green-freeze technology. However, at that time, the green-freeze technology was considered quite controversial technology within the refrigerator industry, and all companies except Foron, a small company at the border of bankruptcy, rejected involvement. The two partners went along with the innovation process: Foron virtually overnight produced the very first prototype of the "Clean Cooler," and Greenpeace simultaneously launched a massive advertising campaign (Stafford et al. 2000). Eventually, Foron's "Clean Cooler" became a huge market success and very quickly generated over 7000 orders due to the grassroots publicity and product endorsement provided by Greenpeace (Stafford et al. 2000).

Furthermore, Foron's "Clean Cooler" won several environmental awards (e.g., the "Blue Angel"). According to Yaziji and Doh (2009), advocacy NGOs in particular typically pressure either individual companies or an entire industry through activism or campaigns while simultaneously playing the role of catalyst, providing companies with new technical knowledge in order to institutionalize sustainable standards through, for example, product development or codes of conduct. Thus, NGOs dichotomy between confrontation and collaboration may function as a catalyst in order to institutionalize new SBMs at the corporate or industrial level (Guay et al. 2004; Yaziji and Doh 2009).

Based on the literature review and the case example outlined above, it is fair to assume that asymmetries in resource dependence and power distributions followed by loss of commitment and mutual trust easily could occur in these regulative innovations if one partner exploits the another partner's vulnerabilities. Given that these activist NGOs and companies often have rather conflicting histories, it may be challenging to establish trust at the management and employee level without "selling out" the NGO partners' credibility and without "selling out" companies' interests in maximizing shareholder value and doing a good business (Argenti 2004). It may also be challenging for both parties to overcome former skepticism or possible "hidden agendas" (Heap 2000) and manage complex networks and collective governance practices among a diverse range of stakeholders on the industrial level (Stafford et al. 2000). Although these collaborations seem to be very successful vehicles toward regulative SBMs, more researchers have discussed whether they really are substantial or just symbolic manifestations in order to increase legitimacy and third-party endorsement (Bowen et al. 2010; Perez-Batres et al. 2012). The level and depth of interaction, integration, and common value creation in terms of Austin and Seitanidis's (2012) collaborative continuum may therefore be questioned.

4.3 SBM Archetype 3: Inclusive Sustainable Business Models

This archetype of business-NGO collaborations is centered at new business opportunities and is tightly embedded within the stream of literature on inclusive business models, defined as "Business [that] includes the poor into a company's supply chains as employees, producers and business owners or develop affordable goods and services needed by the poor. Here, human and business development goes hand in hand" (UNDP 2010). One important example of these inclusive SBMs is the exploration of new emerging low-income markets where the world's 4 billion poorest people, "the bottom of the pyramid" (BOP), are considered as new customers and "blue oceans" with the opportunity for companies to gain new profits (Prahalad and Hart 1999; Esko et al. 2012; Venn and Berg 2013; Boons and Lüdeke-Freund 2013; Prahalad 2013). Inclusive SBMs aimed at the BOP are basically founded in what could be labeled the "access problematic" for citizens in developing countries in gaining access to fulfill their basic needs, such as clean water, electricity, communication and information technology, financial products, and fair trade (Fifka and Idowu 2013; Prahalad 2013). According to Porter and Kramer (2011), it is a matter of shared value, where economic value follows social value and vice versa, which is why these collaborations could be characterized as highly integrated in terms of Austin and Seitanidi's (2012) collaborative continuum.

4.3.1 A Case Example of Inclusive SBM

One on the most cited examples in literature on these inclusive SBMs is the case of micro-credit (Prahalad and Hart 1999) where pioneering companies in the financial sector take sustainable banking to the next level. For example, Grameen Bank, Tridos Bank, and Citigroup provide loans and financial services to people and small enterprises in developing countries that otherwise lack access to the conventional finance system (Fifka and Idowu 2013; Dossa and Kaeufer 2014). Another example in this stream of literature is the establishment of innovative SBMs through supply chain collaborations, for example, in the coffee industry where farmers in developing countries are included in supply chains by Western companies with the ability to sell their products through fair trade if they apply to certain standards (Argenti 2004; Linton 2005; Perez-Alemann and Sandilands 2008).

In supporting institutionalization of fair trade, companies indirectly reduce poverty and asymmetries between suppliers and retailers though sustainable consumption. Although the prerequisite for companies in developing fair trade engagements is access to NGO resources and capabilities related to, for example, training activities aimed at small local farmers in developing countries (Senge et al. 2006), there is some evidence in literature on business-NGO collaborations that these collaborations sometimes emerge from NGO pressures and activism similarly to regulative innovations (Argenti 2004; Linton 2005; Perez-Alemann and Sandilands 2008). It is therefore likely to assume that drivers for companies to enter into fair trade collaborations may comprise a mixture of both legitimacy drivers and resource-based view drivers.

Prahalad and Hart (1999) argue that BOP markets contain profitable business opportunities if companies are willing to adjust their business models and overcome problems in distribution, credit, communication, and education of customers. It is a matter of creativity and radical rethinking of conventional business models and companies often realize that they have to go far beyond incremental adjustment of existing business models used for high-income markets when they are trying to find their pathway through these new markets, combining sustainability, good quality, and low prices (typically 90% price and cost reduction compared with Western markets) (Prahalad and Hart 2002; Schuster and Holtbrügge 2014).

Building trust can be a challenging issue in this archetype of business-NGO collaborations because the NGO partner oftentimes is suspicious of the commercial goals of the business partner (Venn and Berg 2013). Furthermore, business partners often push to move forward and do not want to spend much time on various discussions and dialogues (Schuster and Holtbrügge 2014). Although partners share the same overall mission, for example, providing poor or marginalized people with access to water, cell phones, and so on, there may still be some friction in creating shared value in the collaborative interface (Dahan et al. 2010; Venn and Berg 2013).

4.4 SBM Archetype 4: Social Investment Sustainable Business Models

In recent years, a small but growing part of literature rooted in disciplines of business and society and business strategy has emerged within this archetype of business-NGO collaborations. The most common focus has been to examine how conventional philanthropic collaborations could transform into different areas of business-inspired social investment innovations and community welfare innovations, such as preschool education, minority university education, public education, job training, health care, child cancer treatment, and special services and products aimed at disabled and vulnerable customers (Austin 2000; Warhurst 2005; Holmes and Smart 2009; Eweje and Palakshappa 2011; Jamali et al. 2011). Although this archetype primarily has been practiced in an Anglo-Saxon institutional context where the social welfare system is less developed, there is some evidence that it is on the rise in a global context, taking regulative innovations in terms of social codes of conduct and inclusive business model to the next level.

Competitive advantages gained through this archetype may be when the company is in a position to offer resources that no other companies are able to match (Porter and Kramer 2002). The purpose of these collaborations is therefore often to align local and regional innovative community investments with business strategy to extend the boundaries between core business and society (Warhurst 2005). These insights lead us to understand these collaborations as enablers for social business model innovation at the community level rather than innovation solely seen from a business-centric perspective. Although social investment business model innovations often emerge out of philanthropic community activities, there are differences, as philanthropy is a good and useful thing to do while social investment innovations are deeply embedded within the company strategy, identity, and mission (Austin 2000). Moreover, these business-NGO collaborations are characterized by high levels of integrative value creation, as they evolve toward mutual social goals and missions (Kanter 1999; Austin 2000). In essence, these collaborations could be viewed as highly advanced transformational social business models tightly aligned with the company core business and mission, functioning as catalyst for wider social innovations and solving long-standing problems at the societal level (Rondinelli and London 2003; Le Ber and Branzei 2010).

4.4.1 A Case Example of Social Investment SBM

One case example of social investment SBM is Bestsellers' collaboration with Save the Children, where young people in Bangladesh get access to education through the common Work2Learn project. This means that human labor codes of conduct are supplemented with investments in community educational programs. Another example is seen in the case of the retail chain Coop and their Savannah project, where Coop invests in local schools in collaboration with an NGO, Care, as a prerequisite of training farmers in their supply chain.

The most obvious drivers within these collaborations are based on the resource-based view, gaining access to NGO resources and capabilities in order to develop increased welfare, systemic change, increased community goodwill, and so on (Eweje and Palakshapp 2011), which indirectly may affect the corporate context in terms of better educated and healthier employees and in terms of increased purchasing power because of lower unemployment rates (Kanter 1999; Porter and Kramer 2002). In light of this evidence,

Porter and Kramer (2002, p. 68) argue there is a close link between the corporate competitive context and corporate contributions to society.

Due to the fact that this archetype typically emerges out of conventional philanthropy, it also implies that a range of managerial challenges should be considered to ensure success (Austin 2000). Building trust, eliminating mistrust of the other partner's motives, and transforming conflicts and confusion caused by cultural misunderstandings and differences in governance structures into organizational anchorage and relational capabilities seem to be important managerial challenges (Austin 2000; Googins and Rochlin 2000; Le Ber and Branzei 2010; Eweje and Palakshappa 2011). Employee engagement beyond previous philanthropic engagement is also crucial in fostering trust and learning capabilities at the community level (Austin 2000).

5 Discussion

The literature review and the empirical examples of this study reveal an extensive potential and empirical relevance of business-NGO collaborations in creating SBMs. This chapter builds on the cornerstone literature within business-NGO collaborations combined with the most recent research on SBM. Through the literature review and the case examples, we have identified, discussed, and mapped four different types of business-NGO collaborations and their unique drivers and challenges in creating SBM. A key player in the literature is James Austin (2000), who presented the three stages of business-NGO collaborative interaction, which were later developed into elaborated collaborative continuum consisting of four collaborative stages describing the nature of each of them in terms of level of engagement, co-creation, complexity, and so on (Austin and Seitanidi 2012).

Drivers for strategic decisions in pursuing different types of SBM through business-NGO collaborations are absent in Austin and Seitanidi's collaborative continuum. However, it could be argued from the case examples that different drivers may lead companies toward different types of business-NGO collaborations on the basis of a range of situational conditions. We therefore argue that companies' choice of NGO collaborations within the archetype of regulative innovations is tightly related to NGO criticism and pressures, whereas companies' choice of inclusive business model innovation and social investment innovation is tightly related to access problems for citizens to gain equal access to basic products and welfare services such as electricity, water, information and communication technology, financial products, and fair trade.

By modeling the four archetypes based on Austin and Seitanidi's collaborative continuum, we link strategic options to different drivers and challenges in creating sustainable innovation through business-NGO collaborations. On this basis we put forward the following proposition. Based on the case examples, we therefore stress that companies' choice of marketing innovations and regulative innovations in collaboration with NGO partners is tightly related to legitimacy drivers in terms of third-party endorsement and reputation. On the other hand, companies' choice of inclusive business model innovation and social investment innovation in collaboration with NGO partners is tightly related to resource-based view drivers in terms of gaining access to NGO resources and competencies.

Furthermore, it appears that the business case of sustainable innovations through legitimacy-driven business-NGO collaborations is more visible and measurable in a short-term perspective than in business-NGO collaborations driven by the resourced-based view. The latter are therefore challenged to measure the outcome from a short perspective and from a long perspective. Thus, the complexity of long-term management practice in a short-term business world is a key challenge that needs to be addressed in these collaborations. We therefore argue that legitimacy-driven business-NGO collaborations are related to the managerial challenges of the business case of CSR from a short-term perspective, whereas collaborations driven by the resource-based view are related to the managerial challenges of the business case of CSR from a long-term perspective.

6 Conclusion

The contributions of this chapter constitute a mapping of the archetypes of business-NGO collaborations building on Austin and Seitanidi's collaborative continuum with a discussion of the key drivers and challenges to be considered in generating sustainable innovation through the four different archetypes. The practical implications of this study constitute knowledge applied by companies in their selection, application, and integration of NGOs in SBM projects. The objectives of the companies and NGOs entering into these collaborations should therefore be applied in guiding a proper selection between the different collaborative types. Often, companies are engaged in more than one type of business-NGO collaboration, which may challenge companies in their day-to-day operations and handling of these collaborations. One scenario would be for the companies to handle all collaborations in the same way, which this study questions as the right solution, due to the difference in characteristics and different potentials.

The limitations of this study also reveal key avenues of further research to be pursued. Each of the four business-NGO collaborative types implies and constitutes differences in the way these collaborations should be managed, organized, and measured optimally. This is briefly addressed in the existing research and during the theoretical review. However, despite these early indicators, little theoretical understanding has been offered in exploring the managerial and organizational practices and challenges of how these innovative collaborations evolve and continue to stay innovative. In fact, these R&D processes are highly dependent on NGO capabilities in terms of, for example, on-the-ground legitimacy, knowledge of customer needs, consumer feedback, consumer education, infrastructure, access to local gatekeepers and networks, and so on (Dahan et al. 2010; Esko et al. 2012; Graf and Rotlauf 2012).

Furthermore, very limited research was found on the difference in how business-NGO collaborations are established and managed across national borders or across different industrial contexts. However, differences in national cultures and industrial settings have in other comparative management studies in other research fields revealed numerous differences in how management is carried out. The same differences may be expected and should be examined in an international case study across different industries. Another limitation relates to the fact that there is a general lack of widely accepted definitions applicable to sustainable innovation.

Sustainable innovation as a concept and practice is still evolving, which challenges the development of accepted definitions. However, further research should attempt to address this issue. Additionally, the concepts and definitions of business-NGO collaborations vary. This study attempts to answers the question of defining business-NGO collaborations through mapping and naming four archetypes. Yet the study does not discuss the variety of NGOs or the differences in definitions. The gaps and shortcomings in the existing literature present key areas within the research field in creating sustainable innovation through business-NGO collaborations. Empirical knowledge of how companies successfully manage issues of trust, organize, and measure each of the four archetypes is needed. This is also why the four archetype models and the derived results of the present study will be explored further in relation to the application, management, organization, and measurement of business-NGO collaborations in the four archetypes through a cross-industrial case study.

References

Aagaard, A. 2016. *Sustainable Business—Integrating CSR in Business and Functions*. River Publishers.

Aagaard, A., and S. Ritzén. 2018. Creating and Capturing Sustainable Value Through Sustainable Business Models and Service Innovation. Conference paper presented at the *25th IPDMC: Innovation and Product Development Management Conference*, Porto, Portugal, June 10–13, 2018.

Adams, R., S. Jeanrenaud, J. Bessant, P. Overy, and D. Denyer. 2012. *Innovating for Sustainability. A Systematic Review of the Body of Knowledge*. ON, Canada: Network for Business Sustainability.

Adderly, S., and D. Mellor. 2014. Who's Influencing Whom? Developing Sustainable Business Partnerships. *EuroMed Journal of Business* 9 (1): 60–74.

Angus-Leppan, T., L. Metcalf, and S. Benn. 2010. Leadership Styles and CSR Practice: An Examination of Sense-Making, Institutional Drivers and CSR Leadership. *Journal of Business Ethics* 93 (2): 189–213.

Arenas, D., J. Lozano, and L. Albareda. 2009. The Role of NGOs in CSR: Mutual Perceptions Among Stakeholders. *Journal of Business Ethics* 88 (1): 175–197.

Argenti, P.A. 2004. Collaborating with Activists: How Starbucks Works with NGOs. *California Management Review* 47 (1): 91–116.

Aulakh, P.S., M. Kotabe, and A. Sahay. 1997. Trust and Performance in Cross-Border Marketing Partnerships: A Behavioral Approach. In *Cooperative Strategies, North American Perspectives*, ed. P.W. Beamish and J.P. Killing. San Francisco: The New Lexington Press.

Austin, J.E. 2000. *The Collaboration Challenge: How Nonprofits and Businesses Succeed Through Strategic Alliances*. San Francisco, CA: Jossey Bass Ltd.

———. 2003. Marketing's Role in Cross-Sector Collaboration. *Journal of Nonprofit & Public Sector Marketing* 11 (1): 23–39.

Austin, J.E., and M. Seitanidi. 2012. Collaborative Value Creation: A Review of Partnering Between Non-profits and Businesses: Part 1: Value Creation Spectrum and Collaborative Stages. *Nonprofit & Voluntary Sector Quarterly* 45 (5): 726–758.

Bansal, P. 2005. Evolving Sustainability: A Longitudinal Study of Corporate Sustainable Development. *Strategic Management Journal* 26: 197–218.

Barney, J., and M.H. Hansen. 1994. Trustworthiness as a Source of Competitive Advantage. *Strategic Management Journal* 15: 175–190.

Basil, D.Z., and P.M. Herr. 2003. Dangerous Donations? The Effects of Cause-Related Marketing on Charity Attitude. *Journal of Nonprofit & Public Sector Marketing* 11 (1): 59–76.

Birkin, F., T. Polesie, and L. Lewis. 2009. A New Business Model for Sustainable Development: An Exploratory Study Using the Theory of Constraints in Nordic Organizations. *Business Strategy and the Environment* 18 (5): 277–290.

Bocken, N.M.P., S.W. Short, P. Rana, and S. Evans. 2014. A Literature and Practice Review to Develop Sustainable Business Model Archetypes. *Journal of Cleaner Production* 65: 42–56.

Boons, F., and F. Lüdeke-Freund. 2013. Business Models for Sustainable Innovation: State-of-the Art and Steps Towards a Research Agenda. *Journal of Cleaner Production* 45: 9–19.

Bowen, F., A. Newenham-Kahindi, and I. Herremans. 2010. When Suits Meet Roots: The Antecedents and Consequences of Community Engagement Strategy. *Journal of Business Ethics* 95 (2): 297–318.

Bowman, C., and V. Ambrosini. 2000. Value Creation Versus Value Capture: Towards a Coherent Definition of Value in Strategy. *British Journal of Management* 11: 1–15.

Carroll, A.B., and K.M. Shabana. 2010. The Business Case for Corporate Social Responsibility: A Review of Concepts, Research and Practice. *International Journal of Management Reviews* 12 (1): 85–105.

Charter, M., and T. Clark. 2007. *Sustainable Innovation: Key Conclusions from Sustainable Innovation Conferences 2003–2006*. The Centre for Sustainable Design. University College for the Creative Arts, May 2007. www.cfsd.org.uk.

Chesbrough, H., W. Vanhaverbeke, and J. West. 2006. *Open Innovation: Researching a New Paradigm*. Oxford: Oxford University Press.

Dahan, N.M., J.P. Doh, J. Oetzel, and M. Yaziji. 2010. Corporate–NGO Collaboration: Co-creating New Business Models for Developing Markets. *Long Range Planning* 43 (2/3): 326–342.

Dees, J.G. 1998. Enterprising Nonprofits. *Harvard Business Review* 76 (1): 54–67.

Doh, J.P., and T.R. Guay. 2004. Globalization and Corporate Social Responsibility: How Non-governmental Organizations Influence Labor and Environmental Codes of Conduct. *Management International Review* 44 (2): 7–29.

Dossa, Z., and K. Kaeufer. 2014. Understanding Sustainability Innovations Through Positive Ethical Networks. *Journal of Business Ethics* 119: 543–559.

Dryzek, J.S. 2005. *The politics of the Earth: Environmental Discourses*. Oxford University Press.

Esko, S., M. Zeromkis, and J. Hsuan. 2012. Value Chain and Innovation at the Base of the Pyramid. *South Asian Journal of Global Business Research* 2 (2): 230–250.

Eweje, G., and N. Palakshappa. 2011. Stakeholder Collaboration in New Zealand. *Journal of Corporate Citizenship* 43 (Autumn): 79–101.

Fifka, M.S., and S.O. Idowu. 2013. Sustainability and Social Innovation. In *Social Innovation: Solutions for a Sustainable Future*, ed. T. Osburg and R. Schmidpeter. Heidelberg: Springer.

García, I., J.J. Gibaja, and A. Mujika. 2003. A Study on the Effect of Cause-Related Marketing on the Attitude Towards the Brand: The Case of Pepsi in Spain. *Journal of Nonprofit & Public Sector Marketing* 11 (1): 111–135.

Googins, B.K., and S.A. Rochlin. 2000. Creating the Partnership Society: Understanding the Rhetoric and Reality of Cross-Sectoral Partnerships. *Business and Society Review* 105 (1): 127–144.

Graf, F.S.N., and F. Rotlauf. 2012. Firm-NGO Collaborations, a Resource-Based Perspective. *Z Betriebswirtz* 82: 103–125.

Guay, T., J.P. Doh, and G. Sinclair. 2004. Non-governmental Organizations, Shareholder Activism, and Socially Responsible Investments: Ethical, Strategic, and Governance Implications. *Journal of Business Ethics* 52 (1): 125–139.

Gulati, R. 1995. Does Familiarity Breed Trust? The Implications of Repeated Ties for Contractual Choice in Alliances. *Academy of Management Journal* 38: 85–112.

———. 1998. Alliances and Networks. *Strategic Management Journal* 19: 293–317.

Heap, S. 2000. NGO-Business Partnerships: Research-in-Progress. *Public Management* 2 (4): 555–563.

Holling, C.S. 2001. Understanding the Complexity of Economic, Ecological, and Social Systems. *Ecosystems* 4 (5): 390–405.

Holmes, S., and P. Smart. 2009. Exploring Open Innovation Practice in Firm-Nonprofit Engagements: A Corporate Social Responsibility Perspective. *R&D Management* 39 (4): 394–409.

Inkpen, A.C. 2000. Learning Though Joint Ventures: A Framework of Knowledge Acquisition. *Journal of Management Studies* 37 (7): 1019–1044.

Inkpen, A.C., and S.C. Currall. 1997. International Joint Venture Trust: An Empirical Examination. In *Cooperative Strategies, North American Perspectives*, ed. P.W. Beamish and J.P. Killing. San Francisco: New Lexington Press.

Jamali, D., M. Yianni, and H. Abdallah. 2011. Strategic Partnerships, Social Capital and Innovation: Accounting for Social Alliance Innovation. *Business Ethics: A European Review* 20 (4): 375–391.

Johnson, J.L., J.B. Cullen, T. Sakano, and H. Takenouchi. 1997. Setting the Stage for Trust and Strategic Integration in Japanese-U.S Cooperative Alliances. In *Cooperative Strategies, North American Perspectives*, ed. P.W. Beamish and J.P. Killing. San Francisco: The New Lexington Press.

Jolink, A., and E. Niesten. 2015. Sustainable Development and Business Models of Entrepreneurs in the Organic Food Industry. *Business Strategy and the Environment* 24 (6): 386–401.

Joyce, A., and R.L. Paquin. 2016. The Triple Layered Business Model Canvas: A Tool to Design More Sustainable Business Models. *Journal of Cleaner Production* 135: 1474–1486.

Kanter, R.M. 1999. From Spare Change to Real Change. *Harvard Business Review* 77 (3): 122–132.

Kong, N., O. Salzmann, U. Steger, and A. Ionescu-Sommers. 2002. Moving Business/Industry Towards Sustainable Consumption: The Role of NGOs. *European Management Journal* 20 (2): 109–127.

Kourula, A. 2010. Corporate Engagement with Non-governmental Organizations in Different Institutional Contexts: A Case Study of a Forest Products Company. *Journal of World Business* 45: 395–404.

Koza, M.P., and A.Y. Lewin. 1998. The Co-Evolution of Strategic Alliances. *Organization Science* 9 (3): 255–264.

Le Ber, M.J., and O. Branzei. 2010. (Re)forming Strategic Cross-Sector Partnerships: Relational Processes of Social Innovation. *Business and Society* 49 (1): 140–172.

Lepak, D.P., K.G. Smith, and M.S. Taylor. 2007. Value Creation and Value Capture: A Multilevel Perspective. *Academy of Management Review* 32 (1): 180–194.

Leung, K., and S. White. 2006. Exploring Dark Corners: An Agenda for Organizational Behavior Research in Alliance Contexts. In *Handbook of Strategic Alliances*, ed. O. Shenkar and J.J. Reuer. Thousand Oaks, CA: Sage Publications.

Linton, A. 2005. Partnering for Sustainability: Business–NGO Alliances in the Coffee Industry. *Development in Practice* 15 (3–4): 600–614.

Lodsgård, L., and A. Aagaard. 2017. Creating Value Through CSR Across Company Functions and NGO Collaborations: A Scandinavian Cross-Industry Case Study. *Scandinavian Journal of Management* 33: 162–174.

Lüdeke-Freund, F. 2010. Towards a Conceptual Framework of Business Models for Sustainability. In *ERSCP-EMU Conference*, Delft, The Netherlands, 1–28.

Madhok, A. 1995. Opportunism and Trust in Joint Venture Relationships: An Exploratory Study and a Model. *Scandinavian Journal of Management* 15 (1): 57–74.

Makadok, R. 2001. Appointed Commentary on Priem and Butler. *Academy of Management Review* 26: 498–499.

Makadok, R., and R. Coff. 2002. The Theory Of Value and the Value of Theory: Breaking New Ground Versus Reinventing the Wheel. *Academy of Management Review* 27 (1): 10–13.

Mandell, M.P., and T.A. Steelman. 2003. Understanding What Can Be Accomplished Through Interorganizational Innovations. *Public Management Review* 5 (2): 197–224.

Matten, D., and J. Moon. 2008. 'Implicit' and 'Explicit' CSR: A Conceptual Framework for a Comparative Understanding of Corporate Social Responsibility. *Academy of Management Review* 33 (2): 404–424.

Michelini, L., and D. Fiorentino. 2012. New Business Models for Creating Shared Value. *Social Responsibility Journal* 8 (4): 561–577.

Millar, C., C.J. Choi, and S. Chen. 2004. Global Strategic Partnerships Between MNEs and NGOs: Drivers of Change and Ethical Issues. *Business and Society Review* 109 (4): 395–414.

Morgan, R.M., and S.D. Hunt. 1994. The Commitment-Trust Theory of Relationship Marketing. *Journal of Marketing* 58 (3): 20–38.

Newman, L. 2005. Uncertainty, Innovation, and Dynamic Sustainable Development. *Sustainability, Science, Practice & Policy* 1 (2): 25–31.

Novak, L.I., and T.K. Clarke. 2003. Cause-Related Marketing: Keys to Successful Relationships with Corporate Sponsors and Their Customers. *Journal of Nonprofit & Public Sector Marketing* 11 (1): 137–149.

Osterwalder, A., and Y. Pigneur. 2005. Clarifying Business Models: Origins, Present, and Future of the Concept. *Communications of the Association for Information Systems* 15: 1–25.

Ozman, M. 2009. Inter-firm Networks and Innovation: A Survey of the Literature. *Economics of Innovation and New Technology* 18 (1): 39–67.

Pedersen, E.R.G., W. Gwozdz, and K.H. Hvass. 2016. Exploring the Relationship Between Business Model Innovation, Corporate Sustainability, and Organizational Values Within Fashion Industry. *Journal of Business Ethics*. https://doi.org/10.1007/s10551-016-3044-7.

Pedersen, E.R.G., and J.T. Pedersen. 2013. Introduction: The Rise of Business-NGO Partnerships. *The Journal of Corporate Citizenship* 50: 6–20.

Pedersen, E.R.G., J.T. Pedersen, and Ø.P. Jacobsen. 2011. Partnerskaber mellem virksomheder og NGOer. *Ledelse og Erhvervsøkonomi* 4: 33–48.

Peloza, J., and L. Falkenberg. 2009. The Role of Collaboration in Achieving Corporate Social Responsibility Objectives. *California Management Review* 51 (3): 95–113.

Perez-Alemann, P., and M. Sandilands. 2008. Building Value at the Top and the Bottom of the Global Supply Chain: MNC–NGO Partnerships. *California Management Review* 51 (1): 24–49.

Perez-Batres, L., J. Doh, V. Miller, and M. Pisani. 2012. Stakeholder Pressures as Determinants of CSR Strategic Choice: Why Do Firms Choose Symbolic Versus Substantive Self-Regulatory Codes of Conduct? *Journal of Business Ethics* 110 (2): 157–172.

Porter, M.E., and M.R. Kramer. 2002. The Competitive Advantage of Corporate Philanthropy. *Harvard Business Review* 80 (12): 56–69.

———. 2011. Creating Shared Value. *Harvard Business Review* 89 (1–2): 62–77.

Potts, T., and M. Haward. 2006. International Trade, Eco-Labelling and Sustainable Fisheries—Recent Issues, Concepts and Practices. *Environment, Development and Sustainability* 9: 91–106.

Prahalad, D. 2013. Design Strategy for the Bottom of the Pyramid. In *Social Innovation: Solutions for a Sustainable Future*, ed. T. Osburg and R. Schmidpeter. Berlin and Heidelberg: Springer.

Prahalad, C.K., and S.L. Hart. 1999. Strategies for the Bottom of the Pyramid: Creating Sustainable Innovation. *Working Paper*.

———. 2002. The Fortune at the Bottom of the Pyramid. *Strategy + Business* 26: 1–14.

Ring, P.S., and A.H. Van de Ven. 1992. Structuring Cooperative Relationships Between Organizations. *Strategic Management Journal* 13 (7): 483–498.

———. 1994. Developmental Processes of Cooperative Interorganizational Relationships. *The Academy of Management Review* 19 (1): 90–118.

Rivara-Santos, M., and C. Rufin. 2010. Odd Couples: Understanding the Governance of Firm-NGO Alliances. *Journal of Business Ethics* 94 (1): 55–70.

Rondinelli, D.A., and T. London. 2003. How Corporations and Environmental Groups Cooperate: Assessing Cross-Sector Alliances and Collaborations. *The Academy of Management Executive* 17 (1): 61–76.

Sarkar, M., T. Cavusgil, and C. Evirgen. 1997. A Commitment-Trust Mediated Framework of International Collaborative Venture Performance. In *Cooperative Strategies, North American Perspectives*, ed. P.W. Beamish and J.P. Killing. San Francisco: The New Lexington Press.

Saunders, G.S., and R. Borland. 2013. Marketing-Driven Philanthropy: The Case of PlayPumps. *European Business Review* 25 (4): 321–335.

Schaltegger, S., E.G. Hansen, and F. Lüdeke-Freund. 2016. Business Models for Sustainability: Origins, Present Research, and Future Avenues. *Organization and Environment* 29 (1): 3–10.

Schaltegger, S., F. Lüdeke-Freund, and E. Hansen. 2012. Business Cases for Sustainability and the Role of Business Model Innovation. *International Journal of Innovation and Sustainable Development* 6 (2): 95–119.

Schuster, T. and Holtbrügge, D. 2014. Benefits of Cross-Sector Partnerships in Markets at the Base of the Pyramid. *Business Strategy and the Environment* 23: 188–203.

Senge, P.M., M. Dow, and G. Neath. 2006. Learning Together: New Partnerships for New Times. *Corporate Governance* 6 (4): 420–430.

Sommer, A. 2012. *Managing Green Business Model Transformations*. Berlin: Springer.

Spar, D.L., and L.T. La Mure. 2003. The Power of Activism: Assessing the Impact of NGOs on Global Business. *California Management Review* 45 (3): 78–101.

Stafford, E.R., M.J. Polonsky, and C.L. Hartman. 2000. Environmental NGO–Business Collaboration and Strategic Bridging: A Case Analysis of the Greenpeace-Foron Alliance. *Business Strategy and the Environment* 9 (2): 122–135.

Stubbs, W., and C. Cocklin. 2008. Conceptualizing a 'Sustainability Business Model'. *Organization & Environment* 21 (2): 103–127.

UNDP. 2010. Inclusive Markets Development: Brokering Inclusive Business Models. United Nations, Arrangements and Practices for the Interaction of Non-Governmental Organizations in All Activities of the United Nations System. New York: Report of the Secretary-General, United Nations, 199ara. 1.

Upward, A., and P. Jones. 2016. An Ontology for Strongly Sustainable Business Models: Defining an Enterprise Framework Compatible with Natural and Social Science. *Organization and Environment* 29 (1): 97–123.

Venn, R., and N. Berg. 2013. Building Competitive Advantage Through Social Entrepreneurship. *South Asian Journal of Business Research* 2 (1): 104–127.

Vogel, D.J. 2005. Is There a Market for Virtue? The Business Case for Corporate Social Responsibility. *California Management Review* 47 (4): 19–45.

Waddock, S. 2008. Building a New Institutional Infrastructure for Corporate Responsibility. *Academy of Management Perspectives* 22 (3): 87–108.

Warhurst, A. 2005. Future Roles of Business in Society: The Expanding Boundaries of Corporate Responsibility and a Compelling Case for Partnership. *Futures* 37 (2): 151–168.

Wymer, W.W., and S. Samu. 2003. Dimensions of Business and Nonprofit Collaborative Relationships. *Journal of Nonprofit & Public Sector Marketing* 11 (1): 3–22.

Yaziji, M., and J. Doh. 2009. *NGOs and Corporations: Conflict and Collaboration*. Cambridge: Cambridge University Press.

Yunus, M., B. Moingeon, and L. Lehmann-Ortega. 2010. Building Social Business Models: Lessons from the Grameen Experience. *Long Range Planning* 43: 308–325.

Zaher, A., and J. Harris. 2006. Interorganizational Trust. In *Handbook of Strategic Alliances*, ed. O. Shenkar and J.J. Reuer. Thousand Oaks, CA: Sage Publications.

Zink, K.J., U. Steimle, and K. Fisher. 2008. Human Factors, Business Excellence and Corporate Sustainability: Differing Perspectives, Joint Objectives. In *Corporate Sustainability as a Challenge for Comprehensive Management*, ed. K.J. Zink. Heidelberg: Physica-Verlag.

9

Sustainable Business Models in an Entrepreneurial Environment

Raz Godelnik and Jen van der Meer

1 Introduction

The entrepreneurial space has been undergoing a transformation in the past decade, not only due to developments in technology that have created unprecedented opportunities, but also thanks to the active sharing and dissemination of a growing number of tools and methodologies created to support the complex and risky entrepreneurial process. The Business Model Canvas (BMC) (2010), Lean Canvas (2012), Agile Development (2011), and Customer Development (2005) are some of the main methods that have emerged, providing aspiring entrepreneurs with a clearer roadmap to navigate their way to their desired destination: creating a successful enterprise.

At their core, these new methodologies represent the growing understanding of the difference between a startup and an existing company—

R. Godelnik (✉) • J. van der Meer
Parsons School of Design—The New School, New York, NY, USA
e-mail: godelnir@newschool.edu; vandermj@newschool.edu

© The Author(s) 2019
A. Aagaard (ed.), *Sustainable Business Models*, Palgrave Studies in Sustainable Business In Association with Future Earth, https://doi.org/10.1007/978-3-319-93275-0_9

while the latter executes a business model, the former searches for one (Blank 2013). In addition, these methodologies diverge from a more traditional linear (waterfall model) approach to innovation to an approach that is more agile, iterative, and uses feedback from customers in the early stages of development to test the entrepreneur's initial hypotheses.

While there is almost no empirical evidence regarding the success of the lean startup methodology (Ladd 2016; Nilsen and Ramm 2015), the approach has become popular not only in Silicon Valley, but worldwide, making its way into academia, government, nongovernmental organizations (NGOs), and even large corporations seeking to learn a new mindset that will help them become better innovators ("think like a startup").

The lean startup movement was followed by another movement—the sustainable business models (SBMs)[1] movement, which to some extent was created as a counter-movement. This SBM movement made the case that lean startup is grounded in "business as usual" thinking, driven solely by growth maximization with the ultimate goal of profit maximization without considering the social and environmental impacts of the new venture. In contrast, the SBM movement aims to offer new ways to marry values with value creation, providing entrepreneurs with a roadmap as clear as the one provided by the lean startup movement, but with a different destination in mind: multiple forms of value creation for multiple stakeholders.

These attempts to conceptualize a framework supporting sustainable entrepreneurship (SE) are defined by Schaltegger and Wagner (2011, p. 225) as "the realization of sustainability innovations aimed at the mass market and providing benefit to the larger part of society." While such attempts are supported by a growing body of literature and interest among practitioners, they have failed as yet to generate any significant traction. Growing recognition of the role business models can play as a means of, or even the foundation of, creating value through sustainable innovations has not seemed to improve the adoption rate. One main reason for this lack of take-up is that the discourse regarding SMB tends not to differentiate between startups and corporate environments, adopting de facto the notion that this differentiation is not material and creating a disconnect between SBM thinking and the needs and constraints implicit in the entrepreneurial journey.

We, however, make the case that without proper differentiation and contextualization the SBM framework cannot achieve its full potential to advance sustainable development through innovation, especially in an entrepreneurial environment. We believe there is a clear need to not only connect theory and practice that speak different languages today, but also to make sustainability-driven entrepreneurship a viable path, not just an aspirational goal.

In this chapter, we first discuss this gap by contextualizing the SBM framework in startups, reviewing lean startup adoption in startups, and presenting the key reasons startups choose lean startup over SBM as their guiding philosophy. Then, we explore how a bridge can be built between SBM and lean startup, introducing a new framework that we call "The Lean SBM." Finally, we provide four examples of various applications of the framework already in use, offering signs of practical approaches to integrate SBM in the world of startups.

2 Context: Sustainable Business Models in Startups at the Intersection of Sustainable Business Models and Sustainable Entrepreneurship

This chapter investigates SBM in a very particular context, focusing on their application by entrepreneurs. More specifically, our interest is in entrepreneurs working in startups, which we differentiate from entrepreneurs who innovate inside existing firms (also known as intrapreneurs), reflecting the growing cultural, social, and economic interest in startups.

As illustrated in Fig. 9.1, the space we explore is situated in the overlap between the SBM ecosystem and sustainable entrepreneurship (SE), in which researchers have established clear links between the SBM point of view and SE. Within this area (SBM/SE), we concentrate only on startups, excluding the other part of SBM/SE, which considers established organizations. While our starting point is SBM, we acknowledge that there is a vast literature on SE that does not relate directly to or is grounded in SBM, and therefore is not considered part of the SBM ecosystem.

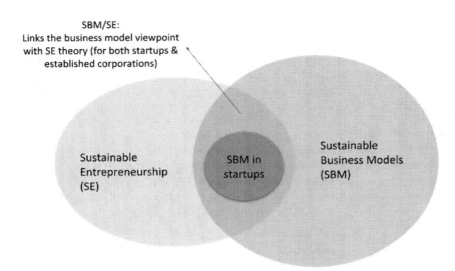

Fig. 9.1 SBM in startups at the intersection of SBM and SE

Nevertheless, our inquiry into SBM in startups is also informed by this literature and we refer to it whenever it helps to further clarify the picture we portray in this chapter; for example, when discussing the very little attention given to the entrepreneurial process in sustainability-driven startups.

Entrepreneurs were considered an integral part of the premise of SBM to "incorporate a triple bottom line approach and consider a wide range of stakeholder interests, including environment and society" (Bocken et al. 2014, p. 42), in the same way as managers and intrapreneurs working in established firms were, reflecting the notion that SBM can both transform existing organizations and help create new ones.

At the same time, de facto, much of the focus of the SBM literature was initially on established organizations, reflecting the focus of preliminary explorations of sustainable development in organizational settings of corporations, either in terms of operationalizing sustainability (Stubbs and Cocklin 2008) or the business case for sustainability (Schaltegger et al. 2012). This initial approach evolved to address startups as well, in most cases not distinguishing it from entrepreneurial activity in established organizations.

This approach is evident, for example, in the New Business Models blueprint that has been published as part of the Reporting 3.0's initiative to create a holistic framework to support the development of a green, inclusive, and open economy. The authors suggest that new business models should not differentiate between entrepreneurs and intrapreneurs, explaining that "in order to scale exponentially, new business models must apply not only to entrepreneurial startups, but also to intrapreneurial transformation of existing business models in even the largest multinational corporations." (Baue and Thurm 2018).

This indivisible approach also reflects that the emphasis of SBM on redefining value creation in organizations with the aim of achieving multiple value creation (social, ecological, economic) for different stakeholders (Jonker 2014a), no matter what the scale of the organization is. This is because "big players can also engage in sustainability-oriented market transformations" (Schaltegger et al. 2016, p. 266). Examples of these transformations can be found in the cases of companies such as Interface (moving from selling carpets to a leasing-based model) and Novelis (applying a circular economy model that is based on a closed-loop recycling system).

Additionally, this approach corresponds with the management literature suggesting that entrepreneurs can also be found in corporations. As Drucker (1985, p. 22) explains in his classic book *Innovation and Entrepreneurship*: "entrepreneurs...create something new, something different; they change or transmute values. An enterprise also does not need to be small and new to be an entrepreneur. Indeed, entrepreneurship is being practiced by large and often old enterprises."

The indivisible approach to entrepreneurs and intrapreneurs in the SBM literature is also reflected in the different tools and frameworks developed in the past decade to support the work on SBM. For example, the flourishing business canvas (evolved from the Strongly Sustainable Business Model Canvas (Upward 2013)), SBM archetypes (Bocken et al. 2014), the value mapping tool (Bocken et al. 2013), and the Business Innovation Kit & Sustainability Innovation Pack, which enables "entrepreneurial teams to explore, dispute about, and co-define business ideas and models for new or existing organisations" (Lüdeke-Freund 2015). Nevertheless, the growing number of tools and frameworks (see Lüdeke-Freund et al. (2016) for an extensive review of SBM tools and frameworks) illustrates the growing attention to the applicability of SBM and the need to provide more guidance regarding how to make this "market device" (Boons and Lüdeke-Freund 2013) work in different contexts.

It is not only SBM scholars who do not separate startups from established firms. In their 2014 report on business model innovation for sustainability, written by two SustainAbility executives, the authors report on the important role large companies have regarding SBM innovation: "Although smaller companies often lead the way in business model innovation, we believe bigger companies have a critical role to play in helping to enhance the impact of the most important innovations" (Clinton and Whisnant 2014, p. 11).

While the majority of SBM scholarship, curricular activity,[2] and practical applications do not distinguish between entrepreneurial activity in startups and established firms, we do see some early signs of interest in making such a distinction. One example is the Lean for Flourishing Startups, co-founded recently by Anthony Upward, who developed the flourishing business canvas, which develops tools to support entrepreneurs working to create flourishing (sustainable) enterprises.

The SBM/SE overlap is grounded in the SBM viewpoint, but it is also informed and influenced by SE research that is not based in SBM (although it may occasionally refer to it). This stream's main focus includes topics such as the entrepreneurs involved in SE; the raison d'être to start SE; the development processes of SE; business orientation; and other aspects that are important for the understanding of SE. Similar to the SBM literature, which is dominated by the notion that the "small versus big" dichotomy (Schaltegger et al. 2016) is a false one, much of the SE research does not differentiate entrepreneurs in startups from intrapreneurs. However, unlike SBM, SE does include a clear sub-stream of research distinguishing between these activities (see Muñoz and Cohen (2018) for an extensive review of SE literature focusing only on startups).

Considered a subset of the entrepreneurship domain (Muñoz and Cohen 2018) SE is, according to Schaltegger and Wagner (2011, p. 225): "the realization of sustainability innovations aimed at the mass market and providing benefit to the larger part of society." The authors make the case that its core SE applies Schumpeter's (1942) idea of creative destruction to sustainability, aiming to replace current processes, products, and services with ones that are better in terms of their social and environmental impacts. The authors provide a four-category typology of sustainability-oriented entrepreneurship: ecopreneurship (environmental entrepreneurship), social entrepreneurship, institutional entrepreneurship, and SE.

Ecopreneurship—focusing on environmental problems. This is a relatively new phenomenon that emerged from the growing understanding in the 1980s of the business value of sustainability. Starting at the beginning of the 1990s, this premise has received growing attention, as reflected in the growing literature covering it (see Schaper (2010) for a detailed list of papers). Schaper (2010) suggests three features common to all ecopreneurial activity: First, they are entrepreneurial activities; second, they have a net positive environmental impact; and finally, they are intentional (i.e. their net positive environmental impact is not accidental but deliberate one, although the level of significance that environmental goals have can vary significantly from one ecopreneur to another).

Social entrepreneurship—focusing on addressing social problems. Of the four, this category is the one probably attracting most attention from scholars. This interest evolved from an early focus on definition and distinctive characteristics to investigating social enterprises' management and performance (Doherty et al. 2014). With the social objective at its core, its definitions range from broad, including both for-profit, non-profit, and hybrid platforms, to narrow, mainly considering non-profit applications (Austin et al. 2006).

Exploring social entrepreneurship through a broader lens and, in particular, the context of commercial entrepreneurship, the duality of

combining social value with financial sustainability has always been one of the main challenges for entrepreneurs trying to overcome the traditional dichotomy between social value creation and financial performance.
Institutional entrepreneurship—focusing on entrepreneurs looking to change institutional settings, transforming exiting societal, regulatory and market institutions, or creating new ones (Schaltegger and Wagner 2011).
Sustainable entrepreneurship—according to Muñoz and Cohen (2018) at its core, SE is about entrepreneurial activities that, at minimum, do not harm the ecological and social environments and are expected to consider and work toward achieving all triple-bottom-line goals.

Muñoz and Dimov (2015, p. 650) provide an important insight into SE: "entrepreneurship is a complex phenomenon; sustainable entrepreneurship is perhaps more so, given the presence of commercially viable ventures that pursue economic, social and environmental outcomes concurrently." This warning, concluding their detailed inquiry into the development process of new sustainable ventures, is to some extent our starting point, as it demonstrates the growing need for SBM to play a supporting role for entrepreneurs involved in sustainable activity. This role is similar to the one lean startup has been playing for entrepreneurs involved in entrepreneurial activity in general. As discussed later in this chapter, as yet, SBM has failed to provide this support.

3 Lean Startup Adoption in Startup Ecosystems

Lean startup methods and the BMC changed how venture founders search and discover opportunities to create value. The insights for these methods were derived from the practical experience of serial entrepreneurs, and their rapid adoption first happened when shared through social media platforms and then applied in university settings (Blank 2013).

To understand the success of lean startup in the entrepreneurial space, we first need to understand its origins and how it has developed.

Lean startup methods are inspired by lean manufacturing methods, which are traced to Shewhart's Plan-Do-Study-Act cycles at Bell Labs—a statistical method for quality control. W. Edwards Deming learned the incremental development methodology directly from Shewhart, which later informed his time with Toyota, developing the primary origin of lean manufacturing methods (Womack et al. 1990). The successful implementation of lean is considered when it is adopted as a philosophy and involves major changes to the entire organization, not just on the factory floor (Bhasin and Burcher 2006).

The Agile Manifesto (2001) was another precursor to lean startup and was created by a group of software developers who had struggled during the previous decades with high-failure software development projects managed through the waterfall linear planning methodology. A more flexible methodology was designed to adapt to the rapidly shifting conditions they had just witnessed. The manifesto tapped into iterative, customer-value-defined methods grounded in lean manufacturing and forged an entire shift in the software industry. This shift inspired the rapid proliferation of agile software development frameworks such as Scrum, Rapid Application Development, and Extreme Programming.

Separate from product development, customer development was developed around that time as an important method, focusing on learning which customers to attract and which markets the customers are in through iterative learning. While writing a memoir about his experiences as a serial stage entrepreneur with both huge successes and failures, Blank (2003) noticed a pattern in his more successful ventures. He documented his empirical approach to identifying and validating hypotheses in his book *The Four Steps to the Epiphany*, which documents the practice of customer development.

The customer development process described in the book includes four key phases:

1. *Customer discovery*: discover who the customers are and what problem the venture can solve, defined in the customer's worldview. Ideally a "hair on fire" problem is the best place to start.
2. *Customer validation*: show the product to the customer and determine if the customer adopts the value proposition.

3. *Customer creation*: create end-user demand beyond early product-market fit, move to heavier marketing spend after initial customers are obtained.
4. *Company building*: informal teams and experiential learning migrate to operational scale and robust organization.

Steve Blank, a serial entrepreneur and Jerry Engel, a venture capital investor, developed the Lean LaunchPad, which presented an iterative approach to discovering and validating customer need and business model viability, providing entrepreneurs with a journey map addressing key steps of the process. After successfully prototyping the Lean LaunchPad as a class at Berkeley's Haas School of Business, the course was adapted at Stanford's Engineering program, connecting the BMC as the core format of the syllabus. With financial support from the VentureWell Foundation, Blank and Engel now train other educators how to teach the Lean LaunchPad curriculum, which has been published online and adopted in over 200 universities worldwide. Blank's software-backed process LaunchPad Central has been adopted by the National Science Foundation, the Department of Defense, and the National Institutes of Health.

Lean Startup was born in the Lean LaunchPad Berkeley class taught by Steve Blank. Eric Reis, an auditing student in the class, observed the methodological overlap with agile software development methods. After launching a successful blog post of the subject, which received great interest from his ecosystem of like-minded software engineering founders, Ries (2011) wrote his first edition of The Lean Startup.

Reis's series of general audience books and talks on the subject, captured and shared in online videos, grew interest in the method, and he is often credited with the movement's overall success. The Lean Startup movement, like the agile movement before it, was embraced as a mindset shift within the software-focused community of startup founders and management teams. Lean Startup Meetup organizers have created their own local events and learning groups in over 94 countries and continue to hold both formal and loose connections to The Lean Startup organization formed by Ries.

In the venture community, the lean startup methods, tools, and practices have become the default shared language for how to organize early-stage activity in finding customer needs, defining competitive advantage, and developing a solution iteratively. Below, we briefly present the main methods, tools, and practices used by startups. It is important to note that while their wide adoption reflects their effectiveness and value for startups, none of these methods, tools, or practices address the issue of sustainability or frame the purpose of a business model with sustainable goals in mind.

3.1 Tools

Business Model Canvas: The BMC was developed from Osterwalder's PhD thesis to propose a business model design template and presented in Osterwalder and Pigneur's (2010) book *Business Model Generation*. Osterwalder et al.'s (2014) subsequent Value Proposition Canvas addressed the application of innovation theory to customer segment definition and value proposition design.

The BMC is a one-page tool for defining a business model, which "describes the rationale of how an organization creates, delivers, and captures value" (Osterwalder and Pigneur 2010, p. 14). The right side of the BMC (the front stage) connects target customer segments to defined value propositions and demonstrates the link between customer relationships and channels to communicate and deliver value. The left side of the BMC (the back stage) focuses on the value chain of the firm: activities, resources, and partner efforts that are combined to deliver the value proposition. Value captured refers to the profit logic of the firm.

Lean Canvas: The Lean Canvas combines lean startup methodology with the canvas format and focuses all early-stage customer discovery on the customer problem. It was created by Maurya (2012) to better fit the entrepreneurial activities, suggesting that the business model elements expressed in the BMC are later-stage concerns once the riskiest assumption, customer value, and customer segment definition are further validated and the venture moves on to company-centric activities.

The Mission Model Canvas: Steve Blank recognized the challenges of adapting the BMC to government-funded projects when he ran a

Hacking for Defense class at Stanford. Blank challenged Osterwalder to create an adaptation of the tool: the Mission Model Canvas. However, the Mission Model Canvas only works in a situation in which the funding for the mission has been secured (such as in a government budgeting cycle), not in the uncertain world of the early-stage startup in search of a business model.

3.2 Practices

Much of the lean startup movement can be observed not just in methods and tools, but also in common practices—defined in the methods but performed as an activity or exercise to develop a core skill repeatedly and regularly in a commitment to continuous innovation.

Minimum viable product (MVP): This is now a common concept employed in accelerators, incubators, and by the earliest stage investors to focus founder energy on building a product with critical features to gather feedback from customers. The focus is not on the product, but the practice of defining the most minimal set of features a customer will pay for. Early-stage teams repeat the cycle of build-measure-learn until they achieve product-market fit, when the core customer finds value in the product. It is "that version of a new product which allows a team to collect the maximum amount of validated learning about customers with the least effort" (Ries 2009).

Get out of the building: Compared with traditional methods of market research, which utilize professionally trained interviewers and analyze results for statistical significance, the "get out of the building" method encourages founders to directly talk to customers. By directly testing hypotheses with users, purchasers, industry experts, and partners, founders learn firsthand if their product and value assumptions are going to be readily adopted or meet resistance. If resistance is met, founders make changes to their MVP and return to immediately receive customer feedback, iterate, and repeat until the problem and solution have been fully validated (Blank 2013).

Running lean: A key emphasis of the lean startup process is moving quickly while learning and testing a vision by measuring how customers behave.

The practice involves documenting Plan A and then identifying the riskiest parts of the plan, systematically testing the plan, and iterating until product-market fit is achieved (Maurya 2012).

Validated learning: A scientific approach to developing a new business that is at the core of the lean startup methodology (Ries 2011).

Build-measure-learn feedback loop: Designed to reference the scientific method of hypothesis-metric-experiment cycle, the lean process begins with the learning goal and ends with a review of results after the hypothesis has been tested (Maurya 2012).

Pivot: A pivot is a key change in a business model assumption, based on interpreting results from customer feedback (Ries 2011; Blank 2013).

Fail fast: The most misunderstood and maligned practice within the lean startup movement is the focus on celebrating failure. In fact, founders are encouraged to celebrate early failure, or "failing fast," meaning that the team stops developing elements of the product that the customer will not value or that do not advance the path to a viable business model. Thus, waste of human time and material resources is avoided, meaning the team can refocus their energy and capital on discovering features and services that will be adopted by customers.

Find a hair-on-fire problem: Building on the Jobs-to-be-Done theory (Christensen et al. 2005), once identified, founders are often encouraged to keep searching until the pain points are so painful that they resemble a "hair on fire" problem. The reason for finding a high priority pain point is that your customer is actively and immediately searching for the perfect solution to put the fire out, and those customers are more likely to accept a not-yet-fully-tested MVP to see if the solution works.

Focus on the early innovator: Startups often fail when they define solutions for a large market, meaning they are not specific in defining their earliest customer segment. Based on the diffusion of innovations theory (Rogers 1962), founders are encouraged to find the early innovator visionaries and then early adopter enthusiasts who are willing to take a risk on a newly emerging technology. Once the first innovators adopt the product and service, the early venture can then move beyond the visionaries to reach early pragmatists, ultimately to cross the "chasm" to a larger market (Moore 1991).

4 The Gap (Or: Why Startups Embrace Lean, Not Sustainable Business Models)

Regarding the entrepreneurial space, it is evident there is a problem with the application of SBM in an entrepreneurial setting. If we think of the lean startup and SBM as two stores competing for the attention of potential customers (i.e. startups), the first is "buzzing and humming" with activity, while the second is nearly empty most of the day with only a few visitors here and there showing some interest in the different offers. Not only that, but it seems as if even entrepreneurs who are interested in embedding sustainability in various forms in their startup are "shopping" in the lean startup store, finding its offerings (i.e. tools, methods, and practices) more relevant and valuable than the ones offered at the SBM store. The bad news is that without significantly increasing the number of customers, SBM advocates cannot make any significant difference in this context. The good news, however, is that this is fixable. In order to fix it and close the gap between the two "stores" (which is discussed in the following section) we need to figure out first what is broken, or, in other words: why startups embrace lean, not SBM.

Here are the reasons we believe to be the main drivers behind the gap:

1. *The economic system*: We need to face the harsh reality—startups operate in an economic system that is still mainly profit-driven and grounded in shareholder primacy. While lean startup and SBM offer new approaches to innovation, lean startup does it within the parameters of the dominant economic paradigm (zeroing in on customers), while SBM tries to disrupt it (by considering a wide range of values and stakeholders). "The missing centrality of profit generation in sustainable business models" (Dentchev et al. 2016, p. 1) appears to make it more, not less, difficult for SBM entrepreneurs navigating their way in an economic system that is still optimized for "business as usual" considerations.

2. *The dominance of venture capital*—Venture capital (VC) investment in 2017 reached approximately $165 billion across 11,042 deals.[3] These numbers illustrate the power VC has on the world of startups and the principles shaping it. One of these principles is that, from a VC perspective, a sustainable startup is almost an oxymoron. Jason Calacanis, a

prominent angel investor and one of the more vocal representatives of the VC ecosystem, said the following in his podcast *This Week in Startups* in reply to a question "Is the word 'sustainable startup' a no-go for an angel?" (Calacanis 2018):

> If you use words like benefit, sustainable, social good in your pitch you may get high fives from your friends and you may get a lot of hugs and kisses and just way to go and thumbs up from your friends at parties, but you're going to disqualify yourself for the large part from getting funding. The whole idea of venture capital and angel funding is to get a massive return…If you're trying to come out of the gate and saying I'm doing a non-profit in a for-profit kind of function, a for-profit vehicle, that just looks bad…you will negate 99 out of 100 meetings. People will not take the meeting if you use these trigger words…Don't trigger a greedy investor to think that you are not greedy and you don't want to make a lot of money or they will not fund you.

This state of affairs places SBM at a clear disadvantage compared with lean startup, which is perfectly aligned with the priorities of VCs and angels. Clearly, any entrepreneur searching for funding (in other words, all entrepreneurs other than those who bootstrap their startup) must take this under serious consideration.

3. *Understanding that Startup ≠ Established firm*—SBM seems to apply an approach based on the idea that tools and frameworks, from the value mapping tool to Reporting 3.0's New Business Models Blueprint, can be used in and adjusted to entrepreneurial or intrapreneurial contexts as needed. This idea of using the same general tool or framework but with different lenses in different situations is very much the opposite of lean startup's starting point: "Start-ups are not smaller versions of large companies" (Blank 2013, p. 67). Lean startup understands what SBM has not yet: entrepreneurs and managers deal with different challenges and need different tools, methods, and practices to address them, not to mention a very different mindset.

4. *(Lack of) understanding the entrepreneurial process*—this is one of the main differences between the two approaches. The lean startup approach defines startup as an experiment and the entrepreneurial process as validated

learning. Eric Ries (2011) laid out this vision in his book *The Lean Startup*: "Startups exist not just to make stuff, make money, or even serve customers. They exist to learn how to build a sustainable business. This learning can be validated scientifically by running frequent experiments that allow entrepreneurs to test each element of their vision" (8–9). While Ries's description of startups' goals may be somewhat aspirational (his understanding of "sustainable business" is probably a narrower one, only in terms of business viability), it reflects a disciplined approach toward the process. This process not only prioritizes experimentation and iteration, but also provides entrepreneurs with a clear general framework for their work: begin by framing your assumptions using the BMC; then, start testing them with customers using the customer development method; apply agile development techniques to build MVP to maximize your learning; and continue using the build-measure-learn feedback loop until you figure out the right business model for your startup.

The SBM story is very different. In general, there has been a struggle to identify how to best incorporate SBM principles into the entrepreneurial journey. The SBM literature addressing the process does it by either describing it in broad strokes, without getting too much into its fine details, or by focusing only on a modification of a specific component of the process (e.g. the BMC with alternatives such as the flourishing BMC (Upward and Jones 2016) and the Clover Business Model Canvas (Jonker 2014b)), paying little or no attention to the other parts. Both approaches suffer often from either a high level of complexity or an oversimplification of the entrepreneurial process, making it difficult to utilize them in practice. From a design viewpoint, we believe that, in both cases, the perspective of the entrepreneur is not well-embedded into these approaches, perhaps reflecting the fact that they were mostly developed by scholars with limited entrepreneurial experience, which is the exact opposite of the lean startup (with the exception of Alex Osterwalder).

There are a few attempts to provide SBM entrepreneurs with a more holistic view of the process, combining SBM and lean startup components; for example, the Business Model Thinking framework laid out by Lüdeke-Freund et al. (2016), or the Flourishing Enterprise Strategy Design Method developed by Upward and Davies (n.d.). However, these nascent frameworks are at a very early stage and need further development to become more applicable.

5. *Innovation is difficult.* Sustainable innovation is extremely difficult—there is a significant difference between considering the value created for customers, echoing the point Peter Drucker (1985) made that the ultimate purpose of a business is to create a customer, and considering the multiple values created (and destroyed) for a wider group of stakeholders (Bocken et al. 2015). This difference is key to understanding that SBM application in startups is difficult, complex, and resource consuming.

Furthermore, the SBM approach requires entrepreneurs to consider not only the startup they are trying to build, but also its entire value network. As Jonker (2014a) notes, it is quite impossible for any organization on its own to create multiple values. Doing so requires collaboration between different organizations, stakeholders, and constituents, or, in Jonker's (2014a, p. 37) words: "It implies organising not only inside—but also between—organisations." This need of meso-level consideration and collaboration adds even more complexity to the already complex challenge of building a startup.

The bottom line is that both lean startup and SBM offer ways to address the entrepreneurial journey, but while the lean startup's path has focused on ways to make the journey easier, less risky, and potentially more successful, SBM has been taking a more conceptual approach, and is less concerned about how to make the journey work in practice (Table 9.1).

Table 9.1 Comparing the lean startup "shop" vs. the sustainable business model "shop"

Core differentiators	Lean startup	SBM
Alignment with the current economic system	✓	X
Easy access to VC funding to reduce early-stage risk	✓	X
Understanding the unique challenges of startups	✓	✓
Providing clear process based on easy-to-use tools and methods	✓	X
Adopted by startup incubators and accelerators seeking a methodology for more viable outcomes	✓	X
Spread through startup founders, investors, and practitioners sharing practices and tools through social media	✓	X
Making entrepreneur's life easier and less risky	✓	X

5 Bridging the Gap

After identifying the different elements behind the SBM and lean startup approaches leading to a far greater adaptability of lean startup by startups, we want to lay the ground for ways to bridge this adaptability gap, enabling SBM to potentially play a more influential role in the entrepreneurial space. To do so, the SBM approach should move from its theory-heavy, practice-light positioning to a more balanced position that is grounded both in theory and in the perspective of its users (i.e. entrepreneurs). Thus, we use Eric Ries's (2011) vision-strategy-product formulation of the entrepreneurial journey as a starting point. This framework provides a clear workflow, in which the entrepreneur begins by articulating the destination (or the North Star) she/he has in mind, then forms a strategy to reach the destination, including a business model and a validated learning process to test assumptions. The product is what the entrepreneur ends up building. As Maurya (2017) points out, this framework corresponds with Simon Sinek's (2009) Golden Circle, moving from the "why" (vision), to the "how" (strategy), to the "what" (product), and thus providing a more disciplined and orderly process of new product building. While this process suggests linearity, it is iterative in its nature, based on feedback loops between the different elements, and accepting the need to make changes or even pivots when necessary.

We use this pyramid formation to create a new framework entitled "The Lean SBM Framework" (see Fig. 9.2), which can be applied for SBM in entrepreneurial environment. After explaining the different elements of the Lean SBM, we provide four examples of different applications of this framework.

Vision—as in Ries's pyramid, the first level to be addressed in the Lean SBM framework is "vision." However, SBM requires more than just understanding the destination; it requires the entrepreneur to produce clarity regarding her/his values, destination, and the ecosystem she/he wants to be part of.

   1. *Values*—following Braungart and McDonough's (2013, p. 80) point of the need to begin with values because "the later you

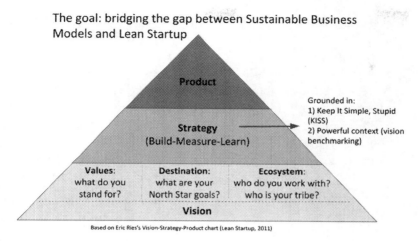

Fig. 9.2 The lean SBM framework

consider values in this process, the less likely values will be considered at all," we believe any new enterprise with sustainability in mind should begin by defining, clarifying, and prioritizing the values it stands for. While this is a valuable exercise for every entrepreneur, in the case of sustainable entrepreneurs this is critical, reflecting the notion of values as "enablers and drivers of innovation" (Breuer and Lüdeke-Freund 2016, p. 9). The reason for this exercise is not only to be intentional about shaping the startup's culture, but also, as Quayle (2017, p. 20) points out, making values explicit helps "communicate more consistently with others in decision making, oversight, and accountability assessments."

2. *Destination*—the North Star goals articulated by the entrepreneur should be grounded in the concept of "preferable future," one that is subjective and driven by value judgments (Voros 2001). The concept should articulate the entrepreneur's normative understanding of sustainability and be explicit, clarifying grand ideas such as "solving environmental and social problems of unsustainability by means of the exploration and exploitation of market opportunities created with innovative business models" (Schaltegger et al. 2016, p. 268).

>   A clearer destination helps create a clear roadmap for the next stage, as well as an effective accountability tool to be used later as the startup progresses.
> 3. *Ecosystem*—the Lean SBM framework requires the entrepreneur to be very intentional about the ecosystem her/his startup will be part of, reflecting an understanding of the systemic nature of the innovation process and that companies do not innovate in isolation, "but in collaboration and interdependence with other organizations" (Edquist 2006, p. 2). The framework resonates with Jonker's (2014a, p. 37) viewpoint that "sustainability is determined as an organisational challenge organised between organisations, between stakeholders, and between other constituents."

Overall, there needs to be a clear alignment between the values and the destination defined by the entrepreneur and those of the stakeholders she/he chooses to work with to meet her/his goals. Beyond the stakeholders, there needs to be a consideration of the place. The entrepreneurial journey is shaped not just by the different nodes in the ecosystem and the type of relationships it has with them, but also by the place where it operates and the culture dominating it. These different elements and considerations require the entrepreneur to identify the "tribe" (i.e. business ecosystem with a clear normative approach to innovation and a set of unique characteristics differentiating it from other ecosystems) that can best support the realization of her/his mission. Picking the right tribe can be critical to shaping the environment in which the startup operates, and thus its chances to succeed eventually.

> *Strategy*—the "how" part of the entrepreneurial journey has always been the Achilles heel of the SBM approach, especially in comparison with lean startup, which offers entrepreneurs a clear path forward. Therefore, the Lean SBM framework offers a different approach to sustainability-led startups based on following the lean startup process (i.e. framing assumptions on a BMC, testing them with the customer development method, building MVP to maximize learning, and using an overall build-measure-learn feedback loop until the right business model is found). The aspired sustainability qualities of the startup are shaped by

the vision—strong values, clear destination, and choosing a proper ecosystem to anchor the strategy and ensure the lean tools, methods, and practices are utilized to advance SBM goals. This combination uses the best of both worlds—a strong SBM context with a clear and effective lean startup content, while avoiding the pitfalls of both approaches, from weak process (SBM) to lack of normative anchoring and subjecting the process to the unsustainable VC culture (lean startup).

In laying out the Lean SBM approach to strategy, we emphasize the following two elements: (1) the keep it simple, stupid (KISS) principle; and (2) the power of context.

1. *The "keep it simple, stupid" (KISS) principle*—we find this design principle, suggesting that systems perform best if they are kept simple, to be very applicable here given the difficulty to apply SBM to an entrepreneurial journey that is already demanding in itself. As Schick et al. (2002, p. 66) point out: "Starting a new business venture with an extensive ecological orientation is not easy and often is even more difficult than starting a conventional business enterprise." Simplicity is not a goal in itself, but a means to increase usability of the strategy. This approach resonates with Norman (2011), who suggests the perceived trade-off between simplicity and complexity is false as there is no zero-sum game between the two and that "the design challenge is to manage complexity so that it isn't complicated" (53).
2. *The power of context*—context is a powerful force in shaping the path of startups; a similar idea realized in two different contexts can evolve into two very different directions. The SBM context, informed by the entrepreneur's values, choice of destination, and ecosystem/tribe selection, shapes the environment in which the startup operates, the different actors it establishes relationships with (investors, partners, advisors, incubators, suppliers, community, etc.), what it considers to be success, how it measures that success, and last but not least, the context serves as a benchmark to evaluate the startup's progress.

All these factors can help operationalize SBM thinking through "standard" lean tools, methods, and practices converging validated learning with normative goals. We believe these same factors can also ensure the flexibility required in the case of different levels of sustainability orientations, corresponding with Schaper's (2010) different levels of significance for environmental goals in ecopreneurial activity.

Product—this level concerns the "what" element of the journey, encompassing the product or service the startup is creating. The "what" is a manifestation of the vision and the strategy the startup used to realize its vision, reflecting the different choices the entrepreneur made along the way. This level demonstrates the convergence of the lean startup and SBM approaches: first, it should demonstrate a product-market fit, either in a steady state or, more likely, as part of a dynamic development and improvement of the product, observing and adapting to the customers' ever-changing needs; second, it should demonstrate sustainability qualities, or how the product creates value in social and environmental terms in clear and measurable ways.

There are already some interesting examples echoing the Lean Startup framework, and while the number of these examples is relatively small, and while their application of the framework varies, these examples provide an indication of the possibilities for this framework. From our perspective, these examples are a manifestation of what Bloch (1995) describes as the "not yet," representing evolving ideas about the possibilities for a desired future.

Example 1: B-Corps—Kickstarter The term "B-Corp" is often used to refer to both benefit corporations and Certified B Corporations. For the purposes of this case study, we are referring to benefit corporations: a new type of legal entity designed to produce a public benefit in addition to driving shareholder value. In the United States (US), benefit corporations are now authorized by 33 states and the District of Columbia.

The directors of B-Corps agree to consider the interests of those stakeholders affected by the company who are not shareholders. The company is obligated to report to shareholders on social and environmental performance, and shareholders can bring lawsuits to enforce the company's public benefit mission.

Originally founded as a C-corporation, or standard private for-profit entity, Kickstarter re-incorporated to become a public benefit corporation in 2015. Kickstarter's original intention was to provide early access to project capital for ideas that needed to get off the ground. As part of its benefit corporation charter, Kickstarter transparently outlines the company's mission: "to create tools and resources that help people bring their creative projects to life, and that connect people around creative projects and the creative process" ("Charter—Kickstarter" 2018).

5.1 Applying the Lean SBM Framework

Vision: The vision for Kickstarter was clear from the beginning of the company and later augmented and codified within their B-Corp structure. Helping creative projects come to life was the stated vision on the first day of launch and remains true today.

Values: Kickstarter chose the B-Corp status to more formally establish how the company's operation reflects their values. Listed in their B-Corp charter are commitments regarding data and data sharing, privacy rights, lobbying policies, transparency of data policies, tax management strategies, and efforts to limit environmental impact inside the company and within their larger ecosystem of creator customers. The company is also committed to a percentage profit contribution of 5% after-tax profit donated to arts and music education and organizations addressing systemic inequality.

Destination: Kickstarter's North Star can be measured in project funds committed, the number of projects funded, and projects completed. As part of the B-Corp reporting promise, Kickstarter continually updates its performance metrics: $3,586,284,343 has been pledged to creative projects on Kickstarter; 14,399,334 people have backed a Kickstarter project; 300,000+ part-time and full-time jobs have been created by Kickstarter projects; and 141,188 creative projects have been brought to life through Kickstarter ("Kickstarter.com" 2018).

Ecosystem: Kickstarter's stakeholder community has consistently focused on the creative community they serve. In searching for early investment, Kickstarter founders were honest about their intention to grow at the pace the community demands, and to not seek aggressive growth paths and quick exit strategies. Despite this stance, Kickstarter attracted funding from Chris Sacca, a well-known angel investor, and Union Square Ventures, an investor in Uber and Twitter. While these investors typically do seek high growth high return outcomes, all the members of the board were unanimous in Kickstarter's decision to shift to a B-Corp and legally commit to serving its employees and creator community.

Strategy: Kickstarter was encouraged by investors and other advisors to consider business model pivots. That is, to take on corporate customers who want to generate product innovation; brand sponsors who want to back brand-relevant creative projects; and to be more receptive to all types of products in a similar manner to their competitor Indiegogo, which accepts medical devices and other types of complex product development. While Kickstarter made some attempts to establish brand relationships and try other value propositions, the management team returned to the core offering and continued to refocus their energies on their primary customer: the creator.

Product: Unlike most tech companies, who continue to pivot, combine, and recombine new business models throughout their early growth, Kickstarter has maintained a steady state. Since Kickstarter first instituted the 5% project fee structure six months after launching, it has not radically changed the business model or value proposition.

Learnings: Kickstarter is a unique technology company story because the founders had a clearly defined vision from the very beginning that has remain unchanged. The original vision and values were aligned as early as their first MVP launch. The company has benefited financially by committing to its core creator community through the B-Corp structure. More importantly, future management team and board decisions are positively constrained within a range of strategic choices that further align to the values of this community. Kickstarter is a virtuous vision-values-destination-ecosystem story well aligned around a stable product and strategy.

Example 2: Nordic Startup Ecosystem—Applegirl The Nordic countries of Europe, specifically Norway, Denmark, Finland, and Sweden, have expanded government and regional investment activities into early-stage startups. As a result of participation in startup cohorts such as Innovation Norway, Nordic Innovation House, the Female Entrepreneur of the Year Awards, and other related programs in these countries, we have observed a specific context for startups seeking SBM.

The first context is embedded in the criteria for selecting startups to support. Countries such as Norway have explicit policies for seeking industries outside of oil and gas exploration and further diversifying the Nordic economy. The legal and regulatory context of Nordic countries often creates conditions for SBM to thrive. At the same time, these companies' early customers, who usually reside within these countries demonstrate a greater awareness and interest in sustainability strategies.

Applegirl is an early-stage startup that is only just beginning their customer discovery process. Founded by American design student, Hannah Michaud in the Copenhagen School of Design and Technology (KEA), the company is situated in a regional environment with a strong interest in sustainable material supply. The company began with a prototyping process for how to transform agricultural apple waste into a potential material supply and is engaged in customer discovery to determine the first ideal customer segment to launch a product offering.

5.2   Applying the Lean SBM Framework

Vision: Applegirl's vision is to generate a source of materials from waste streams and provide a foundation for a regenerative economy. This vision positively constrains the range of plausible futures to those that rely on SBM for growth.

Values: At the earliest stages of the company's process, Applegirl is committed to sustainable manufacturing in a circular economy framework.

Destination: The company founder envisions other products and processes emerging in future iterations and is focused on creating a leather replacement product from apple waste as a first viable product.

Ecosystem: Applegirl has sought funding and support from regional sources within Denmark and the Nordic regions, which allows time for the process of deliberate customer discovery. In other local contexts, a company such as Applegirl would be encouraged to deploy quickly and minimally to demonstrate progress. However, in this case, the founder is permitted more time to engage in process and material research, as well as the early-stage search of a business model.

Strategy: Applegirl is only just initiating its build-measure-learn cycle of iterative business model discovery. The company's near-term strategic goal is to emergently uncover the most viable launch customer segment through extensive customer discovery interviews, refining its initial material prototype, and further developing its prototype into product as it validates the core value proposition.

Product: Applegirl initially pursued packaging and packaging-product designers as its primary product and early customer segment. After speaking directly to the packaging design ecosystem, the founder determined that this product format would not align with the vision and values of the company. The packaging industry suffers from commoditization and does not encourage new material development that may change or elevate cost structures. The benefit of Applegirl's sustainability story would be either invisible to the customer or not valued in the end-user experience.

The founder is continuing her search for an early-stage customer segment and most recently discovered interior designers' needs for innovative wall coverings. The team is now engaged in building relationships with interior designers and determining other options for entering the wall coverings market. While Applegirl is at the initial stages of understanding how to strategically enter this market, the founder's values are aligned to this choice. This customer segment and product form factor may be a promising launching point for the company. The end-user customer is more likely to highly value the sustainability story and appreciate the material quality of the product, and the primary influencer, the interior designer, appears to be actively searching for innovative sustainable materials to incorporate into designs.

Learnings: The Applegirl case demonstrates how SBM can be pursued at the earliest stages of the company and to make strategic choices that maximize sustainable and financial outcomes or effectively deal with the trade-offs. Beginning with an insight into how to create a useful material from agricultural waste, the options for customer discovery and solution development remain open for further opportunity identification, validation, and refinement. As the founder continues her search for an SBM, the vision-values-destination-ecosystem articulation will help as decision criteria for future product and strategy choices as the company grows.

Example 3: Platform Co-ops—Stocksy United Platform cooperatives (also known as platform co-ops) provide an alternative economic model for the Internet era, connecting the cooperative model with the digital economy. Grounded in a human-centered approach, this type of organization is based on shared ownership, democratic governance, and enhanced solidarity (Scholz 2016). The movement has been building up in the last decade, aspiring to create a clear alternative to the Ubers, Aribnbs, Facebooks, and Amazons of the world by offering shared ownership and governance as a remedy for the exploitative, "business as usual" practices found in these platforms.

Perhaps the most well-known example of the platform cooperativism movement, Stocksy United is an artist-owned, multi-stakeholder co-op based in Victoria, British Columbia, Canada. Stocksy was founded in 2013 by stock photo industry veterans Brianna Wettlaufer and Bruce Livingstone, who were the team behind iStockphoto, which was acquired by Getty Images in 2006 for $50 million. The two were disheartened by the trends in the industry, in which profit-making was prioritized over photographers, who were paid very poorly for their work and had little control over their images. They decided to create an alternative marketplace for photographers, which would pay them fairly and make sure their needs are considered, choosing a cooperative structure to make it happen. Stocksy pays photographers 50–75% of sales, which is much higher than industry rates, and is also committed to distributing 90% of its profit at the end of each year to its members (Cortese 2016).

5.3 Applying the Lean SBM Framework

Vision: Stocksy was formed to create an alternative approach to traditional stock photo companies, an approach that is more humane and empathetic to photographers, with the belief that this will generate better products. Incorporating as a cooperative was a way to solidify the vision, create a collaborative culture, and provide photographers with control via ownership and participation in governance.

Values: Stocksy was founded on the understanding of the importance of having a strong community that serves the needs of its members first as the basis of a healthy business. Another important value for the founders was pragmatism, which manifests itself in the idea that a co-op structure requires a focus on both the product and the community from the early stages, and that building a successful business is about finding the right balance between the two (Sylvester-Bradley 2017).

Destination: Stocksy's North Star is to create a business model that allows photographers to make a sustainable living from their work, demonstrating that freelancing in general and stock photography specifically does not have to be a race to the bottom. So far, the company has been consistently progressing toward its destination, with improved financial results that are translated to growing income to its members. Its revenue in 2016 was $10.7 million, with $4.9 million paid in royalties to contributing shareholders (Marshall 2017), up from $7.9 million in revenue and $4.3 million in royalties in 2015. In 2015, Stocksy paid its first dividends of $200,000 to member artists who sold images that year (Cortese 2016).

Ecosystem: Wettlaufer and Livingston used their own money to start Stocksy, with the understanding that VC funding would not serve well a business with a long-term view. At the core of the Stocksy ecosystem is its structure as a multi-stakeholder cooperative. Stocksy has three classes of shareholder: founders and advisors (capped at five people); staff (which was added later, capped at 20); and artist members (capped at 1000). The latter level is highly selective—it currently includes about 980 members who were selected in a robust application process from over 10,000 applicants. The capping of the number of members is intentional to create a more supportive and less competitive environment for the photographers.

Strategy: While Stocksy is grounded in a sustainable vision and focuses on its members' needs, it was created, from the beginning, with a similar focus on its customers' unique needs, with a clear goal in mind: "How do we make that as easy and as personal as possible for them?" (Van Tol 2017). This dual focus was reflected, for example, in its early decision not to offer customers a subscription model. Regarding this model as a "lose-lose" proposition, confusing to customers, and reducing photographers' royalties significantly, Stocksy offers customers simple upfront pricing for royalty-free licensing, allowing the company to focus on providing quality over quantity and pay its members higher compensation.

Product: Stocksy has been relatively consistent with its business proposition, especially after validating a product-market fit for its royalty-free licensing model, as well as the founders' core assumption that it can create a virtuous cycle between the community and the products it creates. While the product offerings have not changed much, Stocksy has been considering changes in its structure that will allow it to scale while not compromising the quality of the products and jeopardizing the spirit and intent behind its creation. One proposal that was considered was to create a non-membership class, while another was to increase the membership cap.

Learnings: Stocksy has been able to create a successful business proposition on every level, including member satisfaction, revenue growth, and its organizational health (Schor 2017), attributing its success to its cooperative model and dual focus on its members and customers. As co-founder and CEO, Wettlaufer pointed out: "At a time when some stock imagery companies are slashing artist royalties and others suffer from bloated, outdated collections, Stocksy's success proves that clients at the major design firms and Fortune 500 companies we serve agree that the combination of fair pay combined with meticulous curation equals a far better product" (Udziela 2016).

While the platform cooperativism movement celebrates Stocksy's success, it is yet to be proven whether this success is uniquely driven by elements such as the dual focus on community and high-quality products, business acumen, and no need for initial external funding, or whether it can be replicated in other contexts, such as co-ops of low-wage workers (Schor 2017).

Example 4: The Zebra Movement—Tinsel The Zebra movement was created to provide a viable alternative to the unicorn model. Unicorns are privately held startups with a valuation of at least $1 billion, once considered a rare event and celebrated by the mainstream startup community. In contrast, the Zebra movement is creating a "new system to help entrepreneurs build companies for purpose and profit" (Brandel et al. 2018). The movement is looking to change the narrative around entrepreneurship from disruption to repair, and is grounded in deep understanding of the systemic failure of the current entrepreneurial ecosystem in the US to support women and minority founders. In addition, the movement focuses on the funding component of the innovation system, acknowledging that it is not suited to serve companies looking to create both profit and social value.

Based in San Francisco, Tinsel makes tech jewelry for women, starting with The Dipper—the world's first audio necklace. Tinsel was founded in 2014 by Aniyia Williams, who was joined by Monia Santinello, Tinsel's other co-founder. Williams learned very quickly the difficulties of being a black female founder in Silicon Valley, especially when it comes to securing funding (she was rejected by 98 out of 100 investors she approached), leading her eventually to join the Zebra movement and become one of its outspoken leaders.

Vision: Tinsel's vision has two main components. The first component focuses on its product development and design: "We're different than other companies in the wearables space in two ways: we use fashion and technology to serve an essential purpose, and our products are created for women by women who are dedicated to delivering quality products, uncompromising in the details" (Tinsel press release). The other component focuses on the company level, in which Williams's vision for Tinsel evolved from initially looking to build a unicorn to eventually aspiring to create a Zebra. This evolution followed different experiences, including her becoming a new mother and a residency with Code2040, a non-profit working to increase black and Latinx representation and leadership in tech, leading her to acknowledge the initial vision was not aligned with her values.

Values: While Tinsel's values have evolved together with Williams' vision for the company, they have been grounded in a human-centered approach to innovation, both at the product and company level.

Destination: Tinsel's North Star is to make wearable jewelry for women while embedding in the process the Zebra movement's values and vision, demonstrating the ability of Zebras to be profitable and make an impact.

Ecosystem: Williams' former boss, Voxer CEO Tom Katis was the initial influence on Tinsel's ecosystem, investing in the company and providing Williams with access to his network. Later, the company's ecosystem was shaped, in particular, by the network Williams developed, which reflected her hybrid focus on making high-quality, fashionable products, a values-based process (i.e. responsible manufacturing), and community. Williams acknowledges of the value of community, especially for entrepreneurs who are considered to be the "other" in the tech industry, or in her words are not "a young, white straight man" (Walravens 2017), suggesting that "others" need to embrace their uniqueness and build a tribe around it. This thinking has led her to join and take an active part in the Zebra movement as well as founding Black & Brown Founders, non-profit supporting Black and Latinx entrepreneurs.

Strategy: Tinsel's journey has been shaped by lean startup thinking. The journey began with Williams identifying multiple pain points regarding the use and style of her headphones, leading to her idea of housing "great-sounding earbuds in a necklace like structure to keep them both ready-to-use and inconspicuously fashionable" (Hockenson 2016). With bootstrapped funding and initial investment from Katis, Williams built, together with Monia Santinello, her co-founder, a lean operation, quickly learning the different aspects involved in developing this particular product. In 2015, Tinsel created a successful Indiegogo campaign to test interest in the product, to raise funding for manufacturing, and to receive feedback from backers regarding The Dipper, which later helped the company further refine the product.

Product: Tinsel's first product, The Dipper, has undergone iterations based on initial customer feedback and is already being manufactured in China (responsibly, according to Tinsel's website) and sold online in two colors. The company plans to add more designs and launch new collections every season in a similar way to other fashion brands. Tinsel's product seems to balance values with value creation—it is produced responsibly but with fashion trends in mind. It is designed and developed by women-led diverse teams, but at the same time pays attention to customer feedback, and, finally, while it is interested in expansion, Tinsel follows a slower and more careful growth philosophy to ensure the company continues developing sustainably.

Learnings: Tinsel has been evolving as a Zebra experiment, reflecting the Zebra movement's agenda as well as the challenges it faces building an alternate ecosystem for entrepreneurs interested in pursuing both profit and purpose. While this journey is far from over, it already demonstrates a couple of important lessons: first, an understanding of the importance of funding choices and funding itself in the entrepreneurial process and the need to build an alternative funding ecosystem that can cater to and support entrepreneurs who are not interested in building the next unicorn; second, the power of building an active network of actors supporting each other—it is not only important to find your tribe, but you also need to become an active tribe member to make it stronger and more valuable.

Finally, it is possible to design and execute a lean development process in a for-profit startup environment that is grounded in values. Based on her experiences at Tinsel, Williams (2017) presented the following flow for such a process: (1) Talk to yourself; (2) Talk to other people; (3) Start building a community of people who care about the problem you work on; (4) Build your prototype; (5) Launch, let people try it and see it; (6) Keep iterating; (7) Get money by finding how to leverage and monetize your community; (8) Seek more funding from resources aligned with your worldview. Overall, Williams recommends founders to bear four things in mind: "keep iterating, keep making your customers happy, keep creating value, and keep the money flowing" (Williams 2017).

6 Summary

A startup is "a human institution designed to create a new product or service under conditions of extreme uncertainty" (Ries 2011, p. 8). If we agree with this sentiment, then startups are perhaps best positioned to generatively create new value in new ways within growing material resource constraints and within rapidly changing social, cultural, and economic conditions. However, the SBM theories and frameworks, to date, have addressed companies both large and small with the same set of theories. This approach has resulted in little to show in terms of tools and practices that are useful and applicable to early-stage startups. Moreover, the SE literature does not help startup founders to evaluate and address the trade-offs that can occur when making early-stage choices between ecological and social value creation and financial performance. The theories remain underutilized by founders seeking more practical support for the daily reality of choice-making and experimentation in a resource-constrained environment.

At the same time, the lean startup movement, while undeniably popular and practical, provides little opportunity for entrepreneurs interested in creating sustainable added value to exercise critical reflective thinking regarding the most difficult decisions. How does a founder stay on course when customer, market, and investor forces suggest potential routes away from their original hypotheses? In practice, lean startup curricula and practices often lead founders to abandon their original vision when they face early resistance from customers and investors and to pursue problem and pain points that are more obvious to their customers but not rooted in or connected to the major problem of spaces of sustainability and social impact they originally sought. Or worse, founders leave their original intent in place, but unexamined, as they throw themselves into the work of prototyping, MVP development, and company building. Founders are encouraged and incentivized to move quickly, break things, and ask for forgiveness later, only at which point do they examine the original mission statement and values that led them to these outcomes.

The Lean SBM Framework offers a practice-based approach for startup founders. By embedding key guiding principles within the core vision, strategy, and product framework of the lean startup pyramid, we encourage entrepreneurs to persevere in the face of early resistance and to further overcome the dichotomy between sustainable value creation and financial performance.

Essentially, founders adopt a regular reflective practice to ensure their vision is made manifest through the strategic experimentation of iterative customer discovery/agile development cycles. Choices become easier when values are clearly aligned and understood by founders and early-stage employees. Founders who can articulate their values to generate a range of preferable futures and define a clearer North Star destination are able to effectively account and be accountable for their progress. Finally, startups that identify customers, investors, and early employees who acknowledge and accept the vision, values, and destination of the firm will serve as a cohesive force to pull the company's offerings onto the market and to ultimately generate and transform the economic system.

The examples provided by platform co-ops, B-Corps, Zebra movement, and Nordic startups provide some promising signs for new directions in which a KISS context-driven framework can make SBM a more preferable choice for entrepreneurs. The true test, however, will be if and when incubators, universities, and other influential actors adopt this approach, leading the way to making sustainable startups the rule rather than the exception.

Notes

1. Also known as Business Models for Sustainability (BMfS), or New Business Models (NBM).
2. For example, a new Master in Entrepreneurship and Sustainable Innovation (M.Sc.) was launched in 2018 by ESCP Europe Business School Berlin, and its objectives mention that is meant to cater both potential entrepreneurs and intrapreneurs interested to learn sustainable innovation skills (https://bit.ly/2DPqNaf).
3. Source: PwC/CB Insights MoneyTree™ Report Q4 2017 (https://pwc.to/2EKyqAW).

References

Austin, James, Howard Stevenson, and Jane Wei-Skillern. 2006. Social and Commercial Entrepreneurship: Same, Different, or Both? *Entrepreneurship Theory and Practice* 30 (1): 1–22. Wiley/Blackwell.

Baue, B., and R. Thurm. 2018. Blueprint 4. Integral Business Model Design for Catalyzing Regenerative & Distributive Economies. *Reporting 3.0.*

Bhasin, Sanjay, and Peter Burcher. 2006. Lean Viewed as a Philosophy. *Journal of Manufacturing Technology Management* 17 (1): 56–72. Emerald Group Publishing Limited.

Blank, Steve. 2003. *The Four Steps to the Epiphany: Successful Strategies for Products That Win*. First. Lulu Enterprises Incorporated.

———. 2013. Why the Lean Start-Up Changes Everything. *Harvard Business Review* 91 (5): 63–72.

Bloch, Ernst. 1995. *The Principle of Hope*. Cambridge, MA: MIT Press.

Bocken, N., P. Rana, and S.W. Short. 2015. Value Mapping for Sustainable Business Thinking. *Journal of Industrial and Production Engineering* 32 (1): 67–81.

Bocken, N., S. Short, P. Rana, and S. Evans. 2013. A Value Mapping Tool for Sustainable Business Modelling. Edited by Gilbert Lenssen, Mollie Painter, Aileen Ion. *Corporate Governance: The International Journal of Business in Society* 13 (5): 482–497. Emerald Group Publishing Limited.

Bocken, N., S.W. Short, P. Rana, and S. Evans. 2014. A Literature and Practice Review to Develop Sustainable Business Model Archetypes. *Journal of Cleaner Production* 65 (Feb.): 42–56. Elsevier.

Boons, Frank, and Florian Lüdeke-Freund. 2013. Business Models for Sustainable Innovation: State-of-the-Art and Steps towards a Research Agenda. *Journal of Cleaner Production* 45: 9–19.

Brandel, Jennifer, Mara Zepeda, Astrid Scholz, and Aniyia Williams. 2018. Zebras Unite To Fix What Unicorns Broke. *Medium*. https://bit.ly/2F6Y2rQ.

Braungart, Michael, and William McDonough. 2013. *The Upcycle: Beyond Sustainability—Designing for Abundance*. Farrar, Straus and Giroux: North Point Press.

Breuer, Henning, and Florian Lüdeke-Freund. 2016. *Values-Based Innovation Management: Innovating by What We Care About*. Palgrave Macmillan.

Calacanis, Jason. 2018. E802: All #AskJason! Minimizing Burn Rate, SV Mental Health, Self-Funding to Series A, Equity Splits, 'sustainability' Stigma, Solo-Founding, Founder/angel Bad Habits, Product+Services & More|This Week in Startups. *This Week in Startups*. https://bit.ly/2ElyK7l.

"Charter—Kickstarter." 2018. Accessed April 4. https://www.kickstarter.com/charter.
Christensen, Clayton, Scott Cook, and Taddy Hall. 2005. Marketing Malpractice: The Cause and the Cure. *Harvard Business Review* 83 (12): 74–83.
Clinton, L., and R. Whisnant. 2014. *Model Behavior—20 Business Model Innovations for Sustainability*. London: SustainAbility.
Cortese, Amy. 2016. A New Wrinkle in the Gig Economy: Workers Get Most of the Money—The New York Times. *The New York Times*. https://nyti.ms/2JhgsYt.
Dentchev, Nikolay, Rupert Baumgartner, Hans Dieleman, Lára Jóhannsdóttir, Jan Jonker, Timo Nyberg, Romana Rauter, et al. 2016. Embracing the Variety of Sustainable Business Models: Social Entrepreneurship, Corporate Intrapreneurship, Creativity, Innovation, and Other Approaches to Sustainability Challenges. *Journal of Cleaner Production* 113 (Feb.): 1–4.
Doherty, Bob, Helen Haugh, and Fergus Lyon. 2014. Social Enterprises as Hybrid Organizations: A Review and Research Agenda. *International Journal of Management Reviews* 16 (4): 417–436.
Drucker, P. 1985. *Innovation and Entrepreneurship*. New York: Harper & Row.
Edquist, Charles. 2006. *Systems of Innovation: Perspectives and Challenges*. Oxford: Oxford University Press, January.
Hockenson, Lauren. 2016. How Tinsel Founder Aniyia Williams Built a Hardware Startup from Scratch While Pregnant. *The Next Web*. https://bit.ly/2uQT1lI.
Jonker, Jan. 2014a. Changing the Logic of Value Creation/changer La Logique de Création de Valeur. Toulouse, France: Toulouse Business School, Chaire d'Excellence Pierre de Fermat, Région Midi-Pyrénées. http://repository.ubn.ru.nl/handle/2066/131208.
———. 2014b. *New Business Models: Collaborating to Create Value*. The Hague: Academic Service.
"Kickstarter.com." 2018. https://www.kickstarter.com/.
Ladd, Ted. 2016. The Limits of the Lean Startup Method. *Harvard Business Review*.
Lüdeke-Freund, Florian. 2015. 'Sustainability Innovation Pack' (Beta)—Facilitation Tool for Sustainable Innovation. *SBM Blog*. https://bit.ly/2q5D9WI.
Lüdeke-Freund, F., L. Massa, N. Bocken, A. Brent, and J. Musango. 2016. Business Models for Shared Value: Main Report.
Marshall, Aase. 2017. Elevating an Industry: The Stocksy United Story|Co-operatives First. *Co-operatives First*. https://bit.ly/2El5uxH.
Maurya, Ash. 2012. *Running Lean: Iterate from Plan A to a Plan That Works*. O'Reilly.

———. 2017. A 3×3×3 Perspective for Getting Your Vision, Strategy, and Product Aligned. *Medium*. https://bit.ly/2pcQYF8.

Moore, Geoffrey A. 1991. *Crossing the Chasm: Marketing and Selling Technology Products to Mainstream Customers*. HarperBusiness.

Muñoz, Pablo, and Boyd Cohen. 2018. Sustainable Entrepreneurship Research: Taking Stock and Looking Ahead. *Business Strategy and the Environment* 27 (3): 300–322. https://doi.org/10.1002/bse.2000.

Muñoz, Pablo, and Dimo Dimov. 2015. The Call of the Whole in Understanding the Development of Sustainable Ventures. *Journal of Business Venturing* 30 (4): 632–654. Elsevier.

Nilsen, Gaute Terland, and Nicolay Arguillere Ramm. 2015. Lean Startup: A Success Factor? A Quantitative Study of How Use of the Lean Startup Framework Affects the Success of Norwegian High-Tech Startups. University of Oslo.

Norman, Donald A. 2011. *Living with Complexity*. MIT Press.

Osterwalder, Alex, and Yves Pigneur. 2010. *Business Model Generation: A Handbook for Visionaries, Game Changers, and Challengers*. OSF.

Osterwalder, Alex, Yves Pigneur, Greg Bernarda, and Alan Smith (Designer). 2014. *Value Proposition Design: How to Create Products and Services Customers Want*. John Wiley & Sons.

Quayle, Moura. 2017. *Designed Leadership*. Columbia University Press.

Ries, Eric. 2009. Lessons Learned: Minimum Viable Product: A Guide. *Startup Lessons Learned*.

———. 2011. *The Lean Startup: How Today's Entrepreneurs Use Continuous Innovation to Create Radically Successful Businesses*. New York: Crown Business.

Rogers, Everett. 1962. *Diffusion of Innovations*. New York: Free Press of Glencoe.

Schaltegger, Stefan, Florian Lüdeke Freund, and Erik G. Hansen. 2012. Business Cases for Sustainability: The Role of Business Model Innovation for Corporate Sustainability. *International Journal of Innovation and Sustainable Development* 6 (2): 95.

Schaltegger, Stefan, Erik G. Hansen, and Florian Lüdeke-Freund. 2016. Business Models for Sustainability. *Organization & Environment* 29 (1): 3–10. Los Angeles, CA: SAGE Publications.

Schaltegger, Stefan, and Marcus Wagner. 2011. Sustainable Entrepreneurship and Sustainability Innovation: Categories and Interactions. *Business Strategy and the Environment* 20 (4): 222–237. John Wiley & Sons, Ltd.

Schaper, Michael. 2010. *Making Ecopreneurs: Developing Sustainable Entrepreneurship*. Edited by Michael Schaper. Second. Gower/Ashgate Pub.

Schick, Hildegard, Sandra Marxen, and Jürgen Freimann. 2002. Sustainability Issues for Start-up Entrepreneurs. *GMI* 38: 66.

Scholz, Trebor. 2016. *Platform Cooperativism: Challenging the Corporate Sharing Economy*. New York: Rosa Luxemburg Stiftung.

Schor, Juliet. 2017. Lecture—Juliet Schor. Platform Cooperativism 2017. https://bit.ly/2GDuyli.

Schumpeter, Joseph Alois. 1942. *Capitalism, Socialism and Democracy*. New York: Harper & Brothers.

Sinek, Simon. 2009. *Start with Why: How Great Leaders Inspire Everyone to Take Action*. Portfolio.

Stubbs, Wendy, and Chris Cocklin. 2008. Conceptualizing a 'Sustainability Business Model'. *Organization & Environment* 21 (2): 103–127. Los Angeles, CA: SAGE Publications.

Sylvester-Bradley, Oliver. 2017. 'Creating a Financial Model That Benefits the Many over the Few'—A Q&A with Brianna Wettlaufer, CEO of Stocksy. *The Open Coop*. https://bit.ly/2uPt0Dd.

Udziela, Kara. 2016. Platform Co-Op, Stocksy United, Doubles Revenue to $7.9M|Business Wire. *BusinessWire*. https://bit.ly/2uPstBd.

Upward, A. 2013. *Towards an Ontology and Canvas for Strongly Sustainable Business Models: A Systemic Design Science Exploration*. York University Toronto, Ontario.

Upward, Antony, and S.N. Davies. n.d. Realizing the Flourishing Imperative (Working Title). In *Rethinking Strategic Management: Competing Through a Sustainability Mindset*, ed. T. Wunder. Heidelberg, Germany: Springer International.

Upward, Antony, and Peter Jones. 2016. "An Ontology for Strongly Sustainable Business Models." *Organization & Environment* 29 (1): 97–123. Los Angeles, CA: SAGE Publications.

Van Tol, Alex. 2017. Why Stocksy United's CEO Is a Rebel With a Cause—Douglas Magazine. *Douglas*. https://bit.ly/2Gy5hNv.

Voros, Joseph. 2001. A Primer on Futures Studies, Foresight and the Use of Scenarios.

Walravens, Samantha. 2017. Rewriting the Playbook for Black and Brown Founders. *Forbes*. https://bit.ly/2q9a7qb.

Williams, Aniyia. 2017. How to Launch a Company When Investors Ain't Writing Checks. *Medium*. https://bit.ly/2iZDVV3.

Womack, James P., Daniel T. Jones, and Daniel. Roos. 1990. *The Machine That Changed the World: The Story of Lean Production—Toyota's Secret Weapon in the Global Car Wars That is Revolutionizing World Industry*. Free Press.

10

Organizational Identity and Value Triangle: Management of Jungian Paradoxes to Enable Sustainable Business Model Innovation

Roberto Biloslavo, David Edgar, and Carlo Bagnoli

1 Introduction

Experts agree that innovation is the only feasible business strategy to meet the challenge faced by international competitors, societal and environmental challenges. In addition to product and process innovation, business model (BM) innovation has taken on even more importance, resulting in the (re)configuration of the value chain and value system, and redefining relationships with business partners and other stakeholders.

R. Biloslavo (✉)
Faculty of Management, University of Primorska, Koper, Slovenia
e-mail: roberto.biloslavo@fm-kp.si

D. Edgar
Department of Business Management, Glasgow School for Business and Society, Glasgow, UK
e-mail: D.A.Edgar@gcu.ac.uk

C. Bagnoli
Department of Management, Ca'Foscari University, Venezia, Italy
e-mail: bagnoli@unive.it

The innovation goal from a sustainable point of view is not only to play better than others, but to change the rules of the game (Kim and Mauborgne 1998) by solving the paradox between greater value for stakeholders (i.e., society, nature, and future generations) and economic profit (Epstein et al. 2015). Incremental product and process innovations have certainly brought cleaner, more efficient, socially conscious products and services, but for the most part have failed to grow beyond a premium-priced or green-lifestyle niche. Alternatively, many novel or radical innovations have failed because they were unable to compete within the constraints of an existing or traditional BM.

As sustainability trends and challenges continue to shift the foundations of our current BMs, incremental innovation will become less effective in enabling companies to adapt and succeed. Only a comprehensive innovation of BMs will allow the development of entirely new value propositions tailored to the demands of and for sustainable business (Baldassarre et al. 2017). Such BMs are identified as sustainable business models (SBMs). SBMs reconcile how a company creates and delivers value for its multiple stakeholders while capturing some value for itself. The value includes *economic value* (i.e., economic growth such as profit or return on investments), *social value* (i.e., poverty alleviation, social justice, equality, or well-being), and *environmental value* (i.e., the use of resources at a rate at which they can be renewed). An innovation that supports transition of BM to SBM is called sustainable business model innovation (SBMI). The question that arises now is what kind of innovation is a sustainable innovation? In general, it can be a technology push innovation or a market pull innovation. The latter results from the identified needs of customers and are usually known as incremental changes, while technology push innovations are generally considered as radical changes (Verganti 2009). However, in our view SBMI is more than anything else a *meaning innovation* (Battistella et al. 2012), that is, it attributes new meaning to the products (e.g., sustainable or green products, or socially responsible products) and to other elements of the BM (e.g., sustainable processes, renewable resources). Usually SBMI starts from the product (e.g., bottom of the pyramid) or processes (e.g., servitization) with the change in meaning of one component of the BM resulting in a knock-on effect on all other BM components (i.e., we cannot have a green product

Organizational Identity and Value Triangle: Management...

without a green BM). Besides considering congruence among BM components the organization must take special care to keep meaning at the BM level compatible with the register of meanings at the level of organizational identity (i.e., strategic meanings). According to Nag et al. (2007), organizational identity influences business orientation and firm strategy and thus, we believe, the organization's BM (see Fig. 10.1).

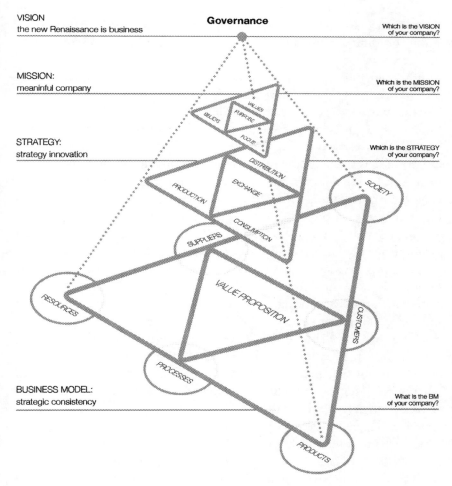

Fig. 10.1 The value tetrahedron

Organizational identity acts as a guide for organizational action (Ashforth and Mael 1996; Kogut and Zander 1996) and can influence the innovation activities pursued. SBMI could not happen if not supported by a proper organizational identity, implying strategic meaning must correspond to the sustainable meaning at the level of SBM. This is supported by Hamilton and Gioia (2009, p. 436), who claim "Sustainability is a multifaceted concept that presumes a dynamic balance among economic, environmental, and social goals … an enduring shift toward sustainable organizational practice requires that sustainability become a fundamental, indispensable part of an organization's identity."

While attributing an identity to an organization is problematic for some (Gioia 1998), many authors agree that some form of organizational identity exists independent of individual members, as a social construct formed through members' cognition and emotions (Scott and Lane 2000). From a strategic perspective, organizational identity is difficult to imitate and as such could enhance organization effectiveness and performance and serve as a source of sustained competitive advantage (Barney et al. 1998). According to De Wit and Meyer (2005), identity is answering four key questions: Why does the firm exist (i.e., purpose)? What is of fundamental importance for us (i.e., values)? What are our driving assumptions (i.e., beliefs)? and Where does the firm operate (i.e., scope)? As such, organizational identity influences what is interpreted as urgent or not, and what are opportunities or threats (Kovoor-Misra 2009).

A transformative innovation process, like the SBMI, starts not from the end goal but from the question "Why do we exist?" and has implications for "what we should do." According to Navis and Glynn (2010), sustainable organizational practices often require some fundamental changes in the organization's character or identity, that is, not only in what organizations do, but also in what they are and how they see themselves or their essential nature. As such, identity shapes and directs strategic change. It determines which sustainability issues are noticed, which are not, and which are perceived feasible to be resolved (Dutton et al. 1994; Gioia and Thomas 1996). In some cases, organizational identity does not have the characteristics to support development of a SBM and needs to change in order to embrace sustainability. However, an organizational identity characterized by centrality, endurance, and distinctiveness (Hatch and Yanow 2008), even if subject to evolution and change (Fiol 2002), is in contrast to an innovation process characterized by variability and novelty. Anthony and Tripsas (2016) say that this "presents a fundamental tension between organizational identity and innovation" (p. 417). This tension is even more evident in a sustainable organization and represents a focal point for our contribution as we believe organizational identity can be a key driver for SBMI for two reasons. First, in the midst of changes organizations need to have an anchor represented by its identity that allows proper sense-making and sense-giving of the business context. Second, a company must not dilute its identity by adapting it to a continuously changing external context, but rather transform the context to affirm its own identity and in doing so be ready to change when needed.

Organizations as socio-technical systems evolve and constantly change through renewal. A sustainable system must constantly "sacrifice" its components to support its own existence, that is, sustainability. In the case of organizations, that means keeping organizational identity "unchanged"[1] but allowing other organizational components like strategy and BMs to be readily dissipated and reorganized (i.e., innovate). This describes SBMI as a top-down process that starts with strategic meanings. However, according to paradox theory, this happens when organizations attend to the competing demands of different strategic goals, strategy options, and market demands (Smith and Lewis 2011). The world of organizations is full of paradoxes[2]; while some of them are generic (e.g., paradox of change and stability [March 1988]), others are industry-specific and/or organizational-specific. Organizational paradoxes derive from the specific organizational history, cultural context, and organization's goals and strategies that the latter chose and executed or tried to execute during its operation. Paradoxes are present at different space and time levels of the organization including its goals, strategy, structures, cultures, systems, practices, processes, and business areas. Strategic meaning at the level of organizational identity elucidates how an organization accepts and engages with the complexities and contradictions of competing alternatives simultaneously, that is, paradoxes (Lüscher and Lewis 2008). This represents the third way of managing paradoxes beside temporally separating and shifting between alternatives, and spatially separating alternatives within different organizational boundaries (Lewis 2000; Poole and Van de Ven 1989).

While substantial amounts of research exist about the importance of organizational identity for organization's performance, impacts on the design and implementation of strategy, and innovation activities, only limited work deals with strategic meanings in relation to sustainability, and even fewer about the relationship between strategic meaning and BMs (e.g., Battistella et al. 2012). As such, there is no conceptual framework for understanding the impact of strategic meanings on SBMI in a way to enable decision-makers to achieve competing sustainability objectives simultaneously. So, we seek to develop such a framework by exploring emerging streams of research applied to paradox and corporate sustainability (e.g., Brooks et al. 2018; Hahn et al. 2014, 2016, 2018; Van der Byl and Slawinski 2015) and research into competing demands of interdependent sustainability issues (Gao and Bansal 2013), which display typical characteristic of paradoxes (Smith 2014). The significance of a paradoxical approach for understanding corporate sustainability is explained by Hahn et al. (2010) who claim that conflicts between the three dimensions of corporate sustainability "represent the rule rather than the exception" (p. 218) and by Van der Byl and Slawinski (2015) who assert that "a paradox lens is well-suited to sustainability research, given that sustainability requires a systems view of organizations" (p. 72).

Sustainability paradoxes are clearly evident in cases like The Coca-Cola Company trying to deal with the tension between its core BM, based on its identity, and the social issue of obesity (Iivonen 2018), or with Wal-Mart's identity of "Everyday low price" which drives a BM on increased consumption of raw materials but seeks extensive environmental sustainability (Cascio 2006). On the other hand, the strategic meaning of Ikea expressed by "Create a better daily life for the majority of people" is very well suited to SBM.

In order to better understand the relation between organizational meanings and the paradoxical nature of organization, we applied a Jungian dialectical approach. The integration of Jungian dialectics with the method of the paradoxes is made on the fact that, at the root of the Jungian theories, there is a very similar concept of the "*coincidentia oppositorum.*" Jung, in fact, always reasons for paradoxes and elaborates his theories starting from antithetical elements, which are in constant conflict with each other and that must find a synthesis in something "higher." We found that the results of the Jungian typological analysis applied on paradoxes on the organizational identity level are convergent with those proposed by the authors of the paradoxical approach, but it gives us a better sense for practical actions and application.

Our main hypothesis is that in order to implement SBMI sustainability must be fully integrated into the core of what an organization purports to be, which means three key conditions are met:

1. organizational identity has as a founding value social sustainability;
2. at the level of organizational identity a "*balance*" between values (ethics) and economic thinking exists;
3. the balance is achieved with a Jungian function of intuition pervading the elements of organizational identity like scope and beliefs.

This chapter explores the concepts of SBMI, organizational identity, and paradoxes. In our perspective, BMs represent frames that managers develop to organize not only "the way organization makes money" but also the way through which they convey organizational identity, meanings, and culture. Special attention is then drawn to Jung's dialectical approach as a conceptual framework for understanding and categorizing organizational identity and explaining its impact on SBMI. In the empirical part, the research methodology is presented followed by a presentation of the Muji case study and key findings, before concluding remarks are given together with the suggestions for further research.

2 Literature Review

2.1 Sustainability, Innovation, and Business Model

2.1.1 Sustainable Business Model and Sustainable Business Model Innovation

Since the 1990s internet boom, various authors have positioned the term BM as a key concept in understanding organizations but at the same time have voiced concerns that the rapid proliferation of the concept has created an abundance of meanings. There is a degree of consensus that the BM is a model of the "systems of activities" (Martins et al. 2015, p. 100) but they differ in their "understanding of how firms develop such systems" (ibid. p. 100) and why. Based on available definitions, it seems that the BM is a "practical thing" that has useful and analytical value for entrepreneurs and companies to run a business, and a "real-world challenge for entrepreneurial managers" (Wirtz et al. 2010). Analyzing the BM means first of all understanding that it refers to a complex system, which acts as a guideline for operational activities and at the same time constitutes the corporate framework. In fact, from a business strategy point of view, BMs do nothing more than concretize it, working as a frame of reference that directs and coordinates all the levers and their implementation as in a puzzle. In doing this, it is necessary to maintain a fundamental consistency between strategy orientation and operative decisions that pervade the whole system and components that create and capture value.

On the other hand, Haggege and Collet (2011) discuss ontological, systemic, choice/consequence, and narrative perspectives. BM understood as a narrative represents a story that explains the basic business logic applied by an organization (Haggege and Collet 2011) and captures the "real-life" or "lived" experience of the business. While narrative represents a possible approach to understanding the BM we also recognize that in a similar fashion to the field of strategy process, the theoretical evolution of BMs has resulted in three schools (Martins et al. 2015), broadly mapping onto the schools of strategy. These schools are the rational positioning school, the evolutionary learning school, and the cognitive school, although organizations may shift between schools as their BM evolves over time (Mitchell and Coles 2003). For the purpose of our study, we have employed the narrative perspective to explicate the mental representation of how a company co-creates value with its stakeholders in line with Battistella et al.'s (2012) view.

It has been claimed that business model innovation (BMI) has a greater impact on profit margins than other types of innovation (Pohle and Chapman 2006), and has become the new basis of competition, replacing product features and enhanced benefits (Spieth et al. 2014). BMI considers the BM instead of products or processes as the subject of innovation (Baden-Fuller and Haefliger 2013) seeking new and novel ways of creating and delivering value to a customer and making profits from it. BMI supports firms exploiting new opportunities in three different ways (Johnson 2010): (1) by supporting the development of new value propositions; (2) by tackling new customer segments that have traditionally been overlooked by existing value propositions; and (3) by entering entirely new industries.

Independent of the degree of innovativeness, BMI requires that at least one of the three BM dimensions— value creation, value delivery, or value capture—is changed by some degree (Baden-Fuller and Haefliger 2013; Baden-Fuller and Mangematin 2013; Johnson et al. 2008). The role of BMI in promoting sustainability is to analyze BM from the point of view of the triple bottom line (i.e., economic, social, and environmental) and modify its components to improve the long-term benefits the firm is delivering to society and itself (Joyce and Paquin 2016).

Taking a broad perspective, sustainable innovation can be considered as the development of something new that improves performance in all the three dimensions of sustainable development at the same time. Sustainable business model innovation has emerged as a model that offers innovative solutions to minimize the adverse environmental impacts of the value chain, maximize societal and environmental benefits, and generate new value propositions that promote market needs and economic value while serving society and the natural environment (Bocken et al. 2014). The aim of SBMI is similar to BMI but its focus is on SBM instead of classical BM. Various definitions of SBM are presented in Table 10.1.

According to Zott et al. (2011), adopting SBM approach helps understand how businesses can create value not only to customers but also to other stakeholders, society, and/or the natural environment and how this value is captured or distributed across a broad set of stakeholders. While Schaltegger et al. (2012) say SBMs are those which integrate economically relevant sustainability concerns with business success or competitive advantages. Hence, SBMs are important in driving and implementing corporate innovation for sustainability; they can help embed sustainability into business purpose and processes, and serve as a key driver of competitive advantage (Bocken et al. 2014).

Table 10.1 Definitions of SBM

Authors	Year (page)	Definition of SBM
Baldassarre et al.	2017 (pp. 176–177)	"… a sustainable business model has the potential of going beyond incremental innovation and/or the improvement of operational and technological efficiency. The core of a sustainable business model is a sustainable value proposition; namely, a value proposition that allows simultaneous value creation for multiple stakeholders, including shareholders, suppliers and partners as well as the environment and society"
Bocken et al.	2013 (pp. 484–485)	"Sustainable business models seek to go beyond delivering economic value and include a consideration of other forms of value for a broader range of stakeholders. They have been defined as business models that create competitive advantage through superior customer value while contributing to sustainable development of the company and society"
Bocken et al.	2014 (p. 44)	"… sustainable business models use both a systems and firm-level perspective, build on the triple bottom line approach to define the firm's purpose and measure performance, include a wide range of stakeholders, and consider the environment and society as stakeholders. Extending this, a sustainable business model aligns interests of all stakeholder groups, and explicitly considers the environment and society as key stakeholders."
Caldera et al.	2017 (p. 1556)	"A sustainable business model is described as a business model that bring about competitive advantage by providing excellent customer value and is instrumental in the sustainable development of the company as well as the society."
Schaltegger et al.	2016 (p. 269)	"A business model for sustainability helps describing, analyzing, managing and communicating (i) a company's sustainable value proposition to its customers and all other stakeholders, (ii) how it creates and delivers this value, (iii) and how it captures economic value while maintaining or regenerating natural, social and economic capital beyond its organizational boundaries."

2.1.2 Value Triangle Business Model

Drawing extensively from existing literature on BMs and SBMs, the BM framework termed "Value Triangle" (VT) was developed (Biloslavo et al. 2018). The VT presumes firms co-create value within a business ecosystem that includes society and natural environment (see Stubbs and Cocklin 2008). More specifically the VT represents how a firm co-creates and co-delivers value with its stakeholders within a circular value system and captures some economic value from it. Based on the VT, the Value Triangle Business Model (VT BM) canvas was developed that allows a visual presentation of SBM to be used in practice (see Fig. 10.2).

The VT BM canvas includes nine components, which are:

1. *Society*: the various stakeholders whom the firm establishes and maintains mutually beneficial relationships including natural environment with its ecosystem services.
2. *Value proposition*: firm's statement to co-create and co-deliver value for its stakeholders.
3. *Customers*: the different group of people or organizations that the firm aims to reach and serve.

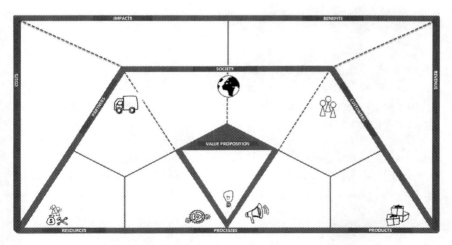

Fig. 10.2 Value triangle business model canvas

4. *Products*: the bundle of goods and services that create values for customers.
5. *Key operational activities*: key operational activities include inbound logistics (i.e., procurement and supply channels), R&D, and operations as well as marketing and outbound logistics (i.e., distribution and communication channels).
6. *Resources*: capital types used by the firm: financial (e.g., cash used in transactions), manufactured (e.g. semi-products, infrastructure), intellectual (e.g., patents, tacit knowledge), human (e.g., labor, skills, motivation), social and relationship (e.g., shared norms, brand loyalty), and natural capital (e.g., clean air, biodiversity).
7. *Partners*: the network of suppliers and partners that makes the BM work.
8. *Benefits*: benefits are divided among benefits delivered to society and environment (i.e., public and partner value) and revenue sources by which firm captures some economic value for itself.
9. *Costs*: costs are divided between costs that represents the negative impact of firm's outcomes and outputs on society and environment and cost drivers that impact the financial aspects of firm's performance.

2.2 Organizational Identity

Organizational identity can be regarded as a collection of physical and psychological features of a certain object that make the object different from or similar to other objects of the same kind (Bromley 1993). A broad definition of organizational identity refers to what members of the organization perceive, feel, and think about their organizations and is subjective (Ind 1990). It is formed based on the history of the organization, its beliefs and the business philosophy, the character of the technology in the organization, the property of the organization, the personality of leading people, the ethical and cultural values, and the strategies of the organization. The study of definitions by Alessandri (2001) highlights definitions of identity that differ in the basic postulates, "from the tangible to the intangible, from the tactical to the strategic" (p. 174), but what they all have in common is the fact that organizational identity is connected to the manner in which the organization presents itself to the public (Alessandri 2001), both internally and externally. The most commonly used concepts in the literature are the terms "corporate identity" and "organizational identity." We will consider organizational identity as something that pertains to organizational members and is constructed by them. Corporate identity relates to how the organization identity is communicated to its stakeholders, especially external stakeholders, an aspect that we consider less relevant for the scope of our contribution.[3]

Identity brings out the strategic meanings that are historically formed and unique for each individual company. They are intimately linked to the raison d'être of the company and represents the point of view it has toward the culturally constructed world. The core of these meanings constitutes a system of meaning and sense-making for the top management that orients the business strategy development and helps to deeply perceive the implications of the decisions.

Organizational identity develops through time (e.g., "Think different" in the case of Apple) by proposing possible answers to industry paradoxes (e.g., "simple interface vs. complex algorithm" in the case of Apple) and to organizational paradoxes (e.g., "product closed vs. open shop" in the case of Apple) that the company is seeking to solve. According to the model developed by Nag et al. (2007), culture and organizational knowledge are deeply embedded in organizational practices and therefore attempts at innovation can fail due to the reciprocal and recursive deterrent constituted by the interaction between culture, knowledge, and organizational practices. In summary, the creation of the organizational identity is divided into four processes that lead it to interact with the organizational culture (internally) and the brand image (externally) (Hatch and Schultz 2002). Identity is expressed in the image perceived by external stakeholders through the functional and symbolic attributes of products, modes of communication, and so on. The image in turn is mirrored in the identity by modifying it. At the same time, the identity is reflected in the culture of the organization through organizational structure, operative systems, and mechanisms. The culture in turn is expressed in the identity reinforcing it or not. The company must build a coherent circle between culture, identity, and image to pursue strategic consistency, a fundamental prerequisite for overcoming organizational resistance to innovation, above all meaning innovation, and being appreciated (and not only) in the market. In that view sustainability and corporate social responsibility provide a specific context for organizational identity construction as sustainability influences identity and identity orientations (Hamilton and Gioia 2009; Morsing and Roepstorff 2015). While other context may imply the same, the sustainability context is specific because it implies a commitment and promise of improving social and environmental issues together with the economic one (Morsing and Roepstorff 2015). Indeed, considering the expectation of larger society for more socially and environmentally responsible behaviors of private companies is very important. Verganti's (2009, p. 56) claim: "The way we give meaning to things depends heavily on our values, our beliefs, our principles and our traditions. In other words, they reflect our cultural model. And this, in turn, reflects what happens in our private and in our society." is highly pertinent here.

Having clarified the importance of organizational identity for sustainable innovation success (Anthony and Tripsas 2016), we can move on to defining the ideal identity type of a sustainable[4] company, starting, however, as a rhetorical expedient, from the definition of the unsustainable company. The unsustainable company is characterized by creating little value for customers as well as for society including nature. Creating little value focuses the company to consider the most effective ways to appropriate the largest part of this value by itself as it believes that the real issue is how to divide value and not how to create more of it. A vicious circle is created, leading to even less value for customers, society, and eventually the company. On the other hand, the sustainable company co-creates a lot of value for customers and society as well as for itself. Creating lots of value focuses the company on the most effective ways to distribute value among stakeholders because it believes that the path to long-term effectiveness is to multiply value created. In this way a virtuous circle is nourished, leading to the creation of even more value for customers and society.

On the basis of the difference between a sustainable and unsustainable company, we can define main traits that characterize mission[5] of the sustainable company and with it its identity.

At the level of *focus*, the sustainable company recognizes how the current context in which it operates is characterized by an exponential acceleration of technological development that leads to perceiving time as a priority with respect to space, and of social change that leads to a contraction of the "real" time and faster rhythms of life in order not to be stuck "out of time." This requires development of durable goods that persist in time and minimize use of non-renewable resources and negative impact on nature. For example, a carpet company, such as interface, must begin thinking of itself as flooring service provider and not as a carpet manufacturer in order to generate alternative solutions to environmentally degrading practices that are standard in the industry (Anderson 1998).

At the level of *beliefs*, the sustainable company recognizes the importance of developing a sustainable esthetic proposal embedded with meaning. This proposal is based on the exclusive variety and variability that the company is able to generate by drawing on its sense of taste and beauty, in order to move from the sale of "cold" products to sale of meaning that relates to green and social issues incorporated into products (Verganti 2009). Esthetics of sustainable companies encompass capacities ranging from an appreciation of "honesty, integrity, support, and compassion" (Issa and Pick 2010, p. 619) to a means of developing the ability to "transcend opposites and contradictions" (Brady and Hart 2006).

At the level of *values*, the sustainable company recognizes the importance of supporting a digital sustainable humanism. The digital revolution, the first cause of time acceleration, leads to questioning all existing BMs, but cannot question the centrality of the person and collaborative relationships between them for the pursuit of a fair and widespread prosperity according to the notion of nature as a whole embracing "mother." Technology is always a means and not an end in itself. The sustainable company is first of all a community that aims to satisfy the needs of people, inside and outside the organization, by pursuing an economic activity that manifests itself through the work and positive attitude of the people involved. The latter is closely linked to social innovation (van der

Have and Rubalcaba 2016) understood as the innovation perpetuated by companies to satisfy social needs that cannot be met, at least according to traditional business logics. Social innovation stimulates facing problems in a different way that can lead to creating new markets in which it is possible to deliver social value as well as generate economic profit (e.g., Grameen Danone).

Finally, at the level of *scope* the sustainable company recognizes the importance of pursuing cultural transformation to escape from product commoditization that characterizes fast-changing mass markets. The company moves from producing and distributing goods and/or services, to guiding transformative experiences that involve the cognitive and emotional sphere of customers, positively altering their "status quo" and satisfying their higher human needs as need for love, belonging, esteem, and self-actualization. However, the ideal identity can be considered as the final goal and sustainable companies can somehow divert from it as, according to paradox theory, they respond to different and unique organizational and market demands in virtuous and repeating cycles of tension and resolution (Smith and Lewis 2011).

2.3 Sustainability and Paradoxes

According to Handy (1994), any complex society is very much characterized by paradoxes that can be only accepted and not resolved. Lewis (2000) says paradoxes are posing competing demands that require ongoing responses rather than one-time resolutions. This is especially the case when considering the sustainable development of organizations. A profound commitment to sustainability is, for most companies, a constant negotiation process of tensions and challenges arising among internal and external stakeholders and their interest. It is certainly not a topic characterized by agreement and according to Bansal (2002) sustainable development is characterized by a multitude of different economic, environmental, and social objectives that all appear desirable in isolation but are "inextricably connected and internally interdependent" (p. 123) as well as contradictory. These are the same characteristics shared by organizational paradoxes.

The term paradox is from the Greek word "paradoxon" that means contrary to expectations, existing belief, or perceived opinion. According to Quinn and Cameron (1988), Lewis (2000), Schad et al. (2016), and Smith and Lewis (2011), contradiction and interdependency lie at the heart of paradoxical tensions. In that view, Schad et al. (2016) define "paradox as persistent contradiction between interdependent elements. This definition identifies two, core characteristics of paradox: contradiction and interdependence, which together inform the boundaries of paradox to sharpen the lens, while also broadening the tent" (p. 10). Similarly, Lewis (2000) says organizational actors experience tension because the inherent conflicting characteristic of paradox where its elements "seem logical in isolation but absurd and irrational when appearing simultaneously" (p. 760) and Poole and Van de Ven (1989) described paradoxes as "interesting tensions, oppositions, and contradictions between theories which create conceptual difficulties" (p. 564). Even as paradox involves a dynamic and constantly shifting relationship between alternative poles, the core elements of contradiction and interdependence remain. Smith and Lewis (2011) argue that the paradoxes are always intrinsic and socially constructed. Paradoxical relationships emerge during the act of organizing that creates contexts in which the two poles of the paradox arise—an element and its opposite. These opposing forces are interdependent, defined one from the other. However, paradoxical relationships can sometimes remain latent, becoming salient only through the external environmental conditions of scarcity, plurality, and change that highlights the contradictory nature of the tensions, making them salient to organizational actors and their sense-making process.

There are different paradoxes related to sustainable development and sustainable company that reside at different organizational levels as well as at different temporal and spatial scales. Some of them are presented in Table 10.2.

By defining a coherent organizational identity, management is in a position that enables creating opportunities for growth and sustainable development that could be accepted and pursued by organization's members, business partners, and other stakeholders (i.e., a coherent identity "solves"[6] inherent paradoxes).

Table 10.2 Paradoxes and sustainability

Paradox	Description
Identity (continuity) vs. *Change* (discontinuity)	*Identity* as continuity in tradition, an essential starting point for change. *Change* as discontinuity, an essential final destination for a new identity.
Profit (value capturing) vs. *Social responsibility* (value creation)	*Profit* as a stimulus to pursue individual profit through the appropriation of the greatest part of created value. *Social responsibility* as a means of pursuing social responsibility through the distribution of created value.
Compete (node/individual) vs. *Collaborate* (relationship)	*Compete* with the other nodes of the network to divide the total value created. *Collaborate* with the other nodes of the network to multiply the total value created.
Unique (local, craft) vs. *Universal* (global, industrial)	*Unique* as a craft product of local culture, which must succeed in preserving local know-how. *Universal* as an industrial product of globalized civilization, which must succeed in enhancing local know-how.
Physical (analogic) vs. *Virtual* (digital)	*Physical* as an anchor to a tangible backbone that offers certainties (resilience, reliability, and efficiency) from which to start to face the digital future. *Virtual* as a precondition to make the system dynamic (fast, nimble, and adaptive) and dissolving the boundaries of the physical.
Valorizing (art, preserving the essential) vs. *Creating* (technology, recombine the elements)	*Valorizing* the (artistic) tradition understood as a created value to be preserved in order to compete and win in traditional market spaces. *Creating* (technological) innovation intended to create new value; an ability to win without competing by creating new market spaces.

Beside purpose one of the main components of organizational identity is represented by key values that in the case of a sustainable company, express the duty to preserve the environment, support sustainable development, and demonstrate the social responsibility of the company. These enduring values can be evident through appropriate leadership decisions about BM components that may require sacrifice of short-term financial gains or end of business relations if the latter are considered to be eco-unfriendly or socially unacceptable. While regarding beliefs, the main paradox is represented by an assumption of the importance of competition (i.e., promoting long-term collaboration vs. exploiting bargaining power) that can be internally oriented versus employees or externally to other stakeholders including society.

2.4 Coincidentia Oppositorum

The attempt to apply the theories elaborated by the Swiss psychiatrist Carl Gustav Jung (1875–1961) to the definition of the identity of a company is moving along different directions, in a territory still largely unexplored. The starting point is the theory of psychological types (Jung 1921/1991). Jung hypothesizes that, at the base of our way of perceiving and interpreting the world, there are four fundamental cognitive functions: Sensing, Intuition, Thinking, and Feeling. The first two would be "perceptive," that is, they would concern the way we acquire information: when we do it through the five senses, we are using Sensing; when—starting from the concrete data—we imagine a situation that does not yet exist, we are instead resorting to Intuition. The information acquired must then be processed, through the two "judging" functions: when we express a judgment on the basis of an impersonal logic, we are adopting the typical patterns of Thinking; when we express a judgment on the basis of moral values and feelings, we are moving within the Feeling. Jung then hypothesizes the existence of two different mental attitudes: the extroversion, which manifests itself when the psychic energy is oriented mainly toward the external world; and introversion, which focuses instead on the inner world. By combining the four cognitive functions with the two mental attitudes, we obtain the eight psychological types:

1. *Extroverted sensing*: focuses on direct perception, new and intense experiences;
2. *Introverted sensing*: focuses on indirect perception, experiences already known and consolidated;
3. *Extroverted intuition*: focuses on the connections of the external world, interdisciplinary perspectives and innovative projects;

4. *Introverted intuition*: focuses on the connections of the inner world, the interpretations of the individual and collective unconscious;
5. *Extroverted thinking*: focuses on linear reasoning and all that is organized down to the smallest detail;
6. *Introverted thinking*: focuses on a "lateral," destructured and destructuring cognitive perspective;
7. *Extroverted feeling*: focuses on collective values, social relationships, and the intense expression of passions;
8. *Introverted feeling*: focuses on individual values, inner recollection, and the rarefied expression of passions.

Beyond the therapeutic field and selection of personnel, Jungian theory of psychological types has not exhausted its possibilities to be applied to the corporate world. It can also find a useful application to the analysis of the product, to the organizational culture, and to the definition of the company's identity. Regarding the application to SBMs, the first consideration to make is that, given the ethical nature of the discourses related to sustainability, the first cognitive function of reference can only be the Feeling. This function, in fact, uses value judgments that can be collective (Extroverted Feeling) or individual (Introverted Feeling). In the first case, the reflection on sustainability will focus on social value, taking into consideration the impact that the company has on the community in which it is located and on the wider ones to which its products or services are directed. The way in which these communities influence the company's way of being and operating will also be considered, and the social initiatives or humanitarian campaigns launched or supported will be evaluated. Another perspective promoted by the Extroverted Feeling can be the constitution, through social networks or other channels, of a "tribe" gathered around the company and its values. Operating according to the perspective of Introverted Feeling, instead, attention will focus on the individual, regardless of the social context to which it belongs.

The theme of environmental impact also involves the Feeling, but not exclusively. In this case, in fact, the perceptual functions must also be called into question: Sensing and Intuition. The first is fundamental because it allows us to clearly perceive, through our five senses, the natural environment, its needs and the way in which it is possible to live in harmony with it. The second is no less important because, detaching itself from the limited perspective of the contingent reality, it allows us to glimpse future scenarios in which the relationship with the environment is resolved in a positive or negative sense. Even the ways in which eco-sustainable behaviors are realized have a double aspect: one that is more linked to practice, and therefore to Sensing (e.g., proposing products with lower environmental impact); and one more linked to vision, and therefore to Intuition (i.e., to imagine a system that revolutions the disposal of waste). Therefore, the value is always dictated by the Feeling, but the way to pursue it involves, in a priority way, the perceptual functions, namely Sensing and Intuition.

More problematic is the function Thinking, especially if it is identified with economic profit. In reality, the Thinking function is directed toward profit and it runs out in a merely utilitarian view when it works exclusively with Sensing. Sensing, in fact, focuses on the material dimension and aims at the concrete result not different from already known. If the Thinking is used to achieve this result, the way it operates—by definition impersonal—will favor the shortest route to reach the goal, respecting the rules but independently of any other ethical consideration. Different is the case when Thinking works with Intuition, because the latter allows abstraction and therefore looking for unconventional solutions. This is an exquisitely rational evaluation, which may not involve ethics and therefore does not refer to the Feeling function. In this way, what Jung calls *coincidentia oppositorum* is realized, and the tension between Thinking and Feeling is resolved, between the reasons of profit and those of ethics.

Jungian theories, in this sense, can be a useful tool for analysis, because many dynamics designed to resolve conflicts within the psyche seem feasible, with due caution, even to different contexts that transcend the individual dimension. And so, if the polarity between Thinking and Feeling can be addressed by resorting to a perceptive function, it is equally true that, in the Jungian perspective, the development of the person (the cornerstone of a fully "sustainable" vision) must take into account both the dimension emotional that the rational, both the practical and the most visionary, artistic, intuitive.

By attempting to cross the four Jungian cognitive functions with the four constituent elements of the mission as an explication of organizational identity, we can notice that:

- *Purpose* seems to correspond to the Thinking, as:
  - Ideally, the purpose derives directly from values and represents their first focus in a more defined context. This focusing operation is dictated by Thinking, because it is the fruit of a reflection on what the Feeling has assumed as indispensable.
  - In practice, the purpose may precede values, because it is often easier to identify. Later, on the basis of what and how it has been done (i.e., made decisions, actions performed), one can generalize and recognize the values behind these actions.
  - When the Extroverted Thinking prevails, the purpose is based on the universal/managerial logic and leads to a deliberate strategy (planning/positioning school).
  - When Introverted Thinking prevails, the purpose is based on the unique/entrepreneurial logic and leads to an emerging strategy (entrepreneurial/cultural school).

- *Values* seem to correspond to the Feeling, as:
  - They possess abstract and "universal" characteristics.
  - They are something that cannot be renounced; therefore, they are situated within the sphere of Ethics.
  - The value in itself can have a conceptual, intuitive or even sensory connotation, but the decision to favor that particular value with respect to others is dictated by the Feeling.
  - In the case of values generally accepted and recognized by the social context in which one lives, one can speak of Extroverted Feeling (today sustainability is recognized as a value at the level of society).
  - In the case of values that are detached, in whole or in part, from what the social context of reference recognizes as an integral part of one's identity, one can speak of Introverted Feeling (30 years ago sustainability was only a value on individual level).

- *Beliefs* seem to correspond to Extroverted Intuition or Introverted Sensing, because:
  - When beliefs are the result of a way of reading reality by the CEO or top team and of setting the limits of an action within generally accepted rules, we are in the presence of Introverted Sensing. This

function, in fact, is linking the new information with previous knowledge, and tends to rely on past experience and draws from it laws considered to be valid at any time and in every context. This is case of "sectoral recipes" applied to an individual mind-set.
- When beliefs are the result of a "vision" that aims to overcome—or in any case to put into question—the laws and limits derived from previous experience, we find ourselves in the area of Intuition, considering multiple possible solutions or scenarios.

* *Scope* seems to correspond to the Extroverted Sensing or Introverted Intuition, because:

   - The scope seems to operate on the same level as beliefs, as it modifies the beliefs themselves and at the same time is continually modified by them.
   - Ideally, the scope comes from the purpose which, in turn, was determined by values.
   - Of the four elements considered, the scope is the most intimately linked to the concrete reality, to the practical dimension of organization's life. In this sense, it seems close to the Extroverted Sensing.
   - Extroverted Sensing consists in defining the range of action within a range defined by the standard classification of economic activities. On the other hand, Introverted Intuition tends to reduce the multiplicity to the unit in order to create new sectors outside standard classification of economic activities.

3 The Case: Muji

3.1 Research Design

The research method used was a qualitative case study which allowed for an understanding of the complex social constructions of organizational identity and paradoxes (Miles et al. 2014). The case study is presented in the form of a grand narrative in order to express complex context dependent situations (Gubrium and Holstein 2008) in a simple way and draw on the emotional and rational side of the people involved (Weick and

Browning 1986). We analyze organizational identity as narrative constructed through communication, used by organizational members to make sense of the distinct characteristics of the organization.

The data was collected from different sources and analyzed by three researchers independently. The researchers then shared their opinions to obtain an agreed assessment in order to increase the validity of findings and minimizing the bias in objectivity. Gaps and conflicts were resolved by further reviewing the transcripts. The main data sources were a semi-structured interview with top management team, a public lecture delivered by the president of Muji Kanai at Ca' Foscari University, the case study written about Muji by Bagnoli and Biotto (2014) and other publicly accessible sources. All collected data was first analyzed by applying content analysis and then the four Jungian cognitive functions.

3.2 Case Study

3.2.1 Muji Company[7]

Muji is a platform company born in Japan in December 1980. The project takes shape under the name of *Mujirushi Ryōhin*—a Japanese expression that means "brandless quality products"—within a chain of pre-existing shops called *Seiyu*. The creator of Muji was Seiji Tsutsumi, a Japanese entrepreneur with propensity for business and artistic sensibility. He conceived an idea in contrast with that historical moment: proposing to the Japanese society the rediscovery of a lifestyle founded on simplicity and the essentiality, which has always been at the base of the culture of his people. The meeting with the art director Ikko Tanaka has been fundamental for the realization of this vision. The amalgam of their talents and their personalities in a short time produces a first line of 40 articles (31 for kitchen & dining, and 9 home accessories), to which Tanaka confers a clear identity, consistent with the concept of lifestyle wanted by Tsutsumi.

The first independent Muji shop from the Seiyu chain opened in 1983, the first step in worldwide expansion (i.e., more than 300 shops and 100 outlets in 25 countries around the world in 2017). The company now has a solid and unique identity with immediately recognizable design. Essential and timeless, the no-logo products by Muji are designed to meet the needs of consumers, offering purchasing solutions for those who want simple but non-trivial products of quality and at the same time not too expensive. These results are attainable thanks to product functionality and durability, easily adaptable to changes in the lifestyles and in the management of the living space. Muji has become a real lifestyle brand in which rationality and the search for the essential prevail.

As the range of products offered is really very wide, it is difficult to place Muji within a specific product category. It ranges from technological objects, to accessories for men and women, household items, and stationery to furnishing items, all designed to ensure maximum comfort for the customer. The choice of materials with which to make these products is extremely careful and based on their quality, with Muji searching for the best raw materials available regardless of their place of origin. At the same time whenever possible, looking for recycled material that together with the adoption of linear and simple packaging underlines a particular attention toward environmental issues.

According to Kenya Hara, the 53-year-old Japanese art director of Muji, the company has developed "localized esthetics", that is, the Japanese tradition of simplicity has evolved into a distinguished minimalist esthetics. In fact, as the culture of "No Waste" belongs to Muji and goes hand in hand with the philosophy of simplicity; the company is able to offer cost efficiency, management awareness, and attention to the environment. The conservation of resources and the elimination of waste are the two key principles in the eco-design strategies that characterize the product life cycle within the company. The approach adopted by Muji is none other than the translation of the principles of the Japanese philosophy of *Kanketsu*, or the concept of simplicity, in today's language of industrial production. This has given rise to an innovative and unconventional strategy.

3.2.2 Muji's Paradoxes

Tradition vs. Innovation

Muji develops the essence of its products as a form of coherence with the philosophy that inspires it, that in turn represents a direct emanation of traditional Japanese culture. Muji has chosen to be innovative by returning to the origins (Back to the Origin into the Future), to recover basic coherence from the origins, in the belief that only by deliberately pursuing what is pure and ordinary it can achieve what is extraordinary. For this reason, Muji has taken charge of rediscovering and enhancing the craft traditions of the world: *"Imagine something that can be found only there, something we want to stay as it is—because it's best as it is. In this era of worldwide uniformity, MUJI works to preserve global work-life traditions. Respectful of the local natural environment and production methods, wherever possible we visit production areas and procure raw materials unspoiled by homogeneity. In a free market whose ideology demands whiter wool, MUJI has started offering products once again made of natural, undyed alpaca fleece. While our products line is still slight, each item exudes the aesthetic appeal of raw fiber. Despite continuing world tension and our concern with the greenhouse effect causing global warming, we recognize that 'warm' originally meant 'affectionate'. At the very least we want humanity's relationship with the earth to be warm as in 'affectionate'."* (president Kanai).

According to Kanai, the culture is mediating between tradition and innovation and transforms the paradox into apparent one: *"Cultures usually influence each other. Civilization is also important, but culture is more important. For example, do you need to make any innovation of raw ham? Raw ham already has enough wisdom in itself. Nobody can put extra wisdom on raw ham. Culture is just perfect. It is important to focus on these points. We need to have a balance like that."*

Emptiness vs. Fullness

In this case "the emptiness" is a notion of dialectical nature that cannot exist without its opposite complementary, "the full," analogously to light and shadow, life and death. But just as "non-being constitutes the utility" of being, so emptiness constitutes the utility of the full. Muji wanted, with respect to the Japanese esthetic tradition, to focus on the experience of emptiness. According to Morrison et al. (2010, p. 119), "*There is a traditional Japanese aesthetic that sees the utmost richness in what is extremely plain. This plainness is different from the Western notion of simplicity. If we define 'simple' in the West as something that stems from a rational alignment of purpose and use, then perhaps 'emptiness' is the right world for extreme plainness. It is an infinite flexibility that accepts each and every concept and adjusts to any purpose. This concept of 'emptiness' lies at the center of the tea ceremony, ikebana, Noh Theater, Japanese gardens and architecture, and all the other cultural practices that emanate from uniquely Japanese aesthetics. The same is true of MUJI."*

Unique vs. Universal

The tension that this paradox originates increasingly characterizes today's society and wants to go beyond the debate, perhaps a bit stereotyped, on the glocal. One cannot in fact limit its understanding to a simple addition or coexistence of both poles, "local" (understood as a declination of "unique") and global (understood as a declination of "universal"), but it is necessary to imply a transformation of the mode of being and operating companies in the world. It is now clear that the global-local antinomy is in fact the expression of a single socio-cultural metabolism that involves both the concepts as different sides of the same coin. In fact, every experience, every identity, every sensitivity will have to be confronted from a perspective of glocalization, in which the added value of the territorial localization, understood as identity patrimony that grows from below, in an epidemic way, compares and proves compatible with a global dynamic of growth and inter-relationship, which goes beyond territorial borders to propose itself in a constructive logic of global standards of control and quality. It is in this perspective that the dialectic between what is unique and what is or can become universal becomes more relevant. Muji believes that it is being driven by a philosophy that does not belong to it as an exclusive form of possession, but in the form of "unique" meanings that are linked to its identity and the way it belongs to the world. A uniqueness that paradoxically opens up to universality.

3.2.3 Muji's Identity and Strategic Meanings

The dominant characteristic of Muji's **value** is without a doubt essentiality (simplicity). Preventing egoistic behaviors seems to be the main purpose. The beliefs are based on the Japanese tradition of perfection and power of emptiness, while the scope involves a plurality of sectors and is not easily definable. An overlap with the Jungian functions would primarily bring the value of essentiality to Feeling. This value, in reality, lends itself to different readings (it could also be applicable to Thinking or Intuition and Sensing), but the analysis of the Muji case directs us without doubt toward the sphere of Feeling, first with the concept of *Security & Tranquility*:

> *Subtraction rather than addition should not lead to renunciation but to greater wealth. Security is therefore understood as a subtraction to the consumer (and more generally to the stakeholders) of the concerns that can invest them in various ways and in a wider sense of instability and fugacity that are associated with any form of excess. Finally, tranquility helps to mitigate the propensity to give way to excesses and to reinforce the awareness of always having to act responsibly for the wellbeing of the ecosystem.* (Bagnoli and Biotto 2014, p. 31)

The care for individual person that is another expression of Muji's values suggests the function of the Introverted Feeling and is represented through *Respect & Harmony*. Respect & Harmony are consistent with the vision of an interconnected world in which everything is related to each other. It is therefore necessary to operate in full respect of what surrounds us, at every level, be it close or far in space and time. Sustainability is not a set of parameters but an attitude toward a responsible and harmonious lifestyle. The happiness of each individual is seen as a key condition necessary to be in harmony with the world that surrounds them. However, the values of Muji also involve—and above all—the Extrovert side of Feeling function through the concept of *Social Wisdom*:

> *Muji wants to rediscover and resonate the folk wisdom inherent in the social and popular soul. Consistently it draws on the tradition of the folk-crafts society (mingei), which Muji believes has expressed the "superior" ability to live in a simpler way by consuming less resources. The beauty of mingei is an aesthetic rooted in the lifestyles of ordinary people.* (Bagnoli and Biotto 2014, p. 31)

At the level of **purpose**, Muji proposes itself to be an educator of the *Esthetics of living "good enough."* Its purpose is to *act as a provider that educates to a wise way of living, trusting in the intelligence of its consumer. Muji wants to change the "appetite quality" of people towards living, influencing the shape that their desires can take. Muji proposes to anticipate the future of consumption, by incorporating intelligence into desire.* (Bagnoli and Biotto 2014, p. 23)

The affiliation of the purpose to the function of Thinking appears immediately evident. The subtraction operation mentioned above can be now traced back to Thinking and is intimately connected to the value of essentiality. If, as we have seen, Essentiality itself is an ethical value, it is also equally true that it responds to a need for mental clarity and orderliness. In fact, by eliminating everything that is not essential one can create that emptiness necessary for the mind to express itself at its best. To the dimension of Thinking, Muji seems to look from both the introverted and the extrovert perspective. The tendency to subtract, in fact, is closer to introversion, while the desire to insert intelligence into desire refers to extroversion, as an "external" embankment and a containment to the indiscriminate flow of the desires themselves. Muji wants to help improve the whole society: "*We want everybody to recognize the word of MUJI as a worldwide word. If a life will be more beautiful, a society will be better*" (president Kanai). The iron code that Muji imposes itself in the creation and marketing of its products, that favors a systemic (eco-) vision that takes into account the fact that everything is related to everything else, has the connotations of Extroverted Thinking, although its underlying intent is obviously ethical, and therefore traceable to Feeling. All this is well expressed by Hara (2011) who said, "*Customers have different interpretations of MUJI products. Some say they've realized eco-friendly, affordable goods especially fit urban life, while others think they are totally 'away' from design. No matter what kind of comments they are, MUJI accept all of them, an ultimate actualization of so-called 'emptiness'.*"

At the level of **scope**, Muji is placed within the lifestyle sector and more specifically within the "*Lifestyle that feels good.*" As a transversal industrial sector that unites several of them, constituting almost a matrix, the lifestyle recalls the archetypal dimension in which Introverted Intuition moves. The constant search for essential forms (archetypal, in fact) and the fact that Muji promotes a "lifestyle that feels good" also contributes to reinforcing this impression:

> When something "feels good" or "has a good atmosphere" the individuality together with a form of a thing have disappeared. When there is complete unity, the individuality of each thing disappears, so the only expressions you can come up with to describe the situation are, "It's really nice," or "This feels good." These indicate a high level of perfection. (Bagnoli and Biotto 2014, p. 30)

Turning to **beliefs**, we immediately notice that Muji's proposal of "*Less is more*" is fully placed in the cultural context of its country and the esthetics of Su—which means simple or unadorned—and conveys the idea that simplicity is not only modest or frugal, but could be even more attractive than luxury.

> Muji tried to recover and re-propose to the public the traditional Japanese values that have always been a cornerstone of his philosophy. One of these hinges is the elimination of the superfluous, which Muji does not interpret only with a view to costs saving, but as an inherent value in contrast to the rampant consumerism and waste that increasingly characterize broader society. (Bagnoli and Biotto 2014, p. 26)

This attention to the traditional Japanese style refers to the perspective of Introverted Feeling that, using the previous information to decipher the present, draws on past experience, looks at the accumulated knowledge from generation to generation, and gives tradition a not indifferent cognitive value. However, the way Muji approaches traditional style is far from derivative. Rather than revisit a language of the past adapting it with few interventions to the present, Muji seems to extrapolate the syntax to give life to a new language under the banner of "less is more." As we know, this concept represents today the avant garde of design and is a common feature of the most significant entrepreneurial and artistic realities of our time. In this context, therefore, Muji does not limit himself to recovering the best of the Japanese tradition, but also proposes to translate the individual traits into a universal language, which is capable of crossing the boundaries without betraying the original identity. It also contributes to this the search for solutions to everyday challenges that leads to on-the-ground research about how people live. The company regularly visits homes to see how design can lend a helping hand and then incorporates that intelligence into new products. As a result, the customer-stakeholder instead of being just a customer becomes a co-producer and a co-creator of experience integrated into the Muji's BM. From a Jungian perspective, this would be an Extroverted Intuitive operation, that is, in the exact opposite of the Introverted Feeling.

Figure 10.3 is showing how strategic meanings impact the building blocks of Muji's SBM according to the VT BM canvas. Muji could not be consider as a green or hybrid company in the strict sense of the word; nevertheless, it certainly participates in changing the emotional and symbolic content and perception of the lifestyle industry from unsustainable fashion type to a co-creator of a better world.

It seems that Muji has succeeded in resolving the paradox between innovation and tradition, and therefore between Intuition and Sensing, and this it has done by moving in two different directions. On the one hand, it considered Thinking: by deepening the Japanese *Weltanschauung*, it derived a "philosophy" that became an integral part of its identity. On the other hand, it relied on sustainability and therefore on Feeling. This can be seen, for example, in the Found Muji project that

> *aims to identify and disseminate, after reinterpreting them in the "Muji" way, products of everyday use that are characteristic expression of cultures rooted in different parts of the world and still anchored to local craft traditions and ancient folk knowledge. Found Muji aims to interpret and "show the Local from the Global point of view, trying to spread the message on a global level"*. (Bagnoli and Biotto 2014, p. 39)

Indeed, Bagnoli and Biotto (2014, p. 40) recognized that

> *The whole world then becomes a possible research target. In accordance with Muji's philosophy, the strategic goals are: "things have to be discovered, not created", i.e. local objects to be re-discovered and made global. In this sense, the project Found Muji is an operational implementation of the theme "promoting social innovation", similar to an example of social enterprise carried out in collaboration with Japan International Cooperation Agency (JICA). In fact, Muji ensures respect for craftsmanship, local cultures and traditions and prevents the transfer of the population to larger centers (urbanization), preferring to keep the artisanal production distributed on the territory of origin.*

		Strategic meanings					
		Esthetics of living "good enough"	Essentiality – Less is	Lifestyle that feels good	Security & Tranquility	Respect & Harmony	Social wisdom
Part.	System of contractors to whom production is entrusted						
Society	Franchising for areas that are not densely populated						
	Future house project						
	M&As and Joint-venture						
	JICA (Japan International Cooperation Agency)						
Customers	Target audience are women, < 40 years old						
	International distribution						
	Experience store						
Products	Muji apps						
	Lifestyle education program						
	Wide range of products						
	Minimalistic & functional design, essential packaging						
Processes	Muji life						
	Muji mess						
	Design museum						
	Muji.net: Design and networks with user						
	Found Muji: Reinterpreting local cultures						
	World Muji: Design with design leaders						
	Muji awards: Design with unknown designers						
	Muji tagging system						
	Catalogue that tells stories of everyday life						
	PR activities						
	Ethnographic research						
	"Artisan skill competition"						
	"Full soul to one product"						
	Selection of material						
Resources	Ryohin laboratory for living						
	IT infrastructure						
	Brand Muji "No brand"						
	Japanese culture						
	Management control system						
	Product design office						
	Knowledge management to share know-how						
	Category manag., Quality manag., Store manag.						
Value prop.	Design of one's life according to an essential, universal, responsible and sustainable lifestyle						

Fig. 10.3 Impact of strategic meanings on the building blocks of Muji's VT BM canvas

It clearly emerges that Muji, defined by its president Kanai as "a non-innovative company," at least not in the traditional sense, has managed to deal creatively with the paradoxes of tradition vs. innovation, unique vs. universal, fullness vs. emptiness. All MUJI products are calibrated to real needs and demands; they offer neither more nor less than necessary, but exactly what is good enough, understood not as a tension arising from renunciation but as an exercise of anonymous responsibility, which does not call for heroic gestures, charitable auctions, or emotional attitudes. Raw materials are left as crude as possible, with their natural colors, which is even more sustainable. President Kanai summarized these as: "*As many point out, now we are no longer just aware of environmental problems, but we have gone further: we ask ourselves what we can do in our daily lives to deal with them. The same is true for the many problems that exist in the world today: they are nothing but the affirmation of the ego, which in future and globally forecasts requires a logic of 'control of egoism'. These values have already begun to move the minds of today's people and MUJI grows gradually comparing itself with them.*"

4 Conclusion

Our chapter has explored the areas of BMs, sustainability, paradox, and Jungian dichotomies in an attempt to make sense of the potential future innovative and SBMs. We fused the various elements of theory together to attempt to give a greater depth and sense to the field and to show how alternative thinking considering organizational paradoxes can help reframe the BMs of the future. Our case of Muji showed how the company had to deal creatively with the paradoxes of tradition vs. innovation, unique vs. universal, fullness vs. emptiness and how Muji has succeeded in resolving their paradox between Intuition and Sensing by moving in two different directions—Thinking: by deepening the Japanese Weltanschauung and reliance on sustainability—Feeling.

Our work recognizes that each company has its own identity, outlined by its own history, by its own choices and from the objectives it aims to achieve. We recognize that not all companies are able to explain and manage their "soul" in the best way; however, it is certain that identity guides the actions of their own subjective reality by mirroring them. Using Value Triangle and the Jungian dialectics, we believe we have provided a practical tool that can help organizations navigate the complexities of sustainable development and make better sense of their own organizations in a rapidly changing and challenging world. Given the enormous potential benefits that can be gained, managers are advised to consider organizational identity and related strategic meanings as a main leverage for their SBMI initiatives.

The proposed research approach could be repeated with other organizations. In this respect, future studies can extend the range of organizations involved as more empirical evidence is urgently needed given the underdeveloped nature of this field. Another possibility is to consider Jungian theory of psychological types for assessing psychological traits of the members of top management team and see their influence on developing organizational identity and leading SBMI.

Notes

1. We use the notion "unchanged" in a sense of not-transformed but it can be re-interpreted. Re-interpretation as a bridge between the position of the organization in the relevant external environments and the internal meanings formed around cherished organizational values, beliefs, and purpose.
2. Paradox is a "persistent contradiction between interdependent elements" (Schad et al. 2016, p. 6).
3. In the literature about organizational identity, we can find discussion about individual identity and the cognitive link that exists between it and organizational identity; however, we will limit our discussion on organizational level only as we are interested on organizational identity as a shared cognitive schema.
4. An ideal type sustainable organization is in our view an organization that persists in time.
5. Johnson and Scholes (2002, p. 239) define a mission statement as "a generalized statement of the overriding purpose of an organization. It can be

thought of as an expression of its raison d'être." Similarly, Leuthesser and Kohli (1997) say that mission is necessary in helping a company form its identity, purpose, and direction.

6. As such, paradoxes cannot be solved but could be only navigated through "both-and" thinking toward "workable actions" that prevent possible paralysis or drift to the one pole of paradoxes. We will use the notion of "solving" for purely practical reasons of transparency and ease of understanding. As Lüscher and Lewis (2008, p. 234) say, a positive outcome of "working through" paradox is achieved not by "eliminating or resolving paradox, but [by] constructing a more workable certainty."

7. Description of Muji is based on Internet contribution by Peron, A. 2015. *Muji, la filosofia del design essenziale e atemporale* (http://www.thismarketerslife.it/stories/muji-la-filosofia-del-design-essenziale-e-atemporale/) and information available on company website.

References

Alessandri, S.W. 2001. Modeling Corporate Identity: A Concept Explication and Theoretical Explanation. *Corporate Communications: An International Journal* 6 (4): 173–182.

Anderson, R.C. 1998. *Mid-course Correction: Toward a Sustainable Enterprise: The Interface Model*. Atlanta, GA: Peregrinzilla Press.

Anthony, C., and M. Tripsas. 2016. Organizational Identity and Innovation. In *Oxford Handbook of Organizational Identity*, ed. M. Pratt, M. Schultz, and B.E. Ashforth, 417–435. Oxford: Oxford University Press.

Ashforth, B.E., and F. Mael. 1996. Organizational Identity and Strategy as a Context for the Individual. *Advances in Strategic Management* 13: 19–64.

Baden-Fuller, C., and S. Haefliger. 2013. Business Models and Technological Innovation. *Long Range Planning* 46 (6): 419–426.

Baden-Fuller, C., and V. Mangematin. 2013. Business Models: A Challenging Agenda. *Strategic Organization* 11 (4): 418–427.

Bagnoli, C., and G. Biotto. 2014. *Il caso Muji, Sincronizzare missione/visione, strategia e modello di business attraverso i significati*. Venice, Italy: Ca' Foscari University.

Baldassarre, B., G. Calabretta, N.M.P. Bocken, and T. Jaskiewicz. 2017. Bridging Sustainable Business Model Innovation and User-Driven Innovation: A Process for Sustainable Value Proposition Design. *Journal of Cleaner Production* 147: 175–186.

Bansal, P. 2002. The Corporate Challenges of Sustainable Development. *Academy of Management Executive* 16 (2): 122–131.

Barney, J., S. Bunderson, P. Foreman, L. Gustafson, A. Huff, L. Martins, R. Reger, Y. Saranson, and L. Stimpert. 1998. A Strategy Conversation on the Topic of Organization Identity. In *Identity in Organizations: Building Theory Through Conversations*, ed. D.A. Whetten and P.C. Godfrey, 99–168. Thousand Oaks, CA: Sage.

Battistella, C., G. Biotto, and A.F. De Toni. 2012. From Design Driven Innovation to Meaning Strategy. *Management Decision* 50 (4): 718–743.

Biloslavo, R., C. Bagnoli, and D. Edgar. 2018. An Eco-critical Perspective on Business Models: The Value Triangle as an Approach to Closing the Sustainability Gap. *Journal of Cleaner Production* 174: 746–762.

Bocken, N., S. Short, P. Rana, and S. Evans. 2013. A Value Mapping Tool for Sustainable Business Modelling. *Corporate Governance: The International Journal of Business in Society* 13 (5): 482–497.

Bocken, N.M.P., S.W. Short, P. Rana, and S. Evans. 2014. A Literature and Practice Review to Develop Sustainable Business Model Archetypes. *Journal of Cleaner Production* 65 (15): 42–56.

Brady, F.N., and D.W. Hart. 2006. An Aesthetic Theory of Conflict in Administrative Ethics. *Administration & Society* 38 (1): 113–134.

Bromley, D.B. 1993. *Reputation, Image and Impression Management*. Oxford: John Wiley & Sons.

Brooks, S., S.B. Ivory, and S.B. Brooks. 2018. Managing Corporate Sustainability with a Paradoxical Lens: Lessons from Strategic Agility. *Journal of Business Ethics* 148 (2): 347–361.

Caldera, H.T.S., C. Desha, and L. Dawes. 2017. Exploring the Role of Lean Thinking in Sustainable Business Practice: A Systematic Literature Review. *Journal of Cleaner Production* 167: 1546–1565.

Cascio, W.F. 2006. Decency Means More Than "always low prices": A Comparison of Costco to Wal-Mart's Sam's Club. *Academy of Management Perspectives* 20 (3): 26–37.

De Wit, B., and R. Meyer. 2005. *Strategy Synthesis: Resolving Strategy Paradoxes to Create Competitive Advantage*. 2nd ed. London: Thomson.

Dutton, J.E., J.M. Dukerich, and C.V. Harquail. 1994. Organizational Images and Member Identification. *Administrative Science Quarterly* 39 (2): 239–263.

Epstein, M., A.R. Buhovac, and K. Yuthas. 2015. Managing Social, Environmental and Financial Performance Simultaneously. *Long Range Planning* 48 (1): 35–45.

Fiol, C.M. 2002. Capitalizing on Paradox: The Role of Language in Transforming Organizational Identities. *Organization Science* 13 (6): 653–666.

Gao, J., and P. Bansal. 2013. Instrumental and Integrative Logics in Business Sustainability. *Journal of Business Ethics* 112: 241–255.

Gioia, D.A. 1998. From Individual to Organizational Identity. In *Identity in Organizations: Developing Theory Through Conversations*, ed. D. Whetten and P. Godfrey, 17–31. Thousand Oaks, CA: Sage.

Gioia, D.A., and J.B. Thomas. 1996. Identity, Image and Issue Interpretation: Sensemaking During Strategic Change in Academia. *Administrative Science Quarterly* 41 (3): 370–403.

Gubrium, J.F., and J.A. Holstein. 2008. Narrative Ethnography. In *Handbook of Emergent Methods*, ed. S.N. Hesse-Biber and P. Leavy, 241–264. New York: Guilford Press.

Haggege, M., and L. Collet 2011. Exploring New Business Models with a Narrative Perspective. Paper presented at the *18th International Product Development Management Conference*, The Netherlands: Delft, June 5–7, 2011.

Hahn, T., F. Figge, J. Pinkse, and L. Preuss. 2010. Trade-offs in Corporate Sustainability: You Can't Have Your Cake and Eat It. *Business Strategy and the Environment* 19 (4): 217–229.

———. 2018. A Paradox Perspective on Corporate Sustainability: Descriptive, Instrumental, and Normative Aspects. *Journal of Business Ethics* 148 (2): 235–248.

Hahn, T., J. Pinkse, L. Preuss, and F. Figge. 2016. Ambidexterity for Corporate Social Performance. *Organization Studies* 37 (2): 213–235.

Hahn, T., L. Preuss, J. Pinkse, and F. Figge. 2014. Cognitive Frames in Corporate Sustainability: Managerial Sensemaking with Paradoxical and Business Case Frames. *Academy of Management Review* 39 (4): 463–487.

Hamilton, A., and D.A. Gioia. 2009. Fostering Sustainability-Focused Organizational Identities. In *Exploring Positive Identities and Organizations*, ed. L.M. Roberts and J.E. Dutton, 435–460. New York: Routledge.

Handy, C. 1994. *The Age of Paradox*. Boston, MA: Harvard Business School Press.

Hara, K. 2011. The Design Guru of MUJI on His Uniquely Japanese Aesthetic. Accessed November 18, 2017. http://www.globaltimes.cn/content/661909.shtml.

Hatch, M.J., and M. Schultz. 2002. The Dynamics of Organizational Identity. *Human Relations* 55 (8): 989–1017.

Hatch, M.J., and D. Yanow. 2008. Methodology by Metaphor: Painting and the Study of Organizational Identity. *Organization Studies* 29 (1): 23–44.

Iivonen, K. 2018. Defensive Responses to Strategic Sustainability Paradoxes—Have Your Coke and Drink It Too! *Journal of Business Ethics* 148 (2): 309–327.

Ind, N. 1990. *The Corporate Image. Strategies for Effective Identity Programmes*. London: Kogan Page.

Issa, T., and D. Pick. 2010. Ethical Mindsets: An Australian Study. *Journal of Business Ethics* 96 (4): 613–629.

Johnson, M.W. 2010. *Seizing the White Space: Business Model Innovation for Growth and Renewal*. Boston, MA: Harvard Business Press.

Johnson, M.W., C.M. Christensen, and H. Kagermann. 2008. Reinventing Your Business Model. *Harvard Business Review* 86: 50–59.

Johnson, G., and K. Scholes. 2002. *Exploring Corporate Strategy*. 6th ed. London: Prentice Hall.

Joyce, A., and R.L. Paquin. 2016. The Triple Layered Business Model Canvas—A Tool to Design More Sustainable Business Models. *Journal of Cleaner Production* 135 (1): 1474–1486.

Jung, C.G. 1991. *L'uomo e i suoi simboli*. Milano: Tascabili Editori Associati.

Kim, C.W., and R. Mauborgne. 1998. Value Innovation: The Strategic Logic of High Growth. *Harvard Business Review* 75 (1): 102–112.

Kogut, B., and U. Zander. 1996. What Firms Do? Coordination, Identity, and Learning. *Organization Science* 7 (5): 502–518.

Kovoor-Misra, S. 2009. Understanding Perceived Organizational Identity During Crisis And Change: A Threat/Opportunity Framework. *Journal of Organizational Change Management* 22 (5): 494–510.

Leuthesser, L., and C. Kohli. 1997. Corporate Identity: The Role of Mission Statements. *Business Horizons* 40 (3): 59–66.

Lewis, M.W. 2000. Exploring Paradox: Toward a More Comprehensive Guide. *Academy of Management Review* 25 (4): 760–776.

Lüscher, L.S., and M.W. Lewis. 2008. Organizational Change and Managerial Sensemaking: Working Through Paradox. *Academy of Management Journal* 51: 221–240.

March, J.G. 1988. *Decisions and Organizations*. Cambridge, MA: Basil Blackwell.

Martins, L.L., V.P. Rindova, and B.E. Greenbaum. 2015. Unlocking the Hidden Value of Concepts: A Cognitive Approach to Business Model Innovation. *Strategic Entrepreneurship Journal* 9 (1): 99–117.

Miles, M.B., A.M. Huberman, and J. Saldana. 2014. *Qualitative Data Analysis: A Methods Sourcebook*. 3rd ed. Thousand Oaks, CA: Sage.

Mitchell, D., and C. Coles. 2003. The Ultimate Competitive Advantage of Continuing Business Model Innovation. *Journal of Business Strategy* 24 (5): 15–21.

Morrison, J., N. Fukasawa, and K. Hara. 2010. *Muji*. New York: Rizzoli.

Morsing, M., and A. Roepstorff. 2015. CSR as Corporate Political Activity: Observations on IKEA's CSR Identity–Image Dynamics. *Journal of Business Ethics* 128 (2): 395–409.

Nag, R., K.G. Corley, and D.A. Gioia. 2007. The Intersection of Organizational Identity, Knowledge and Practice: Attempting Strategic Change Via Knowledge Grafting. *Academy of Management Journal* 50 (4): 821–847.

Navis, C. and Glynn, M. A. 2010. How New Market Categories Emerge: Temporal Dynamics of Legitimacy, Identity, and Entrepreneurship in Satellite Radio, 1990–2005. *Administrative Science Quarterly*, 55 (3): 439–471.

Pohle, G., and M. Chapman. 2006. IBM's Global CEO Report 2006: Business Model Innovation Matters. *Strategy & Leadership* 34 (5): 34–40.

Poole, M. S. and Van De Ven, A. H. 1989. Using Paradox to Build Management and Organization Theories. *Academy of Management Review*, Vol. 14, No. 4, pp. 562–578.

Quinn, R.E., and K.S. Cameron. 1988. *Paradox and Transformation: Toward a Framework of Change in Organization and Management*. Cambridge, MA: Ballinger.

Schad, J., Lewis, M W., Raisch, S. and Smith, W. K. 2016. Paradox Research in Management Science: Looking Back to Move Forward. *The Academy of Management Annals*, Vol. 10. No. 1, pp. 5–64.

Schaltegger, S., F. Lüdeke-Freund, and E.G. Hansen. 2012. Business Cases for Sustainability: The Role of Business Model Innovation for Corporate Sustainability. *International Journal of Innovation and Sustainable Development* 6 (2): 95–119.

———. 2016. Business Models for Sustainability: A Co-Evolutionary Analysis of Sustainable Entrepreneurship, Innovation, and Transformation. *Organization & Environment* 29 (3): 264–289.

Scott, S. G. and Lane, V. R. 2000. A Stakeholder Approach to Organizational Identity. *Academy of Management Review*, Vol. 25, No. 1, pp. 43–62.

Smith, W.K. 2014. Dynamic Decision Making: A Model of Senior Leaders Managing Strategic Paradoxes. *Academy of Management Journal* 57 (6): 1592–1623.

Smith, W.K., and M.W. Lewis. 2011. Toward a Theory of Paradox: A Dynamic Equilibrium Model of Organizing. *Academy of Management Review* 36 (2): 381–403.

Spieth, P., D. Schneckenberg, and J.E. Ricart. 2014. Business Model Innovation—State of the Art and Future Challenges for the Field. *R&D Management* 44 (3): 237–247.

Stubbs, W., and C. Cocklin. 2008. Conceptualizing a "Sustainability Business Model". *Organization & Environment* 21 (2): 103–127.

Van der Byl, C.A., and N. Slawinski. 2015. Embracing Tensions in Corporate Sustainability: A Review of Research From Win-Wins and Trade-Offs to Paradoxes and Beyond. *Organization & Environment* 28 (1): 54–79.

van der Have, R. P. and Rubalcaba, L. 2016. Social Innovation Research: An Emerging Area of Innovation Studies?. *Research Policy*, Vol. 45, No. 9, pp. 1923–1935.

Verganti, R. 2009. *Design-Driven innovation. Cambiare le regole della competizione innovando radicalmente il significato dei prodotti e dei servizi*. Rizzoli Editore.

Weick, K. E. and Browning, L. D. 1986. Argument and Narration in Organizational Communication. *Journal of Management*, Vol. 12, No. 2, pp. 243–259.

Wirtz, B.W., O. Schilke, and S. Ullrich. 2010. Strategic Development of Business Models: Implications of the Web 2.0 for Creating Value on the Internet. *Long Range Planning* 43 (2–3): 272–290.

Zott, C., Amit, R. and Massa, L. 2011. The Business Model: Recent Developments and Future Research. *Journal of Management*, Vol. 37, No. 4, pp. 1019–1042.

11

Performance Management and Enterprise Excellence Through Sustainable Business Models

Rick Edgeman

Enterprise excellence and sustainability movements have developed along near parallel timelines. Adroit use of enterprise excellence systems has significantly enhanced performance across an array of domains, including financial, human ecology, operations and supply chain, and other areas. Insubstantially considered among these domains are social and environmental performance.

Similarly, although the triple bottom line (TBL) is core to enterprise sustainability, many adherents of sustainability approach its people and planet domains with ardor, yet virtually neglect its profit domain.

R. Edgeman (✉)
Department of Management, Robbins College of Business & Entrepreneurship, Fort Hays State University, Hays, KS, USA

Department of Business & Technology, Aarhus University, Aarhus, Denmark

Department of Technology & Innovation, Faculty of Engineering, Southern Denmark University, Odense, Denmark
e-mail: Rick.Edgeman@fhsu.edu

Sustainable enterprise excellence (SEE) merges these movements. A SEE model that adds resilience and robustness (SEER2) and associated maturity assessment regimen are introduced as means of driving triple top line (TTL) enterprise strategy through to TBL performance.

1 When We Live: An Introduction to the Anthropocene Age

The world and age in which we do and will live—the *Anthropocene age*—is and will be rife with wicked social, environmental, economic, and technical challenges—challenges that reside not wholly in any single of these domains, but rather simultaneously in two or more. Alternatives to living in such a world include resolving at least some of the most critical of these challenges … or … extinction, with some espousing the belief that we are on the precipice of the world's sixth great extinction (Kolbert 2014).

Many of these are wicked challenges that resist solution and are or seem difficult or impossible to surmount. Solution resistance has multiple causes, among which are opposing or misaligned demands of multiple influential parties with competing interests. An implication of competing interests is that no single solution is likely to fully satisfy all involved or affected parties—so that a "solution" is either born of compromise or is "winner-takes-all" in nature. Other sources of solution resistance include multifaceted requirements that are incomplete, contradictory, or chameleon-like. It is at best difficult to clearly define wicked challenges and determine their boundaries.

Wicked challenges exist in all fields of endeavor, but are perhaps nowhere more important or more in need of urgent full or partial solutions than in intersecting social and environmental domains. The activities of many enterprises contribute to the creation or growth of many social or environmental dilemmas, with such contributions due to factors such as natural resource consumption, and various social, environmental, and economic impacts of those activities. Although governmental involvement in limiting or partially solving such challenges or dilemmas is common and often necessary, it is also necessary for enterprises to bring their formidable resources to bear—with perhaps the most formidable resource an enterprise can harness and leverage being its intellectual capabilities.

> *Beware of people preaching simple solutions to complex problems. If the answer was easy, someone more intelligent could have thought of it a long time ago—complex problems invariably require complex and difficult solutions.* (Herbert 2006)

> *Our agenda, by necessity, is as complex and encompassing as the problems we face: beware of politicians promising simple solutions.* (Etzioni and Bowditch 2006)

Complex problems require complex solutions. Although it may prove fruitful to break a complex problem into constituent elements, unless those elements are independent of one another, the sum of independent solutions will not provide an adequate solution for the whole: complex problems must be approached in light of their complexity. Presented herein is a complex systems approach to modeling and assessing complex solutions to complex problems that plague humanity.

2 Continuously Relevant and Responsible Enterprises

We here set out on an ambitious enterprise journey. It is a journey without end, an asymptotic one that will ever demand next steps. It is the journey toward becoming a *continuously relevant and responsible enterprise* (*CR2E*). It is a journey simultaneously demanding attention to economic sustainability of the enterprise, as well as to its social and environmental responsibilities, imprints, and influence.

Successful sojourners will reap financial or other strategic benefits deriving from consciously and continuously action that delivers micro- and-macro-level results that are transparent, ethical, relevant, and responsible toward primary stakeholders specifically, society at large, other stakeholders of import such as policymakers, and the natural environment.

Financial and other strategic benefits support economic sustainability of the enterprise, while relevant and responsible strategy on behalf of society and the natural environment support the social and ecological dimensions of sustainability. Strategy is intended here in its most basic form, that is, *strategy is commitment to a set of coherent, mutually reinforcing policies and behaviors aimed at achieving a specific competitive goal* (Pisano 2015).

In all, the call is for excellence spanning the traditional TBL people (society), planet (ecological), and profit dimensions (Elkington 1998). The term "bottom" in the TBL connotes end-of-the-pipe performance and impacts. Continuously relevant and responsible enterprises will of necessity be concerned with the TBL, and intentionally so. Intention implies forethought and forethought suggests that the CR2E produces TBL performance by first formulating and deploying TTL strategy (McDonough and Braungaart 2002), that is, economically sound, socially equitable, and ecologically sensitive—with the intent of bringing about superior people, planet, profit positive performance, and impacts that can be further improved and sustained.

How might an enterprise best embark on this journey? With relatively limited formal attention to societal and environmental sustainability, many organizations have benefited from rigorous application of "excellence models", such as those underlying the Shingo Prize (Plenert 2017), EFQM Excellence Award (Escrig and de Menezes 2015), America's Baldrige National Performance Excellence Award (Bou-Llusar et al. 2009), and similar highly evolved ones. These models are generically known by various names, notable among which are *business excellence, enterprise excellence, performance excellence, operational excellence,* and *organizational excellence models.*

Rigorous use of an enterprise excellence model demands that an enterprise dedicate itself to the foundational core values and principles of the model; understand the vision of excellence supported by the model and apply the criteria by which progress toward excellence is made; and regularly and rigorously assess all relevant enterprise strategies, activities, and results relative to those criteria.

This active learning process assumes cause-and-consequence relationships—that is—*if* the model is intelligently adapted and applied (cause), *then* specific intended results will come to pass (consequences). As such, this approach is undertaken for multiple purposes, perhaps foremost of which are to appropriately adjust and adapt strategy; to improve near-term performance by identifying and implementing current best practices; and to formulate and deploy strategies leading to next best practices and sources of competitive advantage.

Deeper examination of most enterprise excellence models reveals them to be relatively void societal and environmental sustainability considerations. As such, existing core values, principles, criteria, and assessment regimes associated with such models must be reconceived to *elevate* societal and environmental performance to statures on par with economic and selected other performance domains such as innovation and market share. Doing so leads to the more comprehensive concept of SEE. In general:

> *Sustainable enterprise excellence is a consequence of ongoing attainment of balance among the competing and complementary interests of key stakeholder segments. In addition to more commonly noted stakeholder segments such as customers, shareholders, and policy makers, SEE deeply integrates society as an explicit stakeholder and the natural environment as an implicit one. Attainment of such balance increase the likelihood of superior and sustainable competitive positioning and hence long-term enterprise success.*
>
> *This is accomplished through an integrated approach to organizational design and function emphasising innovation, operational, customer-related, human capital, financial, marketplace, societal, and environmental performance.*

In contrast to "enterprise excellence only" definitions and models, SEE emphasizes depth and breadth of socially and environmentally responsible strategy, actions, and outcomes; innovation; and clear acknowledgment of the necessity of balancing the competing and complementary interests of diverse enterprise stakeholders that specifically include society, governmental authorities, and—via surrogates—the natural environment. SEE is seen as fundamental to an enterprise becoming *continuously relevant and responsible*. From a mathematical perspective, we would say that SEE is necessary to the enterprise becoming continuously relevant and responsible. But is it sufficient? That is, does SEE ensure continuous relevance and responsibility? To be sufficient, it must ensure enterprise longevity. Though SEE will contribute to such longevity, it does not ensure longevity and hence is not sufficient. For that reason, *resilience* and *robustness* are added to the portfolio of what is required of the CR2E. Successful and sustainable *management for excellence* delivers an enterprise, that is:

- *Sustainable* to the extent it creates and maintains economic, ecological, and social value for itself, its stakeholders, society at large, and policymakers;
- *Resilient* to the extent it possesses capacity to self-renew through innovation by adapting its responses to negative shocks and challenges over time;
- *Robust* to the degree it is highly resistant or immune to a critical subset of such shocks and challenges;
- *Excellent* when its governance, leadership, and strategy as deployed through people, processes, partnerships, and policies deliver sustained superior performance and impact in enterprise critical areas such as enterprise human ecology, innovation, financial, social, ecological, enterprise intelligence gathering, analytics, and supply chain management (Edgeman 2015; Edgeman et al. 2015a, b).

Having described SEER2, it remains to identify a portfolio of relevant core principles and values, establish criteria by which enterprise progress toward these can be reasonably assessed, and develop a reporting regime capable of indicating the degree to which those criteria are fulfilled. Credible assessment of enterprise progress toward SEER2 *must* yield actionable information in the forms of insight and foresight, else assessment would only be useful for historic and not improvement purposes.

While many possible SEER2 models can be conceived, an obvious need is for a model useful to enterprises ranging from small to large, from simple to complex, and from socially and environmentally naive to relatively advance with respect to each. By "model", we intend not only a model *per se*, but supporting core values, principles, assessment criteria, scoring regime, and—importantly—a mechanism that provides useful insight into recent performance and foresight that can be used to enhance future SEER2 performance.

The more simply such a model can be expressed, and the more broadly applicable its values, principles, criteria, and assessment regime are, the more likely it is that it will be of value to enterprises. We will refer to the model provided herein as a *Springboard to SEER2*. This model will represent a refinement and extension of an earlier model referred to as the Springboard to SEE (Edgeman and Eskildsen 2014). Differences between these two models are intended to reflect issues that have become either more relevant or more obvious over the past handful of years.

3 Sources from Whence Core Values and Principles May Be Derived

There are abundant and rich sources available from which core values, principles, and criteria related to all important SEER2 elements can be extracted or derived. Sources from which criteria, principles, and values pertinent to social and environmental responsibility may be drawn include documentation and websites associated with the *United Nations Global Compact*, the *United Nations Principles of Responsible Management Education*, the *Global Reporting Initiative*, the *United Nations Agenda 2030 Sustainable Development Goals*, *Business Actions for Sustainable Development*, the *International Chamber of Commerce*, the *Organisation for Economic Cooperation and Development*, and the *World Business Council on Sustainable Development*. Similarly, principles, values, and criteria widely acknowledged as critical to enterprise excellence can be gleaned from the *EFQM Excellence Model* of the *European Foundation for Quality Management*, the *Shingo Operational Excellence Model* from the *Shingo Institute*, Baldrige National Quality Award site of the United States National Institute of Standards and Technology, and numerous additional sources. While there is something unique provided within each of these sources, there is in total significant overlap among their core values, principles, and criteria.

The target of the *Springboard to SEER2 model* is to enable relatively straightforward assessment of progress toward *SEER2* and hence progress on an enterprise's journey toward becoming *continuously relevant and responsible*. The journey is one already populated by some travelers and is one on which many more will embark. If our fellow travelers are limited to social and environmental responsibility professionals and other advocates, then our footprint will be shallow, our journey lonely, and our progress slow. Simply put, unless our traveling companions include a critical mass of influential and highly committed policymakers and enterprises, the sustainability needle will remain largely unmoved.

4 Why Are We Here Today? A Changed and Changing World

The world is changed and changing. Though change is inevitable, some changes—both internal and external to the enterprise—can be influenced by enterprise strategy and activities. In instances where influence can be exerted, it is almost certain that—even if *"change for the better"* occurs, *"better change"* is possible. Better change is a function of factors that include relevant piece-by-piece knowledge; knowledge of interactions among those pieces; pertinent experience; collection and interpretation of stakeholder perspectives, and where, how, and why those perspectives converge or diverge; knowing which, where, why, when, and how compromises can and should be made and communicated.

What sort of changes or challenges are we talking about? Big ones. Really big ones. Changes in the built environment, social, ecological, economic, technological, and political domains or that span a subset of these. Changes that affect the strategies, activities, and performance requirements of public sector, for-profit, not-for-profit, and for-benefit enterprises and entities (Sabeti 2011). Anthropogenic changes—ones due in large to human activity (Edgeman 2018). Many-faced wicked challenges where progress relative to one face degrades another face, or creates a new challenge. From among these a brief list—all of which are supremely worthy of enterprise attention—includes:

- The rise to greater prominence of ethical investors and consumers whose investment and consumption choices are guided by social or ecological morality (Erragragui and Lagoarde-Segot 2016);

- Greater public awareness of and disdain for unscrupulous behavior by corporate leaders (Johnson 2018);
- Increased concern for the plight of women, children, and minorities (Carpenter 2016; Thébaud 2015);
- Increased awareness and loathing of modern slavery in multiple supply chains, including slavery in supply chains, agriculture, fishing, construction, domestic service, and apparel industries. Some estimates of the number of people subject to some form of slavery globally exceed 40 million—believed to be the highest number of slaves in human history, with slaves found in higher or lower percentages in almost all nations (Davidson 2015);
- Use of conflict materials, many of which are critical to important communication, computing, and entertainment technologies (Voland and Daly 2018);
- Greatly diminished (known) reserves of key minerals and metals critical to technological advancement—some of which are conflict materials;
- Rapid global growth of the middle class and both middle class and base of the pyramid (BOT) consumerism (Prahalad 2005);
- Increasing effort to destabilize and isolate rogue regimes (Chomsky 2015; Wunderlich 2017);
- Climatological volatility and ecological degradation;
- Food insecurity and water scarcity. It is estimated that more than 1.2 billion people worldwide are subject to water scarcity, a number expected to grow to about 1.8 billion by 2025—at which time a full two-thirds of the global population is expected to be subject to the either water scarcity or the somewhat less severe condition of water stress. The U.S. Director of National Intelligence estimates that 40% of the world's fresh water supply will be consumed by 2030. California's groundwater reserve is being depleted at the rate of approximately one *trillion* liters annually. See: http://the-generation.net/water-the-currency-of-the-future/. This combines with highly water-intensive food, beverage, and apparel preferences that contribute to water scarcity (Liu et al. 2017);
- Increasing desertification, and ocean acidification, and rising ocean levels (Halpern et al. 2015);

- Aging populations and populations growing too rapidly in some areas and too slowly in other regions to economically and culturally sustain those regions;
- Public health threats including self-induced ones such as the growing opioid addiction challenge in the United States;
- Refugees from conflict or environmentally impacted areas;
- Increasing radicalism/extremism (Kruglanski et al. 2014).

These are substantial challenges, many of which are fully or partially attributable to human activity—individually, collectively, and—in many instances—at enterprise levels. This suggests that it is incumbent on humanity broadly and enterprises specifically to attempt to fully or partially solve or navigate these challenges. The criticality of organizations is identified simply by noting that approximately one-half of the world's 100 largest economies are organizations—not nations.

5 Frogs and Snowballs: Changes and Challenges

The previously cited changes and challenges, many of which are anathema, could be added to *ad infinitum*. Some changes happen seemingly without notice. Limited warning should not excuse limited preparation, though it may stem from lack of adequate intelligence or surveillance. For these and other reasons, risk management and mitigation have risen to prominence in recent years (Olson and Wu 2015). Other challenges or changes evolve very slowly, imperceptible to most, until fully realized or irreversible. The principle behind this is illustrated by the myth of the *frog in the kettle* wherein, placed in boiling water, a frog will leap from danger whereas, placed in tepid water that is slowly brought to a boil, the frog will remain in the water and perish. Albeit untrue, this story illustrates that inadequate ability to perceive or assess the immediate, short-term, and long-term impacts of change influences whether and how information is acted upon. Further, the story illustrates that large-scale differences can be accomplished by *slow* change or by an appropriately sequenced and executed series of individually small, but collectively large changes.

Many of the previously cited changes and challenges fit this profile. Consider, for example, accelerating atmospheric concentration of greenhouse gases, much of which is due to industrialization coincident with global population growth, that is, acceleration due to accumulated human activity across many generations. It was not until 1804 that global human population reached one billion—a period of approximately 200,000 years (Stringer and Galway-Witham 2017). Global population reached 2 billion by 1927, 3 billion by 1959, 4 billion by 1974, 5 billion in 1987, 6 billion in 1999, 7 billion in 2011, and—at this writing—about 7.6 billion. It is projected that global population will reach 8 billion people by 2025, 9 billion people by 2040, and 11 billion people by the turn of the next century (http://www.theworldcounts.com/counters/shocking_environmental_facts_and_statistics/world_population_clock_live). Population growth at this pace and scale has contributed to growth in atmospheric concentration of greenhouse gases at a rate far exceeding the atmosphere's natural exchange or filtration ability. Given current trends and technologies, many greenhouse gases currently in the atmosphere will persist for many generations, a factor partially responsible for recent and projected changes in global temperature swings and other climate phenomena over recent and coming years—part of a vicious cycle (Edgeman 2017) that includes accelerating melting of polar ice and permafrost thawing that release methane and carbon dioxide—common greenhouse gases—into the atmosphere (Nauta et al. 2015).

Global economic development and population growth are coincident with the global economy projected to multiply an estimated 26 times this century. This will exert significant strain on food production and natural resources that include water and soil (Dietz and Stern 2015; Jones and Warner 2016). Strain on resources and environmental stresses are among key motivators of servitization, wherein services supplement or replace traditional product offerings, with some services intended to prolong product life cycles, resulting in reductions in both resource depletion and greenhouse gas generation associated with extraction and production processes (Baines et al. 2017; Raddats et al. 2016). Beyond population growth, economic development is driven by such factors as rapid growth of the middle class, and of BOT consumption. The BOT is defined as the four billion people in the world subsisting on 2 USD/day or less (Anderson and Markides 2007; Hart and Christensen 2002; Prahalad 2005).

Many of the changes and challenges cited herein are insidious in their progression—much like the proverbial snowball rolling downhill, which grows and grows and grows, increasing in its size, mass, and capacity for devastation as its surface area grows exponentially with its radius. Relative to issues cited thus far herein, the snowball represents challenges such as food insecurity, water and other natural resource depletion, population growth, growth in atmospheric concentration of greenhouse gases, ocean acidification, and increasing desertification. The speed of the "snowball" is critical, as speed determines the size and mass to which the snowball grows—and, importantly, the scope, scale, and speed of responses needed from individuals, enterprises, governments, or societies.

6 Hope on the Horizon?

A good deal of research and development has been devoted to solving many of the changes and challenges cited herein. While many of the generated solutions are proven ones, they are still only partial relative to the magnitude of the challenges or changes they address and, as such, significant work remains. Moving forward, work includes *intentional* and *routine* embedding of research, innovation, and development of such solutions or application thereof in enterprise strategy. Examples of technology-based solutions addressing one or more of the challenges and changes cited include the following examples:

- Precision drip technology that delivers water only where needed (Tal 2013);
- Efficient water desalination technology that provides water for human consumption, agricultural use, and increase of forest canopy in arid regions such as the Middle East (Tal 2013);
- Clean and renewable energy technologies;
- 3D printing technology (additive manufacturing) with applications ranging from surgical to home construction (Gardan 2016; Segars 2018);

- Communications technology that facilitates remote employment and reduces transportation demand;
- Dramatically more fuel- or energy-efficient automobile and mass transit services;
- Smart technology regulates fuel consumption/energy use;
- Creation of new materials such as graphene that have multiple important or potential applications, such as clean-up of nuclear waste, ultra-fast data upload, rapid charging of portable devices, ultra-effective water filtration, greater product durability and hence longevity, bionic technology that could make it possible for people with catastrophic injuries to regain full functionality in certain cases, and more (https://gizmodo.com/5988977/9-incredible-uses-for-graphene);
- Rapidly advancing computing technology that is likely to deliver better solutions to climate change more rapid development of drought-resistant food sources, and greatly enhanced national security and crime-fighting capability. Currently, the world's fastest supercomputers process at petascale speeds (1,000,000,000,000,000 calculations/second, that is, one quadrillion) with exascale computers in development (1,000,000,000,000,000,000 calculations per second, that is, a quintillion calculations/second)—about one trillion times more powerful than the fastest consumer laptop available (https://www.recode.net/2017/6/20/15812270/china-fastest-supercomputer-us-exascale-department-energy-intel-nvidia-ibm).
- Adaption of e-reader and Apple IPad technology to greatly reduce the need for and number of print materials in home, libraries, schools, and beyond which concurrently reducing built environment footprint and urban sprawl (Edgeman et al. 2015a).

It is left to the reader to further correlate these with the previously supplied list of challenges and changes. The point is not that every enterprise can or should focus on solutions as significant as these. Rather, the point is that integration of intentional and routine consideration of significant challenges and changes in the life of the enterprise can and ultimately will deliver important breakthroughs. On the other hand, lack of intentionality in this regard is likely to contribute to the continued growth and potential for devastation of the various "snowballs" threatening humanity.

7 Why or How Can Enterprise Excellence Be of Value in This Struggle?

Enterprise excellence theory and models are built on foundations laid by the quality movement and principles and practices of total quality management (Oakland 2014). Among those principles and practices are ones related to lean enterprise (Koenigsaeker 2013) and Six Sigma philosophy and methods (Hammer 2002). These are well-known for being highly pragmatic in their origins and in common application. Given the very real nature of challenges and changes such as those cited herein, pragmatism is important since there is great and perhaps urgent need to derivation of equally pragmatic solutions.

Lean is often-focused on waste reduction and elimination, with high-efficiency also front-and-center. Lean is often associated with *kaizen*, a Japanese word ordinarily translated as continuous improvement but interpreted as incremental improvement. It is of value to note that *kaizen* does not preclude breakthrough improvement, whether through a series of incremental improvements, or by a singular act. Six Sigma is well-known for its focus on variation reduction, superior operational performance, and improved financial performance.

Each of these can be generally construed as positive. The issue at hand is one of leveraging these inherent positives, while also adapting or redirecting the priorities or targets of the methods. This effort can be aided by examining the previously provided cited challenges and changes, identifying key themes, and surmising lean and Six Sigma implications. Doing so leads to the following observations and implications regarding future lean and Six Sigma practice, with the recommendation of an immediate start to integration:

- Alternative forms of currency. Traditional currencies such as $, ¥, €, and £ generally serve as surrogates for goods, services, opportunities, or experiences. While many opine that "anything can be monetized", monetization will almost always sacrifice information with the loss of information leading to a transformed version of the issue at hand. Other forms of currency that are more apt for some of the cited chal-

lenges and changes can be identified: food, water, warmth, improved natural environment, more secure social environment, leisure time, and many others;
- Shift from the (financial) bottom line, to multiple bottom lines, with the TBL that emphasizes social, ecological, and economic (people, planet, profit) performance providing a possible starting point. Of course, "performance" is "end of the pipe" in nature so that if these are to result intentionally, it will be as a result of associated TTL strategy that prioritizes social equity, ecological responsibility, and economic wisdom (Edgeman et al. 2015b). This implies movement to mixed currency models that more holistically represent problem characteristics and solution outcomes;
- Waste elimination and reduction emphases must—sometimes—be redirected. Wastes of special concern become those associated with negative social and/or ecological consequences. Currencies associated with these need to be direct measures, rather than monetized or—more accurately—should use the "real" currency: water usage, greenhouse gas emissions, food wastage, and so on. Similarly, rather than simply minimizing variation and improving financial performance, solutions might *include* focus on minimizing water usage, maximizing food production, yielding cleaner air, minimizing transportation of people and products, and so on.
- Design for Six Sigma (DFSS) will become more prominent. This forecast is driven by acknowledging that "tweaking" existing technologies may not deliver solutions that are "fast enough, efficient enough, and big enough";
- Biomimicry—learn from nature and incorporate learnings in your solutions (Deldin and Schuknecht 2014). Nature is inherently lean and highly inventive. In developing its ultralight (99.98% air) metal, Boeing fundamentally used a lattice design similar to that found in spiderwebs, honeycombs, and the bones of birds. Velcro adapted the means of attachment cockleburs use. Much regarding efficient heating and cooling of architectural structures can and has been learned from the design of termite mounds. Reed beds provide highly effective water filtration systems. There are many lessons in biomimicry of value in both lean and DFSS.

- Consciously incorporate large-scale systems thinking in product, process, service and system design, and improvement efforts with the objective of more conscious consideration of important interactions and points of leverage (Ackoff 1994).
- Integrate Design for the Circular Economy (Bocken et al. 2016) with Design for Six Sigma. For thousands of years humanity engaged in *linear* economic practice (take, make, use, waste). More recently, *reuse* economic practices have developed (take, make, use, recycle, eventually waste). At present, there is growing emphasis on development of circular economy products and practices where inputs are divided into biological and technological components or nutrients. Circular economy practices are take, make, use, separate into technological and biological components, reuse and repurpose these as possible, and minimize waste with the goal of zero waste of either technological or biological components. In some sense, an intent of circular economy theory and practice is that waste generated by one product, process, service, or system provides nutrients (inputs) for subsequent products, processes, services, or systems.

Humanity itself is at—perhaps past—a tipping point. At many levels, including the process and system levels, individual levels, enterprise levels, and other, we must determine or whether or how to confront the challenges and changes that have brought us to this juncture. There are of course many considerations involved: what challenges or changes should be confronted, with what priority, with how much urgency, and more.

Having addressed these considerations we must ask and answer some critical questions that lead to understanding of the drivers and direction of change; impacts of change; levers of change that individuals, enterprises, governments, or societies can influence or control; relationships or interactions among those levers; desired future states; and strategies and actions leading to those desired future states.

These are very much the sort of questions and considerations—albeit on a grander scale—that lean and Six Sigma approaches are built to address—the rules of the game so to speak.

It is important to identify prominent changes, challenges, and trends so that one can know the game one is playing, and learn its rules and nuances. In many regards, the "game" is the same one it has always been—survival. What has changed are the specific threats to survival. If lean and Six Sigma approaches are to help win the game, they will need to be appropriately adapted. Given the broad and deep influence each of these has experienced, such adaption is strongly recommended.

8 What Does This Have to Do with Enterprise Excellence?

On the face of the matter, this has little to do with enterprise excellence, though it is a simple matter to connect prior discussion to sustainability and, in turn, sustainable business models (SBMs). What has been documented are many of the challenges humanity faces, some of the causes of those challenges, technologies, and other approaches to combating these challenges—and these have much to with sustainability and with what enterprises can accomplish when their face is set toward, rather than away from such challenges.

Positioning the *Springboard to SEER2 model* as a sustainable business model suggests that it must support not only continuously relevant and responsible enterprise actions and results, but should also serve to orient an organization toward significant social and environmental challenges. First, however, this implies a certain understanding of what constitutes a SBM.

Like any model, a sustainable business model is a map—an inevitably imprecise abstraction of reality. As late quality management guru W. Edwards Deming aptly stated, "all models are wrong, but some are useful" (Sterman 2002).

The issue is not whether a given model is correct as, inevitably, it is not. Instead, the issue is whether and to what degree a model is of value or useful. A model's value and utility are reflected by the extent to which its application:

- enables leadership to more intelligently allocate and transfer resources to minimize risk by balancing key elements of risk (aversion, acceptance, and containment);

- informs and builds an organizational culture that delivers performance and impacts consistent with organizational mission, vision, purpose, strategy, and expectations that are improving at a pace at or beyond that needed to ensure survivability;
- promotes organizational agility so that the enterprise is able to quickly respond to signaled change, moving people, and other resources where needed quickly;
- promotes enterprise resilience and robustness;
- promotes ongoing innovation; and
- enables accurate forecasts of future performance.

These characteristics are interrelated and should thus be jointly considered.

Business models depend on particular external conditions. For the business model to be sustainable, those conditions must align with a thriving economy that consistently delivers social progress made within the context of environmental boundaries. Example considerations might include whether the business model enables complete decoupling of economic growth from environmental damage, and whether it relies on fair or unfair terms of trade. These conditions imply that a sustainable *business* model must:

- be *commercially successful* in that it must be based on strategy and tactics that create both sufficient value for customers and sufficient profit for the enterprise;
- is *future-ready* in the sense that it promotes enterprise agility, thus rendering the enterprise both more resilient and more robust to volatility in its competitive landscape;
- promotes societal sustainability since it is not possible for an enterprise to be sustainable in the long run if the society it serves is not built on a sustainable economy.

Strategy matters. The enterprise must know how it will compete and how it will create the conditions necessary to be part of a sustainable society, with five widely recognized generic competitive strategies including (Porter 1980):

- *Low-cost provision*—striving to achieve lower overall costs than rivals on products or services that attract a broad spectrum of consumers;
- *Broad differentiation*—differentiation of offerings in the enterprise's product and service portfolio from those of rivals via attributes that appeal to a broad spectrum of consumers;
- *Focused low-cost*—concentration on narrow price-sensitive consumer segments and on costs to offer lower-priced products and services;
- *Focused differentiation*—concentration on narrow consumer segments accomplished via meeting specific requirements and preferences within those niche segments;
- *Best-cost provision*—delivers more value to consumers by providing upscale product and service attributes at a lower investment level that demanded by rivals.

These strategies are strongly influenced by five primary forces (Porter 2008):

- Rivalries among existing competitors;
- The threat of new entrants in the competitive landscape;
- The threat of substitute/replacement products or services;
- The bargaining power of suppliers; and
- The bargaining power of consumers.

It can be gleaned from this that the notion of *competitive excellence* is fundamentally embedded in SEER2. As such, when it is derived, our *Springboard to SEER2* must simultaneously support:

- Development and/or application of relevant technologies that address social or ecological challenges;
- SEER2;
- Continuously relevant and responsible actions and results;
- Competitive excellence.

There are of course synergies among these so that a model for any one of the four will to an extent support each of the other three.

9 Toward a Model: The House of Sustainability

Recall that a model is a map, an abstraction, or reduction of reality that emphasize only selected essential features. Features regarded as essential depend on the purpose of the map and the perspective of the mapmaker. A single reality can usually be interpreted from several perspectives, with a given map representing one or more perspectives. A map's usefulness depends on a number of factors, many of which have been previously cited. In addition, a map's utility depends on the match between user needs, features emphasized, level of resolution, and the flexibility or adaptability offered by the map relative to perturbations in its corresponding (real) landscape.

A model is a map and the goal is to provide a map for management of enterprises willing to relentlessly and rigorously pursue excellence.

Enterprises are complex systems and their *management is understood* to entail *mastering the complexity of designing, controlling, and developing the strategies, activities, and relationships of purpose-oriented entities.* Excellence includes socially, ecologically, and economically relevant, responsible, and superior performance and impacts, paths to such performance and impacts, and strategy and governance that identifies possible such paths and selects from among them. This requires better understanding of and reaction to social trends and processes in that enterprises must attend to more stakeholders than in the past when shareholder expectations were paramount, customers were royalty, and little else mattered. This magnifies the importance of being able to accurately forecast production and service demands along with innovation and design directions, all with the intention of positioning enterprises to get in front of, rather than lag change. An enterprise need not always be first to market or highly innovative, but in the longer run, the value of its strategy depends on the accuracy with which it forecasts or anticipates changes.

Figure 11.1 introduces a newly developed strategy tool that will be referred to as a *house of sustainability* (HOS) that some may recognize of as a loose adaptation of the house of quality (HOQ) that is fundamental to the quality function deployment (Hauser and Clausing 1996). Its

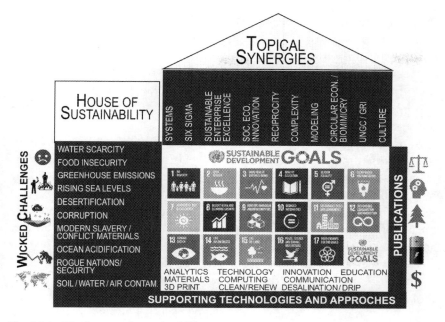

Fig. 11.1 The house of sustainability

rows and columns represent, respectively, selected key challenges cited herein faced by humankind, and selected means of addressing those challenges, only some of which have been heretofore discussed. The "roof" of the HOS is intended to represent relationships among various means of addressing challenges that could be represented symbolically by, for example, +, 0, and − to represent means that are synergistic, unrelated, and at cross-purposes, respectively. Wherever synergies among means exist it may be possible to produce multiplicative results, whereas means working at cross-purposes require careful evaluation of compromises that may need to be made. The body of the HOS, that is, where means and challenges intersect might ordinarily be used to denote the strength of the relationships between various means and challenges and hence the likelihood of success in addressing a given challenge. Relationship strengths are ordinarily represented as 0 (no relationship), 1 (weak relationship), 3 (moderate relationship), and 9 (strong relations rather than record strengths in the body of the HOS, the choice has been made here to simply provide the 17 sustainable development goals (SDGs) of associated with the United Nations Agenda 2030. This choice has been made only for the purpose of indicating that there exist significant relationships between the challenges recorded as rows of the HOS and the 17 SDGs so that the same means used to address the cited challenges can—with appropriate forethought—be deployed by an enterprise to simultaneously address SDGs.

Summing strengths across columns indicates the collective abilities of the identified means to address a given challenge, whereas summing the strengths across rows to yield column totals will indicate the overall value of a given means to address multiple challenges—first—searching for key relationships between critical challenges identified herein, and possible means of attacking those challenges. These are represented by the row and column elements of Fig. 11.1.

Both enterprise relevance and enterprise responsibility are addressed by the HOS. In this sense, the HOS can be used as a strategy deployment tool that can aid deployment social and environmental elements of enterprise TTL strategy as a means of—later—achieving TBL performance and impacts.

10   Structured Enterprise Excellence Models

Essentially all enterprises adhere to some extent to enterprise-specific guiding principles. These shape the culture of the enterprise, here defined as the collection of behaviors within the enterprise. Such principles influence enterprise strategy, that must then be deployed, with the intent of yielding defined performance. Excellence models emphasize excellent performance and SEE models deliberately incorporate social and environmental performance.

Figure 11.2 provides a generic SEE model. The "sustainable" designation of this model is driven by overt inclusion of social and environmental concerns in both enterprise strategy and results (performance). As such, the model emphasizes TTL strategy and TBL performance or results. This does not preclude inclusion of other strategy or performance areas. As but a few examples of possible additional inclusions, many

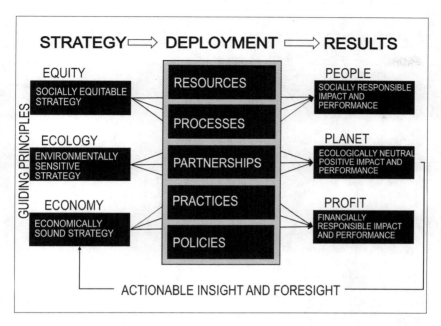

Fig. 11.2 A generic sustainable enterprise excellence model

enterprises incorporate innovation or supply chain considerations. It is in part via such inclusions that resilience and robustness can be integrated to yield a SEER2 model.

11 Guiding Principles, Sustainable Culture, and Worthy Sustainability Goals

Though most enterprises will identify some guiding principles that are contextually tied to their history or to their competitive landscape, other such principles are likely to be ones embraced by a large array of entities. Among more commonly embraced guiding principles that are consistent with social and environmental sustainability are the 10 principles of the United Nations Global Compact or UNGC (https://www.unglobalcompact.org/). The UNGC is a voluntary initiative based on chief executive officer commitments to implement universal sustainability principles and to take steps

Table 11.1 The United Nations Global Compact 10 principles

UNGC principle	Brief description
Human rights	
Principle 1	Support and respect the protection of internationally proclaimed human rights.
Principle 2	Make sure the business is not complicit in human rights abuses.
Labor	
Principle 3	Uphold the freedom of association and the effective recognition of the right to collective bargaining.
Principle 4	Uphold elimination of all forms of forced and compulsory labor.
Principle 5	Uphold the effective abolition of child labor.
Principle 6	Uphold elimination of discrimination in respect to employment and occupation.
Environment	
Principle 7	Support a precautionary approach to environmental challenges.
Principle 8	Undertake initiatives to promote greater environmental responsibility.
Principle 9	Encourage the development and diffusion of environmentally friendly technologies.
Anti-corruption	
Principle 10	Work against corruption in all its forms, including extortion and bribery.

to support United Nations goals, including the 17 United Nations Sustainable Development Goals (UN SDGs) portrayed in Fig. 11.1. There are almost 13,000 UNGC signatories, of which almost 10,000 are businesses—many of which are large, highly recognizable multinational corporations such as Royal Dutch Shell plc, Microsoft, Intel, Rio Tinto plc, General Motors Company, Volvo, ABB Ltd., various Siemens units that include Siemens Gamesa Renewable Energy, General Electric, Anheuser-Busch, Renault, Tesco plc, Arla Foods amba, and LEGO (https://www.unglobalcompact.org/what-is-gc/participants/).

The UNGC Ten Principles are cited in Table 11.1 (https://www.unglobalcompact.org/what-is-gc/mission/principles), with the brief description of each principle intended to begin with "businesses should".

Various other principles might qualify as core or guiding for any given enterprise. The Shingo Institute—the administrative home of the Shingo Prize for Operational Excellence—has noted that enterprises they have observed to be sustainable over the long run are ones with exceptional and sustainable culture, where culture is shared, pervasive, enduring, and generally implicit—though it may be reinforced via codes of conduct or other formal mechanisms. Generally, culture may be thought of as the tacit social order of the enterprise that is reflected in the collection of behaviors, beliefs, and attitudes resident in the enterprise and principles identified as critical to (enterprise) cultural sustainability include pervasive practice of mutual respect, humility of leadership, routine practice of scientific and critical thinking, unity of purpose, and shared vision—often referred to as constancy of purpose, and the ability to perceive and act systemically (Plenert 2017).

An enterprise's culture is observable and the aforementioned principles manifest in two primary dimensions: how people interact, which ranges along a spectrum from independently to interdependently, and how they individually and collectively respond to change, which spans a spectrum anchored at one end by stability and at the other end by flexibility. If these are set as two axes in a two-by-two matrix, then eight critical elements of enterprise life emerge: purpose, caring, order, safety, authority, results, enjoyment, and learning (Groysberg et al. 2018a). Each of these is associated with specific advantages and disadvantages and most enterprises will strongly emphasize and support one or two of these eight elements—notably caring and results—and will devote less attention and assign lower importance to the others. It is of value for an enterprise to be able to profile, evolve (shape), align (convergence), and understand salient contextual factors and conditions associated with their cultures if they are to develop a sustainable culture. A highly relevant and easily applied set of diagnostics that can be used to aid an enterprise in development of a sustainable culture can be found in the work of Groysberg et al. (2018a, b, c, d, e).

The 17 UN SDGs are cited in Table 11.2. The SDGs are highly integrated into the UNGC's multi-year strategy to drive business awareness and action in support of achieving the SDGs by 2030 and are described at https://www.unglobalcompact.org/sdgs/17-global-goals#sdg1, with links provided for those seeking further elaboration. In examining the UNGC 10 principles and the 17 UN SDGs, it is of value to consciously consider the synergies among the two sets, and to identify elements that might be explicitly included in a sustainable business model.

Table 11.2 United Nations Sustainable Development Goals for agenda 2030

UN SDG	Brief description
SDG 1	*No poverty*: End poverty, in all its forms, everywhere.
SDG 2	*Zero hunger*: End hunger, achieve food security and improved nutrition, and promote sustainable agriculture.
SDG 3	*Good health and well-being*: Ensure healthy lives and promote well-being for all, at all ages.
SDG 4	*Quality education*: Ensure inclusive and equitable quality education and promote life-long learning opportunities for all.
SDG 5	*Gender equality*: Achieve gender equality and empower all women and girls.
SDG 6	*Clean water and sanitation*: Ensure availability and sustainable management of water and sanitation for all.
SDG 7	*Affordable and clean energy*: Ensure access to affordable, reliable, sustainable, and modern energy for all.
SDG 8	*Decent work and economic growth*: Promote sustained, inclusive, and sustainable economic growth, full and productive employment, and decent work for all.
SDG 9	*Industry, innovation, and infrastructure*: Build resilient infrastructure, promote inclusive and sustainable industrialization, and foster innovation.
SDG 10	*Reduce inequalities*: Reduce inequality within and among countries.
SDG 11	*Sustainable cities and communities*: Make cities and human settlements inclusive, safe, resilient, and sustainable.
SDG 12	*Responsible consumption and production*: Ensure sustainable consumption and production patterns.
SDG 13	*Climate action*: Take urgent action to combat climate change and its impacts.
SDG 14	*Life below water*: Conserve and sustainably use the oceans, seas, and marine resources for sustainable development.
SDG 15	*Life on land*: Protect, restore, and promote sustainable use of terrestrial ecosystems, sustainably manage forests, combat desertification, halt and reverse land degradation, and halt biodiversity loss.
SDG 16	*Peace and justice strong institutions*: Promote peaceful and inclusive societies for sustainable development, provide access to justice for all, and build effective, accountable, and inclusive institutions at all levels.
SDG 17	*Partnerships for the goals*: Strengthen the means of implementation and revitalize the global partnership for sustainable development.

From a business model perspective, the UNGC 10 principles can be used to inform enterprise strategy and actions (or behaviors) and hence also culture. The 17 UN SDGs, which in total have 169 designated targets, or some relevant subset thereof can be regarded as omnibus performance goals toward which—at least in part—enterprise performance should be oriented.

It is of course the case that if an enterprise is to be economically sustainable, it must create value for its shareholders or other financially invested stakeholders. The challenge is, ultimately, for an enterprise to do well economically, while also doing good relative to societal and environmental concerns. This creates several challenges (Consolandi and Eccles 2018), among which are the following:

- There are not—unlike with financial performance—universal standards used to measure an enterprise's ecological, social, and governance (ESG) performance.
- This has led to a proliferation of NGOs and data vendors attempting to fill this voice and that enterprises and investors alike must determine which portfolio of measures to use, as well as how to calculate and interpret those measures.
- Enterprise skepticism remains as to whether shareholders will reward positive ESG performance over the longer term.
- ESG measures address enterprise performance, while the 17 SDGs and associated 169 targets are related to societal and ecological improvement. A bridge clearly liking these must be built.
- Investor focus is typically riveted on enterprise financial performance and many enterprises struggle to understand, let alone communicate how positive ESG performance maps to positive financial performance.
- Strong investor—corporate community collaboration must be established if strong progress is to be made toward achieving the 2030 SDGs.

It is of value to recognize that any specific business sectors more naturally align with furthering progress toward fulfillment of some SDGs, than with other SDGs. Core to identification of natural alignment is the ability to relate *materiality* of ESG results with SDG impacts, where materiality is associated with issue of importance to investors.

While such relationships are clearly important to social and ecological relevance and responsibility, they are equally critical to economic survivability and hence the economic sustainability of the enterprise. Table 11.3 summarizes the 3 SDGs most naturally aligned to various

Table 11.3 Business sector alignment with United Nations Sustainable Development Goals

Business sector	Naturally aligned SDGs (unordered)
Consumption	2, 4, 13
Financial	4, 9, 10
Health care	3, 4, 15
Infrastructure	11, 14, 15
Nonrenewable Resources	11, 12, 14
Renewable Resources and Alternative Energy	11, 12, 13
Resource Transformation	12, 13, 14
Services	2, 4, 5
Technology and Communications	5, 9, 16
Transportation	3, 12, 14

business sectors, while Table 11.4 cites the three business sectors best positioned to address each of the first 16 SDGs (Consolandi and Eccles 2018)—with the 17th SDG omitted as it essentially addresses collaboration, rather than commonly identified social or ecological goals.

A brief review of Table 11.3 reveals that selected SDGs are strongly aligned with multiple business sectors, whereas multiple SDGs are not strongly aligned with any particular business sector. A given enterprise—regardless of its native business sector—may of course be intentionally structured and oriented to address any given SDG.

Although SDGs 1, 6, 7, and 8 are not represented in Table 11.3, it is fair to note that SDG 6 (clean water and sanitation) and SDG 7 (affordable and clean energy) are not only important from social and environmental perspectives, but are targets of numerous highly successful companies or are highly prioritized by some nations or regions. Similarly, the aforementioned growth of the middle class and BOT consumption are global indicators of progress toward poverty alleviation (SDG 1) and of economic growth (SDG 8).

The intention of Tables 11.3 and 11.4 is to provide some guidance to an enterprise as to where it is likely to experience greatest social or ecological success or impact, as measured against the UN SDGs. This can be of value in formulating an enterprise-specific sustainable business model.

Table 11.4 Three most important business sectors relative to each United Nations Sustainable Development Goal

UN SDG	Sectors most important to SDG (unordered)
SDG 1	Consumption, Health Care, Nonrenewable Resources
SDG 2	Consumption, Health Care, Nonrenewable Resources
SDG 3	Consumption, Health Care, Resource Transformation
SDG 4	Consumption, Health Care, Services
SDG 5	Consumption, Health Care, Technology and Communications
SDG 6	Consumption, Health Care, Nonrenewable Resources
SDG 7	Health Care, Nonrenewable Resources, Resource Transformation
SDG 8	Health Care, Nonrenewable Resources, Resource Transformation
SDG 9	Health Care, Resource Transformation, Technology and Communications
SDG 10	Financials, Health Care, Technology and Communications
SDG 11	Health Care, Nonrenewable Resources, Renewable Resources, and Alternative Energy
SDG 12	Consumption, Nonrenewable Resources, Resource Transformation
SDG 13	Consumption, Renewable Resources and Alternative Energy, Resource Transformation
SDG 14	Consumption, Nonrenewable Resources, Resource Transformation
SDG 15	Consumption, Health Care, Resource Transformation
SDG 16	Health Care, Resource Transformation, Technology and Communications

Source: Adapted from Consolandi and Eccles (2018)

12 A SEER2 Model for the Continuously Relevant and Responsible Enterprise

Assumed here as a given is that any true sustainable business model will consciously and deeply embed a TTL orientation in its strategy and TBL orientation in its performance. How this is accomplished, the relative balance among triple top and bottom line dimensions, specific strategic details, and alignment to various UN SDGs will vary from enterprise-to-enterprise. Strategy elements are integrated in ways that mean strategy principally targeting one area is likely to intersect strategy principally targeting one or more other areas. Foregoing discussion suggests that useful additions to sustainable business model strategy might commonly include, for example, cultural sustainability, technology development and adoption, innovation (broadly construed), resilience, robustness, and supply chain strategy. Collecting these elements and other aforementioned ones

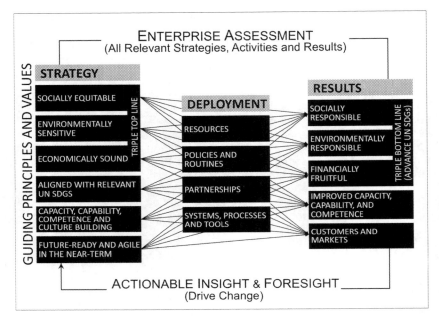

Fig. 11.3 Sustainable enterprise excellence, resilience and robustness model

allows formation of a SEER2 model such as the one portrayed in Fig. 11.3, though of course many alternative SEER2 models might be derived.

The SEER2 model of Fig. 11.3 may be regarded as an extension of the generic SEE model of Fig. 11.2. Rather than generic guiding principles and values, ones in the model of Fig. 11.3 are intended to explicitly include or be deeply informed by the UNGC 10 principles and the cited principles associated with a sustainable enterprise culture. Non-exhaustive strategy emphases, deployment means, and results areas cited in Fig. 11.3 are elaborated in Tables 11.5, 11.6, and 11.7.

Guiding principles inevitably impact strategy—else they are not "guiding" in nature. As but one example, embracing mutual respect as a guiding principle will demand that strategy drives the enterprise toward more complete gender equity, a UN SDG. Similarly, guiding principles such as practice of scientific and critical thinking, and thinking and acting systemically, lead almost surely to incorporation of analytics as a strategy component and, also, to technology- or innovation-oriented strategy.

Table 11.5 Representative SBM and SEER2 strategic emphases

Strategy emphases	
Emphasis	Rationale
Socially equitable	Social equity is core to sustainable business models (SBMs) and part of triple top line strategy.
Ecologically sensitive	Ecological sensitivity is core to SBMs and triple top line strategy.
Economically sound	Economic success is critical to any for-profit enterprise and is in many cases the primary of the triple bottom lines. It is key to enterprise survivability in both the near- and long-terms.
Aligned with relevant UN SDGs	Approximately 10,000 business signatories to the United Nations Global Compact embrace its 10 principles and in turn affirm working toward the UN sustainable development goals (UN SDGs) that are consistent with their mission, vision, and purpose.
Capacity, capability, competence, and culture building	Capacity, capability, and competence are foundational to customer and market success in both the near- and long-terms. These impact agility, resilience and robustness, and demand investment in human ecology—thus contributing to (enterprise) cultural sustainability and in turn enterprise sustainability. These are drivers of employee satisfaction, loyalty, and retention.
Future-ready/agile in the near-term	Agility contributes to enterprise resilience in that it enables more rapid response in volatile environments in the form of course corrections. Future readiness implies adept scanning of the competitive horizon and preparation in advance of changes.
Analytical and innovative	Properly implemented and executed, analytics enable both more informed risk/cost-benefit analysis and more timely decision-making, hence contributing to both resilience and robustness, in addition to financial prudence. Innovation is broadly intended here and includes but is not limited to new product and service offerings. Innovation can include, for example, business model innovation that better orients the enterprise toward the communities it serves, customers, and markets. Given triple top line orientation and alignment of the enterprise with both UN Global Compact Principles and relevant UN Sustainable Development Goals, at least some portion of the innovation should be social-ecological innovation (SEI) in nature, with positive social or environmental ramifications.

Table 11.6 Selected means by which strategy may be deployed, usually in combination

Deployment means	
Means	Rationale
Resources	Key resources useful in strategy deployment include enterprise human ecology, financial resources, and material resources.
Policies and Routines	Policies and routines are intended to influence or determine all major decisions and actions occurring within their boundaries. Routines are repetitive, recognizable patterns of interdependent actions (social replicators) that—typically—are carried out by multiple actors. Many enterprise routines serve as material expressions of policies.
Partnerships	Partnerships address who an enterprise is willing to collaborate with as well as the relative commitments expected from and benefits that accrue to each partner. Key to partnerships are synergistic concerns, leverage of partner capabilities, and minimization of the weaknesses or gaps in one's own enterprise.
Systems, Processes, and Tools	Systems, processes, and tools, as intended herein, form a hierarchy. From a systems perspective, enterprises are systems of people. *Overall* enterprise behavior depends on the structure of entire enterprise, not the sum of its parts. More commonly systems are collections of subsystems or processes, integrated to accomplish a larger, more omnibus objective. Within its contextual boundaries, each subsystem or process requires inputs and produces outputs, enabled by tools, each of which is intended to achieve specific outcomes. Systems are composed of processes; processes are composed of tools. The *House of Sustainability* is included in this portfolio.

Each UNGC principle maps to socially and environmentally oriented strategy, and to strategic alignment of the enterprise with contextually relevant UN SDGs. Enterprise strategy must be deployed. How thoroughly and how well it is deployed impacts how fully it is realized.

Most of the means of deployment cited in the center portion of Fig. 11.3 are all-purpose in nature in the sense of being useful in deploying any sort of strategy. In contrast, the *HOS* introduced herein is of explicit value in deploying innovation, technology, or other strategy related either directly or peripherally to the UN SDGs.

Ultimately, strategy is formulated and deployed with the objective of achieving specific outcomes or results. SEER2 targets the TBL and other

Table 11.7 Representative results targeted by SBM and SEER2 models

Results (performance and impacts) areas	
Area(s)	Rationale
Socially responsible	Sustainable business model (SBM) and SEER2 consciously pursue socially responsible results. Such results are consistent with the UN Sustainable Development Goals (UN SDGs).
Environmentally responsible	SBM and SEER2 intentionally pursue environmentally responsible results. Such results naturally advance the UN SDGs.
Financially fruitful	Most enterprises, and particularly for-profit and for-benefit enterprises, must perform in financially sustainable ways, else they cease to exist. To the extent that issues such as employment creation and gender equality are supported, financially fruitful results are consistent with the UN SDGs.
Improved capacity, capability, and competence	Improved capacity, capability, and competence are pursued as means of rendering the enterprise more agile, resilient, and robust. This is accomplished in part via improved inventiveness and innovativeness that target social-ecological results, as well as financial ones.
Customers and markets	Positive customer results include improved customer satisfaction, loyalty, retention, and enterprise advocacy executed by customers. These are strongly related to enhanced market performance that may be reflected in such measures as market share, new customers and contracts, and reduced customer defection rates. Each of these correlates positively to financial performance.

contextually relevant results—examples of which include relevant customer and marketplace outcomes, human ecology (employee) results, supply chain performance, innovation performance, enriched enterprise culture, and the trio of improved capacity, capability, and competence that reflect values deeply held by learning organizations (Lichtenthaler 2009).

Social-ecological innovation (SEI) prominence in SBMs and SEER2 traces to its ability to reduce enterprise fragility in general and its financial system in particular (Klemkosky 2013) and hence contribution to enterprise resilience and robustness. SEI is innovation with social and/or ecological targets and has the ability to make critical contributions to SBMs and SEER2 in many regards, not least of which is its role in value creation:

- SEI efforts will in some instances be generally consistent with lean approaches that focus on reducing cost, risks, waste, and delivering proof-of-value (Schrettle et al. 2014).
- SEI will in other instances direct attention to redesign of selected products, processes, or business functions to optimize their performance and hence advance from doing old things in new ways to doing new things in new ways—that is, to value creation.

13 Springboard to SEER2 Assessment

Springboard models provide simple, accessible technology used to conduct regular, rigorous, comprehensive, and systematic assessment of all relevant enterprise strategy, activities, and results. *Relevant* is here understood to mean "relevant to whatever the model seeks to discover", whereas *comprehensive* implies thorough examination and discovery of intelligence relevant to areas assessed by the model. Chief among self-assessment aims are that it should provide feedback and foresight to the enterprise that stimulates improvement, informs strategy, and contributes to the possibility and greater likelihood—if not reality—of identification, strategic selection, and implementation of *best* and *next best* practices and sources of competitive advantage.

Each strategy emphasis, deployment means, and results area can be assessed using maturity scales. Maturity scales can range from relatively crude to highly detailed, with an intermediate level represented by a 1-to-5 scale. The primary challenge is to develop credible maturity scales for each of element assessed. More credible scales will deliver more credible, more useful assessments, and the intent of such scales is to enable more useful assessment of inherently qualitative or "soft" characteristics. Table 11.8 provides an example maturity scale for deployment via systems, processes, and tools.

Figures 11.4 through 11.8 provide a simple graphical assessment summarization of enterprise SEER2 strategy emphasis, deployment means, and results. The figures provide assessment "dials" for each of strategy, deployment, and results with each dial being, essentially, a radar chart. It is left to the enterprise to determine the relative importance or weight of strategy, deployment, and results as well as differentiation in the importance of the

Table 11.8 Example maturing scale for the systems, processes, and tools deployment means

Deployment maturity rating	Deployment means: systems, processes, and tools (SPT)
1	*Very low maturity*: low awareness and capability
The enterprise generally has little or no coordination across its systems, processes, and tools. Tools are used primarily as needed, with only vague understanding of the process in which they are applied. Similarly, processes are not optimized and a fire-fighting approach is used, rather than a solid process improvement approach. Processes are treated independently, rather than being understood as part of a larger system. Low-hanging and ground fruit is abundant.
2	*Low maturity*: sporadic or reactive capability
There is increasing coordination in the use of tools within the context of the processes in which they are applied. Process improvement approaches are consistently used in pockets across the enterprise or enterprise unit. Coordination of multiple processes within a system is practiced by some. There are many low-hanging fruit opportunities.
3	*Moderate maturity*: early systematic approaches
Tools are generally well-understood and appropriately used. Process improvement approaches are widely and routinely used. Increasing process optimization effort and some system optimization effort, especially with respect to the most important processes and systems. Systems-level awareness is common and increasing.
4	*High maturity*: aligned and partially integrated
Tool refinement is common. Process improvement and innovation approaches are well-understood and practiced almost universally. Process and systems improvement effort is a clear job expectation. Systems-level understanding is high, with processes in multi-process systems well-coordinated among the most important systems. The value of systems optimization to the enterprise is acknowledged. There is broad and increasing use of process and system optimization tools and methods. Seen as benchmark-quality by many external entities.
5	*Very high maturity*: clear, consistent, and pervasive SPT integration and alignment
There is clear understanding of the use of tools within processes and strong emphasis on and consistent practice of process improvement, optimization, and innovation. Process mapping is routinely practiced. The relationship among processes within systems is well-understood, and there is clear emphasis on overall system optimization. Related systems are coordinated. Widely acknowledged as best-in-class or world-class.

Fig. 11.4 SEER2 strategy assessment dial

various strategic emphases, deployment means, and results areas since—otherwise—the enterprise will be using a naive approach that fundamentally assumes that "all areas are equally important". It is suggested that weights—especially those associated with strategy and results—be assigned in collaboration with key stakeholders, policymakers, and communities. Use of this approach will yield a more relevant and useful assessment.

Each of the strategy, deployment, and results assessment dials presented in Figs. 11.4, 11.5, and 11.6 can be augmented with a strengths-weaknesses-opportunities-threats (SWOT Plot) narrative, a generic form of which is provided in Fig. 11.7. The purpose of the N-E-W-S labels circling the SWOT Plot narrative is twofold: first—the letters correspond to compass directions (North, East, West, South) and second—these are purposely stated in this order due to the objective of SWOT analysis, to provide "news" in the form of actionable insight and foresight. Linking the SWOT Plot narratives with the corresponding dials, and collecting these in a single combined graphical-and-narrative format that will be referred to as a *SEER2 NEWS Report Assessment Dashboard*, a generic portrayal for which is provided in Fig. 11.8.

Performance Management and Enterprise Excellence... 353

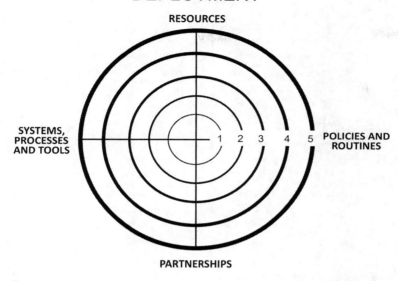

Fig. 11.5 SEER2 deployment assessment dial

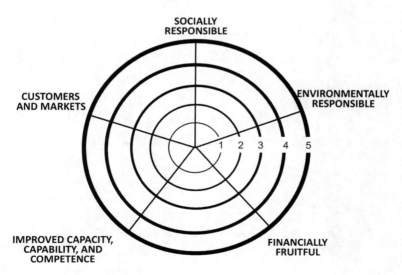

Fig. 11.6 SEER2 results assessment dial

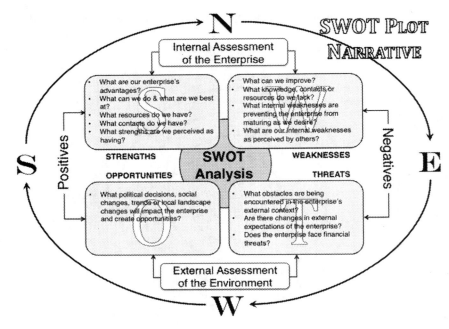

Fig. 11.7 Generic SWOT Plot narrative

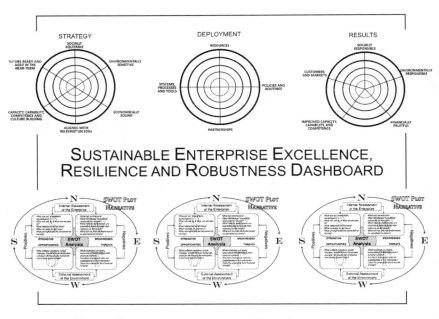

Fig. 11.8 SEER2 NEWS Report Assessment Dashboard

14   Summary

Assessment provides an enterprise health review, the primary expectation of which is provision of ample and *actionable* insight and foresight. Astute enterprises are able to attain significant improvement and implement best and next best practices, strengthening existing or identifying new sources of competitive advantage. Central to this effort is the ability to meaningfully estimate enterprise maturity with respect to relevant strategy, deployment, and results.

SEER2 are hallmarks of high-performing organizations that thrive in good times and that successfully navigate more turbulent ones via pursuit of continuously relevant and responsible strategies, activities, and results. As such, SEER2 models are SBMs. Widespread adoption of SEER2 practices is critical to long-term sustainable enterprise success and that is of course motivating to the stakeholders of most enterprises. Equally holds promise for the sustainability of not only the enterprise, but also society and the natural environment.

References

Ackoff, R.L. 1994. Systems Thinking and Thinking systems. *System Dynamics Review* 10 (2–3): 175–188.

Anderson, J., and C. Markides. 2007. Strategic Innovation at the Base of the Pyramid. *MIT Sloan Management Review* 49 (1): 83–88.

Baines, T., A.Z. Bigdeli, O.F. Bustinza, V.G. Shi, J. Baldwin, and K. Ridgway. 2017. Servitization: Revisiting the State-of-the-art and Research Priorities. *International Journal of Operations & Production Management* 37 (2): 256–278.

Bocken, N.M.P., I. de Pauw, C. Bakker, and B. van der Grinten. 2016. Product Design and Business Model Strategies for a Circular Economy. *Journal of Industrial and Production Engineering* 33 (5): 308–320.

Bou-Llusar, J.C., A.B. Escrig-Tena, V. Roca-Puig, and I. Beltrán. 2009. An Empirical Assessment of the EFQM Excellence Model: Evaluation as a TQM Framework Relative to the MBNQA Model. *Journal of Operations Management* 27 (1): 1–22.

Carpenter, R.C. 2016. *'Innocent Women and Children': Gender, Norms, and Protection of Civilians*. London: Routledge.

Chomsky, N. 2015. *Rogue States: The Rule of Force in World Affairs*. Chicago, IL: Haymarket Books.

Consolandi, C., and R.G. Eccles. 2018. Supporting Sustainable Development Goals is Easier than You Might Think. *MIT Sloan Management Review*. Big Idea: Sustainability Blog, 15 February 2018. Accessed March 31, 2018. https://sloanreview.mit.edu/article/supporting-sustainable-development-goals-is-easier-than-you-might-think/.

Davidson, J.O. 2015. *Modern Slavery: The Margins of Freedom*. London: Palgrave Macmillan.

Deldin, J.M., and M. Schuknecht. 2014. The AskNature Database: Enabling Solutions in Biomimetic Design. In *Biologically Inspired Design*, ed. D. McAdams and R. Stone, 17–27. London: Springer.

Dietz, S., and N. Stern. 2015. Endogenous Growth, Convexity of Damage and Climate Risk: How Nordhaus' Framework Supports Deep Cuts in Carbon Emissions. *The Economic Journal* 125 (583): 574–620.

Edgeman, R. 2015. Strategic Resistance for Sustaining Enterprise Relevance: A Paradigm for Sustainable Enterprise Excellence, Resilience and Robustness. *International Journal of Productivity and Performance Management* 64 (3): 318–333.

———. 2017. Routinizing Peak Performance and Impacts Via Virtuous Cycles. *Measuring Business Excellence* 21 (3): 261–271.

———. 2018. Urgent Evolution: Excellence and Wicked Anthropocene Age Challenges. *Total Quality Management & Business Excellence*. https://doi.org/10.1080/14783363.2018.1430510.

Edgeman, R., A. Bøllingtoft, J. Eskildsen, P. Kallehave, and T. Kjærgaard. 2015a. Sustainable Enterprise Excellence and the Continuously Relevant & Responsible Organization. *International Journal of Social Ecology & Sustainable Development* 4 (4): 65–76.

Edgeman, R., and J. Eskildsen. 2014. Modeling and Assessing Sustainable Enterprise Excellence. *Business Strategy and the Environment* 23 (3): 173–187.

Edgeman, R., J. Eskildsen, and A. Neely. 2015b. Translating Triple Top Line Strategy into Triple Bottom Line Performance. *Measuring Business Excellence* 19 (1): 1–12.

Elkington, J. 1998. Partnerships from Cannibals with Forks: The Triple Bottom Line of 21st Century Business. *Environmental Quality Management* 8 (1): 37–51.

Erragragui, E., and T. Sagoarde-Segot. 2016. Solving the SRI Puzzle? A Note on the Mainstreaming of Ethical Investment. *Finance Research Letters* 18: 32–42.

Escrig, A.B., and L.M. de Menezes. 2015. What Characterizes Leading Companies Within Business Excellence Models? An Analysis of "EFQM Recognized for Excellence" Recipients in Spain. *International Journal of Production Economics* 169: 362–375.

Etzioni, A., and A. Bowditch. 2006. *Public Intellectuals: An Endangered Species?* Lanham, MD: Rowan & Littlefield Publishing.

Gardan, J. 2016. Additive Manufacturing Technologies: State of the Art and Trends. *International Journal of Production Research* 54 (10): 3118–3132.

Groysberg, B., J. Lee, J. Price, and J.Y.D. Cheng. 2018a. The Leader's Guide to Corporate Culture: How to Manage the Eight Critical Elements of Organizational Life. *Harvard Business Review* 96 (1): 44–52.

———. 2018b. What's Your Organization's Cultural Profile: A Worksheet and Questions to Get You Started. *Harvard Business Review* 96 (1): 53.

———. 2018c. How to Shape Your Culture: Steps for Setting an Aspirational Target. *Harvard Business Review* 96 (1): 54.

———. 2018d. Convergence Matters: When Employee's Views of the Culture Align, Engagement and Customer Orientation Benefit. *Harvard Business Review* 96 (1): 55.

———. 2018e. Context, Conditions, and Culture: Consider Geographic Region, Industry, Strategy, Leadership, and Organizational Design. *Harvard Business Review* 96 (1): 56–57.

Halpern, B.S., M. Frazier, J. Potapenko, K.S. Casey, K. Koenig, C. Longo, J.S. Lowndes, et al. 2015. Spatial and Temporal Changes in Cumulative Human Impacts on the World's Ocean. *Nature Communications* 6, Article 7615. https://doi.org/10.1035/ncomms8615.

Hammer, M. 2002. Process Management and the Future of Six Sigma. *MIT Sloan Management Review* 43 (2): 26–32.

Hart, S.L., and C.M. Christensen. 2002. The Great Leap: Driving Innovation from the Base of the Pyramid. *MIT Sloan Management Review* 44 (1): 51–56.

Hauser, J.R., and D. Clausing. 1996. The House of Quality. *IEEE Engineering Management Review* 24 (1): 24–32.

Herbert, S. 2006. Tangled Up in Blue: Conflicting Paths to Police Legitimacy. *Theoretical Criminology* 10 (4): 481–504.

Johnson, C.E. 2018. *Challenges of Leadership: Casting Light or Shadow*. 6th ed. Thousand Oaks, CA: Sage Publishing.

Jones, G.A., and K.J. Warner. 2016. The 21st Century Population-Energy-Climate Nexus. *Energy Policy* 93: 206–212.

Klemkosky, R.C. 2013. Financial System Fragility. *Business Horizons* 56 (6): 675–683.

Koenigsaeker, G. 2013. *Leading the Lean Enterprise Transformation*. 2nd ed. Boca Raton, FL: CRC Press.

Kolbert, E. 2014. *The Sixth Extinction: An Unnatural History*. New York: Henry Holt.

Kruglanski, A.W., M.J. Gelfand, J.J. Bélanger, A. Sheveland, M. Hetiarachchi, and R. Gunaratna. 2014. The Psychology of Radicalization and Deradicalization: How Significance Quest Impacts Violent Extremism. *Political Psychology* 35 (S1): 69–93.

Lichtenthaler, U. 2009. Absorptive Capacity, Environmental Turbulence, and the Complementarity of Organizational Learning Processes. *The Academy of Management Journal* 52 (4): 822–846.

Liu, X., J.J. Klemeš, P.S. Varbanov, L. Čuček, and Y. Qian. 2017. Virtual Carbon and Water Flows Embodied in International Trade: A Review on Consumption-Based Analysis. *Journal of Cleaner Production* 146: 20–28.

McDonough, W., and M. Braungaart. 2002. Design for the Triple Top Line: New Tools for Sustainable Commerce. *Corporate Environmental Strategy* 9 (3): 251–258.

Nauta, A.L., M.M.P.D. Heijmans, D. Blok, J. Limpens, B. Elberling, A. Gallagher, B. Li, et al. 2015. Permafrost Collapse After Shrub Removal Shifts Tundra Ecosystem to a Methane Source. *Nature Climate Change* 5: 67–70.

Oakland, J.S. 2014. *Total Quality Management and Operational Excellence: Text with Cases*. 4th ed. New York: Routledge.

Olson, D.L., and D.D. Wu. 2015. *Enterprise Risk Management*. 2nd ed. Singapore: World Scientific.

Pisano, G.P. 2015. You Need an Innovation Strategy. *Harvard Business Review* 93 (6): 44–54.

Plenert, G. 2017. *Discover Excellence: An Overview of the Shingo Model and Its Guiding Principles*. Boca Raton, FL: Productivity Press.

Porter, M. 1980. *Competitive Strategy*. New York: Free Press.

———. 2008. The Five Competitive Forces that Shape Strategy. *Harvard Business Review* 86 (1): 78–93.

Prahalad, C.K. 2005. *The Fortune at the Bottom of the Pyramid: Eradicating Poverty Through Profits*. Philadelphia, PA: Wharton School Publishing.

Raddats, C., T. Baines, J. Burton, V.M. Story, and J. Zolkiewski. 2016. Motivations for Servitization: The Impact of Product Complexity. *International Journal of Operations & Production Management* 36 (5): 572–591.

Sabeti, H. 2011. The For-benefit Enterprise. *Harvard Business Review* 89 (11): 98–104.

Schrettle, S., A. Hinz, M. Scherrer-Rathje, and T. Friedli. 2014. Turning Sustainability into Action: Explaining Firms' Sustainability Efforts and Their Impacton Firm Performance. *International Journal of Production Economics* 147 (Part A): 73–84.

Segars, A.H. 2018. Seven Technologies Remaking the World. *MIT Sloan Management Review, Executive Guide*. Accessed March 9, 2018. https://sloanreview.mit.edu/projects/seven-technologies-remaking-the-world/?switch_view=PDF.

Sterman, J.D. 2002. All Models are Wrong: Reflections on Becoming a Systems Scientist. *Systems Dynamics Review* 18 (4): 501–531.

Stringer, C., and J. Galway-Witham. 2017. Paleoanthropology: On the Origin of Our Species. *Nature* 546: 212–214. https://doi.org/10.1038/546212a.

Tal, A. 2013. Shifting Sands: Land and Water Management in the Middle East. *Harvard International Review* 35 (2): 37–41.

Thébaud, S. 2015. Business as Plan B: Institutional Foundations of Gender Inequality in Entrepreneurship Across 24 Industrialized Countries. *Administrative Science Quarterly* 60 (4): 671–711.

Voland, T., and S. Daly. 2018. The EU Regulation of Conflict Minerals: The Way Out of a Vicious Cycle? *Journal of World Trade* 52 (1): 37–63.

Wunderlich, C. 2017. Deligitimisation à la carte: The 'rogue state' Label as a Means of Stabilizing Order in the Nuclear Non-proliferation Regime. Resistance and Change in World Politics. In *Resistance and Change in World Politics: Global Issues*, ed. S. Gerthiess, S. Herr, K. Wolf, and C. Wunderlich. Cham; London: Palgrave Macmillan.

12

Summary and Concluding Remarks: The Next Step for Sustainable Business Models

Annabeth Aagaard

Global sustainability challenges and requirements present unique, new business opportunities, but at the same time they also challenge the existing structures of companies and the way value is created, captured and measured in businesses today. These changes influence (or force) organizations to change their ways of organizing, managing, collaborating, and engaging with all types of stakeholders and ecosystems, presenting a need for new theoretical models and empirical understandings of business modeling in today's interconnected society across institutional boundaries and international borders.

The aim of *Sustainable Business Models: Innovation, Implementation, and Success* is to contribute to the knowledge of the concept, value creation (VC), implementation, management, and evaluation of sustainable business models (SBMs). In bridging the theoretical understanding of SBMs to empirical findings and case examples, the book explores how

---

A. Aagaard (✉)
Aarhus University,
Herning, Denmark
e-mail: aaa@btech.au.dk

the concept of SBM is applied and integrated in practice, as stressed as an insufficiently researched area by several authors. Through the chapters of the book, different aspects of SBMs are explained and discussed in further elaboration and exploration of the concept and of how SBMs are developed, integrated, and actively managed in creating sustainable value.

In the introductory Chap. 1, the concept of SBM is identified by bridging the existing theory of (traditional) business models and business model innovation with central theories and frameworks of SBM. In assessment of business models, the chapter presents a framework for theorists and practitioners to determine the sustainability of a business model. This framework can be applied in identification of new and SBM opportunities and in comparing the sustainability of business models within individual or across different companies. The elaboration of the concept, new patterns, and typologies of SBMs are further explored in Chap. 2, which also consolidates the currently available knowledge about so-called business model patterns that have the potential to support solutions to ecological and social problems, such as greener products, new mobility systems, or social enterprises. This consolidation leads to a new pattern taxonomy that can be used to support SBM innovation and sustainability innovation. In empirical exploration of the concept, a database of 45 patterns is developed, and these are evaluated and classified by international experts, resulting in a typology of 11 groups. This typology is further refined and prepared to serve as a SBM innovation tool and classification for both theorists and practitioners to apply.

The growing trends of digitalization and use of data and Internet of Things (IoT) in driving digital transformation of new and existing businesses emphasize the research gap of using digitalization in sustainable business development and SBM. Thus, the focus of Chap. 3 is on how to design SBMs while exploring IoT-enabled strategies to drive sustainable consumption. Over the years, SBMs, and in particular product service systems (PSS), have been positioned as a way to achieve greater levels of sustainability. In this chapter, the focus is on PSS in the consumer market with high environmental impact attributed to the use phase of the life cycle. For such systems, total life cycle sustainability performance is highly dependent on the behavior of the user. The research analyzes examples from practice to explore the possibility of using IoT technology to enable sustainable behavior through user interactions built into the PSS design. A framework for business model assessment is developed based on design for sustainable behavior strategies and IoT capabilities. This framework is applied to existing case companies to identify gaps and opportunities. The study finds that the application of IoT to drive sustainable consumption in PSS is currently limited. Several underexplored strategies are identified with the potential to boost sustainability performance of PSS in the use phase. Thus, future research could explore the actual implementation of such strategies, including the value proposition offered to consumers.

Developing the strategic and tactical processes of implementing SBM is a key research area and presents a number of research gaps for further research to pursue. Thus, the focus of Chap. 4 is on sustainability goal setting with a value-focused thinking (VFT) approach. As stressed in the chapter, firms are increasingly setting themselves business goals, which are more and more sustainability-oriented. The rationale behind setting these goals, however, is unclear. Is the improvement in sustainability the fundamental purpose of the firm's business, or is sustainability just an opportunity to improve some of the firm's competitive factors, such as reputation and image—that is, is it just a means to achieve economic success? An approach called VFT is helpful in clarifying the strategic goal-setting process and the role of sustainability goals in it, and in connecting values to firms' strategic decision-making. This chapter explores the process of how a VFT approach can be applied in making the sustainability-related goal setting more transparent so that decisions are based on the values a firm wants to follow. The approach supports the early phases of SBM innovation, and it facilitates developing value propositions that are in line with the fundamental values of the firm.

For companies to continuously develop their business in a sustainable fashion, new mechanisms and processes have to be adopted to ensure a steady stream and portfolio of ideas for SBM. Therefore, Chap. 5 explores SBM ideation and development of early ideas for SBM. The chapter stresses that the development of early ideas into sustainable business ideas and models that have a positive impact in society and on the environment is a challenge. It may, however, be facilitated by the use of tools, although many well-known tools used for business modeling (e.g., the

Business Model Canvas) do not examine the challenges that exist in the very early phases of development of ideas that aim at rendering research or innovative ideas into business ideas and also consider sustainability aspects from societal and environmental perspectives. Therefore, this chapter discusses an ideation tool that enables the involvement of many stakeholders and takes into account various perspectives already in the very early stages of the development of a business model. The Impact Canvas (IC) tool is targeted for early ideation, testing, and development of business ideas. The focus lies on the impact of the business solution in society and on the environment while also addressing customer needs in detail. It is suitable for existing businesses as well as pre-start-ups and research teams. The IC tool was created by a diverse group of practitioners supporting spin-offs and start-ups in the university environment and has since been introduced and deployed in other business communities.

The conceptualization of VC lies at the heart of business models. However, as business model innovation and business model ecosystems are more and more influenced by various stakeholders, emphasis has to be put on multiple VC through SBMs, as is the focus of Chap. 6. In conventional business models, this concept of VC is limited to a one-dimensional value, namely finance, for a limited scope of actors—mostly nominated as stakeholders or shareholders. These models are constructed from an organization-centric perspective. The rise of so-called SBMs has initiated a debate on broadening the dimensionality of VC, leading to an emerging perspective of multiple VC. This necessitates the design of business models that enable the creation of more than one value for a broad range of constituents simultaneously. Underpinning this development, three archetypes of business models appear: asset-based, community-based, and material-based. In comparison to conventional business models, the perspective here is multi-actor. Changing from an organization-centric to a multi-actor perspective also gives rise to a broadening connotation of VC, leading to a spectrum of different types of value. This spectrum goes from value destruction to forms of value preservation and creation to value restoration. This line of thought is elaborated upon in our forthcoming contribution.

With the United Nation's Sustainable Development Goals comes a global request for greener and more environment-friendly business development that stress effective use, recycling and reuse of resources as well as minimization of waste and pollution. These goals, together with the environmental development of the world, have given rise to the concept of circular economy (CE), which has emerged as an attractive concept for both industry and society. Thus, Chap. 7 emphasizes CE as a lever for SBMs as CE holds promises of reducing the negative impacts from our natural resource usage, while allowing or even supporting economic growth of firms. Still, it is a vague and highly challenging model for organizations to adopt, and empirical research hardly exists regarding actions in industry. Chapter 7 outlines the model of CE and describes how the model is applied in different settings as in policy-making, changes in society, and in industry. An emphasis will be put on how it challenges current business models in industry. Specifically, the chapter focuses on the challenges that occur due to CE and due to the required business model innovation based on recent research in industry.

Collaborations, networks, and partners are key in developing sustainable businesses and business models, as the main company may not possess the knowledge, skills, or resources to fully leverage, develop, and implement SBM on their own. Thus, the use of collaborative innovation and partnerships in developing the proper foundation for SBMs is the focus of Chap. 8. The specific emphasis of the chapter is on the effective identification and integration of non-governmental organizations (NGOs) in creating the necessary knowledge transfer, trust, and legitimacy when building new SBM innovations. Through case examples from international companies and their collaborations with NGOs, the drivers and challenges, archetypes of SBMs, and the managerial implications of these business-NGO collaborations are mapped and discussed theoretically and empirically. As a result, the chapter presents four archetypes of SBMs through business-NGO collaborations for companies to apply in determining which type of collaboration to engage in and which challenges to be aware of in managing these collaborations successfully.

A majority of the extant literature emphasizes SBM in established companies. However, social entrepreneurship is a central research field in the area of sustainable business and SBM. Therefore, the objective of Chap. 9 is to explore the concept of SBM in an entrepreneurial environment. The dichotomy between corporations and start-ups has led to the creation of new tools and frameworks designed specifically for the latter. This trend has also been echoed in academic literature on business model innovation focusing on high-tech entrepreneurial ventures and how this form of innovation creates entrepreneurial opportunities. At the same time, while there has been a remarkable progress in the research around SBMs, we have not seen yet similar attempts to create tools and frameworks that cater specifically to the needs of entrepreneurs looking to create sustainable start-ups. With the new breed of entrepreneurs who seek to address sustainability challenges at the start of their venture formation, this chapter clarifies the specific needs of this environment, exploring the elements of lean start-up tools that potentially can be considered for sustainable entrepreneurship, while presenting successful examples that can be used to prototype new tools and frameworks, and finally suggesting new directions on the ways SBMs should be considered in an entrepreneurial context.

The corporate implementation of SBM requires strategic management, and the focus of Chap. 10 is therefore on managing the strategic dualities to enable SBM. The chapter adds a new lens and richness to the paradoxical nature of SBMs by building on the need for more interdisciplinary approaches and greater appreciation of strategic paradoxes and dualities. In doing so, the authors of the chapter apply a paradoxical lens to the most frequently cited business model frameworks and explore the conventional understanding of the business models based on the assumption that conflict exists between profit and business responsibility. Consequently, the chapter proposes a new SBM framework named "Value Triangle." It includes, as core elements, society incorporating the natural environment and future generations and three types of co-created and co-delivered value: public, partner, and customer. To explain the framework, a range of different sustainable case studies are presented, offering a new perspective on designing SBMs and navigating the dualities that exist in sustainable business.

In determining successful implementation, VC, and strategic management of SBM, we need to talk evaluation and measurement of performance and excellence. Chapter 11 therefore discusses performance management and enterprise excellence through SBMs. Skilled use of enterprise excellence systems has been shown to significantly boost performance across an array of key domains, including financial, human capital, operations and supply chain, and other areas. Notably absent are social and environmental performance, with their absence attributable to the inadequate emphasis on enterprise excellence of these domains. Similarly, although the triple bottom line is core to the sustainability movement, many adherents of sustainability approach its people and planet domains with ardor, yet virtually neglect its profit domain. A simple model of sustainable enterprise excellence and accompanying maturity assessment regimen are introduced and advanced as a means of merging these movements to drive an equity, ecology, and economy triple top line strategy to produce triple bottom line people, planet, and profit performance with innovation and organizational design playing pivotal roles in both the model and its assessment.

Through the chapters of *Sustainable Business Models: Innovation, Implementation, and Success*, the book elaborates upon the concept of SBMs as well as widens the scope and the understanding of what SBMs are and can become—how they can be innovated and implemented in different ways and through various collaborations in ensuring a successful and sustainable performance and impact.

One clear conclusion from this publication is that this concept is still evolving, as what is considered sustainable in the mindsets of society changes over time, continuously raising the bar for SBM. With the growing power of consumers, end-users, social media, and NGOs, these and other stakeholders play an increasing role in setting the standards and boundaries for what is considered sustainable business and what is not. Thus, SBMs will only be sustainable if the stakeholders of the ecosystems consider them as such. This also implies the necessity of open innovation and open business models in pursuing the full potential of what sustainable business can become. The inclusion of the stakeholders and the ecosystem in business model innovation is crucial in providing more interconnected SBMs that support the sustainability of the entire value chain and across ecosystems. With the growing need and request for SBM comes the strategic, tactical, and operational challenges of ideation, implementation, adoption, VC, and collaborations in ensuring the successful performance and impact of SBMs. Consequently, the majority of the chapters of the books have emphasized these issues by presenting case examples of or frameworks for how to overcome some of these managerial and strategic challenges. However, more research is needed in exploring successful integration and ensuring sustainable impact across companies and sectors.

The majority of existing literature has addressed the use and development of SBM in established companies. However, the research field and empirical cases of successful social entrepreneurs and start-ups are growing and underline the potentials of this area, now and in the future. With more companies starting up with fundamentally sustainable mindsets, business models, and strategies, new frameworks and models will have to emerge too, and new ways of differentiating products, services, and business models will be established.

One very timely and relevant research area is the use of data and digitalization in the further development of sustainable business and SBM innovation. Through the use of big data, businesses can optimize their business processes, portfolios, and functions (e.g., production, logistics, sales) in making smarter, more efficient, less resource-consuming and polluting business choices. In addition, through the interconnectivity between users, businesses, society, and other stakeholders, entire ecosystems can start making more sustainable, socially and environmentally friendly decisions and developments that cross sectors and boarders. For the reader who seeks more knowledge on the use of data and digitalization for sustainability, we suggest another Palgrave Macmillan publication, *Digital Business Models—Driving Transformation and Innovation (2018)*.

So how do we expect the field of SBM to develop in the next coming years—theoretically and empirically? As more and more companies are forced by society and stakeholders to pursue sustainability in their businesses, strategies, and VC, sustainability will become more and more mainstream over time. This challenges companies to be more radical in their sustainability approaches and in their SBM innovation to be able to differentiate and compete globally. Thus, new frameworks and models may have to be invented in exploring, developing, and deploying more radical SBM. Also, the growing trends of social entre/intrapreneurs provide new venues for entrepreneurial research and processes as well as for the development of frameworks and models in managing, facilitating, and assessing these social entre/intrapreneurs and social enterprises. The new trends of sustainable/social intra/entrepreneurship also open up the SBMs and innovation processes of companies and networks allowing for new types and forms of collaboration across new and multiple stakeholders to be explored both theoretically and in practice. This widens our interest in the unique ecosystems of SBM.

From a global perspective, the optimal sustainable and circular developments in businesses would require a higher level of interconnectivity, as ecosystems are dependent and influence each other and the use of resources across the national and global value chains. Data can be the leverage in attaining the optimum sustainability through interconnectivity across the ecosystems and value chains of businesses and society. However, digital technologies should not be applied for the sake of technology, but from a human-centric perspective and for the sake of transparency while building the proper strategy and decision platforms for effective development and adoption of SBMs in businesses and society. And in doing so, companies as well as governments will need to consider the issues of General Data Protection Rights (GDPR) and the social consequences of increased digital transformation. Particularly in determining how to avoid the possibility of digitalization creating an A-team and a B-team of citizens and employees—those with or without (the right) digital skills. New venues for sustainability research and SBMs may therefore address and provide answers to how to ensure sustainable, digital transformation that incorporates the longitudinal, human, social and environmental effects of digitalization. Thus, new venues for research and practices in sustainable (digital) business development, performance, and growth are present and will keep evolving. However, in any case multiple stakeholders across global societies will have to come together to legislate, motivate, educate, facilitate, and move businesses and organizations across sectors and borders in a sustainable direction now and in the times to come.

Index

A

Alexander, Christopher, 27–29, 33, 35, 36, 39, 40, 42, 51, 52, 54
Alexandrian form, 28, 33–39, 45, 56
Anthropocene age, 318–319
Architecture, 28
Artefact/artifacts, 31
Assessment, 10, 12, 362, 363, 367

B

B-Corps, 260–262, 272
Beehive model, 163, 165–166, 169
Bottom of the pyramid (BOP), 216, 224
  market, 225
Business model (BM), 1–19, 26–56, 277, 278, 281–288, 291, 294, 307, 309, 362–368
  ecosystem, 364, 367
  elements, 191, 192, 195, 196, 204, 205
  for sustainability, 41, 211–231
Business model innovation (BMI), 1–3, 5, 17, 18, 26, 28, 31, 34, 48–56, 102, 115, 184, 191, 200, 203–205, 362, 364, 366, 367
Business modelling
  Business Innovation Kit (BIK), 37, 48–52
  business model canvas, 34, 37, 38, 40, 45, 46, 48, 54
  digital business modelling, 52–55
  Smart Business Modeler, 52–55
  Strongly Sustainable Business Model Ontology, 37
  triple layered business model canvas, 37, 45

Business model pattern, 362
  circular economy business model pattern, 28, 40, 46, 54
  circular economy pack, 54
  food waste prevention pattern, 28, 44, 45
  pricing pattern, 38, 48–52
  revenue pattern, 43, 48–52
  sustainability pack, 27, 50, 54
  sustainable business model pattern, 26–56
Business-NGO collaboration, 211–231, 365
Butterfly model, 163, 166–169

C

Canvas tool, 126, 128, 129, 135, 138–143
Card sorting, 47–48
Case study, 44–46
Circular business, 64
Circular business models, 159, 175
Circular economy (CE), 77, 161, 165, 173, 174, 181–194, 196–206, 332, 365
Circularity, 153, 160, 163, 167–171, 174, 175
Classification
  business model types, 26
  empiricist philosophy, 44
  essentialist philosophy, 44
  taxonomy, 44, 47, 48, 56
  typology, 43, 44, 46, 56
Collaboration, 365, 367, 369
Collaborative continuum, 217–220, 224, 228, 229

Collaborative innovation, 217, 219, 228
Community, 28, 32, 36, 45, 46, 48, 54
Conversion, 161, 167–169, 173
Corporate social responsibility (CSR), 17, 217, 229
Corporate sustainability, 26, 28
CSR, *see* Corporate social responsibility

D

Data triangulation, 44
Debonding, 159
Decomposition, 159
Delphi survey, 47–48
Design, 26–56
Digital transformation, 362, 369

E

Early idea development, 120–146
Eco-efficiency, 162, 173–175
Enterprise excellence, 317–355
Enterprise excellence systems, 366
Experiment, 200, 203, 205–206

F

Future-Fit Business Benchmark, 104, 107–112

G

Guiding principles, 338–344, 346

I

Ideation, 363, 364, 367
  process, 120–146
  tool, 131
Implementation, 361, 363, 366
Inclusive business models, 213, 224–226, 229
Inclusivity, 153, 160, 163, 167–170, 175
Innovation, 362, 365–367, 369
Innovation team, 201–203, 206
Innovative research and business ideas, 120–122, 127–131, 136, 140
Insight and foresight, 322, 352, 355
Integration, 365, 368
Internet of Things (IoT), 62, 63, 67, 69, 73–78, 80–85, 362, 363
IoT, *see* Internet of Things

K

Knowledge for action, 29, 30, 32, 56
Knowledge transfer, 27

L

Lean startup, 240, 241, 246, 256, 258, 260, 269, 271
Life cycle perspective, 189, 190, 205
Lifespan extension, 159–161

M

Morphological analysis, 46–47
Multi-actor, 156, 163–169
Multidisciplinary team, 120, 121, 124, 131, 136–138, 141
Multiple value creation, 151–175

N

NGO, *see* Non-governmental organization
Non-governmental organization (NGO), 213, 216, 217, 221–223, 225–231, 365, 367
Nordic startups, 262–263, 272

O

Open innovation, 56, 129

P

Pattern
  definition, 33, 34, 41–42
  language, 28–43, 48, 55, 56
  library, 54, 55
  theory, 27–29, 44
Performance management, 366
Platform cooperatives, 265, 267
Post-growth, 44, 45
Problem-solution combination, 28, 33, 34, 42
Product life cycle, 61, 62, 75
Product-service system (PSS), 362, 363
Purpose, 90–94, 96, 97, 100–102, 104, 113

R

Recycle, 183–186, 189–191, 198, 199, 201, 202
Recycling, 161, 173
Reduce, 184, 189, 194, 201
Research agenda, 26–56
Resource parameters, 182, 188–191, 195–196, 205

374 Index

Reuse, 183–185, 187, 189–191
Revenue model, 191, 192, 195, 196, 199, 200, 202, 204, 205

S

Servitization, 159, 160, 170, 173, 175
Shingo Operational Excellence Model, 323
Simon, Herbert, 31
Smart devices, 62, 63, 69–73, 78
Social-Ecological Innovation (SEI), 347, 349, 350
Social inclusion, 163
Social innovation, 8
Social investment, 219, 226–229
Societal challenges, 151–175
Stakeholder relationship pattern, 28, 44, 45
Starfish model, 163–165, 169
Startups, 26, 48, 52, 53, 239, 240, 246–260, 271, 272, 364–366, 368
Strategic management, 366
Strategy, 182, 187, 190, 197–199, 203, 205–206
Substitution, 161–162, 167, 168, 173
Sustainability, 1, 3–6, 8, 9, 11–19, 26, 31, 42, 49, 52, 61–65, 68, 76, 80, 83, 84, 211–213, 215, 225, 361–364, 366–369
　assessment, 12
　decision-making, 90–92, 94–103, 105, 106, 113
　evaluation, 4, 11–14, 16–18
　goal setting, 89–115
　management, 90, 91, 95–101, 103–113, 115

　science, 90, 91, 95, 96, 99, 101, 113
　strategy, 96, 98, 100–102, 112–114
Sustainable and impactful ideas, 120–146
Sustainable behaviour, 63, 68–69, 73–78, 81–85
Sustainable business, 8, 17
Sustainable business model innovation (SBMI), 3, 6–8, 17–19, 48–55, 211–231, 362, 363, 365, 368
Sustainable business models (SBMs), 1, 26–56, 61–85, 97, 102, 104, 115, 169, 211–231, 277–310, 361–369
Sustainable consumption, 61–85
Sustainable Development Goals (SDGs), 153, 158, 364
Sustainable entrepreneurship (SE), 240–246, 284
Sustainable innovation, 1, 4, 5, 8, 16, 240, 245, 255, 278, 283–288, 290
Sustainable organisation, 29–32, 42, 56
Sustainable PSS, 62, 64, 73–75
Sustainable value, 9, 11, 12, 14
Sustainify/sustainification, 153, 160, 161, 163, 167, 168, 174, 175

T

Theory building, 45
Transaction, 152, 154, 161
Transition, 151–153, 163, 165, 171, 174, 175

U

United Nations Agenda 2030 Sustainable Development Goals, 323, 338
United Nations Global Compact (UNGC), 323, 339–342, 346–348

V

Value capture, 3, 5, 9–13, 15–16
Value creation (VC), 1–19, 26, 41, 42, 45–47, 152, 154, 156, 158, 159, 162, 163, 165, 168–175, 361, 364, 366–368
Value cycle, 158
Value delivery, 2, 5, 9
Value-Focused Thinking (VFT), 89–115, 363
Value preservation, 161, 171, 173, 175
Value proposition, 5–14, 191, 195, 196, 204–206
Value restoration, 173, 175
Values, 89–115
Values-based business model, 48

W

Wicked problem, 153–154, 156, 158, 170, 173–175
Workshop, 36, 49, 51, 52, 54

Z

Zebra movement, 268–270, 272